The Middle English Breton Lays

Middle English Texts

The Middle English Texts Series is designed for classroom use. Its goal is to make available to teachers and students texts which occupy an important place in the literary and cultural canon but which have not been readily available in student editions. The series does not include those authors such as Chaucer, Langland, the Pearl-poet, or Malory, whose English works are normally in print in good student editions. The focus is, instead, upon Middle English literature adjacent to those authors that teachers need in compiling the syllabuses they wish to teach. The editions maintain the linguistic integrity of the original work but within the parameters of modern reading conventions. The texts are printed in the modern alphabet and follow the practices of modern capitalization and punctuation. Manuscript abbreviations are expanded, and u/v and j/i spellings are regularized according to modern orthography. Hard words, difficult phrases, and unusual idioms are glossed on the page, either in the right margin or at the foot of the page. Textual and explanatory notes appear at the end of the text, along with a glossary. The editions include short introductions on the history of the work, its merits and points of topical interest, and also include briefly annotated bibliographies.

The Middle English Breton Lays

Edited by
Anne Laskaya and Eve Salisbury

Published for TEAMS
(The Consortium for the Teaching of the Middle Ages)
in Association with the University of Rochester

by

Medieval Institute Publications

WESTERN MICHIGAN UNIVERSITY

Kalamazoo, Michigan— 2001

Library of Congress Cataloging-in-Publication Data

The Middle English Breton lays / edited by Anne Laskaya and Eve Salisbury.
p. cm. -- (Middle English texts)
Includes bibliographical references.
ISBN 1-879288-62-1 (alk. paper : paperbound)
English poetry--Middle English, 1100-1500. 2. Romances, English--Celtic influences. 3. Romances, English--French influences. 4. Knights and knighthood--Poetry. 5. Brittany (France)--Poetry. 6. Romances, English. I. Laskaya, Anne, 1953- II. Salisbury, Eve. III. Consortium for the Teaching of the Middle Ages. IV. Series: Middle English texts (Kalamazoo, Mich.)
PR2064.M45 1995
821' . 109--dc20 95-38170
CIP

ISBN 1-879288-62-1
ISBN 978-1-879288-62-1

P 9 8 7 6

Cover design by Elizabeth King

Printed in the United States of America

Contents

Preface

Middle English Breton Lays makes available to teachers and students for the first time in this form an important body of poetry worthy of attention for a variety of reasons. Seven of the eight narrative poems in this volume constitute a group of Middle English lays that have been distinguished by their identification in some way as Breton: *Sir Orfeo, Sir Degaré, Lay le Freine*, Thomas Chestre's *Sir Launfal, Sir Gowther, Emaré*, and the *Erle of Tolous*. The eighth poem, *Sir Cleges*, is not acknowledged by scholars to be a Breton lay, but rather is simply classified as a short romance. Our decision to place it within this particular group of poems is based upon common topoi that render it compatible with the Middle English Breton Lays. Although Chaucer's Franklin's Tale and Wife of Bath's Tale are recognized as part of the English Breton lay group, we have chosen to exclude them because they are edited so often elsewhere. Reference to Chaucer, however, occurs throughout the volume, and he remains an important touchstone for discussions of the genre as well as for any study of late medieval English culture.

With the exception of Thomas Rumble's *Breton Lays in Middle English*, these poems have usually been subsumed within the gargantuan corpus of romance. A number of collections, most notably French and Hale's *Middle English Metrical Romances*, Maldwyn Mills' *Six Middle English Romances*, Donald Sands' *Middle English Verse Romance*, A. C. Gibbs' *Middle English Romances,* and most recently Jennifer Fellows' *Of Love and Chivalry*, indicate this tendency. The scholarship on the lays is also frequently immersed in discussions of medieval romance, various other genres, and related subject matter. Needless to say, the study of the Middle English Breton Lays as a group is rendered somewhat daunting by these practices. But while it is our aim to create convenience where it has been absent, this volume is also intended to promote further study of various issues which present themselves clearly only when the poems are understood as a group.

The introductions and notes to each of the poems attempt to render this volume more inclusive than either Rumble's edition (a collection of the poems without notes) or Mortimer J. Donovan's *The Breton Lay: A Guide to Varieties* (a critical study without the poems). For each poem, we point to a large body of secondary materials that explore the historical realities of the medieval past, a time not exclusively reserved for knights, ladies, and chivalric romance, but a time of dynamic social and political change. It is our hope that this edition will provide a means by which these realities may be more fully addressed and the lack of current critical discourse on many of these important poems redressed.

The collaboration has been both rewarding and productive. We have divided the material evenly between us with each responsible for four poems including individual introductions and notes (Laskaya: *Sir Orfeo, Emaré, Sir Launfal*, and *Lay le Freine*; Salisbury: *Sir Degaré, Sir Gowther, Erle of Tolous, Sir Cleges*). We have also shared the production of prefatory material, the general introduction, the glossary, and the appendices. In this way we have been able to cope with and finally overcome a continental separation — Eugene, Oregon, to Rochester, New York — that even the use of e-mail and Federal Express could not completely eradicate. Admittedly, there are variations in the ways we have approached the texts, but we have resisted uniformity, preferring instead to encourage discussion by retaining our differences.

We are grateful to the National Endowment for the Humanities for assistance in the production of this volume. We would also like to thank the following: the Trustees of the National Library of Scotland for permission to use the Auchinleck MS in the preparation of *Sir Orfeo, Sir Degaré, Lai le Freine* as well as Advocates 19.3.1 for *Sir Gowther*; the British Library for permission to work from the Cotton Caligula MS in the preparation of *Emaré*; the Syndics of Cambridge University Library for the use of Cambridge Ff. 2.38 in the preparation of *Erle of Tolous;* and the Bodleian Library at Oxford for permission to work from Bodleian 6922 for *Sir Cleges*. We would both especially like to thank Russell A. Peck for his meticulous reading and prodigious commentary and Alan Lupack, Curator of the Robbins Library and second reader, for providing often obscure research materials. Eve's special thanks go to Ronald B. Herzman, mentor and colleague at SUNY Geneseo, and Graham Drake, also at Geneseo, for their critical assessments; to Sarah L. Higley, whose trial run of these materials in the classroom proved invaluable; to Karen Saupe and Jennifer Church for their expertise in the intricacies of Word Perfect; and especially to daughter Meghan whose cooperation and patience contributed to the timely completion of the project. Anne's special thanks go to James W. Earl, colleague and Director of the Medieval Studies Program at the University of Oregon; to the students in her senior seminar on Chivalry and to those in her Romance course for their careful reading and response; to Christy Bradford-Racy for her assistance on bibliographic searches; to the staff of the University of Oregon Knight Library who, in the midst of a major building renovation and expansion project, helped locate research materials not readily available; and especially to family and friends: Suzanne Lesley Gerhardt, Christine Antonetti, and Suzanne Gatch for their love, friendship, and support. Lastly, Anne thanks her mother, Janet Houser, for all those childhood reading hours which provided faith in the human imagination, joy in the presence of ambiguity, and pleasure in the magic of fiction.

Introduction

What is a Breton lay and why is its designation in Middle English important? Without the identification of "Middle English," the Breton lay may refer to any of the poems produced between approximately 1150 and 1450 which claim to be literary versions of lays sung by ancient Bretons to the accompaniment of the harp.[1] The subsequent codification of the literary genre is attributed to the Anglo-Norman writer Marie de France whose twelve lays immortalize this tradition of Breton storytelling in the twelfth century.[2] Set in Brittany, Wales, or Normandy, Marie's lays address matters of courtesy, chivalry, and courtly love, concerns of interest to her multilingual, aristocratic audience.[3] Old French imitations of her lays followed in the thirteenth century with varying degrees of success; many of them are now lost.[4] The Middle English lays – *Sir Orfeo, Sir Degaré, Lay le Freine, Erle of Tolous, Emaré, Sir Gowther, Sir Launfal* – were composed sometime between the late thirteenth or early fourteenth and the early fifteenth century. Of them only Thomas Chestre's *Sir Launfal* and the anonymous *Lay le Freine* may be considered translations or adaptations of Marie's poems.[5]

---

[1] The French lais include: *Desiré, Melion, Graelent, Doon, Guingamor, Tydorel, Tyolet, Haveloc, L'Espine, Le Cor, Nabaret, Le Trot, L'Ombre, Le Conseil, L'Amours, Aristote, Le Vair Palefroi, L'Oiselet, L'Espervier, Narcisse, Le Lecheor, Ignauré*, and the twelve lays of Marie de France.

[2] See Robert Hanning and Joan Ferrante, translators, *The Lais of Marie de France* (New York: E. P. Dutton, 1978). Marie's lays include: *Guigemar, Equitan, LeFresne, Bisclavret, Lanval, Deus Amanz, Yonec, Laüstic, Milun, Chaitivel, Chevrefoil, Eliduc.* There are translations or other versions in Old Norse, Middle High German, Italian, French, and Latin (*Laüstic* may be found in Alexander of Neckham's *De naturis rerum*).

[3] There are several examples of translation from Old French into Breton and English, which suggest the multilingual, cosmopolitan nature of Marie's audience.

[4] See Mortimer J. Donovan, *The Breton Lay: A Guide to Varieties* (Notre Dame, IN: University of Notre Dame Press, 1969), pp. 65–120. The acknowledged source for *Sir Orfeo, Lai d'Orfée,* is not extant.

[5] See A. C. Spearing, "Marie de France and Her Middle English Adapters," *Studies in the Age of Chaucer* 12 (1990), 117–56.

Defining the Middle English Breton lay as a distinct genre has been a nagging concern of modern scholars. In an early attempt, A. C. Baugh offers the following:

> whether a given short romance is called a Breton lay or not depends mainly on whether it says it is one, has its scene laid in Brittany, contains a passing reference to Brittany, or tells a story found among the lais of Marie de France.[6]

The lays themselves support this definition: *Sir Degaré* is set in Brittany, *Lay le Freine* and *Sir Launfal* are "found among the lais of Marie de France," while the others make some "passing reference" to Brittany or a lost Breton source. But the poems also call themselves *contes*, stories, *gestes*, and romances, a tendency that suggests that the Middle Ages felt no clear need for generic types. Needless to say, this has created confusion among scholars about the validity of calling Middle English Breton lay a genre at all.

Most scholars see the lays as a shortened form of romance.[7] John Finlayson, for instance, looks to length as a means of differentiating these poems from other romances in Middle English. For Finlayson, the poems constitute a "sub-genre of romance" equivalent in their relation to the longer romances as short story is to novel.[8] This is certainly a valid distinction since these poems all run between eight hundred to twelve hundred lines, a mere third the length of romances such as *Bevis of Hampton, Havelok the Dane,* and *King Horn*. They also follow the general pattern of romance – separation and reunion – or, as Northrop Frye views it, a journey of descent followed by ascent and a corresponding resolution of the hero or heroine's identity, purpose, and place in the world.[9] The poems often fall into some pattern based on story type or linguistic model depending on the particular critic's criteria

---

[6] See A. C. Baugh, ed., *A Literary History of England*, vol. 1 (New York: Appleton-Century-Crofts, 1948), p. 196.

[7] See John B. Beston, "How Much Was Known of the Breton Lai in Fourteenth-Century England?" in *The Learned and the Lewed: Studies in Chaucer and Medieval Literature,* ed. Larry D. Benson (Cambridge, MA: Harvard University Press, 1974), pp. 319–36. See also Paul Strohm, "The Origin and Meaning of Middle English Romaunce," *Genre* 10 (1977), 1–28.

[8] See John Finlayson, "The Form of the Middle English Lay," *Chaucer Review* 19 (1984–85), 352–68.

[9] See Northrop Frye, *Secular Scripture: A Study of the Structure of Romance* (Cambridge, MA: Harvard University Press, 1976).

for evaluation.[10] Yet the attempt to impose a single formulaic pattern on these texts in order to determine a genre has been thwarted by their resistance to conform to any single cohesive system. As Finlayson concludes, "the lay in Middle English is not a uniform sub-type of romance distinguishable by a manner of treatment and by particular combinations of motifs."[11]

Since the composition period of the Middle English lays spans approximately one hundred years, even within the group there are distinctions to be made. While the earlier lays – *Sir Orfeo, Sir Degaré, Lay le Freine* – may be identified by octosyllabic couplets, the later – *Erle of Tolous, Sir Launfal, Emaré, Sir Gowther* – may be identified by their tail-rhyme stanzas.[12] The first group, in imitation of Marie's octosyllabic poems, is more suggestive of the Breton minstrel tradition she codified in her lais; the second group reflects a native English stanzaic practice used in several other Middle English romances. Both varieties are emphatically metrical with rhythmic features undeniably musical, perhaps, as some scholars reckon, something analogous to folk music intended to be performed in public places by minstrels.[13] Certainly the relationship of these English poems to music and minstrelsy is important. In *Sir Orfeo*, for instance, Orfeo finds pleasure and solace in his harp as he grieves the loss of his bride, while in *Sir Cleges*, the hero's identity is revealed in a memorable scene of minstrelsy. None of the other poems contain such overt references to music, though in some cases they provide a courtly ethos against which the drama is played out. But since these are literary texts undoubtedly intended to be

---

[10] See Kathryn Hume, "The Formal Nature of Middle English Romance," *Philological Quarterly* 53, 2 (1974), 158–80. Hume argues that there are two types of romance: Type A comprises the armor-clad folk tales, a most attractive group which celebrates achievement, joy, and order. Type B displays their heroes against a significant background, usually a specific swatch of history or pseudo-history. See also Susan Wittig, *Stylistic and Narrative Structure in Middle English Romances* (Austin: University of Texas Press, 1978) and G. V. Smithers, "Story-patterns in Some Breton Lays," *Medium Aevum* 22 (1953), 61–92. Smithers distinguishes between three types of recurring story patterns: Type I include those in which there is contact between a mortal and a supernatural being; Type II include those in which a mortal and a supernatural being have a child; Type III include a father/son combat. In *Chivalric Romances: Popular Literature in Medieval England* (Bloomington: Indiana University Press, 1983), Lee C. Ramsey subsumes the lays into a study of chivalric romances and classifies them by themes such as child exile, superman, fairy princess, and "gentils and vilains."

[11] See Finlayson, pp. 366–67.

[12] See Mortimer J. Donovan's comparison of the two forms in *The Breton Lay: A Guide to Varieties*. Chaucer's Franklin's Tale, and Wife of Bath's Tale, written in decasyllabic couplets, require a third formal category.

[13] See Constance Bullock-Davies, "The Form of the Breton Lay," *Medium Aevum* 42 (1973), 18–31. See also Rachel Bromwich, "A Note on the Breton Lays," *Medium Aevum* 26 (1957), 36–38.

read aloud, the verbal repetitions, rhyming patterns, and exhortations to "listen," all capture the vibrant cadences of oral performance.

With much critical attention turned to matters of "form," it is not surprising that other crucial generic features have been overlooked or even subtly discounted. Subject matter and its treatment, for instance, has been cast aside as having "nothing distinctive" to offer.[14] Neither has there been much attention paid to the extra-literary environment in which these poems were produced. To define the genre then we must not only take into consideration the formal nature of these narratives, i.e., stylistic and structural features, but their discursive nature, the social and ideological contexts which contribute to their generic identity.[15] Furthermore, a genre as elusive as Middle English Breton Lay demands consideration of its interaction with an actual audience whose interests and concerns are their subjects.[16]

The Prologue to *Lay le Freine* is a good place to begin an examination of internal generic attributes because it characterizes the subject matter that is shared by many of the English lays:

> We redeth oft and findeth ywrite –
> And this clerkes wele it wite – *know*
> Layes that ben in harping
> Ben yfounde of ferli thing. *marvelous*
> Sum bethe of wer and sum of wo, *war*
> And sum of joie and mirth also,
> And sum of trecherie and of gile,
> Of old aventours that fel while;
> And sum of bourdes and ribaudy, *jokes; ribaldry*
> And mani ther beth of fairy.
> Of al thinges that men seth,
> Mest o love, for sothe thai beth. *Most*
> (lines 1–12)

The Prologue's beginning posits an audience of readers who share in a particular tradition of storytelling – "layes that ben in harping" – that addresses a number of

---

[14] See A. C. Baugh, p. 196.

[15] See Kevin Brownlee and Marina Scordilis Brownlee, *Romance: Generic Transformation from Chrétien de Troyes to Cervantes* (Hanover, NH: University Press of New England, 1985).

[16] For discussions of audience interaction with Chaucer's work, see Paul Strohm, *Social Chaucer* (Cambridge, MA: Harvard University Press, 1989); R. W. Hanning, "The Audience as Co-Creator of the First Chivalric Romances," *Yearbook of English Studies* 11 (1981), 1–28.

marvelous happenings: war, woe, joy, happiness, treachery, guile, adventure, bawdiness, ribaldry, the fairy world, and most of all, love. These subjects are familiar to a medieval audience not only from literary narratives "they redeth oft," but from the realities of medieval life. Difficult social problems especially within the family – incest, rape, abandonment, illegitimacy – as well as issues of the larger community – inheritance, exile, orphanage, poverty, violence, social mobility, punishment, rehabilitation, territorial disputes – are subjected to analysis and transformation. "Treachery and guile," which in life may go unpunished, are punished in the lays according to exacting standards of justice. "Adventures" provide the narrative impetus, spelled with occasional humor and comic relief. Plausible social contexts lend the poems an air of realism, while, at the same time, infusions of the marvelous and strange cast an aura of enchantment about them. In some poems – *Sir Orfeo, Sir Launfal, Lay le Freine, Sir Degaré* – the enchantments are of the Celtic fairy world; in others – *Erle of Tolous, Emaré, Sir Gowther*, *Sir Cleges* – they are predominantly miraculous and Christian. In the paradoxes of medieval metaphysics, when death could be life and life, death; when madness could be holiness and criminality the sign of a saint; when supernatural spirits could mate with mortals and transformation could be a possibility of everyday life, the unexpected and magical becomes the norm.[17] The Otherworld, Celtic or Christian, could exist in a subterranean realm or in the heavens, or even just beyond the reach of a hand. When two spheres of reality are perceived to coexist so intimately, the boundaries between them are often indistinguishable.

But the subject matter of most concern, as the Prologue to *Lay le Freine* suggests, is love. This may not be particularly surprising, considering the importance of love to romance, but there are subtle distinctions to be made between love in these poems, the longer Middle English romances, and Marie's lais for that matter. These Middle English lays are not the courtly love stories of Marie de France – stories of arranged marriages, and subsequent longing for happiness and fulfillment outside its parameters – but rather stories of lovers whose happy ending resides in marriage. Five of these poems end in marriages – *Sir Gowther, Sir Degaré, Erle of Tolous, Lay le Freine*, and *Sir Launfal*,[18] while the others – *Sir Orfeo, Emaré*, and *Sir Cleges* – end in marital reunion. Because of their shorter length they intensify and emphasize the importance of truth in love, both for its stabilizing influence on the family unit

---

[17] See Aron Gurevich, *Medieval Popular Culture: Problems of Belief and Perception*, translated by János M. Bak and Paul A. Hollingsworth (Cambridge, MA: Cambridge University Press, 1988), p. 176.

[18] Sir Launfal "marries," is separated from the fay, and then reunited after a year.

and its concommitant stabilization of a larger community.[19] They address both the personal and social in ways different from Marie de France's Norman, aristocratic orientation.

Since many of these poems "beth of fairy," the positing of another time and place, the employment of what might be called a psychology of displacement is a necessary component of their storytelling strategy. The fairytale beginnings disrupt ordinary perceptions of time and allow the audience to reperceive the present by removing it from the events of the moment. The "once upon a time," so familiar to us in our own fairytales, signals imminent entry into an otherworldly environment, where trouble invariably accompanies enchantment, where actual reality is subject to transformation by magic as well as merit.

In the late Middle Ages, Brittany provided fertile soil for the English imagination. The legendary forest of Brocéliande, the open plains and big sky, its rocky coasts and otherworldly remoteness were features that inspired writers like Chaucer whose own version of a Breton lay, the Franklin's Tale, features the rocks of Brittany's coast in a test of marital fidelity. Chaucer's invocation of the Breton tradition at the beginning of the tale effectively removes his audience from their place in the present to sometime in a distant past:

> Thise olde gentil Britouns in hir dayes
> Of diverse aventures maden layes,
> Rymeyed in hir firste Briton tonge; *Rhymed*
> Whiche layes with hir instrumentz they songe,
> Or elles redden hem for hir plesaunce. *read them; their*
> And oon of hem have I in remembraunce.
> (F 709–14)

It is generally agreed that Chaucer knew and made use of the Auchinleck manuscript containing three of the early lays: *Lay le Freine, Sir Orfeo*, and *Sir Degaré*.[20] Some scholars suggest that he was making the most of a current vogue, capitalizing on the appeal of the "old-fashioned," sentimental nostalgia invoked by the genre. Kathryn Hume more definitively asserts that he was capitalizing on the magical ethos associ-

---

[19] See Susan Wittig, *Stylistic and Narrative Structures in Middle English Romances* (Austin: University of Texas Press, 1978), p. 179. Wittig posits a "common model" for romance, composed of "two major linking structures (separation-restoration, love-marriage)." The Middle English Breton lays, because of their brevity, emphasize the latter of these formations.

[20] See Laura A. Hibbard [Loomis], "Chaucer and the Breton Lays of the Auchinleck MS," *Studies in Philology* 38 (1941), 14–33.

ated with the Breton tradition.[21] Both perspectives address a process of poetic appropriation not uncommon in medieval literature. But there is more going on here than a sentimental journey into an enchanted pagan past. Rather, Chaucer seems to be reclaiming a tradition that had migrated with the ancient Celts from Britain to Brittany in the fifth century. As Emily Yoder suggests, Breton lays "were considered to be ancient stories of the British people who inhabited the main island of Britain" and are not to be confused with stories told by contemporary late medieval Bretons, inhabitants of Brittany located across the English Channel.[22] Yet the "olde gentil Britons" to whom Chaucer refers are the progenitors of the Breton tradition. The two seemingly separate groups – Britons and Bretons – share the same genealogy and cultural heritage. The very interchangeability of the terms "Briton" and "Breton" underscores that kinship relation as does the dual connotation of *Bretaigne* (both Britain and Brittany or Little Britain as it came to be known). The facts of rivalry between France and Britain for Brittany, the claims of both on its sovereignty, and its strategic importance in the Hundred Years War (1337–1453), infuse a seemingly innocuous poetic act with political motive.[23] The "matter of Britain" (i.e., Arthurian legend), dominated by French writers such as Chrétien de Troyes, Robert de Boron, Wace, Marie de France, and others since the twelfth century, was ripe for English reclamation in the fourteenth century. The Middle English Breton lays are part of an agenda for reinstating a cultural heritage.

Both French culture and its aristocratic language, brought to England in the eleventh century by the invading Normans, were, by the fourteenth and fifteenth centuries, systematically displaced by the cultural forces of England. After the deposition of Richard II, whose love of French culture and language was well-known and ridiculed by his detractors, his successor, Henry IV, made English the official

---

[21] Kathryn Hume, "Why Chaucer Calls the Franklin's Tale a Breton Lai," *Philological Quarterly* 51.1 (1972), 365–79. Hume argues that there are three typical features of the lay which Chaucer knew and used: (1) "a concern with love and with what the Franklin calls 'gentilesse,' (2) the frequent use of magic (both fairie and other) as a plot device, and (3) an a-Christian ethic" (p. 366).

[22] See Emily K. Yoder, "Chaucer and the 'Breton' Lay" *Chaucer Review* 12 (1977/78), 74–77.

[23] See Desmond Seward, *The Hundred Years War: The English in France, 1337–1453* (New York: Atheneum, 1978), p. 79. Although Brittany remained neutral during the war, there were claims to her sovereignty made by both England and France. Many English garrisons were stationed there and, according to Seward, Brittany was the site of one of the most memorable events of the war. Called the "Combat of the Thirty" it was a staged event, a chivalric tournament between thirty English soldiers and thirty French soldiers. Suggested by the English garrison commander, the idea was to come to some determination of military superiority without a fullblown battle. The French won, killing nine English soldiers including the garrison commander and taking the rest prisoner.

language of Britain.[24] After 1362, with the opening of Parliament in English, rather than French, the dominance of French in England rapidly diminished. English poets could no longer presuppose a bilingual or multilingual audience, but rather they focused on an English-speaking audience:

Bifel a cas in Breteyne,	*Once upon a time; Brittany*
Whereof was made *Lay le Frain*;	
In Ingliche for to tellen ywis	*i.e., I will tell you in English*
of an asche for sothe it is. . .	*ash*
(*Lay le Freine* prologue, lines 23–26)	

The anonymous poet of *Lay le Freine* does not presume that his audience knows the heroine's French name means "asche" in English, but rather explicitly defines it.

One minor geographic change that the poet of *Lay le Freine* makes from Marie's version – where Brittany becomes the "west cuntre" of England – accrues added significance in view of the processes of reclaiming the heritage. Orfeo's removal from a mythical place in ancient Greece to Winchester, the ancient Anglo-Saxon capital, *Emaré's* bringing a tale "out of Brittany," and the changes that render *Sir Launfal* more "public" and "concrete" within a fourteenth-century English context, all suggest an agenda very unlike Marie's. These discernible changes in orientation, as A. C. Spearing suggests, imply a process of adapting Marie's lais to an English "lay" audience in order to speak to their concerns.[25] What Susan Crane suggests about insular romance holds true for the English lays: "[they] are attuned to the realities of English life," with voices shaped to answer England's questions.[26]

Because of the social and political events of the period, some of those questions have to do with issues such as class identity, personal identity, and positioning within society. Perhaps that is one reason there are so many identifiable folktale motifs that figure significantly in the reconstructed action of these poems – the Calumniated Queen or Persecuted Wife of *Erle of Tolous* and *Emaré*; the Wish Child or Devil's Contract of *Sir Gowther* and *Sir Orfeo*; the Spendthrift Knight and Strokes Shared of

[24] For a thorough discussion of the complexities of linguistic displacement in England, which also included Latin, see M. T. Clanchy, *From Memory to Written Record* (Cambridge, MA: Harvard University, 1979). See also John H. Fisher, "A Language Policy for Lancastrian England," *PMLA* 107 (1992), 1168–80.

[25] See A. C. Spearing, "Marie de France and her Middle English Adapters," pp. 117–56.

[26] See Susan Crane, *Insular Romance: Politics, Faith, and Culture in Anglo-Norman and Middle English Literature* (Berkeley: University of California Press, 1986), p. 12.

Sir Cleges; the Father/Son Combat of *Sir Degaré*, for example.[27] Folktales bring with them the tensions inherent within a particular social environment; they constitute the venue by which, according to Jack Zipes, "common people perceived nature and their social order."[28] Drawing much of their social *energia* from folktale, these poems reflect a perception of nature and the social order as seen through the eyes of the "common people." But rather than consistently upholding traditionality, as Carol Fewster claims for Middle English romance,[29] they affirm the dominant values of a dynamic society and an urgent necessity to redefine its norms.

The regional differences among the lays, differences determined by dialect, have fueled speculation about the composition of the actual audience for whom these poems were intended. *Lay le Freine,* whose dialect is similar to Chaucer's, is placed near London or Middlesex, as is *Sir Orfeo. Sir Launfal* and *Sir Degaré* are thought to derive from somewhere in the South Midlands, and *Erle of Tolous*, *Emaré,* and *Sir Gowther* are thought to have originated in the Northeast Midlands.[30] These regional and dialectical differences, as some scholars suggest, probably identify corresponding differences in audience. While some posit an audience derived from the new mercantile class of wealthy, semi-aristocratic wool merchant houses of East Anglia, others would define the audience in terms of what K. B. McFarlane calls the "fallen gentry."[31] John B. Beston posits two separate groups: for the earlier couplet lays a "rather sophisticated audience, familiar with the courtly tradition," and for the tail-

[27] Mortimer J. Donovan's suggestion that a shift in emphasis of the Middle English lays from *courtesie* to *aventure* signals "retrogression and tends to reduce the lay to a folktale" is a significant if rather negative recognition of the relation of the lays to folktale. See *The Breton Lay: A Guide to Varieties*, p. 122.

[28] See Jack Zipes, *Breaking the Magic Spell: Radical Theories of Folk and Fairy Tales* (Austin: University of Texas Press, 1979; rpt. New York: Methuen, 1984), p. 5.

[29] See Carol Fewster, *Traditionality and Genre in Middle English Romance* (Cambridge, MA: D. S. Brewer, 1987), p. 30.

[30] The issue of origin is still under contention. Variations occur even among versions of the same poem.

[31] See Derek Pearsall, "The Development of Middle English Romance," *Medieval Studies* 27 (1965), 91–116. See also Harriet Hudson "Middle English Popular Romances: The Manuscript Evidence," *Manuscripta* 28 (1984), 67–68. Hudson uses the term "fallen gentry" as defined by K. B. McFarlane in *The Nobility of Later Medieval England: The Ford Lectures for 1953 and Related Studies* (Oxford: Clarendon Press, 1973).

rhyme lays "a somewhat crude but robust audience."[32] Eamon Duffy claims that the audience, at least by the late fifteenth century, is composed of a wider segment of society accounted for by "the spread of literacy down the social scale, even to many women."[33] It is not surprising then that the production of these manuscripts corresponded with a growing demand for reading materials – reading materials congruent with the concerns of an increasingly diverse audience.

The poems that we have chosen to present derive from five manuscript anthologies. Beginning with the Auchinleck MS, compiled possibly in 1330 in a London bookshop,[34] we derive *Sir Orfeo, Lay le Freine*, and *Sir Degaré*; later manuscripts – Cambridge University Library Ff. 2.38, British Library Cotton Caligula A.ii, National Library of Scotland Advocates 19.3.1, and Oxford's Bodleian Library 6922 (Ashmole 61) – supply the others.[35] Of the group, Auchinleck reigns first and foremost both in content and presentation. Although thirteen items have been lost, this manuscript contains 334 leaves (voluminous by medieval standards) and a total of forty-four narratives which Laura Hibbard Loomis categorizes as follows: eighteen romances, one chronicle and a list of Norman barons, two pious tales of the miracle type, eight legends of saints and other holy legends, one visit to the Otherworld, one humorous tale, two debates, one homily, two monitory pieces, three works of religious instruction, and three of satire and complaint. As her summary suggests, the romances, a genre in which she includes *Sir Orfeo* and *Lay le Freine*, dominate the manuscript and point to the popularity of such narratives for its fourteenth-century audience.[36]

---

[32] See John B. Beston, "How Much Was Known of the Breton Lai in Fourteenth-Century England?" in *The Learned and the Lewed*, ed. Larry D. Benson (Cambridge, MA: Harvard University Press, 1974), pp. 319–36.

[33] See Eamon Duffy, *The Stripping of the Altars: Traditional Religion in England, c. 1400– c. 1580* (New Haven: Yale University Press, 1992), p. 68. For further discussion of literacy in England see JoAnn Moran, *The Growth of English Schooling 1340–1548* (Princeton: Princeton University Press, 1985); James Westfall Thompson, *The Literacy of the Laity in the Middle Ages* (Berkeley: University of California, 1938; rpt. New York: Burt Franklin, 1963). See also Carol M. Meale, ed. *Women & Literature in Britain, 1150–1500,* Cambridge Studies in Medieval Literature 17 (Cambridge, MA: Cambridge University Press, 1993).

[34] See Laura A. Hibbard [Loomis], "The Auchinleck Manuscript and a Possible London Bookshop of 1330–1340," *PMLA* 57 (1942), 595–627.

[35] Cambridge Ff. 2.38 (*Erle of Tolous)*; Cotton Caligula (*Sir Launfal* and *Emaré)*; Advocates 19.3.1 (*Sir Gowther)*; Bodleian Ashmole 61 (*Sir Cleges)*.

[36] See Derek Pearsall, "Middle English Romance and its Audiences," in *Historical & Editorial Studies in Medieval & Early Modern English for Johan Gerritsen,* eds. Mary-Jo Arn and Hanneke Wirtjes with Hans Jansen (Groningen: Wolters Noordhoff, 1985), pp. 37–47. Pearsall notes that the

Cambridge Ff. 2.38, compiled in the late fifteenth or early sixteenth century, is equally voluminous, containing forty-three items including *Bevis of Hampton, Guy of Warwick, Eglamour of Artois, Octavian, Le Bone Florence of Rome, Robert of Sicely, Syr Tryamoure, Sir Degaré*, saints' lives such as those of Margaret, Thomas, Edmund; Mirk's Festial; a collection of homilies; devotional works such as *The Assumption of the Virgin*; *The Seven Sages of Rome*, which is a collection of didactic narratives; and other miscellaneous items. Cotton Caligula A.ii, compiled from 1451–60, contains thirty-eight items including *Chevaliere Assigne, The Siege of Jerusalem, Octavian, Libeaus Desconus, Isumbras, Eglamour of Artois, Emaré, Launfal Miles* (*Sir Launfal*), *Susannah and the Two Elders*, Lydgate's *Stans Puer ad Mensam*, his piece on table manners, and *The Chorle and the Bird*, medical remedies, saints' lives, seventeen devotional works, and several didactic items. Advocates 19.3.1, compiled in the late fifteenth century, more modestly contains Lydgate's *Stans Puer ad Mensam* and *The Life of Our Lady*, *Sir Isumbras*, *Sir Gowther*, and *Amadace of Gaul*, though its length (432 leaves) might suggest greater diversity. The late fifteenth century Bodleian 6922 (Ashmole 61) boasts thirty-nine items in 162 leaves and includes *Sir Cleges* (found between *Tale of an Incestuous Daughter* and *The Founding of the Feasts of All Saints and All Souls*), *Erle of Tolous, Kyng Orfew (Sir Orfeo), Lybeaus Desconus*, *Isumbras*, didactic works such as *A Father's Instruction to His Son, A Good Wife Instructs Her Daughter, Twelve Points for Purchasers of Land,* three of Lydgate's works (*Stans Puer ad Mensam, Rammeshorne,* and *The Governans of Man* [dietary advice]), and fourteen devotional items including personal morning and evening prayers. What we are witnessing when we examine the contents of these manuscripts, compiled over the course of more than a century, is not only evidence of increased demand, but also a diversification of literary tastes. From the "highly literary" Auchinleck to the more pious and devotional materials in the later manuscripts there seems to be a marked change in the concerns of a newly literate English audience. Though the new demands may be more pious and practical, the Middle English Breton lays, as well as the instructive romances, remain a part of the new directions.

These manuscript anthologies stand as important indicators both of England's burgeoning literacy and of an increasing privatization of reading for an audience interested in redefining social norms.[37] Frances McSparran and P. R. Robinson

Auchinleck MS is the medieval equivalent of a "coffee-table" book, probably intended for private household use.

[37] See Janet Coleman, *Medieval Readers and Writers, 1350–1400* (New York: Columbia University Press, 1981). Coleman argues that the extension of the "middle class" marked a corresponding increase in manuscript patronage. The newly literate were interested in "what concerned pious men of commerce, eager to establish law and order, principles of morality and peace" (p. 71).

posit an audience of "devout and literate layfolk" and conclude that the Cambridge MS functioned as "family reading in a pious middle-class household." Derek Pearsall notes evidence of "more attention to the needs of private readers in the presentation and lay-out of the texts."[38] Whatever reading audience the compilers of these manuscripts had in mind, it is clear that these voluminous collections served many functions: the romance narratives could be read aloud for entertainment and instruction in familial matters; the didactic items could be used for the instruction of children; and the devotional works could address the need for private reading and meditation in the edification of one's own soul. What the diverse contents of these manuscripts seem to indicate is the beginning of a new kind of reading – one more private than public, more family oriented than not.[39] If a genre can finally be determined by its interaction with an audience then these poems are "English" Breton lays largely because they point to a renewed interest in the nuclear English family and the shaping of distinctly English family values.

Select Bibliography

Beston, John B. "How Much Was Known of the Breton Lai in Fourteenth-Century England?" In *The Learned and the Lewed: Studies in Chaucer and Medieval Literature*. Ed. Larry D. Benson. *Harvard English Studies* 5. Cambridge: Harvard University Press, 1974. Pp. 319–36. [Claims that the Breton lay was not as well-known in fourteenth-century England as many have claimed.]

Bromwich, Rachel. "A Note on the Breton Lays." *Medium Aevum* 26 (1957), 36–38. [Notes the relationship of Marie's lais to Welsh sagas told in the ninth and tenth centuries.]

Bullock-Davies, Constance. "The Form of the Breton Lay." *Medium Aevum* 42 (1973), 18–31. [Discusses structure and stylistic elements of the genre and includes an analysis of the Briton/Breton manner of musical performance.]

Crane, Susan. *Insular Romance: Politics, Faith, and Culture in Anglo-Norman and Middle English Literature.* Berkeley: University of California Press, 1986. [Delineates distinguishing features of English romance.]

---

[38] See Derek Pearsall, "Middle English Romance and its Audiences," p. 42.

[39] See Harriet Hudson, p. 77.

——. “The Franklin as Dorigen.” *Chaucer Review* 24 (1989/90), 236-52. [Argues that the Franklin and Dorigen share analogous positions in society.]

——. *Gender and Romance in Chaucer’s Canterbury Tales*. Princeton: Princeton University Press, 1994. [Discusses the Franklin’s Tale and Breton lay genre.]

Donovan, Mortimer J. *The Breton Lay: A Guide to Varieties.* Notre Dame: University of Notre Dame Press, 1969. [Comparative study with emphasis on the French *lais*.]

Finlayson, John. “The Form of the Middle English Lay.” *Chaucer Review* 19 (1984–85), 352–68. [Locates the genre within romance.]

Hudson, Harriet. “Middle English Popular Romances: The Manuscript Evidence.” *Manuscripta* 28 (1984), 67–78. [Discusses the provenance of romance manuscripts and their probable audience.]

Hume, Kathryn. “Why Chaucer Calls the *Franklin’s Tale* a Breton Lai.” *Philological Quarterly* 51 (1972), 365–79. [Offers reasons for Chaucer’s use of Breton lay that go beyond those generally accepted.]

——. “The Formal Nature of Middle English Romance.” *Philological Quarterly* 53 (1974), 158–80. [Distinguishes three types of romance based upon the hero’s ability to fulfill his destiny.]

Johnston, Grahame. “The Breton Lays in Middle English.” In *Iceland and the Mediaeval World: Studies in Honour of Ian Maxwell*. Eds. Gabriel Turville-Petre and John Stanley Martin. Victoria, Australia: Wilke, 1974. Pp. 151–61. [Argues that the differences among the English lays discourages study of the English lays as a group.]

Loomis, Laura A. Hibbard. “The Auchinleck Manuscript and a Possible London Bookshop of 1330–1340.” *PMLA* 57 (1942), 595–627. [Study of internal evidence to date and locate the manuscript’s production in a commercial scriptorium in London.]

——. “Chaucer and the Breton Lays of the Auchinleck MS.” *Studies in Philology* 38 (1941), 14–33. [Discusses evidence of the influence of the Auchinleck MS particularly on the Franklin’s Tale and Wife of Bath’s Tale.]

Pearsall, Derek. "The Development of Middle English Romance." *Mediaeval Studies* 27 (1965), 91–116. [Follows the growth and development of the genre from 1240 to 1400.]

——. "Middle English Romance and Its Audience." In *Historical and Editorial Studies in Medieval and Early Modern English for Johan Gerritsen.* Ed. Mary-Jo Arn and Hanneke Wirtjes, with Hans Jansen. Groningen: Wolters-Noordhoff, 1985. Pp. 37–47. [Discusses a range of possible audiences from urban to provincial.]

Shippey, T. A. "Breton *Lais* and Modern Fantasies." In *Studies in Medieval English Romances: Some New Approaches*. Ed., Derek Brewer. Cambridge: D. S. Brewer, 1988. Pp. 69–91. [Relates Marie's lais to a small group of fantasy novels recently written for children.]

Smithers, G. V. "Story-Patterns in Some Breton Lays." *Medium Aevum* 22 (1953), 61–92. [Distinguishes three types of recurring patterns.]

Spearing, A. C. "Marie de France and Her Middle English Adapters." *Studies in the Age of Chaucer* 12 (1990), 117–56. [Comparative study of Marie's *Le Fresne* and *Lanval* with their Middle English adaptations.]

Strohm, Paul. "*Storie, Spelle, Geste, Romaunce, Tragedie*: Generic Distinctions in the Middle English Troy Narratives." *Speculum* 46 (1971), 348–59. [A useful study of genre as perceived by medieval writers.]

——. "The Origin and Meaning of Middle English Romaunce." *Genre* 10 (1977), 1–28. [Discusses the use of the term from the twelfth through the fifteenth centuries and addresses such related terms as *storie*, *geste*, and *lay*.]

——. *Social Chaucer*. Cambridge, MA: Harvard University Press, 1989. [Provides a social context for Chaucer's work and includes a useful discussion of audience.]

Yoder, Emily K. "Chaucer and the 'Breton' Lay." *Chaucer Review* 12 (1977–78), 74–77. [Discusses the distinctions between the terms *Briton* and *Breton* and Chaucer's use of the former in the Franklin's Tale.]

Zipes, Jack. *Breaking the Magic Spell: Radical Theories of Folk and Fairy Tales*. Austin: University of Texas Press, 1979; rpt. New York: Methuen, 1984. [Breaks away from conventionally accepted psychoanalytical theories, offering instead a socio-politically oriented (i.e., Marxist) theory for the interpretation of folk narratives.]

Sir Orfeo

Introduction

The Auchinleck manuscript, a tremendously important anthology dating from about 1330–40, contains the earliest known Middle English version of *Sir Orfeo*. The manuscript was apparently compiled for affluent but non-aristocratic readers.[1] It includes a wide variety of materials, many of which are extant only in this MS; all the texts of the Auchinleck are in English. The manuscript provides considerable information on literacy and book-production in the early fourteenth century, and it has received particular attention because there is some evidence which suggests that Chaucer may have owned it.[2]

The author of *Sir Orfeo* is unknown. The language of the text suggests that it was composed in the late thirteenth or early fourteenth centuries within the Westminster-Middlesex area. No immediate source for the poem is known. Most scholars assume that an Old French source existed at one time. References to a musical lay of Orpheus can be found in several Old French texts: the twelfth-century romance, *Floire et Blanceflor* refers to "le lai d'Orphey" (line 855); the *Lai de l'Espine* mentions "Le lai lor sone d'Orphei" (line 181); and the Vulgate *Prose Lancelot* indicates the existence of a "lay d'orfay."[3] Some scholarly efforts have been made to find connections between *Sir Orfeo* and a number of other texts, including Boethius' *De Consolatione Philosophiae*, King Alfred's Old English translation of Boethius, Walter Map's

---

[1] For information on the MS see the facsimile edition, *The Auchinleck Manuscript: National Library of Scotland Advocates' MS. 19.2.1*, intro., Derek Pearsall and I. C. Cunningham (London: Scholar Press, 1977); E. Kölbing, "Vier Romanzen-Handschriften," *Englische Studien* 7 (1884), 177–201; and A. J. Bliss, "Notes on the Auchinleck Manuscript," *Speculum* 26 (1951), 652–58.

[2] See Laura Hibbard Loomis' articles: "Chaucer and the Breton Lays of the Auchinleck Manuscript," *Studies in Philology* 38 (1941), 14–33; "Chaucer and the Auchinleck Manuscript: Thopas and Guy of Warwick," in *Essays and Studies in Honor of Carleton Brown* (New York: New York University Press, 1940), pp. 111–28; and "The Auchinleck MS and a Possible London Bookshop of 1330–40," *PMLA* 57 (1942), 595–627. See also *Sources and Analogues of Chaucer's Canterbury Tales*, ed. W. F. Bryan and Germaine Dempster (Chicago: University of Chicago Press, 1941), pp. 486–559.

[3] The passages from these texts are cited in *Sir Orfeo*, ed. A. J. Bliss (Oxford: Clarendon Press, 1966), pp. xxxi–xxxii.

De Nugis Curialium, and more. None of these is conclusive. What is certain is that *Sir Orfeo* presents a Breton Lay on a classical theme. The Orpheus myth is, of course, well known throughout the Western world. Whether as lover, musician, or priestly wisdom figure, Orpheus can be found represented in ancient Greek art and literature from as early as the sixth century B.C., and the narrative can be found in a number of different ancient cultures.[4] Orpheus is also well-represented by authors known to the medieval world, including Virgil, Ovid, Horace, Boethius, the anonymous author of the Hellenistic Jewish *Testament of Orpheus*, Clement of Alexandria, Fulgentius, and later William of Conches, Nicholas Trivet, Boccaccio, the anonymous author of the *Ovide Moralisé*, Pierre Bersuire, Christine de Pizan, and Robert Henryson, just to name a few.[5] The power of the Orpheus myth to resonate through time and within both classical and medieval literatures has led to a number of divergent interpretations of the lay of *Sir Orfeo*; it has been read within Christian contexts, Celtic-folktale contexts, as well as within historical, philosophical, psychological, intertextual, and poetic contexts.

The basic narrative of unassuaged grief and the image of Orpheus the magical or shamanistic harper originates in classical literature. For the late Middle Ages, the best known classical sources would have been Ovid's *Metamorphoses* X and Virgil's *Georgics* IV (as well as the numerous commentaries on them). Through medieval commentaries, Christian re-readings of the narrative became well-known: 1) Orpheus's backward glance and his consequent loss of Eurydice becomes emblematic for temptation and sin; or 2) Orpheus becomes a Christ figure and the tale foretells

---

[4] See Emmet Robbins' essay, "Famous Orpheus," in *Orpheus: The Metamorphosis of a Myth*, ed. John Warden (Toronto: University of Toronto Press, 1982), pp. 3–23. See also Joan M. Erikson, *Legacies: Prometheus, Orpheus, and Socrates* (New York: Norton, 1993); William K. C. Guthrie, *Orpheus and Greek Religion: A Study of the Orphic Movement*, rev. ed. (New York: Norton, 1966; rpt. Princeton University Press, 1993); Elizabeth A. Newby, *A Portrait of the Artist: the Legends of Orpheus and Their Use in Medieval and Renaissance Aesthetics*, Harvard Dissertations in Comparative Literature (New York: Garland, 1987); *The "Vulgate" Commentary on Ovid's Metamorphoses: The Creation Myth and the Story of Orpheus*, ed. Frank T. Coulson (Toronto: Pontifical Institute of Mediaeval Studies, 1991); *Le Mythe d'Orphée aux Animaux et ses Prolongements dans le Judaisme, le Christianisme et l'Islam*, ed. Andre Dupont-Sommer (Rome: Accademia nazionale dei lincei, 1975).

[5] See the comprehensive study by John Block Friedman, *Orpheus in the Middle Ages* (Cambridge: Harvard University Press, 1970); also Klaus Heitmann, "Orpheus im Mittelalter," *Archiv für Kulturgeschichte* 45 (1963), 253–94; Kenneth R. R. Gros Louis, "Robert Henryson's *Orpheus and Eurydice* and the Orpheus Traditions of the Middle Ages," *Speculum* 41 (1966), 643–55. *Orpheus, the Metamorphosis of a Myth*, ed. John Warden (Toronto: University of Toronto Press, 1982), especially the essays by Eleanor Irwin, "The Songs of Orpheus and the New Song of Christ," pp. 51–62); and Patricia Vicari, "*Sparagmos*: Orpheus among the Christians," pp. 63–83.

redemption. The lay of *Sir Orfeo* blends these received cultural materials with both Celtic and Germanic folk materials, especially the Celtic journey to the Otherworld, thereby producing what Jeff Rider terms "a hybrid super-myth."[6]

Sir Orfeo situates the action not in classical Greece but in medieval England. Heurodis is not actually killed (as she is in most classical and medieval versions); she is, instead, abducted by the fairy king so that she resembles "the taken" mortals common in Irish *aithed* narratives. Once Heurodis is taken, Orfeo (anachronistically a ruler of a medieval kingdom) appoints his loyal steward to rule in his stead. Additionally, he instructs the people to elect a parliament and name a new king if they ever learn of his death. Donning the pilgrim's cloak, he renounces his kingdom and all his wealth and retreats into self-imposed poverty and exile. The only object he carries with him from his courtly life into his new life is his harp. When he plays his harp, "whereon was al his gle" (line 267), he comforts himself and charms the beasts of nature. After ten years, he happens to spy Heurodis riding a palfrey with the fairy king's hunting party and follows after her. Here we do not travel to Hades or Hell but to the Celtic Otherworld "in at a roche" (line 347). Knocking at the gate of the Otherworld palace, Orfeo, dressed as a begging minstrel, gets past the porter, past the tableau of the dead, and offers to sing for the fairy king. When the fairy king offers the "rash boon" found so frequently in folklore narratives, Orfeo sees his chance and asks for Heurodis. With a bit of hesitation, the fairy king relents and the two mortals are reunited. The fairy king places no taboo about looking back on Orfeo as he does in the classical version. Instead of the traditional backward glance which loses Eurydice forever, the fourteenth-century Breton lay hero leads his Heurodis back home. Disguising himself once more as a beggar, he tests his steward's loyalty and regains his throne.

As with many Breton lays, this narrative recreates folklore motifs: the journey to the Otherworld, the man who loses his wife/lover, the rash boon, the exile-return pattern, and the testing of the loyal steward. The lay creates a double narrative in which the loss of the queen precipitates the loss of the kingdom, and the private recuperation of the queen precipitates the public recuperation of the kingdom. It has

---

[6] Jeff Rider, "Receiving Orpheus in the Middle Ages: Allegorization, Remythification and *Sir Orfeo*," *Papers on Language & Literature* 24 (1988), 356. On the complex relationship of medieval authors to tradition, see Lee Patterson, *Negotiating the Past: The Historical Understanding of Medieval Literature* (Madison: University of Wisconsin Press, 1987). Alexandre Leupin suggests that "medieval writers show neither idolatrous respect for a tradition . . . nor the anguish of innovation conceived as rupture: at every turn the old is rejuvenated within the new, and the new is the incessant transformation of a textual 'already there'"; see his chapter, "Absolute Reflexivity: Geoffrey of Vinsauf's *Poetria Nova*," in his book, *Barbarolexis: Medieval Writing and Sexuality*, trans. Kate M. Cooper (Cambridge: Harvard University Press, 1989), p. 22.

often been noted that the poem's structure is built upon antitheses: loss and restoration, sorrow and joy, wealth and poverty, the calm beauty of the lush, warm garden and the grief of the stark, cold or indifferent "wildernes," the elegance of the fairy world and the macabre tableau of the death courtyard, the brutality of nature and the civilizing force of art. But contrast is also problematic. More than one scholar has noticed the way the eerie Otherworld seems to mirror the medieval court world of the poem. And more than one scholar has examined the oppositions with a deconstructive turn. Even the task of interpreting the major characters unravels a plethora of possibilities. The fairy king, for example, abducts Heurodis, but he is not overtly identified as evil in the poem; instead, he operates outside and beyond the human framework of understanding. He can be read as a demonic figure, particularly if we invoke a medieval Christian framework. But invoking other frameworks will produce other readings: he can serve as an image of fate, a representative of death, an adversary who comes to life to punish sin, a pre-Christian divinity or spirit, a rupture in meaning, the representative of artifice, irrationality, "king of textuality," and more.[7]

A similar complexity or instability of meaning can be found in Pierre Bersuire's *Reductorium Morale* (c. 1325–1337), a text roughly contemporaneous with *Sir Orfeo*. Written in Latin, this moralized encyclopedia offers opposing interpretations of the Orpheus figure. First, Bersuire imagines Orpheus as a Christ-figure:

> Let us speak allegorically and say that Orpheus, the child of the sun, is Christ the son of God the Father, who from the beginning led Eurydice, that is, the human soul to himself. And from the beginning Christ joined her to himself through his special prerogative. But the devil, a serpent, drew near the new bride, that is, created *de novo*, while she collected flowers that is, while she seized the forbidden apple, and bit her by temptation and killed her by sin, and finally she went to the world below. Seeing this, Christ-Orpheus wished himself to descend to the lower world and thus he retook his wife, that is, human nature, ripping her from the hands of the ruler of Hell himself; and he led her with him to the upper world, saying this verse from Canticles 2:10, "Rise up, my love, my fair one, and come away.[8]

[7] "King of textuality" is a phrase and an idea developed by Roy Michael Liuzza in his article, "*Sir Orfeo*: Sources, Traditions, and the Poetics of Performance," *Journal of Medieval and Renaissance Studies* 21 (1991), 269–84.

[8] The Latin reads: *Dic allegorice quod Orpheus, filius solis, est Christus, filius dei patris, qui a principio Euridicem .i. animam humanam per caritatem & amorem duxit ipsamque per specialem prerogativam a principio sibi coniunxit. Veruntamen serpens, diabolus, ipsam novam nuptam .i. de novo creatam, dum flores colligeret .i. de pomo vetito appeteret, per temptationem momordit, & per peccatum occidit, & finaliter ad infernum transmisit. Quod videns Orpheus Christus in infernum personaliter*

Then, immediately following this allegorization, he imagines that Orpheus represents sinful humanity:

> Or let us say that Orpheus is a sinner who, by the bite of the serpent, that is, by the temptation of the Devil, lost his wife, that is, his soul, when she was indiscreetly collecting flowers, that is, applying her mind to the flux of *temporalia*. But he recovered her spiritually when he descended to the lower world through thought and through the power of his sweet measured words. Fear alone of infernal punishment made him penitent for his sins and thus he regained his wife through grace . . . . But many are there who look backward through love of temporalia just as a dog returns to his vomit, and they love their wife too much, that is, the recovered soul, and so they favor their concupiscence and return the eyes of their mind to it and so they put her by and Hell receives her again. So says John 12:25, "He that loveth his life shall lose it."[9]

Similar instability in meaning can be found in the *Ovide Moralisé*, also dating from around the same time as *Sir Orfeo*. But the instability of meaning found in the commentaries on the myth stem from juxtaposing different avenues of interpretation; within *Sir Orfeo*, the ambiguities arise, not in a chronological listing of different interpretations but by the simultaneous interweaving and resonance of different innuendoes and possibilities.

If anything in the poem forms a stable center, it is the harp. More than any character, the harp is the central image of the poem, since, from beginning to end, its presence is known. The harp was a powerful metaphor in classical and medieval culture. As a Pythagorean model of perfect harmony and proportion, its strings came to represent the music of the spheres: a metaphor for the harmonious cosmos. It was also associated with the spiritual life, the power of grace, heavenly music, and the

---

voluit descendere & sic uxorem suam .i. humanam naturam rehabuit, ipsamque de regno tenebrarum ereptam ad superos secum duxit, dicens illud Canticorum .ii. "Surge, propera amica mea & veni." Pierre Bersuire, *Metamorphosis Ovidiana, moraliter explanata* (Paris, 1509), fol. LXXXv. Both English and Latin passages are edited and cited in Friedman, pp. 127–28.

[9] The Latin reads: *Vel dic quod Orpheus est peccator, qui scilicet morsu serpentis, .i. diaboli temptatione, uxorem suam .i. animam perdit dum indiscrete ad colligendum flores .i. ad congreganda fluxibilia temporalia intendit, sed tamen ipsam spiritualiter recuperat quando ad inferos per considerationem descendit & per orationem dulciter modulatur. Solus enim timor infernalis supplicii facit de vitiis poenitere & et sic facit uxorem per gratiam rehaberi . . . Verumtamen multi sunt qui quia retro per amorem temporalium respiciunt, & tanquam canis ad vomitum mentaliter revertuntur, & ipsam uxorem scilicet animam recuperatam nimis diligunt ita quod concupiscentiis eius favent & ad ipsam mentis oculos retrovertunt ipsam iterum amitunt & infernus eam recipit. Io. xii. "Qui amat animam suam perdet eam"* (fol. LXXIIIr). Cited and translated in Friedman, pp. 128–29.

harmony of the spirit. Michael Masi notes, "Compared to the music of the reed and other wind instruments, [the harp] was the instrument of grace and goodness, not of sensuality and ribaldry. It was a sacred instrument and the quality of its music was not to be confused with the secular entertainment of other music."[10] Certainly for a medieval Christian audience, the image could easily resonate with the numerous citheras of Old Testament kings and prophets, especially with the lyre of the psalm-writer, King David. In *Sir Orfeo*, the harp charms the animals, brings harmony where there was hostility, and is the one item which Orfeo carries over from his kingly world into his beggar world. It is also the one object which is shared by both character and poet; it bridges the fictional world of the lay and the actual world of the lay minstrel. Furthermore, the harp succeeds where armies of men fail; it charms the fairy king and is essential for Heurodis' recovery and for Orfeo's restoration. The orphic song emphasizes the power of art, eloquence, poetry, music, and rhetoric. Like Amphion, the legendary builder of Thebes, who charmed the stones of the city into place with his harp, Orfeo and his harp can represent functions of culture, language, and civilization. In an eleventh-century poem by Thierry of Saint-Trond, Orpheus, "trusting with all the power of his spirit in the divinity of his art, bravely took what he desired from [the Otherworld of] Styx. Thus art, aided by firm purpose, vanquished nature."[11] Nicolas Trivet, who wrote a commentary on Boethius (c. 1305) contemporaneous with *Sir Orfeo*, also emphasizes this aspect of the narrative. Trivet writes: "By Orpheus, we should understand the part of the intellect which is instructed in wisdom and eloquence . . . . Orpheus, then, by his sweet lyre, that is of his eloquence, brought the wicked, brutal, and wild animals/men of the wood to the law of reason."[12]

---

[10] Michael Masi, "The Christian Music of *Sir Orfeo*," *Classical Folia* 28 (1974), 19. Masi also points to John Hollander, *The Untuning of the Sky* (Princeton: Princeton University Press, 1961), pp. 31–36.

[11] Thierry of Saint-Trond's poem is cited in Peter Dronke, "The Return of Eurydice," *Classica et Mediaevalia* 23 (1962), 199; and in Friedman, pp. 165–66. The Latin reads: *Numine sic artis fidens industria mentis, / Fortiter extorsit a Styge quod voluit. / Sic ars naturam vicit, studio mediante, / Virtuti dominae cedere cuncta probans.* The full text of the poem is in F. W. Otto, *Commentarii critici in codices Bibliothecae Academicae Gissensis Graecos et Latinos* (Giessen: G. F. Heyeri, 1842), pp. 163–65.

[12] Cited in Friedman, pp. 110–11. The Latin reads: *Orpheum intelligitur pars intellectiva instructa sapientia et eloquentia . . . . Iste autem per suavitatem citharae id est eloquentiae impies brutales e silvestres reduxit ad normam rationis.* See also Thomas Aquinas, *Commentary on the De Anima of Aristotle*, Lib. I, Lec. xxi.

Where the brilliant Otherworld is characterized by visual artifice and stasis, Orfeo's song breaks into its suspended motion and charms Heurodis back to life. As Roy M. Liuzza comments, "Heurodis must be resurrected by the voice of the singer just as the written word, in medieval linguistic thought, must be revived by the voice of the reader/performer."[13] But even the harp, the powerful central image of the lay doesn't have the last word or final sound. Any semiotic system we bring to this poem will fail to capture all the meanings of the text. As Jeff Rider comments, "What makes *Sir Orfeo* so remarkable is the degree of critical response it has generated, the high praise it has earned, and the almost utter lack of accord among critics as to its interpretation. The poem seems to be remythified with each reading; each reading makes us feel that the previous one, even yesterday's, was inadequate."[14]

Select Bibliography

Manuscripts

National Library of Scotland MS Advocates 19.2.1, fols. 299a (stub)–303ra; also known as the Auchinleck MS (A). [A folio volume of 332 vellum leaves, most of its illuminations have been excised, and the manuscript has been damaged by the loss of many leaves which have been cut away completely.]

British Library MS Harley 3810, fols. 1a–10a (H).

Bodleian Library MS Ashmole 61, fols. 151a–156a (B).

Facsimile Edition

The Auchinleck Manuscript. National Library of Scotland. Advocates MS. 19.2.1. With introduction by Derek Pearsall and I. C. Cunningham. London: Scolar Press, in association with The National Library of Scotland, 1979.

---

[13] Roy M. Liuzza, "*Sir Orfeo*: Sources, Traditions, and the Poetics of Performance," *Journal of Medieval and Renaissance Studies* 21 (1991), 282.

[14] Jeff Rider, p. 361.

Sir Orfeo

Editions

Bliss, A. J., ed. *Sir Orfeo.* London: Oxford University Press, 1954. 2nd ed. Oxford: Clarendon Press, 1966. [Prints all three MSS. Reconstructs a thirty-eight line prologue for A out of the prologue to *Lay le Freine* and H and B.]

Wallace, Sylvia Crowell, ed. "*Sir Orfeo*: An Edition." Ph.D. dissertation, Yale University, 1963.

Zielke, Oscar, ed. *Sir Orfeo: Ein englisches Feenmärchen aus dem Mittelalter.* Breslau: Koebner, 1880. [Uses A with twenty-four line prologue derived from H and prologue to *Lay le Freine* (A fol. 261a).]

Collections

Burrow, John A., ed. *English Verse 1300-1500.* Longman Annotated Anthologies of English Verse, Vol. I. London: Longman, 1977. Pp. 4–27. [Text based on A with Bliss's thirty-eight line prologue.]

Cook, A. S. *A Literary Middle English Reader.* Boston: Ginn, 1915; rpt. Boston: Ginn, 1943, pp. 88-107. [Follows A, adding a ten line prologue.]

Dunn, Charles W., and Edward T. Byrnes, eds. *Middle English Literature.* New York: Harcourt Brace Jovanovich, 1973. Pp. 216–30. [Twenty-four line prologue, from Zielke.]

Ford, Boris, ed. *The Age of Chaucer The Pelican Guide to English Literature* I. Baltimore: Penguin, 1955. Pp. 271–88.

French, Walter Hoyt, and Charles Brockway Hale, eds. *The Middle English Metrical Romances.* 2 vols. New York: Prentice-Hall, 1930; rpt. New York: Russell & Russell, 1964. Vol. I. Pp. 321–41. [Uses A as base text, with twenty-four line prologue from Zielke.]

Garbáty, Thomas J., ed. *Medieval English Literature.* Lexington, Mass: Heath, 1984. Pp. 349–64. [A text with twenty-four line prologue, as in French and Hale.]

Gibbs, A. C., ed. *Middle English Romances*, York Medieval Texts. London: Edward Arnold; Evanston: Northwestern University Press, 1966. Pp. 84–103. [A text with twenty-four line prologue.]

Haskell, Ann S., ed. *A Middle English Anthology*. Garden City: Anchor, 1969. Pp. 247–62. [A text with no prologue.]

Rumble, Thomas, ed. *The Breton Lays in Middle English*. Detroit: Wayne State University Press, 1965. Pp. 207–26. [Uses Ashmole 61 as base text.]

Sands, Donald B., ed. *Middle English Verse Romances*. New York: Holt, Rinehart and Winston, 1966. Pp. 185–200. [A text with no prologue.]

Schmidt, A. V. C., and Nicolas Jacobs, eds. *Medieval English Romances*. New York: Holmes & Meier, 1980, Vol. I. Pp. 151–71. [A text with twenty-four line prologue.]

Sisam, Celia and Kenneth, eds. *The Oxford Book of Medieval English Verse*. London: Oxford University Press, 1970. Pp. 76–98. [A text with twenty-four line prologue.]

Sisam, Kenneth, ed. *Fourteenth Century Verse and Prose*. Oxford: Clarendon Press, 1921; rpt. with corrections, 1975. Pp. 13–31.

Related Studies

Brouland, Marie-Thérèse. *Sir Orfeo: le substrat celtique du lai breton anglais*. Paris: Didier Erudition, 1990. [Identifies Celtic folktales and mythic symbols which reside in *Orfeo* and which have parallels in other texts. A catalogue of episodes, objects, and characters *Sir Orfeo* shares with other texts stemming from Celtic materials.]

Doob, Penelope B. R., *Nebuchadnezzar's Children: Conventions of Madness in Middle English Literature*. New Haven: Yale University Press, 1974. Pp. 158–207. [Argues that "the poem can be fully understood only when one grasps the traditions that seem to have influenced its conception: the commentaries, the Christian uses of the Orpheus legend, and especially the convention of the Holy Wild Man" (p. 165).]

Friedman, John B. *Orpheus in the Middle Ages*. Cambridge: Harvard University Press, 1970. [Examines the Orphic narrative as it appears in numerous literary, philosophical, theological, and historical texts written in the Middle Ages and their various uses and interpretations of the myth. See also his article, "Eurydice, Heurodis, and the Noon-Day Demon." *Speculum* 41 (1966), 22-29.]

Grimaldi, Patrizia. "*Sir Orfeo* as Celtic Folk-Hero, Christian Pilgrim, and Medieval King." In *Allegory, Myth, and Symbol*, ed. Morton W. Bloomfield, *Harvard English Studies* 9. Cambridge: Harvard University Press, 1981. Pp. 147–61. [Grounding her argument on Northrop Frye's definition of allegory, Grimaldi demonstrates the multiple levels of allegory (literal, allegorical, tropological, and anagogical) in *Sir Orfeo* which point to Celtic folklore, myth, Christianity and socio-political ethics.]

Gros Louis, Kenneth R. R. "The Significance of Sir Orfeo's Self-Exile." *Review of English Studies* n.s. 18 (1967), 245–52. [Although we expect Orpheus to undertake a long search for Eurydice, since that is the case in numerous versions of the narrative, in *Sir Orfeo* this does not occur. Orfeo assumes he has lost his wife and retreats into exile. He does not plan to search for her and is not on any heroic quest; instead, she is mysteriously brought to him. Focusing on the ten years Orfeo lives in the wilderness, Gros Louis reads the lay as a Christianized narrative of penance and purification, the restoration of Heurodis a gift of grace.]

Hynes-Berry, Mary. "Cohesion in *King Horn* and *Sir Orfeo*." *Speculum* 50 (1975), 652–70. [Argues against scholars like Howard Nimchinsky, "*Orfeo, Guillaume*, and *Horn*." *Romance Philology* 22 (1968), 1-14, who see lines of influence between *Sir Orfeo* and the romance of *King Horn*. The similarities are "critically misleading," and "neither . . . can be fairly evaluated using the other as a model" (652). *Horn* is a romance of the action hero and has "little interest in psychology" (670); *Orfeo*, on the other hand, is concerned with emotion and its theme is primarily psychological. These differences resonate in both the structures and aesthetics of both texts.]

Lerer, Seth. "Artifice and Artistry in *Sir Orfeo*." *Speculum* 60 (1985), 92–109. ["Through a close analysis of the vocabulary and possible source material of the Auchinleck version of the poem, this study . . . show[s] how *Sir Orfeo* articulates a vision of art's power to reshape experience" (p. 94). The lay affirms the power of visual arts, horticulture, language, and music to shape order and meaning out of chaos and affirms the restorative and redemptive power of narrative in the face of loss.]

Liuzza, Roy Michael. "*Sir Orfeo*: Sources, Traditions, and the Poetics of Performance." *Journal of Medieval and Renaissance Studies* 21 (1991), 269–84.

[Considers the lay within the oral tradition and argues that "the conscious manipulation of the boundaries between orality and textuality" (p. 272) creates some of its powerful effects.]

Masi, Michael. "The Christian Music of *Sir Orfeo*." *Classical Folia* 28 (1974), 3–20. [Reads the lay as Christian narrative by examining connections between Orpheus and Christ and by exploring the Christian music symbolism found in medieval moral and cosmological concepts of the harmony of the universe. Makes specific connections between the music symbolism in *Sir Orfeo* and Boethius' *De Musica*.]

O'Brien, Timothy D. "The Shadow and Anima in *Sir Orfeo*." *Mediaevalia* 10 (1984), 235–54. [Offers a psychological interpretation of the lay based on Jung's concept of individuation.]

Riddy, Felicity. "The Uses of the Past in *Sir Orfeo*." *Yearbook of English Studies* 6 (1976), 5–15. [Contrary to many studies which ascribe emotional and psychological depth to *Orfeo*, Riddy maintains that the lay emphasizes "outward" and "observable" experiences and behaviors instead. That although the listener may learn from Orfeo, his "is not the kind of character who can be said to 'learn' anything, since he lacks . . . breadth of consciousness" (p. 11). The narrative (rather than the characters) articulates themes of nostalgia and grief and presents a Christian reading which redeems loss and the past.]

Rider, Jeff. "Receiving Orpheus in the Middle Ages: Allegorization, Remythification and *Sir Orfeo*." *Papers on Language & Literature* 24 (1988), 343–66. [Examines "allegorization" and "remythification" as responses to myth evidenced in medieval readings of the Orpheus myth, particularly within the lay of *Sir Orfeo* and as evidenced in modern interpretations of the lay. Focusing on the interplay of "King" and "Faerie," Rider writes: "The fairy king's abduction of Heurodis might thus be seen as the representation of the allegorization, the capture and reduction, of myth, which is eventually liberated and brought back to full life through the artist's efforts" (p. 366).]

Severs, J. Burke. "The Antecedents of *Sir Orfeo*." In *Studies in Medieval Literature in Honor of Professor Albert Croll Baugh*. Ed. MacEdward Leach. Philadelphia: University of Pennsylvania Press, 1961. Pp. 187–207.

Sir Orfeo

We redeth oft and findeth y-write,	*written*
And this clerkes wele it wite,	*these scholars; know*
Layes that ben in harping	*are in song*
Ben y-founde of ferli thing:	*composed about marvelous things*
Sum bethe of wer and sum of wo,	*Some are of war; grief*
And sum of joie and mirthe also,	*gaiety*
And sum of trecherie and of gile,	*guile*
Of old aventours that fel while;	*adventures; happened once*
And sum of bourdes and ribaudy,	*jokes; ribaldry*
And mani ther beth of fairy.	*the Otherworld*
Of al thinges that men seth,	*relate*
Mest o love, forsothe, they beth.	*Most of; in truth*
In Breteyne this layes were wrought,	*Brittany these; made*
First y-founde and forth y-brought,	*composed; produced*
Of aventours that fel bi dayes,	*happened in olden times*
Wherof Bretouns maked her layes.	*their*
When kinges might ovr y-here	*anywhere hear*
Of ani mervailes that ther were,	*marvels*
Thai token an harp in gle and game	*took; minstrelsy*
And maked a lay and gaf it name.	*gave*
Now of this aventours that weren y-falle	*have happened*
Y can tel sum, ac nought alle.	*I; but*
Ac herkneth, lordinges that ben trewe,	*But listen*
Ichil you telle of "Sir Orfewe."	*I will*
Orfeo mest of ani thing	*most*
Lovede the gle of harping.	*glee or music*
Siker was everi gode harpour	*Sure; good*
Of him to have miche honour.	*much*
Himself he lerned forto harp,	*He taught himself to*
And leyd theron his wittes scharp;	*applied*
He lerned so ther nothing was	*in no way*
A better harpour in no plas.	*any place*
In al the warld was no man bore	*born*

That ones Orfeo sat bifore —	*once*
And he might of his harping here —	*hear*
Bot he schuld thenche that he were	*think*
In on of the joies of Paradis,	*one*
Swiche melody in his harping is.	
Orfeo was a king,	
In Inglond an heighe lording,	*high (great) lord*
A stalworth man and hardi bo;	*brave both*
Large and curteys he was also.	*Generous; courtly*
His fader was comen of King Pluto,	*descended from*
And his moder of King Juno,	
That sum time were as godes yhold	*Who once; considered to be gods*
For aventours that thai dede and told.	*did*
This king sojournd in Traciens,	*dwelled*
That was a cité of noble defens —	*fortifications*
For Winchester was cleped tho	*called; then*
Traciens, withouten no.	*denial*
The king hadde a quen of priis	*queen of excellence*
That was y-cleped Dame Heurodis,	*called*
The fairest levedi, for the nones,	*lady indeed*
That might gon on bodi and bones,	*walk [about] in*
Ful of love and godenisse —	*goodness*
Ac no man may telle hir fairnise.	*But; beauty*
Bifel so in the comessing of May	*It happened; beginning*
When miri and hot is the day,	*merry (pleasant)*
And oway beth winter schours,	*away*
And everi feld is ful of flours,	*field*
And blosme breme on everi bough	*blossoms bright*
Over al wexeth miri anought,	*Everywhere grow; enough*
This ich quen, Dame Heurodis	*same*
Tok to maidens of priis,	*two; refinement*
And went in an undrentide	*late morning*
To play bi an orchardside,	*enjoy themselves*
To se the floures sprede and spring	
And to here the foules sing.	*hear; birds*
Thai sett hem doun al thre	*themselves*
Under a fair ympe-tre,	*grafted tree*
And wel sone this fair quene	*very quickly*
Fel on slepe opon the grene.	*asleep*

The maidens durst hir nought awake,	*dared*
Bot lete hir ligge and rest take.	*let her lie*
So sche slepe til after none,	*slept; noon*
That undertide was al y-done.	*Until midday; past*
Ac, as sone as sche gan awake,	*But; began [to]*
Sche crid, and lothli bere gan make;	*loathsome outcry made*
Sche froted hir honden and hir fete,	*rubbed; hands*
And crached hir visage – it bled wete –	*scratched her face; profusely*
Hir riche robe hye al to-rett	*she tore all to pieces*
And was reveyd out of hir wit.	*driven*
The two maidens hir biside	
No durst with hir no leng abide,	*Dared not; longer*
Bot ourn to the palays ful right	*ran; immediately*
And told bothe squier and knight	
That her quen awede wold,	*their; was going mad*
And bad hem go and hir at-hold.	*bade them; seize*
Knightes urn and levedis also,	*ran; ladies*
Damisels sexti and mo.	*[numbering] sixty and more*
In the orchard to the quen hye come,	*hastily came*
And her up in her armes nome,	*their arms took*
And brought hir to bed atte last,	
And held hir there fine fast.	*very securely*
Ac ever she held in o cri	*persisted in one*
And wold up and owy.	*wished [to go]; away*
When Orfeo herd that tiding	*heard*
Never him nas wers for nothing.	*had he been as grieved by anything*
He come with knightes tene	*came; ten*
To chaumber, right bifor the quene,	
And bi-held, and seyd with grete pité,	*beheld [her]; sorrow*
"O lef liif, what is te,	*dear life; with you*
That ever yete hast ben so stille	*Who; yet; calm*
And now gredest wonder schille?	*But; cries strangely shrilly*
Thy bodi, that was so white y-core,	*exquisitely*
With thine nailes is all to-tore.	*torn to pieces*
Allas! thy rode, that was so red,	*face*
Is al wan, as thou were ded;	*pale, as [if]*
And also thine fingres smale	*slender*
Beth al blodi and al pale.	
Allas! thy lovesum eyyen to	*lovely two eyes*

Loketh so man doth on his fo! — *as; foe*
A, dame, ich biseche, merci!
Lete ben al this reweful cri, — *Let be; pitiful*
And tel me what the is, and hou, — *what's bothering you; how*
And what thing may the help now."
Tho lay sche stille atte last — *Then*
And gan to wepe swithe fast, — *very hard*
And seyd thus the King to:
"Allas, mi lord, Sir Orfeo!
Sethen we first togider were, — *Since*
Ones wroth never we nere; — *Never once; angry [with one another]*
Bot ever ich have yloved the
As mi liif and so thou me;
Ac now we mot delen ato; — *must separate apart*
Do thi best, for y mot go." — *I must*
"Allas!" quath he, "forlorn icham! — *utterly lost I am*
Whider wiltow go, and to wham? — *Where will you; whom*
Whider thou gost, ichil with the, — *I will [go]*
And whider y go, thou schalt with me."
"Nay, nay, Sir, that nought nis! — *cannot be*
Ichil the telle al hou it is: — *I will; all how*
As ich lay this undertide — *morning*
And slepe under our orchardside,
Ther come to me to fair knightes, — *two*
Wele y-armed al to rightes, — *quite properly*
And bad me comen an heighing — *bade; in haste*
And speke with her lord the king. — *their*
And ich answerd at wordes bold, — *with*
Y durst nought, no y nold. — *dared not, nor did I want to*
Thai priked oyain as thai might drive;[1]
Tho com her king, also blive, — *their; as quickly*
With an hundred knightes and mo,
And damisels an hundred also,
Al on snowe-white stedes;
As white as milke were her wedes. — *their garments*
Y no seighe never yete bifore — *saw*

---

[1] *They spurred back as [fast as] they might go*

So fair creatours y-core.	*exquisite*
The king hadde a croun on hed;	
It nas of silver, no of gold red,	
Ac it was of a precious ston —	
As bright as the sonne it schon.	
And as son as he to me cam,	
Wold ich, nold ich, he me nam,	*Whether I wished or not he took me*
And made me with him ride	
Opon a palfray bi his side;	*palfrey*
And brought me to his palays,	
Wele atird in ich ways,	*adorned; every way*
And schewed me castels and tours,	*towers*
Rivers, forestes, frith with flours,	*woods with flowers*
And his riche stedes ichon.	*gorgeous steeds each one*
And sethen me brought oyain hom	*afterwards; back home*
Into our owhen orchard,	*own*
And said to me thus afterward,	
"'Loke, dame, tomorwe thatow be	*that you*
Right here under this ympe-tre,	
And than thou schalt with ous go	*us*
And live with ous evermo.	
And yif thou makest ous y-let,	*a hindrance for us*
Whar thou be, thou worst y-fet,	*Wherever; will be fetched*
And totore thine limes al	*torn apart; limbs*
That nothing help the no schal;	
And thei thou best so totorn,	*though (even if) you are so torn*
Yete thou worst with ous y-born.'"	*Yet; will be carried with us*
When King Orfeo herd this cas,	*matter*
"O we!" quath he, "Allas, allas!	*woe*
Lever me were to lete mi liif	*I'd rather lose*
Than thus to lese the quen, mi wiif!"	*lose*
He asked conseyl at ich man,	*advice from each person*
Ac no man him help no can.	
Amorwe the undertide is come	*The next day; high noon*
And Orfeo hath his armes y-nome,	*taken*
And wele ten hundred knightes with him,	
Ich y-armed, stout and grim;	*Each; strong; fierce*
And with the quen wenten he	
Right unto that ympe-tre.	

Thai made scheltrom in ich a side — *a rank of armed men on each*
And sayd thai wold there abide
And dye ther everichon, — *die; everyone*
Er the quen schuld fram hem gon. — *Before; from*
Ac yete amiddes hem ful right — *yet amidst them straightaway*
The quen was oway y-twight, — *snatched*
With fairi forth y-nome. — *enchantment; taken*
Men wist never wher sche was bicome. — *never knew; gone*
Tho was ther criing, wepe and wo! — *Then*
The king into his chaumber is go, — *has gone*
And oft swoned opon the ston, — *swooned; stone (i.e., floor)*
And made swiche diol and swiche mon — *such dole; moan*
That neighe his liif was y-spent — — *almost; ended*
Ther was non amendement. — *no remedy for it*
He cleped togider his barouns, — *called*
Erls, lordes of renouns,
And when thai al y-comen were,
"Lordinges," he said, "bifor you here
Ich ordainy min heighe steward — *I ordain; high*
To wite mi kingdom afterward; — *rule; henceforth*
In mi stede ben he schal — *place*
To kepe mi londes overal.
For now ichave mi quen y-lore, — *I have; lost*
The fairest levedi that ever was bore, — *lady; born*
Never eft y nil no woman se. — *Never again will I see another woman*
Into wildernes ichil te — *I will go*
And live ther evermore
With wilde bestes in holtes hore; — *woods grey*
And when ye understond that y be spent, — *dead*
Make you than a parlement,
And chese you a newe king. — *choose*
Now doth your best with al mi thing." — *do; affairs*
  Tho was ther wepeing in the halle — *Then*
And grete cri among hem alle;
Unnethe might old or yong — *Hardly; young*
For wepeing speke a word with tong.
Thai kneled adoun al y-fere — *together*
And praid him, yif his wille were, — *prayed*
That he no schuld nought fram hem go. — *from them*

"Do way!" quath he, "It schal be so!"	*Enough!*
Al his kingdom he forsoke;	
Bot a sclavin on him he toke.	*Only; pilgrim's mantle*
He no hadde kirtel no hode,	*had neither tunic nor hood*
Schert, ne no nother gode,	*Shirt; goods*
Bot his harp he tok algate	*at any rate*
And dede him barfot out atte gate;	*passed barefoot*
No man most with him go.	*might*
O way! What ther was wepe and wo,	*woe!*
When he that hadde ben king with croun	
Went so poverlich out of toun!	*in such poverty out of his town*
Thurth wode and over heth	*Through; heath*
Into the wildernes he geth.	*goes*
Nothing he fint that him is ays,	*finds; for him; comfort*
Bot ever he liveth in gret malais.	*distress*
He that hadde y-werd the fowe and griis,	*worn the variegated and grey fur*
And on bed the purper biis,	*purple linen*
Now on hard hethe he lith,	*heath; lies*
With leves and gresse he him writh.	*covers himself*
He that hadde had castels and tours,	*towers*
River, forest, frith with flours,	*woodland; flowers*
Now, thei it comenci to snewe and frese,	*although it begins; snow; freeze*
This king mot make his bed in mese.	*must; moss*
He that had y-had knightes of priis	*excellence*
Bifor him kneland, and levedis,	*kneeling; ladies*
Now seth he nothing that him liketh,	*sees; pleases*
Bot wilde wormes bi him striketh.	*snakes; glide*
He that had y-had plenté	
Of mete and drink, of ich deynté,	*delicacy*
Now may he al day digge and wrote	*dig; grub*
Er he finde his fille of rote.	*roots*
In somer he liveth bi wild frut,	*fruit*
And berien bot gode lite;	*berries of little worth*
In winter may he nothing finde	
Bot rote, grases, and the rinde.	*Except roots; bark*
Al his bodi was oway dwine	*away dwindled*
For missays, and al to-chine.	*hardship; chapped*
Lord! who may telle the sore	*sorrow*
This king sufferd ten yere and more?	

His here of his berd, blac and rowe, — *hair; beard; rough*
To his girdel-stede was growe. — *waist*
His harp, whereon was al his gle, — *pleasure*
He hidde in an holwe tre; — *hollow*
And when the weder was clere and bright, — *weather*
He toke his harp to him wel right
And harped at his owhen wille. — *played; own desire*
Into alle the wode the soun gan schille, — *sound began to resound*
That alle the wilde bestes that ther beth
For joie abouten him thai teth, — *gathered*
And alle the foules that ther were — *birds*
Come and sete on ich a brere — *sat; briar*
To here his harping a-fine —
So miche melody was therin; — *much*
And when he his harping lete wold, — *would leave off*
No best bi him abide nold. — *beast; would remain*
He might se him bisides, — *nearby*
Oft in hot undertides,
The king o fairy with his rout — *of fairyland; company*
Com to hunt him al about
With dim cri and bloweing, — *blowing [of horns]*
And houndes also with him berking; — *barking*
Ac no best thai no nome, — *But they took no beast (game)*
No never he nist whider they bicome — *Nor did he ever know where they went*
And other while he might him se — *at other times*
As a gret ost bi him te, — *army; went*
Wele atourned, ten hundred knightes, — *equipped*
Ich y-armed to his rightes, — *All properly armed*
Of cuntenaunce stout and fers, — *appearance*
With mani desplaid baners, — *unfurled*
And ich his swerd y-drawe hold —
Ac never he nist whider thai wold. — *knew not whither; went*
And otherwile he seighe other thing: — *saw*
Knightes and levedis com daunceing
In queynt atire, gisely, — *elegant; skillfully*
Queynt pas and softly; — *Graceful steps*
Tabours and trunpes yede hem bi, — *drums and trumpets went*
And al maner menstraci. — *sorts of minstralsy*
And on a day he seighe him biside — *on a certain day*

Sexti levedis on hors ride,	*Sixty ladies*
Gentil and jolif as brid on ris;	*lively as bird on bough*
Nought o man amonges hem ther nis;	*Not a single man was with them*
And ich a faucoun on hond bere,	*each a falcon on [her] hand bore*
And riden on haukin bi o rivere.	*a-hawking by a*
Of game thai founde wel gode haunt —	*great plenty*
Maulardes, hayroun, and cormeraunt;	*Mallards, heron; cormorant*
The foules of the water ariseth,	
The faucouns hem wele deviseth;	*marked*
Ich faucoun his pray slough —	*Each; prey killed*
That seigh Orfeo, and lough:	*saw; laughed*
"Parfay!" quath he, "ther is fair game;	*By my faith*
Thider ichil, bi Godes name;	*I'll [go]*
Ich was y-won swiche werk to se!"	*I was wont such sport*
He aros, and thider gan te.	*began [to] approach*
To a levedi he was y-come,	
Biheld, and hath wele undernome,	*perceived*
And seth bi al thing that it is	*sees*
His owhen quen, Dam Heurodis.	*own*
Yern he biheld hir, and sche him eke,	*Eagerly; also*
Ac noither to other a word no speke;	*But neither*
For messais that sche on him seighe,	*sadness*
That had ben so riche and so heighe,	*Who; exalted*
The teres fel out of her eighe.	*eye*
The other levedis this y-seighe	*saw*
And maked hir oway to ride —	
Sche most with him no lenger abide.	*might*
"Allas!" quath he, "now me is wo!"	
Whi nil deth now me slo?	*Will not; slay*
Allas, wreche, that y no might	
Dye now after this sight!	
Allas! to long last mi liif,	*too long lasts*
When y no dar nought with mi wiif,	
No hye to me, o word speke.	*Nor she; one*
Allas! Whi nil min hert breke!	*will not*
Parfay!" quath he, "tide wat bitide,	*come what may*
Whiderso this levedis ride,	*Wherever these*
The selve way ichil streche —	*same; hasten*
Of liif no deth me no reche."	*nor; I do not care*

His sclavain he dede on also spac	*pilgrim's gown he put on quickly*
And henge his harp opon his bac,	
And had wel gode wil to gon –	*very good desire*
He no spard noither stub no ston.	*avoided; stump*
In at a roche the levedis rideth,	*Into a rock*
And he after, and nought abideth.	
When he was in the roche y-go,	*gone*
Wele thre mile other mo,	
He com into a fair cuntray	*country*
As bright so sonne on somers day,	*as sun on summer's*
Smothe and plain and al grene –	*Smooth and level*
Hille no dale nas ther non y-sene.	*was not to be seen*
Amidde the lond a castel he sighe,	*saw*
Riche and real and wonder heighe.	*royal; wonderously high*
Al the utmast wal	*All [of] the outermost wall*
Was clere and schine as cristal;	*bright*
An hundred tours ther were about,	
Degiselich and bataild stout.	*Wonderful with strong battlements*
The butras com out of the diche	*buttresses; moat*
Of rede gold y-arched riche.	
The vousour was avowed al	*vaulting; adorned*
Of ich maner divers aumal.	*With every kind of enamel*
Within ther wer wide wones,	*were spacious dwellings*
Al of precious stones;	
The werst piler on to biholde[1]	
Was al of burnist gold.	*burnished*
Al that lond was ever light,	*always*
For when it schuld be therk and night,	*dark*
The riche stones light gonne	*stone's light shone*
As bright as doth at none the sonne.	*noon*
No man may telle, no thenche in thought,	*nor think*
The riche werk that ther was wrought.	*exquisite*
Bi al thing him think that it is	
The proude court of Paradis.	
In this castel the levedis alight;	*dismounted*
He wold in after, yif he might.	*wished to enter if*

[1] *Even the worst (least attractive) pillar you could see*

Orfeo knokketh atte gate;
The porter was redi therate
And asked what he wold hav y-do. *done*
"Parfay!" quath he, "icham a minstrel, lo! *I am*
To solas thi lord with mi gle, *entertain; my minstrelsy*
Yif his swete wille be."
The porter undede the gate anon *undid*
And lete him into the castel gon.
  Than he gan bihold about al,
And seighe liggeand within the wal *lying*
Of folk that were thider y-brought
And thought dede, and nare nought. *seemed dead, but were not*
Sum stode withouten hade, *stood; head*
And sum non armes nade, *had no arms*
And sum thurth the bodi hadde wounde, *through*
And sum lay wode, y-bounde, *mad*
And sum armed on hors sete,
And sum astrangled as thai ete; *they ate*
And sum were in water adreynt, *drowned*
And sum with fire al forschreynt. *shriveled*
Wives ther lay on childe bedde,
Sum ded and sum awedde, *driven mad*
And wonder fele ther lay bisides *wondrous many*
Right as thai slepe her undertides; *Just as; their*
Eche was thus in this warld y-nome, *taken*
With fairi thider y-come. *enchantment brought there*
Ther he seighe his owhen wiif,
Dame Heurodis, his lef liif, *dear life*
Slepe under an ympe-tre —
Bi her clothes he knewe that it was he. *she*
  And when he hadde bihold this mervails alle, *these marvels*
He went into the kinges halle.
Than seighe he ther a semly sight, *fair*
A tabernacle blisseful and bright, *canopy beautiful*
Therin her maister king sete *their*
And her quen, fair and swete.
Her crounes, her clothes schine so bright *Their*
That unnethe bihold he him might. *scarcely*
When he hadde biholden al that thing,

He kneled adoun bifor the king:
"O lord," he seyd, "yif it thi wille were,
Mi menstraci thou schust y-here." *should hear*
The king answered, "What man artow, *are you*
That art hider y-comen now?
Ich, no non that is with me, *Neither I, nor no one*
No sent never after the. *you*
Sethen that ich here regni gan, *Since; reign*
Y no fond never so folehardi man *foolhardy*
That hider to ous durst wende *to us dared come*
Bot that ic him wald ofsende." *Unless I wished him summoned*
"Lord," quath he, "trowe ful wel, *believe*
Y nam bot a pover menstrel;
And, sir, it is the maner of ous
To seche mani a lordes hous — *seek many*
Thei we nought welcom no be, *Although (even if)*
Yete we mot proferi forth our gle." *must offer*
Bifor the king he sat adoun
And tok his harp so miri of soun, *merry; sound*
And tempreth his harp, as he wele can, *tunes; knows well [how to do]*
And blisseful notes he ther gan, *began*
That al that in the palays were
Com to him forto here, *listen*
And liggeth adoun to his fete — *lie*
Hem thenketh his melody so swete. *They think*
The king herkneth and sitt ful stille; *listens; sits quietly*
To here his gle he hath gode wille. *his (Orfeo's); he (the king)*
Gode bourde he hadde of his gle; *Great pleasure; songs*
The riche quen also hadde he. *she*
When he hadde stint his harping, *stopped*
Than seyd to him the king,
"Menstrel, me liketh wel thi gle.
Now aske of me what it be, *what[ever] you wish*
Largelich ichil the pay; *Generously*
Now speke, and tow might asay." *if you wish to find out*
"Sir," he seyd, "ich biseche the *beseech you*
Thatow woldest give me *That you*
That ich levedi, bright on ble, *same; of complexion*
That slepeth under the ympe-tree."

"Nay!" quath the king, "that nought nere!	*that could never be*
A sori couple of you it were,	*ill-matched*
For thou art lene, rowe and blac,	*lean, rough*
And sche is lovesum, withouten lac;	*beautiful; blemish*
A lothlich thing it were, forthi,	*loathly; therefore*
To sen hir in thi compayni."	*see*
"O sir!" he seyd, "gentil king,	
Yete were it a wele fouler thing	*much more disgraceful*
To here a lesing of thi mouthe!	*hear a lie from*
So, sir, as ye seyd nouthe,	*just now*
What ich wold aski, have y schold,	*might ask [for]; I should*
And nedes thou most thi word hold."	*by necessity*
The king seyd, "Sethen it is so,	*Since*
Take hir bi the hond and go;	
Of hir ichil thatow be blithe."	*With; I wish that you be happy*
He kneled adoun and thonked him swithe.	*quickly*
His wiif he tok bi the hond,	
And dede him swithe out of that lond,	*quickly*
And went him out of that thede —	*country*
Right as he come, the way he yede.	*went*
So long he hath the way y-nome	*taken*
To Winchester he is y-come,	
That was his owhen cité;	
Ac no man knewe that it was he.	
No forther than the tounes ende	*further; town's*
For knoweleche no durst he wende,	*Because he did not want to be recognized*
Bot with a begger, y-bilt ful narwe,	*[whose house] was very small*
Ther he tok his herbarwe	*lodging*
To him and to his owhen wiif	*For himself and for*
As a minstrel of pover liif,	
And asked tidinges of that lond,	
And who the kingdom held in hond.	
The pover begger in his cote	*cottage*
Told him everich a grot:	*every scrap*
Hou her quen was stole owy,	*their; away*
Ten yer gon, with fairy,	*ago; by magic*
And hou her king en exile yede,	*into; went*
But no man nist in wiche thede;	*no one knew; country*
And how the steward the lond gan hold,	

And other mani thinges him told.
Amorwe, oyain nonetide, — *The next day, towards noon*
He maked his wiif ther abide; — *stay with the beggar*
The beggers clothes he borwed anon
And heng his harp his rigge opon, — *back*
And went him into that cité
That men might him bihold and se.
Erls and barouns bold,
Buriays and levedis him gun bihold. — *Burgesses (citizens)*
"Lo!" thai seyd, "swiche a man!
Hou long the here hongeth him opan! — *hair; upon*
Lo! Hou his berd hongeth to his kne!
He is y-clongen also a tre!" — *gnarled like*
And, as he yede in the strete, — *went*
With his steward he gan mete,
And loude he sett on him a crie: — *he (Orfeo); him (the steward)*
"Sir steward!" he seyd, "merci!
Icham an harpour of hethenisse; — *I am; from heathendom*
Help me now in this destresse!"
The steward seyd, "Com with me, come;
Of that ichave, thou schalt have some. — *what I have*
Everich gode harpour is welcom me to
For mi lordes love, Sir Orfeo."
In the castel the steward sat atte mete, — *table*
And mani lording was bi him sete;
Ther were trompours and tabourers, — *trumpeters; drummers*
Harpours fele, and crouders — — *many; stringplayers*
Miche melody thai maked alle.
And Orfeo sat stille in the halle
And herkneth; when thai ben al stille,
He toke his harp and tempred schille; — *tuned it loudly*
The blissefulest notes he harped there — *most beautiful*
That ever ani man y-herd with ere —
Ich man liked wele his gle. — *minstrelsy*
The steward biheld and gan y-se, — *began to perceive*
And knewe the harp als blive. — *at once*
"Menstrel!" he seyd, "so mot thou thrive, — *If you wish to thrive*
Where hadestow this harp, and hou? — *did you get; how*
Y pray that thou me telle now."

"Lord," quath he, "in uncouthe thede *unknown land*
Thurth a wildernes as y yede, *went*
Ther y founde in a dale
With lyouns a man totorn smale, *torn in small pieces*
And wolves him frete with teth so scharp. *had devoured*
Bi him y fond this ich harp; *same*
Wele ten yere it is y-go."
"O!" quath the steward, "now me is wo!
That was mi lord, Sir Orfeo!
Allas, wreche, what schal y do,
That have swiche a lord y-lore? *lost*
A, way that ich was y-bore! *O, woe; born*
That him was so hard grace y-yarked, *to him; bitter fortune was allotted*
And so vile deth y-marked!" *[a] death was ordained*
Adoun he fel aswon to grounde; *in a faint*
His barouns him tok up in that stounde *moment*
And telleth him how it geth — *it (the world)*
"It is no bot of mannes deth!" *There is no remedy for man's death!*
King Orfeo knewe wele bi than
His steward was a trewe man
And loved him as he aught to do,
And stont up, and seyt thus, "Lo,
Steward, herkne now this thing:
Yif ich were Orfeo the king,
And hadde y-suffred ful yore *very long ago*
In wildernisse miche sore, *sorrow*
And hadde ywon mi quen o-wy *won away*
Out of the lond of fairy,
And hadde y-brought the levedi hende *gracious lady*
Right here to the tounes ende,
And with a begger her in y-nome, *had placed her*
And were mi-self hider y-come
Poverlich to the, thus stille, *In poverty*
For to asay thi gode wille, *test*
And ich founde the thus trewe,
Thou no schust it never rewe. *should never regret it*
Sikerlich, for love or ay, *Surely; fear*
Thou schust be king after mi day; *should*
And yif thou of mi deth hadest ben blithe, *But if; happy*

Thou schust have voided, also swithe." *been banished immediately*
Tho all tho that therin sete *Then all those*
That it was King Orfeo underyete, *Recognized that it was*
And the steward him wele knewe —
Over and over the bord he threwe, *overturned the table*
And fel adoun to his fet; *his (Orfeo's)*
So dede everich lord that ther sete,
And all thai seyd at o criing: *in one cry*
"Ye beth our lord, sir, and our king!"
Glad thai were of his live; *life*
To chaumber thai ladde him als belive *led him immediately*
And bathed him and schaved his berd,
And tired him as a king apert; *clothed; openly*
And sethen, with gret processioun, *afterwards*
Thai brought the quen into the toun
With al maner menstraci —
Lord! ther was grete melody!
For joie thai wepe with her eighe *their eyes*
That hem so sounde y-comen seighe.[1]
Now King Orfeo newe coround is, *newly crowned*
And his quen, Dame Heurodis,
And lived long afterward,
And sethen was king the steward. *And after [that]*
Harpours in Bretaine after than
Herd hou this mervaile bigan,
And made herof a lay of gode likeing, *made of it; great delight*
And nempned it after the king. *named*
That lay "Orfeo" is y-hote; *called*
Gode is the lay, swete is the note. *Good*
Thus com Sir Orfeo out of his care: *sorrow*
God graunt ous alle wele to fare! Amen!

Explicit

[1] *That [they] saw them [Orfeo and Heurodis] return in safety*

Notes

Abbreviations: A: Auchinleck MS; B: Bodleian Library MS (Ashmole 61); H: Harley 3810; Bl: Bliss; Bu: Burrow; D&B: Dunn & Byrnes; F&H: French & Hale; Ga: Garbáty; Gi: Gibbs; Ha: Haskell; Ru: Rumble; S: Sands; Sc: Schmidt; Si: Sisam; Z: Zielke.

A begins the poem at line 39 of this edition: *Orfeo was a King*, which is the first line to appear in the upper left corner of fol. 300a. The previous page has been cut out of the manuscript. Both H and B begin with lines similar to the opening of *Lay le Freine*, which is found earlier in A, at fol. 261a. There is writing at the top of fol. 300a, which could be a title, though it is in a later hand. Most editors assume that the poem began on 299b. Bl conjectures that thirty-eight lines are missing, noting that the previous page had forty-four lines per column. If the title were written in a larger hand, as titles are elsewhere in the manuscript, and a small illumination were included, that would account for the six lines which, combined with the missing thirty-eight lines would exactly fill the column. He notes that the first twenty-four lines "can be supplied with some certainty," for they reappear in *Lay le Freine,* but that the remaining fourteen must be reconstructed from H and B. But in fact, he follows only the first twelve lines of *Lay le Freine*, then reconstructs mainly from H lines 13–24. The fourteen lines between line 24 and 39 on Orfeo's skills at harping occur later in H, (lines 46ff.). Bl thinks they should precede the introduction of Orfeo at line 39. I follow Bl's reconstruction as does Bu, though the great majority of *Sir Orfeo* editors (Z, D&B, F&H, G, Gi, Sc, and Si) add only twenty-four lines, mainly from *Lay le Freine.* S and Ha follow A and begin at line 39. Ru follows B and thus avoids the problem. For a thorough discussion of the issues involved in reconstructing the prologue to *Sir Orfeo*, see Bl's edition, pp. xlv–xlviii; and his article, "*Sir Orfeo*, lines 1–46," *English and Germanic Studies* 5 (1953), 7–14; and G. Guillaume, "The Prologues of the *Lay le Freine* and *Sir Orfeo*," *Modern Language Notes* 26 (1921), 458–64. Bl argues that the common prologues to *Le Freine* and *Sir Orfeo* suggest that both lays were written by the same author. For a differing opinion, see John B. Beston, "The Case Against Common Authorship of *Lay le Freine* and *Sir Orfeo*," *Medium Aevum* 45 (1976), 153–63.

1 *y-write*. An illumination has been cut out of A 261a that eclipses most of the last word of line 1. Bl has added it based on the catchline at the foot of folio 260d. This opening line stresses literacy; the image is one of the reader reading and exists alongside the high profile given to performance. Taken together, they illustrate the overlapping of orality and literacy in late medieval culture.

Notes

1–26 These lines emphasize the musical and poetic composition of the lay. The end of the text returns to this concern in lines 598–602. The opening to *Sir Orfeo* places the text in the tradition of the Breton Lay and associates the author with a long line of poets going back to "kinges" who, when they heard "Of ani mervailes," they "token an harp in gle and game / and maked a lay and gaf it name" (lines 19–20). The Prologue suggests some features common to the Breton Lay which are also mentioned in Marie de France's *Prologue* to her collection of *Lais* (lines 3–8) and in *Guingemar* (lines 24–6).

10 The word *fairy* here and elsewhere in the poem means "land of the fays" or the "fays" themselves. The word *fay* comes from Old French *fée* derived from the Latin *fata*, "the Fates." For further information on Celtic folktale backgrounds see W. Y. Evans-Wentz, *The Fairy Faith in Celtic Countries* (London: H. Frowde, 1911; rpt. New Hyde Park, New York: University Books, 1966); Howard Rollin Patch, *The Other World: According to Descriptions in Medieval Literature* (Cambridge: Harvard University Press, 1950; rpt. New York: Octagon, 1970); John Rhys, *Celtic Folklore: Welsh and Manx* (Oxford: Clarendon Press, 1901); C. S. Lewis, "The *Longaevi*," chapter six in his *Discarded Image* (Cambridge: Cambridge University Press, 1964), pp. 122–38. See also Dean Baldwin's "Fairy Lore and the Meaning of *Sir Orfeo*," *Southern Folklore Quarterly* 41 (1977), 129–42; John B. Friedman, *Orpheus in the Middle Ages* (Cambridge: Harvard University Press, 1970), pp. 146–210 and 233–40; Dorena Allen, "Orpheus and Orfeo: The Dead and the *Taken*," *Medium Aevum* 33 (1964), 102–11; Patrizia Grimaldi, "*Sir Orfeo* as Celtic Folk-Hero, Christian Pilgrim, and Medieval King," in *Allegory, Myth, and Symbol*, ed. Morton W. Bloomfield (Cambridge: Harvard University Press, 1981), pp. 147–61; and J. Burke Severs, "Antecedents of *Sir Orfeo*." See also notes to line 280 in *Sir Launfal*.

11 *thinges*. A: *thingeth.*

13 A: *In breteyne bi hold time / This layes were wrought so seith this rime.* H reads *In Brytayn this layes arne y-wrytt / Furst y-founde and forthe y-gete.* These lines from A are emended with material borrowed from B to preserve the rhyme pattern. B reads *That in the leys ben y-wrought, / Fyrst found and forth brought.*

17–20 On the traditional association of kings and poets, see Morton W. Bloomfield and Charles W. Dunn, *The Role of the Poet in Early Societies* (Cambridge: D. S. Brewer, 1989).

23–24 The prologue in A from *Lay le Freine* rhymes *Freine* with *sothe to sayn*. H rhymes *that ben trewe* with *Sir Orphewe*. *Sir Orfewe* may be the title, substituting for *Lay le Freine* in the A prologue. H reads *y wol you telle of Sir Orphewe*, assuming "Sir Orfewe" is a proper name for the hero and not a title. I have followed Bl's reconstruction which borrows and alters lines from H.

25 Orfeo's name had a long tradition of being associated with music, art, and the power of eloquence. From the time of Fulgentius, his name had been understood to mean "beautiful voice." See notes to lines 419–52 below.

25–38 These lines, missing in A, are based on H (lines 33–46), occasionally emended from B. The spelling has been adjusted to follow the spellings most often found in A.

26 Harping is often offered as evidence for a hero's nobility and courtly refinement. See *Romance of Horn* (lines 227–44) and the Northern Middle English *Tristrem* (lines 1882–94). The medieval figure of the musician-as-king is also found in Biblical portraits of David. See J. B. Friedman, *Orpheus in the Middle Ages* (Cambridge: Harvard University Press, 1970). The harp was considered the most aristocratic and heavenly of instruments. See F. P. Pickering, *Literature and Art in the Middle Ages* (Coral Gables: University of Miami Press, 1970), pp. 285–301; Curt Sachs, *The History of Musical Instruments* (New York: Norton, 1940), pp. 261–65.

29 *lerned* from B. H has *loved*.

31–33 Multiplication of negatives achieves emphasis in Middle English.

33 *al* from B.

41 A: *T stalworth*.

42 *curteys*, or courteous, in medieval texts does mean "polite," but it carries a much weightier meaning that includes courtly, elite, valuable, upper class, and cultured behaviors as well as generosity.

44 Pluto was, according to classical myth, god of the underworld. Juno was a goddess, the wife of Jupiter, not a king as the author of the poem suggests. These references to the classical Roman deities do not establish a reliable

lineage but do suggest the kind of lineage the author ascribes to Orfeo, placing the story firmly in pre-Christian contexts. See Jean Seznec, *Survival of the Pagan Gods*, trans. Barbara F. Sessions, Bollingen Series 38 (New York: Pantheon, 1961). Interestingly, in Chaucer's Merchant's Tale, Pluto is called "king of Fayerye"; his wife is "Proserpina and al hire fayerye" (IV [E] 2227, 2039).

47–50 Because the poet has set the poem in England, classical and medieval places are conflated; hence, Winchester, the old capital, becomes Thrace.

52 A: *herodis*. Heurodis is associated with vulnerability to captivity or loss. She has been read as temptation, lust, feeling or emotion; as madness, the irrational, the body; as Eve, a Celtic analogue to Guenevere, a Proserpina figure; as the anima within the male self, the Church, the "bride of Christ"; and as the human soul. Fulgentius interpreted her name as stemming from "eur dike" or "profound, deep, or good judgment": "*Euridice uero profunda diiudicatio,*" Fabius Planciades Fulgentius, *Mythologiae* III, x, ed. Rudolf Helm (Leipzig: B. G. Teubneri, 1898), p. 76. Fulgentius read the Orpheus and Eurydice story as an allegory for the musical arts. Mortimer J. Donovan, "Herodis in the Auchinleck *Sir Orfeo*," *Medium Aevum* 27 (1958), 162–65, suggests that "Heurodis" is similar to the "Herodias" who asks for John the Baptist's head. Or, given A's spelling she might also be linked to Herodis, Pilate's wife, who according to myth walked the earth after the crucifixion, yearning to make things right. See notes to lines 463–68 below.

57–72 The fairy king's abduction of Heurodis occurs in May, a time commonly ascribed to fairy activity. In his article, "Fairy Lore and the Meaning of *Sir Orfeo*," *Southern Folklore Quarterly* 41 (1977), 129–42, Dean R. Baldwin identifies several other medieval texts which situate human encounters with fairies in May, often under a tree or in an orchard or forest: the *Ballad of Thomas Rhymer*, Child 37; Gower's *Confessio Amantis* IV: 1282–1328 in *The English Works of John Gower*, ed. G. C. Macaulay EETS e.s. 81 (1900; rpt. London: Oxford University Press, 1957). See also W. Y. Evans-Wentz, *The Fairy-faith in Celtic Countries* (New York: H. Frowde, 1911), p. 124; L. C. Wimberly, *Folklore in the English and Scottish Ballads* (Chicago: University of Chicago Press, 1966), pp. 311–13; and K. M. Briggs, "The Fairies and the Realms of the Dead," *Folklore* 81 (1970), 81–96. Following a postmodern path, Jeff Rider reads the abduction of Heurodis as "the representation of the allegorization, the capture and reduction of myth, which is eventually liberated and brought back to full life through the artist's efforts. Faerie is thus the representation of interpretive power which must destroy artistic harmony and a full aura of potential meaning in order to reveal them and thereby achieve a greater understanding, the power the artist must in turn overcome if he or she is to lead him or herself (or others) out of the wilderness and the poem from the sterile frozen state in which the unmastered imp of interpretation would captivate it" ("Receiving Orpheus in the Middle Ages: Allegorization, Remythification and *Sir Orfeo*," *Papers on Language & Literature* 24 [1988], 366).

57 *Bifel*. A: *Uifel*.

67 In *sprede* the *r* is inserted above the line.

70 The exact meaning of *ympe-tree* has been debated; it has been variously translated as "grafted tree," "orchard tree," and "apple tree." See Constance Bullock-Davies, "'Ympe-tre' and 'Nemeton,'" *Notes and Queries* n.s. 9 (1962), 6–9; Sharon Ann Coolidge, "The Grafted Tree in Literature: A Study in Medieval Iconography and Theology," *DAI* (1977): 2107A Duke University; and her article, "The Grafted Tree in *Sir Orfeo*: A Study in the Iconography of Redemption," *Ball State University Forum* 23 (1982), 62–68. Alice E. Lasater has suggested that the *ympe-tre* corresponds to the grafted tree of Emain found in Irish folklore: "Under the Ympe-Tre or : Where the Action is in *Sir Orfeo*," *Southern Quarterly* 12 (1974), 353–63. The notion of a grafted tree is also reminiscent of the golden bough in Virgil's *Aeneid* (VI: 287–99). *Sir Gowther* (lines 67–72) contains an episode where a woman is accosted by a demon while lying under a tree. See also *Launfal* (lines 223ff.), *Sir Degaré* (lines 70ff.), OF *Guingamor* (lines 422–95), OF *Graelent* (lines 220–79) *Sir Gawain and the Green Knight* (lines 718–25). For a parody, see Chaucer's Sir Thopas (lines 796–806) and the satire against friars in the Wife of Bath's Tale (III D, lines 878–880): "Women may go now saufly up and doun. / In every bussh or under every tree / Ther is noon oother incubus but he [meaning friars]." The *MED* identifies the ympe-tree as a grafted tree or an orchard tree.

75–76 Midday, or noon, was considered a perilous time in both folklore and Christian material. See Friedman *Orpheus*, pp. 187–190, and his article, "Eurydice, Heurodis, and the Noon-Day Demon," *Speculum* 41 (1966), 22–29. It is also in the *hot undertides* (lines 281ff.) that the *king o fairy with his rout* comes out into the wilderness to hunt and is, consequently, seen by Orfeo. See Psalm 91:3–6: "For he will deliver you from the snare of the fowler and from the deadly pestilence; he will cover you with his pinions, and under his wings you will find refuge . . . . You will not fear the terror of the night, or the arrow that flies by day, or the pestilence that stalks in darkness, or the destruction that wastes at noonday." In the *Vulgate* this Psalm (numbered 90) reads: "deliver me from the snare of the hunters . . . from hostile attack, and from the noon-day demon." Friedman cites rabbinical commentary from the Midrash on this noon-day demon: "He has no power when it is cool in the shade and hot in the sun, but only when it is hot in both shade and sun" [Friedman, "Noon-day," p. 28, quoting *The Midrash on Psalms*, trans. William G. Braude (New Haven: Yale University Press, 1959)]. Similar glossing on the Psalm can also be found among Church fathers. *Undertyde* can refer to mid-morning (i.e., 9:00 a.m.), midday (noon), or midafternoon (3:00 p.m.). See *Launfal* (line 227).

78–82 Heurodis' behavior here and in lines 105–12 suggests she has gone mad or is fighting madness; see Penelope B. R. Doob, *Nebuchadnezzar's Children: Conventions of Madness in Middle English Literature* (New Haven: Yale University Press, 1974), p. 12. Doob reads *Sir Orfeo* within a Christian context, but she is concerned, too, to read it within a history of mental illness. She writes, "the onset of the disease is sudden; its symptoms are spectacular; and, whether the madness is purgative or punitive, it is clearly symbolic of and caused by the madman's sin."

82 *reveyd*. A: *reueyd*. Z reads *reneyd*. Si emends to *reveysed*. So too in F&H and S. Bl emends to *reueyed*.

90 *Sexti* suggests a large number; likewise, the number *hundred* suggests an indefinite number in lines 143–44, as does *ten hundred* in line 183.

102–16 Felicity Riddy, "The Use of the Past in *Sir Orfeo*," *Yearbook of English Studies* 6 (1976), 9–10, notes that Orfeo's lament over the impending loss of Heurodis echoes late medieval verse meditations which describe the body of Christ. The contrast between the former beauty of Heurodis and her grotesque self-mutilated present self is similar to the following lines which Riddy cites from *English Lyrics of the XIIIth Century*, ed. Carleton Brown (Oxford: Clarendon Press, 1932), p. 35:

His bodi that wes feir and gent
And his neb suo scene — *his face so radiant*
Wes bi-spit and all to-rend, — *beslobbered; torn*
His rude was worthen grene. — *face had become green*

And from John Grimestone's preaching-book, *Candet Nudatum Pectus* (MS Adv. 18.7.21, 120r):

> Þee lippes pale and reuli þat er weren brith and rede, *rueful; bright*
> Þe eyne þat weren loveli nou ben dimme and dede.

108 A: *al*; H and B have *as*.

129–30 See Ruth 1:16 and H. Bergner, "*Sir Orfeo* and the Sacred Bonds of Matrimony," *Review of English Studies* n.s. 30 (1979), 432–34. Orfeo lives up to his pledge; he follows Heurodis into oblivion, exiling himself, and then, once he sees her, follows her into the fairy kingdom. The verse from Ruth reads: "Wither ever thou gost I schal gon and where thou abidest I and thou together shall abidest." Although Ruth speaks these words, not to her husband, but to her mother-in-law, Naomi, the lines were frequently associated with holy matrimony.

135–40 The fairy world's preliminary contact with Heurodis is unsuccessful. The second meeting with the fairy king, himself, involves Heurodis in a brief journey and tour of the Otherworld, lines 142–63, and concludes with a threat, lines 165–74. The fairy king's motives for abducting Heurodis remain mysterious.

140 A: *Y n durst.* Bl reads: *Y no durst nought*; F&H, S, and Z read: *Y durst nought.*

146 The white horse and the white clothes worn by those who escort or meet the protagonists at the boundary of the Otherworld are common in romance and dream vision literature. See *Launfal*'s Blanchard and notes to *Launfal,* line 326.

150 The crown which is neither silver nor gold but made of some unknown precious gem suggests the Otherworldly nature of the "king," although he is not identified by the narrator as "fairi" until line 193.

156 Although the fairy company apparently rides *stedes* (line 145), Heurodis rides a palfrey. Steeds were strong horses, often used in battles and in jousting; palfreys were small saddle horses used for riding and were not as powerful. This detail reinforces the vulnerability of the human when surrounded by Otherworldly forces.

157–61 Heurodis' brief description of the beautiful Otherworld is upheld but complicated by the more complete description given later in the poem, lines 347–417. Note the tension in the poem's description of the Otherworld: it is beautiful and macabre, terrifying and elegant, hell and faerie simultaneously. See also *Sir Launfal*, *Sir Gawain and the Green Knight*, and the numerous versions of the quest for the Holy Grail to see similar tensions between Christian and non-Christian concepts of the Otherworld in medieval courtly and popular literature. See J. Burke Severs, "The Antecedents of Sir Orfeo"; Dorena Allen, "Orpheus and Orfeo: The Dead and the *Taken*"; C. S. Lewis, *The Discarded Image* (Cambridge: Cambridge University Press, 1964), esp. chapter 6 (pp. 122–38) on "The *Longaevi*," and E. C. Ronquist, "The Powers of Poetry in *Sir Orfeo*," *Philological Quarterly* 64 (1985), 101.

170–74 The fairy king's threat is, apparently, a real one. See lines 388–404. Friedman, *Orpheus*, pp. 193–94, assumes that the fairy king, as a satanic agent, used violence on those humans who resisted him.

174 After this point in the poem, Heurodis never speaks again, though we are privileged to her thoughts in lines 325–26.

187–90 *Scheltrom* comes from the OE *scyld-truma*, a tribal battle formation in which warriors used their shields to create a wall of defense. Once again, the human attempt at resistance proves futile against the power of the supernatural. The knights' willingness to die in battle, protecting the queen, also suggests that the humans are expecting a human enemy and do not realize that the "king" is from fairy until after Heurodis is abducted.

194 Compare lines 288, 296, and 494.

205 Orfeo appoints his steward to rule in his absence. The steward is a high court official from the nobility, but in the conventions of medieval romance, he is often evil. This steward proves otherwise. See J. Eadie, "A Suggestion as to the Origin of the Steward in the Middle English *Sir Orfeo*," *Trivium* 7 (1972), 54–60. Several scholars assume that Orfeo's good judgment is evidenced by the ordination of the good steward: A. M. Kinghorn, "Human Interest in the Middle English *Sir Orfeo*," *Neophilologus* 50 (1966), 359–69; K. R. R. Gros Louis, "The Significance of Sir Orfeo's Self-Exile," *Review of English Studies* n.s. 18 (1967), 245–52. But see Edward D. Kennedy's argument that Orfeo's personal loss inappropriately overwhelms his better judgment: "Sir Orfeo as *Rex Inutilis*," *Annuale Mediaevale* 17 (1976), 88–110.

227–71 Among scholars, considerable disagreement surrounds Orfeo's exile. It can be seen as an act of despair, atonement, or spiritual retreat, or as part of a process of initiation for Orfeo, or as an expression of the great love (or too great a love) Orfeo has for Heurodis. The *sclavin* (pilgrim's garb), the bare feet, and the renunciation of comfort suggest his desire to suffer. The narrator emphasizes "loss" with the repetition of the phrases "He that hadde" luxury "now" has nothing, and with his own reaction: "Lord! who may telle the sore / This king sufferd ten yere and more?" Orfeo does, however, keep his harp, thus retaining some of his former identity. His regimen follows that of ascetic hermits. See Charles Allyn Williams, *The German Legends of the Hairy Anchorite*, University of Illinois Studies in Language and Literature, vol. 18 (Urbana: University of Illinois Press, 1935). Considering the act of exile within folklore tradition, Patrizia Grimaldi notes, "Like the meaning of the voyage of Bran, the meaning of the ten years' journey is not that of a pilgrimage nor is it connected with the expiation of crimes. The stories of 'voyages' *(immram)* told by Irish storytellers were the dramatizations of an initiation process through experience into a more comprehensive view of the world" (p. 154). See also, Dean R. Baldwin: "[Orfeo's] time in the wilderness is, then, best understood not as a time of penance nor of trial nor of purification; rather, Orfeo is (unconsciously) following the tradition of lovers generally and romance lovers in particular until his lady can be restored to him" (p. 137). Baldwin points to *Ywain and Gawain*, ed., Albert B. Friedman and Norman T. Harrington, EETS o.s. 254 (London: Oxford University Press, 1964), lines 1649–56, for support:

An evyl toke him als he stode;
For wa he wex al wilde and wode. *woe*
Unto the wod the way he nome; *took*
No man wist whore he bycome.
Obout he welk in the forest,
Als it wore a wilde beste;
His men on ilka syde has soght
Fer and here and findes him noght. *Far*

Here, Yvain, rejected by his wife, exiles himself, lives on roots and raw meats (lines 1665–70), and is gradually cured of his lovesickness by a magical ointment (lines 1709–1832). K. R. R. Gros Louis, "The Significance," reminds us that Orfeo does not set out to find Heurodis; "in fact, there is no search in the entire poem, nor does Orfeo ever plan to make one. If we do not recognize this crucial fact, we fail not only to see the uniqueness of *Sir Orfeo* in the tradition of the Orpheus myth, but also to understand the intention of its author" (pp.

245–46). Gros Louis stresses Orfeo's humility: "the ten years he spends in the wilderness constitute a kind of penance, and because of it, Orfeo receives a gift of grace — Heurodis is returned to him" (p. 247).

231 See 1 Kings 16:23: "So whensoever the evil spirit from the Lord was upon Saul, David took his harp, and played with his hand, and Saul was refreshed, and was better, for the evil spirit departed from him."

241–56 These lines echo numerous medieval texts on the vicissitudes of fortune. See Boethius's *Consolatio* and Chaucer's *Book of the Duchess*, lines 599–625. See also Lamentations 1: 1–2; 3: 4–6, 28–30; 4: 1–5. Compare with Henryson, *Orpheus and Eurydice*, lines 154-163.

255–60 Several scholars have attributed sources and analogues for these lines. See Geoffrey of Monmouth's *Vita Merlini*, ed. and trans., John J. Parry, *Illinois Studies in Language and Literature* 10 (1925), 243–380:

> Deplangitque uiros nec cessat fundere fletus,
> Pulueribus crines sparsit, uestes que rescidit,
> Et prostratus humi nunc hac illac que uolutat.
> . . . .
> Utitur herbarum radicibus, utitur herbis,
> Vtitur arboreo fructu, morisque rubeti.
> (lines 65–67; 78–79)

Indeed, the episode in *Sir Orfeo* shares much in common with Geoffrey's *Vita Merlini*; Parry translates: "Merlin . . . bewailed the men and did not cease to pour out laments, and he strewed dust on his hair and rent his garments, and prostrate on the ground rolled now hither and now thither . . . . He had now lamented for three whole days and had refused food, so great was the grief that consumed him. Then when he had filled the air with so many and so great complaints, new fury seized him and he departed secretly, and fled to the wood and rejoiced to lie hidden under the ash trees; he marvelled at wild beasts feeding on the grass of the glades; now he chased after them and again he flew past them; he lived on the roots of grasses and on the grass, on the fruit of the trees and on the mulberries of the thicket. He became a silvan man just as though devoted to the woods." In the *Vita Merlini*, the mad Merlin is also subdued and enticed back into civilization by a messenger's harp-accompanied song. See also the description of Merlin in the *Livre d'Artus* in *The Vulgate*

Version of the Arthurian Romance, ed. H. Oskar Sommer (Washington: Carnegie Institute, 1908–16), vii. 125; also available from New York: AMS Press, 1969]:

> [Merlins] si fist uenir par art cers & biches & dains et toutes manieres de bestes sauuages enuiron luj pasturer . . . . [Merlins] dist que il ne meniue fors que herbes & racines de bois ausi come ces autres bestes car [fait il] ge nai cure dautres uiandes & ce sont toutes mes deuices. Ne nai cure dostel auoir fors solement dun chaisne crues ou ge me repose par nuit.

For a Christian context, see Nicholas Love's early fifteenth-century *The Mirrour of the Blessed Lyf of Jesu Christ*, ed. Lawrence F. Powell (Oxford: The Clarendon Press, 1908), p. 85, cited in Doob, p. 186: "And so the lorde of all the worlde gothe all that long weye bare foote and allone . . . . Gode lorde, where ben youre dukes and erles, knightes and barouns, horses and harneises . . . ? Where ben the trumpes and clariouns and alle othere mynstralcie and herbergeres and purveyoures that schulde goo byfore, and alle othere worschippes and pompes of the world as we wrecched wormes usen? Be not ye that highe lorde of whose joye and blisse hevene and erthe is replenesched? Why than goo yee thus sympilly, alone and on the bare erthe? Sothely the cause is for ye be not at this tyme in youre kyngdom, the which is not of this world. For here ye have anentisshed [humbled] youre self, takynge the manere of a servaunt and not of a kyng." Doob reads Orfeo's exile in a Christian context, finding figural similarities between Orpheus and various Holy Wild Men. She also cites (p. 187) St. Ambrose: "We ought to remember how the first Adam was cast out of paradise into the desert in order to notice how the second Adam returned from the desert to paradise . . . . Naked of spiritual graces, Adam covered himself with the leaves of a tree . . . ."

265–71 See Job 30: 30–31: "My skin is become black upon me, and my bones are dried up with heat. My harp is turned to mourning, and my organ into the voice of those that weep."

269–80 The harping consoles the exiled Orfeo, himself, and "tames" the animals. This tradition goes back to shamanistic origins in pre-Christian material as well as to the classical Orpheus and the biblical David. See, for example, John Lydgate, *Reson and Sensualyte*, ed. Ernst Sieper, EETS e.s. 84, 89 (London: Kegan Paul, Trench, Trubner, Ltd., 1901-1903) I, 147, lines 5603–11:

> The harpis most melodious
> Of David and of Orpheous.

Ther melodye was in all
So hevenly and celestiall
That there nys hert, I dar expresse,
Oppressed so with hevynesse,
Nor in sorwe so y-bounde,
That he sholde ther ha founde
Comfort hys sorowe to apese . . .

The taming of the animals by means of the harp and song is one main feature of the Orpheus figure. Boethius, in his *Consolatio*, writes: "Long ago the Thracian poet, Orpheus, mourned for his dead wife. With his sorrowful music he made the woodland dance and the rivers stand still. He made the fearful deer lie down bravely with the fierce lions: the rabbit no longer feared the dog quieted by his song. But as the sorrow within his breast burned more fiercely, that music which calmed all nature could not console its maker. Finding the gods unbending, he went to the regions of hell" (*The Consolation of Philosophy*, Book III, metre 12, trans. Richard Green [Indianapolis: Bobbs-Merrill, 1962)], p. 73). The Latin reads: "*Quondam funera coniugis / Vates Threicius gemens / Postquam flebilibus modis / Siluas currere mobiles, / Amnes stare coegerat, /Iunxitque intrepidum latus / Saeuis cerua leonibus, / Nec uisum timuit lepus / Iam cantu placidum canem* . . . ." King Alfred's translation of Boethius also stresses the power of Orpheus' music: "Once on a time it came to pass that a harp-player lived in the country called Thracia, which was in the kingdom of Crecas. The harper was so good, it was quite unheard of. His name was Orpheus, and he had a wife without her equal, named Euridice. Now men came to say of the harper that he could play the harp so that the forest swayed, and the rocks quivered for the sweet sound, and wild beasts would run up and stand still as if they were tame, so still that men or hounds might come near them, and they fled not. The harper's wife died, men say, and her soul was taken to hell. Then the harpman became so sad that he could not live in the midst of other men, but was off to the forest, and sat upon the hills both day and night, weeping, and playing on his harp so that the woods trembled and the rivers stood still, and hart shunned not lion, nor hare hound, nor did any beast feel rage or fear towards any other for gladness of the music. And when it seemed to the harper that nothing in this world brought joy to him he thought he would seek out the gods of hell and essay to win them over with his harp, and pray them to give him back his wife." *King Alfred's Version of the Consolations of Boethius*, trans. Walter John Sedgefield (Oxford: Clarendon Press, 1900), p. 116. OE text: *King Alfred's Old English Version of Boethius' "De consolatione philosophiae*," ed. Walter John Sedgefield (Oxford: Clarendon Press, 1899), pp. 101–02. See also

J. Burke Severs, "The Antecedents of *Sir Orfeo*," in *Studies in Medieval Literature in Honor of Professor Albert Croll Baugh*, ed. MacEdward Leach (Philadelphia, University of Pennsylvania Press, 1961), pp. 188–90; note 3, 203–04. Although not, apparently, a direct source for the Orfeo-poet, Alfred's account offers an interesting comparison with the Breton lay here. See also Michael Masi, "The Christian Music of *Sir Orfeo*," *Classica Folia* 28 (1974), 3-20.

281–17 Just as the fairy world made contact with Heurodis several times before she was actually abducted, Orfeo witnesses fairies several times before he actually sees and recognizes Heurodis. The fairy occupations — hunting, parading, dancing, making music, and hawking — correspond to the royal activities Orfeo had enjoyed before his exile. Eleanor Hull, "The Idea of Hades in Celtic Literature," *Folklore* 8 (1907), 121–65, maintains that Celtic myth regularly ascribed to its Otherworld activities and objects found in everyday life, as if objects could exist in two worlds at once. The link between fairies, ladies, and falconry has a long tradition. Compare *Sir Launfal,* lines 960–72; *Sir Landevale,* line 447; OF *Le Bel Inconnu*, lines 3840–43; 3936–49. See also D. W. Robertson, Jr., *A Preface to Chaucer* (Princeton: Princeton University Press, 1962), pp. 190–94 and figures 8 and 9.

287 Notably, this hunt appears to be aimless; no game is taken. It seems to resemble the Otherworld condition of suspended life described in lines 389–90.

319–30 For commentary on this recognition scene, see Lewis J. Owen, "The Recognition Scene in *Sir Orfeo*," *Medium Aevum* 40 (1971), 249–53.

331–38 See lines 175–78, 195–200; 542–52.

333 *wreche*. A: *wroche*. H: *wreche*. So too in F&H, Z, and S.

339–54 Whereas Orfeo's first loss of Heurodis is followed immediately by his exile, and journey into the wilderness, this second separation is followed immediately by his journey into the fairy country. This time he is able to see and to follow the fairy company, whereas the initial abduction was, apparently, invisible.

340–41 See lines 129–30.

351–76 See *The Vision of Josaphat.* Josaphat passes over a plain of vast extent, where there are sweet-smelling flowers and strange, wondrous fruits. The leaves of the tree make clear music to a soft breeze and send forth delicate fragrances. A city walled with gold shines with unspeakable brightness. See the description of opulence in Isaiah 2: 7–10, 12, 15: "Their land is filled with silver and gold, and there is no end to their treasures; their land is filled with horses, and there is no end to their chariots. Their land is filled with idols; they bow down to the work of their hands, to what their own fingers have made. And so people are humbled, and everyone is brought low — do not forgive them! Enter into the rock, and hide in the dust from the terror of the Lord . . . For the Lord of hosts has a day against all that is proud and lofty, against all that is lifted up and high . . . against every high tower, and against every fortified wall." See also the description of the city in the OF *Le Bel Inconnu* (lines 1877–1916) and the fortress in *Guingamor* (lines 356–70; 389–91).

360 I have translated this line as "Wonderful with strong battlements." Walls which were "bataild" had indentations which protected the wall's defendants during assault. The *MED* lists meanings for the word "batild" as follows: "a) furnished with (indented) parapets, battlements; also walled, fortified. . . . b) crenelated; c) ornamented or edged with an indented design, notched." The *MED* entry identifies this line from *Sir Orfeo* as an example of the first meaning.

376 *Paradis* occurs only twice in the poem: here, and in line 37 where it describes Orfeo's musical power. The *paradis* of the Otherworld holds beauty and sorrow, just as Orfeo's songs can, but the *paradis* of sound, Orfeo's music, is powerful enough to restore the dead to life and to break the boundaries between the two realms, whereas the beauty of the fairy castle is static and its visual beauty does not restore the dead.

388 *seighe liggeand.* A: *seiȝe ful liggeand.*

387–04 Compare with the formulaic listings of people in purgatory and in heaven from *St. Patrick's Purgatory* or *Owayne Miles* (also found in the Auchinleck). See *St. Patrick's Purgatory*, ed. Robert Easting. EETS o.s. 298 (Oxford: Oxford University Press, 1991), pp. 15 and 27. Stanzas 77–79 include the following lines:

> Sum bi the fet wer honging,
> With iren hokes al brening,
> And sum bi the swere,
> And sum bi wombe and sum bi rigge,
> Al otherwise than y can sigge,
> In divers manere.

And sum in forneise wern ydon,
With molten ledde and quic brunston
Boiland above the fer,
And sum bi the tong hing . . .
And sum on grediris layen there . . .

A similar formulaic listing characterizes souls in heaven in stanzas 153–54:

Sum soule he seyye woni bi selve,
And sum bi ten and bi twelve,
And everich com til other;
And when thai com togiders ywis,
Alle thai made miche blis . . .
Sum he seiye gon in rede scarlet,
And sum in pourper wele ysett,
And sum in sikelatoun;
As the prest ate masse wereth . . .
And sum gold bete al doun.

406 *liif.* A: *liif liif.*

419–52 Orfeo, playing his harp and singing, mirrors the narrator of the lay who, then, becomes "hero of his own poem" (Rider, p. 357). The poem comes to inscribe the symbol of Orfeo as artist. See also Fulgentius (6th c.) *Mythologies* 3:10, cited in *Fulgentius the Mythographer*, trans. Leslie George Whitbread (Columbus: Ohio State University Press, 1971), p. 96: "Now this legend is an allegory (*designatio*) of the art of music. For Orpheus stands for *oreafone* [*oraia phone*], that is, matchless sound, and Eurydice [*eur dike*] is deep judgement . . . ." Fulgentius used the Orpheus-Eurydice myth within a description of the education in the arts. His etymological analysis of the two names associates the characters with abstract concepts. For discussions of poetic self-referentiality, see Ronquist, pp. 100, 110–12; and Lerer, pp. 94 and 106–09. The beauty, opulence, and chamber of horrors all seem undercut once the harper begins to play. The Otherworld and its fairy king become bound to cultural codes and laws and are no longer beyond recognition. The law of "trouthe" and the beauty of art rule even over the fairy king. The association of Orpheus with eloquence can also be seen in Nicholas Trivet (cited on page 22 of this volume).

419–74 See the fifteenth-century *Ovide moralisé*: "By Orpheus and his harp one should understand the persons of our Lord Jesus Christ, son of God and Father, omnipotent in his divinity, and the glorious Virgin Mary in her humanity. He played his harp so melodiously that he drew forth from hell the saintly souls of the saintly fathers who had descended there through the sin of Adam and Eve. . . . And by the harp of the aforementioned Orpheus one should understand twenty-two well-tuned and harmonious strings on which our aforementioned Lord Jesus Christ played while in this world. By ten of these strings one should understand the Ten Commandments of God's laws and by the other twelve strings are signified the twelve articles of the faith of our Lord and Saviour Jesus Christ . . . ." C. de Boer, ed., *Ovide moralisé en prose* (Amsterdam: North Holland, 1954), p. 264. The success Orfeo has retrieving Heurodis is reminiscent of Christ's successful rescue of humanity from the bonds of Hell in the Harrowing of Hell. See Friedman, esp. chapter three; and Peter Dronke, "The Return of Eurydice," *Classica et Mediaevalia* 23 (1962), 198–215.

430 Orfeo tells a bit of a lie here: although he is poor and a minstrel of the woods, he is also Heurodis' husband and a king. His disguise gives him an advantage over the fairy king.

439–41 See lines 249–50. In the same way that Orfeo had tamed the wild animals in lines 270–80, he tames the forces of the Otherworld. See also the late thirteenth-century, northern English *Tristrem* (lines 1882–94), a text which is includcd in thc Auchinleck MS. Tristan is, of course, in many texts throughout Europe associated with harping and musicianship. In the Middle English version, a battle of the musicians takes place after an Irish earl, disguised as a minstrel, wins Ysonde from King Mark. Tristrem, returning from the hunt, finds Ysonde missing, and by the power of his own musicianship, he retrieves the lost Ysonde:

His gle al for to here	
The levedi was sett onland	
To play bi the rivere;	
Th'erl ladde hir bi hand;	
Tristrem, trewe fere,	*companion*
Mirie notes he fand	*Delightful; played*
Opon his rote of yvere,	*ivory*
As thai were on the strand;	*shore*
That stounde	*time*
Thurch that semly sand	*Through; comforting message*
Ysonde was hole and sounde.	
Hole sche was and sounde	
Thurch vertu of his gle.	*efficacy of his music*
(lines 1882–94)	

(*Sir Tristrem* in *Lancelot of the Laik and Sir Tristrem*, ed. Alan Lupack [Kalamazoo: Medieval Institute Publications, 1994], pp. 209–10). See also Peter Lombard's commentary on Psalm 150 (where David plays the harp to praise God): "Laudate eum in cithara, id est ut sponsum quia ab imis liberavit," *Commentarium in Psalmos*, in *PL*, ed. J. P. Migne (Paris, 1854), 191: col. 1291.

449 Z, in his 1880 edition of *Sir Orfeo* (p. 137), notes the similarity between this clothing exchange and a similar episode in *King Horn* (lines 1052–53). It is a similarity more fully explored by Nimchinsky, "*Orfeo, Guillaume,* and *Horn,*" *Romance Philology* 22 (1968), 1–14.

450 *aske.* A: *alke.* So emended by everyone.

463–68 Trouthe must be observed as the fairyland abides by the customs of the ideal medieval court. Kings, especially, must abide by their word. But Orfeo doesn't tempt the king; he flees with Heurodis before the king could possibly martial any resistance. The rash boon is, of course, common in folklore. It also exists within religious writing. See Mark 6:14–29, where Herod makes a rash promise to Herodias' daughter: "Whatsoever thou shalt ask I will give thee, though it be the half of my kingdom." Instead of property or wealth, she asks for the head of John the Baptist: "And the king was struck sad. Yet because of his oath, and because of them that were with him at table, he would not displease her."

477–82 The narrative moves away from its former focus on Orfeo's journey to free Heurodis and becomes a story about the testing of a steward. It has analogues in the return story of Odysseus, whose disguise allows him to test the citizens of Ithaca, who returns first to the lowly swineherd's hut on the edge of town, and whose powerful bow-stringing parallels Orfeo's harp-playing. See also Shakespeare's *Measure for Measure,* where the Duke returns to test his appointed substitute.

482 *no durst wende.* A: *ne durst wende.* F&H and S read *he durst wende*; Bl reads *no durst wende.*

483 *y-bilt ful narwe* is a difficult phrase. See Bl (p. 54); or Angus McIntosh, quoted by M. L. Samuels in his review of Bl, *Medium Aevum* 24 (1955), 60.

497 Orfeo's return occurs around the same time of day as Heurodis' disappearance. See notes to line 75.

519 The steward has continued Orfeo's practice of retaining good musicians, but Orfeo has certainly learned to be wary of appearances. The presence of musicians at meals and celebrations is a convention which usually signifies the civilized world and reflects court culture; see, for example, *Emaré* (lines 388–90). See also the parable of the good steward found in Luke 12: 37–48.

521 A: *trompour.*

522 *Crouders* is a word meaning "croud-players" which derives from the Welsh *crwth*, a Celtic string instrument which was played with a bow and plucked with the fingers. However, the *MED* refers to this line in *Sir Orfeo* and interprets the word as "one who plays the crowd."

527 *blissefulest.* A: *blifulest.*

535–74 Orfeo tells a second falsehood. The first one was a lie of omission; here he tells the steward that he found Orfeo dying of wounds in the wilderness, which is, in a way, true at least psychologically. However, his primary purpose is to explain how he got Orfeo's harp. This also allows him to test the steward fully.

544–45 See lines 333–35.

558–74 In their edition of the poem, Schmidt and Jacobs note: "This long sentence with its eight conditional clauses is structurally reminiscent of lines 241–56."

578 F&H gloss: "Knocked the board off its trestles in his haste" (I, 340).

596 Although the traditional romance ending usually confirms that the happy couple's progeny continue to rule the kingdom, *Sir Orfeo* leaves us only with the information that the loyal steward became king after Orfeo and Heurodis die.

598–99 See lines 18–20.

603–04 The conventional blessing given by the minstrel to the audience carries significant implications at the end of a tale in which song and poetry rescue Heurodis and literally charm away adversity.

Lay le Freine

Introduction

The Middle English *Lay le Freine*, dating from the early fourteenth century, exists in only one manuscript copy, National Library of Scotland Advocates 19.2.1, also called the Auchinleck MS. *Le Freine* is a relatively close translation of Marie de France's 518-line poem, *Lai le Fresne*, which was composed in the late twelfth century. The Middle English version is shorter than the Old French original, being only 408 lines. In the thirteenth century, *Le Fresne* was greatly amplified and transformed into a lengthy Old French romance, the *Roman de Galeran de Bretagne*.[1] The twenty-two line prologue to *le Freine* is also attached to two versions of *Sir Orfeo*, demonstrating the common medieval practice of borrowing material freely from text to text. *Le Freine*, like the Auchinleck *Sir Orfeo*, is damaged and consequently has been, in parts, reconstructed. The dialect features of *Le Freine* are Southern with some East Midland elements; it therefore reads much like Chaucer's writings. The author of the Middle English *Lay le Freine* is unknown.

This short Breton lay focuses on a female protagonist who is abandoned at birth, is raised as a foundling within a convent by a generous abbess, and then becomes the lover of a wealthy nobleman. When the nobleman, Guroun, is pressured to marry a legitimate wife, Le Freine accepts her fate with charitable resignation, even helping to prepare the castle for the wedding festivities. The woman Guroun marries happens to be none other than Le Freine's twin sister, Le Codre. Le Freine's true identity is revealed in the final moments of the narrative when her mother recognizes a beautiful cloth she had used to wrap around her baby daughter when she abandoned her. Guroun, discovering Le Freine's true class identity and lineage, annuls his unconsummated marriage to Le Codre and marries Le Freine. Le Codre, we are told, eventually marries another wealthy nobleman. The conclusion of this lay, like the conclusion of many Breton lays, reunites the protagonist with the family unit and affirms, in its fairytale ending, the triumph of the good. The protagonist's suffering is not as dramatic as that encountered by Emaré or Sir Orfeo, and although she is a foundling,

[1] The standard edition of Marie de France's *Lais* is Jean Rychner, ed., *Les lais de Marie de France* (Paris: Champion, 1969; rpt. 1983). See also *Galeran de Bretagne; roman du XIIIe siècle*, ed. Lucien Foulet (Paris: Champion, 1925; rpt., 1966).

she never suffers the poverty of a Sir Launfal. Still, the unattached, unclaimed, and potentially illegitimate status of Le Freine places her on the margins of her world, in vulnerable circumstances, and certainly in a position to suffer psychologically and socially. Her journey is, however, a nearly steady progression away from isolation and toward connection and legitimacy within the secular community. She moves from the infant carried on the night paths between villages to the infant resting safely within a tree, from the caretaker's home to the convent, and finally from the status of mistress in the nobleman's castle to the status of wife.

The text contains a number of folklore motifs: twin births, the abandoned or exposed child, the tokens which help with recognition and the establishment of identity, the degraded one who turns out to be noble, and the theme of patience rewarded.[2] Although the poem frequently mentions God, it lacks the religious opening and closing lines found in other romances and lays. It is not as secular as *Launfal* but not as religious as *Emaré*.[3] Neither Le Freine's liaison with Guroun within the convent nor Guroun's pretense to holiness for the purposes of a sexual affair receive the narrator's reproof. Still, the story is told as an "ensaumple," and it spins out a moral tale which condemns envy and slander while rewarding silence, patience, and generosity. Le Freine and her mother form the central opposition within the moral framework of the tale. The mother, jealous about the birth of her neighbor's twin sons, spreads rumors that twins can only result from two fathers. In this way, the tale incorporates the widespread superstition that virtuous women produce one healthy child at a time and that multiple births reflect multiple fathers. This superstition finds its way into folktales throughout the world, but its popularity in high and late medieval materials may also reflect the increased regulation of human sexuality which marked the late Middle Ages. In canon law, Gratian's *Decretum* assumed, as did some Synod documents, that sinful sexual unions were the cause of stillbirths, handicaps, deformities, and so on. It did not take much to step from Gratian's ideas to the idea that multiple births came from multiple partners. Obviously, shame, economic pressures, cultural biases, as well as other forces could work to encourage child abandonment. In his work, *The Kindness of Strangers*, John Boswell details the history of child abandonment in the Middle Ages; he writes, "between 1195 and 1295 at least thirteen different councils in England alone passed

[2] See the similarities between this lay and the "Fair Annie" ballads (Child No. 62), Francis J. Child, *The English and Scottish Popular Ballads* (Boston: Houghton, Mifflin and Co. 1883-86), II, 63–83.

[3] See John C. Hirsh, "Providential Concern in the *Lay le Freine*," *Notes and Queries* n.s. 16 (1969), 85–86.

legislation directly or indirectly bearing on the abandonment of children."[4] Although the topos of the exposed child in *Le Freine* can be considered conventional since it is common throughout medieval romance materials, its widespread presence in medieval literature is not simply the function of tradition. Boswell notes, "the recurrence of a topos or even the repetition of narrative details cannot be taken as meaningless or ahistorical simply because they may be derivative. Marriage, murder, and the birth of children do not occur in twentieth-century literature simply in 'imitation' of classical antecedents" (p. 365). In his chapter 10, "Literary Witnesses," Boswell includes *Le Freine* in his discussion of the cultural resonance of child abandonment tales. The correspondence between the fantastic Breton lays and historical context is, of course, complex and subtle, a relationship common sense affirms and yet a difficult relationship to delineate. Still, "the single most characteristic feature of high medieval abandonment literature is its hopefulness . . . exposed children not only survive but flourish; not only overcome the difficulties of being abandoned but rise through them to greatness, becoming popes, . . . saints, kings, and most often [they] are joyfully reunited with their natal parents in the process" (p. 394). Although the codified cultural narrative is hopeful, its relationship to fact is speculation (and, obviously, doubtful). As Boswell notes, "To question the likelihood of these events is to overlook the real message they convey: the need of the societies that composed them, and of individuals within those societies, to believe that abandonment could result in a better life for their children, a need obviously created by an even more basic necessity — the necessity, in the absence of any other acceptable means of family limitation, of abandoning children" (p. 394).

If *Le Freine* participates in the cultural discourse surrounding children, it also functions culturally as one of many medieval narratives which condemn women's speech and laud women's silence. Thematically, *Le Freine*, like *Emaré*, admires "mesure," restraint, and patience. Chaucer's Clerk's Tale, the tale of Griselda, is perhaps the best known fourteenth-century English text on women's patience, but the motif is repeated in the Constance-saga materials, in sermons, tracts, and in many women's saints' lives.[5] Le Freine's mother, providing the medieval stereotype of the jealous, gossiping woman is:

---

[4] John Boswell, *The Kindness of Strangers* (New York: Vintage, 1990), p. 322.

[5] See also Chaucer's Man of Law's Tale, John Gower's Tale of Constance in his *Confessio Amantis*, Boccaccio's tale of Griselda in the *Decameron*, and Alcuin Blamires's edition of medieval texts about women, entitled *Woman Defamed and Woman Defended* (Oxford: Clarendon Press, 1992). Christine de Pisan also records a number of tales of virtuous and silent women in *The Book of the City of Ladies* (the tale of Griselda is found in Book II, ch. 50); her text also includes a defense of women's speech.

A proude dame and an envieous,
Hokerfulliche missegging, *Maliciously mis-saying (slandering)*
Squeymous and eke scorning. *Disdainful; also*
To ich woman sche hadde envie;
Sche spac this wordes of felonie . . . *malice*
(lines 60–64)

Notably, her "missegging" and "wordes of felonie" evoke disdain from other women. They bring on the other women's curses (lines 77–82), her own husband's rebuke (lines 74–76), God's retribution (her own twins) (line 85), and her own extreme moral dilemma (lines 89–136). Her false words create very real consequences. Contrasting the jealous mother's slanderous speech about her neighbor's good fortune in the beginning of the lay is Le Freine's silent generosity toward Le Codre's good fortune at the end of the lay:

Albe her herte wel nigh tobroke,
No word of pride ne grame she spoke.
(lines 353–54)

In fact, while she readies the wedding chamber, she decides it "yll besemed a may so bright" (line 362), so she takes "her riche baudekyn" and lays it across the bed. This quiet act of generosity, this gift from her little inheritance, is, of course, the silent move that opens up the possibility for everyone's redemption. As she gives up one of the only things that has protected her (the cloth), she unknowingly prepares the way for her mother to reclaim her. In the last thirty lines of the poem, Le Freine is called "hende" three times, echoing line 265 when Guroun first meets her at the convent, and she is described as "hende of mouth." Her "gentilesse" is, apparently, the legacy from her father, as her generosity is paralleled in her father's response when he hears of the birth of the twin boys:

The knight therof was glad and blithe,
And thonked Godes sond swithe,
And graunted his erand in al thing,
And gaf him a palfray for his tiding.
(lines 55–58)

The textual crafting of Le Freine's silence is notable, given her role as the title character. Constructed to give voice to others such as the mother, the father, the neighbor's messenger, the maiden who carries Le Freine to the convent, the abbess, Guroun, and his barons, and long before Le Freine, herself, speaks, the text saves or silences her voice until the very end. Le Freine never speaks directly in the text until her mother addresses her in the wedding chamber (line 379), only twenty-nine lines from the end of the narrative. Le Freine's acquisition of a voice in the story and her reclamation of identity, heritage, and family (especially her mother) clearly coincide. She steps into language as she steps simultaneously into kinship, patrimony, and marriage. In other words, she has no voice outside of the established social order.

Select Bibliography

Manuscripts

National Library of Scotland Advocates 19.2.1 (The Auchinleck Manuscript).

The Auchinleck dates from the early-fourteenth century. *Le Freine* is found on folios 261–2 which have considerable damage. The MS is missing lines 121–33 and 341–408. I have followed other editors in supplying these lines from a Middle English re-creation done by Henry William Weber in 1810. Weber based his reconstructions on Marie de France's text. I am indebted to Wattie's critical edition in the preparation of this edition.

Critical Editions

Wattie, Margaret. "The Middle English *Lai le Freine*." *Smith College Studies in Modern Languages* 10.3 (April 1929), i–xxii and 1–27.

Varnhagen, Hermann. "*Lai le Freine*." *Anglia* 3 (1880), 415–23.

Collections

Ellis, George. *Specimens of Early English Metrical Romances*. Rev. ed. by J. O. Halliwell. London: Henry G. Bohn, 1848. Pp. 538–46.

Weber, Henry W. *Metrical Romances of the Thirteenth, Fourteenth and Fifteenth Centuries*, 3 Vols. Edinburgh: Archibald Constable, 1810. I, 357–71.

Rumble, Thomas C. *The Breton Lays in Middle English.* Detroit: Wayne State University Press, 1965. Pp. 80–94.

Lay le Freine

Sands, Donald B. *Middle English Verse Romances*. New York: Holt, Rinehart & Winston, 1966. Pp. 233–45.

Related Studies

Burgess, Glyn S. *Marie de France: Text and Context*. Athens: University of Georgia Press, 1987. [Offers a discussion and summary of the scholarly speculations about Marie de France's identity. Also discusses the Breton lay genre, the historical context, and provides readings of the lays of Marie de France, including *Lai le Fresne* and *Lanval*.]

———. *Marie de France: An Analytical Bibliography*. London: Grant & Cutler, 1977 and Supplement No. 1. London: Grant & Cutler, 1985. [Although keyed to Marie de France's versions of *Le Fresne* and *Lanval*, this bibliography contains entries which have bearing on some aspects of the Middle English version as well.]

Donovan, Mortimer J. "Le Freine." In *The Breton Lay: A Guide to Varieties*. Notre Dame: University of Notre Dame Press, 1969. Pp. 126–39. [Examines the relationship of the Middle English *Le Freine* to Marie de France's *Le Fresne*. Also discusses versification, argues that the prologue belonged to *Sir Orfeo* first and was then borrowed for *Le Freine*, points to the poem's relationship with the "Fair Annie" ballad, and situates *Le Freine* within definitions of the Breton lay genre.]

Freeman, Michelle. "The Power of Sisterhood: Marie de France's *Le Fresne*." In Mary Erler and Maryanne Kowaleski, eds. *Women and Power in the Middle Ages*. Athens: University of Georgia Press, 1988. Pp. 250–64. [Offers a reading of the OF text, emphasizing the power of women characters to revise and transform text, speech, and the world of the lay. Examines "sisterhood" as it resonates between various characters, not simply between Le Fresne and Le Codre.]

Guillaume, Gabrielle. "The Prologues of the *Lay le Freine* and *Sir Orfeo*." *Modern Language Notes* 36 (1921), 458–64. [Argues that the prologue to *Le Freine* was composed by the English author (not borrowed from various French texts as has been argued by others) and that the author of *Sir Orfeo* subsequently borrowed the prologue from *Le Freine*.]

Maréchal, Chantal. "Le *lai de Fresne* et la littérature édifiante du xiie s." *Cahiers de Civilisation Mediévale* 35 (1992), 131–41. [Compares Marie de France's *Fresne* with sermons and other clerical writings to suggest ways the lay contains theological and moral significance. Considers historical documents to argue that the lay reflects authentic cases found in canon law and illustrates transformations of matrimonial institutions of the twelfth century.]

Zupitza, Julius. "Zum *Lay le Freine*," *Englische Studien* 10 (1887), 41–48.

Lay le Freine

We redeth oft and findeth ywrite — *read; written*
And this clerkes wele it wite — *scholars; know*
Layes that ben in harping *are*
Ben yfounde of ferli thing. *marvelous*
Sum bethe of wer and sum of wo, *Some are of war*
And sum of joie and mirthe also, *gaiety*
And sum of trecherie and of gile, *guile*
Of old aventours that fel while; *adventures; happened once*
And sum of bourdes and ribaudy, *jokes; ribaldry*
And mani ther beth of fairy. *the Otherworld*
Of al thinges that men seth,
Mest o love for sothe thai beth. *Most of; in truth*
In Breteyne bi hold time *Brittany in olden times*
This layes were wrought, so seith this rime. *These; made*
When kinges might our yhere *anywhere hear*
Of ani mervailes that ther were, *marvels*
Thai token an harp in gle and game, *took; minstrelsy*
And maked a lay and gaf it name. *gave*
Now of this aventours that weren yfalle, *have happened*
Y can tel sum ac nought alle. *but not all*
Ac herkneth lordinges, sothe to sain, *But listen*
Ichil you telle Lay le Frayn. *I will*
  Bifel a cas in Breteyne *Befell; event*
Whereof was made Lay le Frain.
In Ingliche for to tellen ywis *In English; certainly*
Of an asche for sothe it is; *ash tree*
On ensaumple fair with alle *An example*
That sum time was bifalle.
In the west cuntré woned tuay knightes, *country; lived two*
And loved hem wele in al rightes; *each other*
Riche men in her best liif, *their prime*
And aither of hem hadde wedded wiif. *either; had*
That o knight made his levedi milde *one; lady*

That sche was wonder gret with childe. — *wondrously great*
And when hir time was comen tho, — *then*
She was deliverd out of wo.
The knight thonked God almight, — *thanked*
And cleped his messanger an hight. — *called; in haste*
"Go," he seyd, "to mi neighebour swithe, — *quickly*
And say y gret him fele sithe, — *I greet; many times*
And pray him that he com to me,
And say he schal mi gossibbe be." — *godparent [of my children]*
The messanger goth, and hath nought forgete, — *not forgotten*
And fint the knight at his mete. — *found; table*
And fair he gret in the halle — *greeted*
The lord, the levedi, the meyné alle. — *company*
And seththen on knes doun him sett, — *then; knees; himself*
And the Lord ful fair he gret: — *saluted*
"He bad that thou schust to him te, — *should; come*
And for love his gossibbe be."
"Is his levedi deliverd with sounde?" — *safely*
"Ya, sir, ythonked be God the stounde." — *occasion*
"And whether a maidenchild other a knave?" — *was it; or*
"Tuay sones, sir, God hem save." — *Two sons; them*
The knight therof was glad and blithe,
And thonked Godes sond swithe, — *God's mercy quickly*
And graunted his erand in al thing, — *request*
And gaf him a palfray for his tiding. — *gave; palfrey; news*
Than was the levedi of the hous
A proude dame and an envieous, — *lady*
Hokerfulliche missegging, — *Maliciously slandering*
Squeymous and eke scorning. — *Disdainful; also scorning*
To ich woman sche hadde envie; — *each*
Sche spac this wordes of felonie: — *spoke these; malice*
"Ich have wonder, thou messanger,
Who was thi lordes conseiler, — *counselor*
To teche him about to send
And telle schame in ich an ende, — *shame everywhere*
That his wiif hath to childer ybore. — *two children born*
Wele may ich man wite therfore — *Well; each; know*
That tuay men hir han hadde in bour; — *two; she has had; bed*

That is hir bothe deshonour."[2] *dishonor*
  The messanger was sore aschamed; *sorely ashamed*
The knight himself was sore agramed, *aggrieved*
And rebouked his levedy *rebuked; lady*
To speke ani woman vilaynie.
And ich woman therof might here *each; who might have heard*
Curssed hir alle yfere, *all together*
And bisought God in heven
For His holy name seven *By; seven names*
That yif hye ever ani child schuld abide *if she; bear*
A wers aventour hir schuld bitide. *worse; she; experience*
  Sone therafter bifel a cas *Soon; it happened*
That hirself with child was.
When God wild, sche was unbounde *willed; relieved*
And deliverd al with sounde. *safely*
To maidenchilder sche hadde ybore. *Two girls*
When hye it wist, wo hir was therefore. *she; knew, woe*
"Allas," sche seyd, "that this hap come! *event*
Ich have ygoven min owen dome. *given myself; doom*
Forboden bite ich woman *be it for any*
To speken ani other harm opon. *harm of any other*
Falsliche another y gan deme; *Falsely; did judge*
The selve happe is on me sene. *same event; in me seen*
Allas," sche seyd, "that y was born!
Withouten ende icham forlorn. *Forever I am lost*
Or ich mot siggen sikerly *Either; must surely say*
That tuay men han yly me by; *two; have lain*
Or ich mot sigge in al mi liif *must say; life*
That y bileighe mi neghbours wiif; *lied about*
Or ich mot — that God it schilde! — *must; prevent*
Help to sle min owhen child. *slay; own*
On of this thre thinges ich mot nede *One; I needs must*
Sigge other don in deoe. *Say or do*
  "Yif ich say ich hadde a bileman, *second lover*
Than ich leighe meselve opon; *lie about myself*
And eke thai wil that me se

[2] *That is dishonor for both of them (both husband and wife)*

Held me wer than comoun be.	*worse*
And yif ich knaweleche to ich man	*acknowledge; each*
That ich leighe the levedi opon,	*lied about the lady*
Than ich worth of old and yong	*shall be by*
Behold leighster and fals of tong.	*Thought a liar; tongue*
Yete me is best take mi chaunce,	
And sle mi childe, and do penaunce."	*slay*
Hir midwiif hye cleped hir to:	*quickly summoned*
"Anon," sche seyd, "this child fordo.	*destroy*
And ever say thou wher thou go	*always; wherever*
That ich have o child and namo."	*one; no more*
The midwiif answerd thurchout al	*to all this*
That hye nil, no hye ne schal.[1]	
[The levedi hadde a maiden fre,	*noble*
Who ther ynurtured hade ybe,	*nurtured had been*
And fostered fair ful mony a yere;	*many a year*
Sche saw her kepe this sori chere,	*sad countenance*
And wepe, and syke, and crye, "Alas!"	*sigh*
And thoghte to helpen her in this cas.	*decided to*
And thus sche spake, this maiden ying,	*young*
"So n'olde y wepen for no kind thing:	*I would not weep for this kind of thing*
But this o child wol I of-bare	*one; will; carry away*
And in a covent leve it yare.	*convent leave; quickly*
Ne schalt thou be aschamed at al;	
And whoso findeth this childe smal,	
By Mary, blissful quene above,]	*(see note)*
May help it for Godes love."	
The levedi graunted anon therto,	*agreed*
And wold wele that it were ydo.	*wished indeed; done*
Sche toke a riche baudekine	*embroidered cloth*
That hir lord brought from Costentine	*Constantinople*
And lapped the litel maiden therin,	*wrapped; little*
And toke a ring of gold fin,	*precious*
And on hir right arm it knitt,	*fastened*
With a lace of silke therin plit;	*silk; entwined*
And whoso hir founde schuld have in mende	*mind*

[1] *That she will not nor she shall not (i.e., the midwife agrees to become an accomplice)*

That it were comen of riche kende. *she; noble kin*
  The maide toke the child hir mide *with*
And stale oway in an eventide, *stole; evening*
And passed over a wild heth. *heath*
Thurch feld and thurch wode hye geth *Through field; wood; went*
Al the winterlong night –
The weder was clere, the mone was light – *weather; moon*
So that hye com bi a forest side; *Until*
Sche wax al weri and gan abide. *became; weary*
Sone after sche gan herk *hark (hear)*
Cokkes crowe and houndes berk. *bark*
Sche aros and thider wold. *would go*
Ner and nere sche gan bihold. *Nearer and nearer*
Walles and hous fele hye seighe, *many; she saw*
A chirche with stepel fair and heighe. *steeple*
Than nas ther noither strete no toun,
Bot an hous of religioun, *But*
An order of nonnes wele ydight *nuns; called*
To servy God bothe day and night. *serve*
The maiden abod no lengore, *tarried; longer*
Bot yede hir to the chirche dore, *went; door*
And on knes sche sat adoun,
And seyd wepeand her orisoun: *weeping; prayer*
"O Lord," she seyd, "Jesu Crist,
That sinful man bedes herst, *Who; hears prayers of*
Underfong this present, *Receive*
And help this seli innocent *blessed*
That it mot ycristned be, *may christened*
For Marie love, thi moder fre." *Mary's; mother*
  Hye loked up and bi hir seighe *She*
An asche bi hir fair and heighe,
Wele ybowed, of michel priis; *branched; great excellence*
The bodi was holow as mani on is. *body; many a one*
Therin sche leyd the child for cold,
In the pel as it was bifold, *robe; enfolded*
And blisced it with al hir might. *blessed*
With that it gan to dawe light. *dawn*
The foules up and song on bough, *birds*
And acremen yede to the plough. *farmers went*

The maiden turned ogain anon, *back soon*
And toke the waye he hadde er gon. *she had formerly gone*
The porter of the abbay aros,
And dede his ofice in the clos, *prayers; vestry*
Rong the belles and taperes light,
Leyd forth bokes and al redi dight. *made ready everything*
The chirche dore he undede, *undid*
And seighe anon in the stede *place*
The pel liggen in the tre, *robe lying*
And thought wele that it might be
That theves hadde yrobbed sumwhare,
And gon ther forth and lete it thare. *left*
Therto he yede and it unwond, *went; unwound*
And the maidenchild therin he fond. *found*
He tok it up betwen his hond, *hands*
And thonked Jesu Cristes sond; *mercy*
And hom to his hous he it brought, *home*
And tok it his douhter and hir bisought *gave*
That hye schuld kepe it as sche can, *she; care for; knew how*
For sche was melche and couthe theran. *with milk; knew about nursing*
Sche bad it souke and it nold, *suck; would not*
For it was neighe ded for cold. *nearly dead*
Anon fer sche alight *fire; lit*
And warmed it wele aplight. *[the babe] well at once*
Sche gaf it souke opon hir barm, *gave; bosom*
And sethen laid it to slepe warm. *then*
And when the masse was ydon, *mass*
The porter to the abbesse com ful son *went immediately*
"Madame, what rede ye of this thing? *advise you about*
Today right in the morning,
Sone after the first stounde, *hour*
A litel maidenchild ich founde
In the holwe assche ther out, *hollow*
And a pel him about.
A ring of gold also was there.
Hou it com thider y not nere." *don't know*
The abbesse was awonderd of this thing. *amazed*
"Go," hye seyd, "on heighing, *she; in haste*
And feche it hider, y pray the. *bring it here*

It is welcom to God and to me.
Ichil it help as y can *I will*
And sigge it is mi kinswoman." *say; my*
The porter anon it gan forth bring
With the pal and with the ring.
The abbesse lete clepe a prest anon, *summoned*
And lete it cristin in funston. *had it christened at the font*
And for it was in an asche yfounde, *because; ash tree*
Sche cleped it *Frain* in that stounde. *named; occasion (time)*
(The Freyns of the "asche" is a *freyn* *French*
After the language of Breteyn;
Forthe *Le Frein* men clepeth this lay *Therefore*
More than *Asche* in ich cuntray). *each*
This Frein thrived fram yer to yer.
The abbesse nece men wend it were. *kinswoman (niece); thought*
The abbesse hir gan teche and beld. *bring up*
Bi that hye was of twelve winter eld, *By the time she; old*
In al Inglond ther nas non *was not at all*
A fairer maiden than hye was on. *she; one*
And when hye couthe ought of manhed, *knew about human nature*
Hye bad the abbesse hir wis and rede *bade; instruct; advise*
Whiche were her kin, on or other, *Who*
Fader or moder, soster or brother.
The abbesse hir in conseyl toke,
To tellen hir hye nought forsoke, *she was not forsaken*
Hou hye was founden in al thing, *discovered; precise detail*
And tok hir the cloth and the ring, *gave*
And bad hir kepe it in that stede; *place*
And ther whiles sche lived so sche dede.
Than was ther in that cuntré
A riche knight of lond and fe, *with land and income*
Proud and yong and jolive, *full of life*
And had nought yete ywedded wive. *yet*
He was stout, of gret renoun, *bold*
And was ycleped Sir Guroun. *named*
He herd praise that maiden fre,
And seyd he wald hir se. *would; see*
He dight him in the way anon, *set himself*
And joliflich thider he come; *gaily*

And bad his man sigge verrament	*bade; say truly*
He schuld toward a turnament.	
The abbesse and the nonnes alle	*nuns all*
Fair him gret in the gest halle,	*Graciously; guest*
And damisel Freyn, so hende of mouth,	*sweet*
Gret him faire as hye wele couthe;	*Greeted; well knew*
And swithe wele he gan devise	*quickly; did discern*
Her semblaunt and her gentrise,	*appearance; breeding*
Her lovesum eighen, her rode so bright,	*lovely eyes; complexion; clear*
And comced to love hir anon right,	*commenced*
And thought hou he might take on	*how*
To have hir to his leman.	*to [be] his lover*
He thought, "Yif ich com hir to	
More than ichave ydo,	*I have to do*
The abbesse wil souchy gile	*suspect guile*
And voide hir in a litel while."	*remove; an instant*
He compast another enchesoun:	*composed; strategy*
To be brother of that religioun.[1]	
"Madame," he seyd to the abbesse,	
"Y lovi wele in al godenisse,	*love you; goodness*
Ichil give on and other,	*I shall; one*
Londes and rentes, to bicom your brother,	*Lands; rents; become*
That ye schul ever fare the bet	*better*
When y com to have recet."	*reception*
At few wordes thai ben at on.	*With; agreed*
He graythes him and forth is gon.	*gets himself ready*
Oft he come bi day and night	
To speke with that maiden bright.	
So that with his fair bihest,	*promise*
And with his gloseing atte lest,	*flattery at last*
Hye graunted him to don his wille	*She; do his desire*
When he wil, loude and stille.	
"Leman," he seyd, "thou most lat be	*forsake*
The abbesse, thi nece, and go with me.	*kinswoman*
For icham riche, of swich pouwere,	*such power*

[1] *To pretend to be a monk of that same religious order*

The finde bet than thou hast here."[1]
The maiden grant, and to him trist, *acceded; trusted*
And stale oway that no man wist. *stole; knew*
With hir tok hye no thing *took; nothing*
Bot hir pel and hir ring. *Except*
When the abbesse gan aspie *realized*
That hye was with the knight owy, *away*
Sche made morning in hir thought, *mourning*
And hir biment and gained nought. *lamented*
So long sche was in his castel
That al his meyné loved hir wel. *household*
To riche and pouer sche gan hir dresse, *She spoke so with rich and poor*
That al hir loved, more and lesse. *all loved her, both high and low*
And thus sche lad with him hir liif *led*
Right as sche hadde ben his wedded wiif. *as if*
His knightes com and to him speke,
And Holy Chirche comandeth eke,
Sum lordes douhter for to take,
And his leman al forsake; *lover*
And seyd him were wel more feir *told; [it] would be; proper*
In wedlok to geten him an air *heir*
Than lede his liif with swiche on *lead; such a one*
Of was kin he knewe non. *Of whose; not one*
And seyd, "Here bisides is a knight *here nearby*
That hath a douhter fair and bright
That schal bere his hiritage; *bear; heritage*
Taketh hir in mariage!"
Loth him was that dede to do, *Reluctant; deed*
Ac atte last he graunt therto. *But; agreed*
The forward was ymaked aright, *agreement; properly*
And were at on, and treuthe plight. *accorded; pledged*
Allas, that he no hadde ywite, *had no knowledge*
Er the forward were ysmite *Before; agreement; struck*
That hye and his leman also *she (his bride); lover*
Sostren were and twinnes to! *Sisters*
Of o fader bigeten thai were, *one; begotten*
Of o moder born yfere. *together*

[1] *Better could be provided for you than you have here*

That hye so ware nist non,
For soth y say, bot God alon.[1]
The newe bride was grayd with alle   *made ready*
And brought hom to the lordes halle.
Hir fader com with hir, also
The levedi, hir moder, and other mo.   *many others*
The bischop of the lond withouten fail
Com to do the spusseayl.   *espousal*
[That maiden bird in bour bright,
Le Codre sche was yhight.   *called*
And ther the guestes had gamen and gle,   *merriment; glee*
And sayd to Sir Guroun joyfully:
"Fairer maiden nas never seen,
Better than Ash is Hazle y ween!"   *suspect*
(For in Romaunce *Le Frain* "ash" is,   *French*
And *Le Codre* "hazle," y-wis.)   *I know*
A gret fest than gan they hold   *feast*
With gle and pleasaunce manifold.
And mo than al servauntes, the maid,
Yhight Le Frain, as servant sped.   *Called*
Albe her herte wel nigh tobroke,   *Although; heart*
No word of pride ne grame she spoke.   *anger*
The levedi marked her simple chere,   *The mother noticed*
And gan to love her, wonder dere.   *very dearly*
Scant could sche feel more pine or reuth   *Scarcely; pain; compassion*
War it hir owen childe in sooth.   *Were*
Than to the bour the damsel sped,   *bower*
Whar graithed was the spousaile bed;   *readied; wedding*
Sche demed it was ful foully dight,   *thought; poorly made*
And yll besemed a may so bright;   *ill-befitted a maiden*
So to her coffer quick she cam,   *went*
And her riche baudekyn out nam,   *brocaded cloth withdrew*
Which from the abbesse sche had got;
Fayrer mantel nas ther not;
And deftly on the bed it layd;
Her lord would thus be well apayd.   *pleased*
Le Codre and her mother, thare,

---

[1] *That they were so, no one knew, / Except God alone, for truth I say*

Ynsame unto the bour gan fare, *Together; to go*
But whan the levedi that mantyll seighe, *saw*
Sche wel neighe swoned oway. *fainted*
The chamberleynt sche cleped tho, *chamberlain; called then*
But he wist of it no mo. *knew; nothing*
Then came that hendi maid Le Frain, *gentle*
And the levedi gan to her sain, *lady did; speak*
And asked whose mantyll it ware. *was*
Then answered that maiden fair:
"It is mine without lesing; *lying*
Y had it together with this ringe.
Myne aunte tolde me a ferli cas *marvelous thing*
Hou in this mantyll yfold I was,
And hadde upon mine arm this ring,
Whanne I was ysent to norysching." *upbringing*
Then was the levedi astonied sore: *very astonished*
"Fair child! My doughter, y the bore!"
Sche swoned and was wel neighe ded, *dead*
And lay sikeand on that bed. *sighing*
Her husbond was fet tho, *fetched then*
And sche told him al her wo,
Hou of her neighbour sche had missayn, *slandered*
For sche was delyvered of childre twain; *Because*
And hou to children herself sche bore; *two*
"And that o child I of sent thore, *sent off*
In a convent yfostered to be;
And this is sche, our doughter free;
And this is the mantyll, and this the ring
You gaf me of yore as a love-tokening."
The knight kissed his daughter hende *eagerly*
Oftimes, and to the bisschop wende: *went*
And he undid the mariage strate, *immediately*
And weddid Sir Guroun alsgate *instead*
To Le Frain, his leman, so fair and hend.
With them Le Codre away did wend, *go*
And sone was spousyd with game and gle, *soon*
To a gentle knight of that countré.
Thus ends the lay of tho maidens bright,
Le Frain and Le Codre yhight.] *called*

Notes

Abbreviations: E: Ellis; H: Holthausen; L: Laurin; S: Sands; V: Varnhagen; W: Wattie; Wb: Weber; Z: Zupitza.

1–22 These lines also appear in both fifteenth-century manuscripts of *Sir Orfeo*. Although they are a composite of material taken from various lais of Marie de France, they do not appear in her lais. See Guillaume, pp. 459–60. For notes on the prologue and its use with *Sir Orfeo*, see the notes for *Orfeo*, lines 1–38. Interestingly, the prologue, like the exordium to scholarly books, tells us its own form of who, what, where, how, and why. Who told the tales? The Breton kings (so although the text doesn't claim an author, it tries to underwrite its authority by claiming to have come from lays composed by kings). Where was the tale from? Breteyne and its courtly worlds. When? In olden times. How was the tale told? Kings heard of marvelous things, picked up a harp, and preserved those marvels in lays. What? Lays can tell of many things: war, woe, joy, happiness, treachery, guile, bawdiness, jokes, the fairy world, but most of all, of love. The introduction then focuses on its own specific subject, a fair "ensaumple" from long ago. For a discussion of authority, rhetoric, and prologues in theological and scholarly medieval texts (as well as their influence on literary forms), see A. J. Minnis, *Medieval Theory of Authorship*, 2nd ed. (Philadelphia: University of Pennsylvania Press, 1988). Obviously, the Middle English lays are somewhat removed from court and university; still, the use of the extensive introduction is connected with the tradition of the prologue in other literary genres and venues.

1 The first line suggests a literate audience, stressing reading and writing, as does the word *clerk* in line 2, although much of the lay also stresses the oral transmission of the text (see, for example, lines 20–22, 25, 233–34, 334, 347–48, 408). The MS is blurred at the end of line 1. W emends this to read [ywri]te. I follow her reading.

8 This line highlights the ancient quality of the lay, an emphasis found frequently within the texts included in this volume, to establish authority. See Chaucer's short poem, "The Former Age."

11 *thinges.* MS: *thingeth.*

26 The ash tree as a symbol for the protagonist contrasts with the hazel tree symbol used for Le Freine's sister, Le Codre. Lee Ramsey, discussing Marie de France's version of the story, notes that the ash does not bear fruit and is used for Le Freine because she cannot give Guroun a legitimate heir, until her lineage is known [*Chivalric Romances: Popular Literature in Medieval England* (Bloomington: Indiana University Press, 1983), p. 114]. Perhaps irony is intended, since the ash tree first bears the child in its branches (its fruit) and because Le Freine will turn out to be the prized wife. The differences in the connotations of the twins' names contributes to the problems of signs and human abilities to read them which forms a theme within the text. Where their bodies are so similar, their names artificially set them apart as opposites. The *Dictionary of Folklore, Mythology, and Symbols* (New York: Funk and Wagnalls, 1949), vol 1, p. 80, connects the "ash" in Scandinavian mythology to the tree of the world, Yggdrasil; the gods ripped the Ash out of the ground and formed it into Ask, the first man. In English and Scottish folklore, the ash is said to have healing powers and its sap a protection against witchcraft. The magical qualities of the tree are also recorded in Pliny who claims that snakes will not crawl over leaves from an ash tree and that a rod made from the ash tree, if it draws a circle in the dirt around a snake, will confine it so that it dies of starvation. See note to line 342 below.

29 MS: *knighteth*. Wb, V, and W all substitute "s" as I have. The West Country is often associated with Wales and with the Celtic fairy world. *Le Freine* does not, however, contain miraculous events or objects; the only things close to magic are the ring and the robe, said in Wb's continuation to have been marvelous love tokens first given Le Freine's mother by her father (lines 397–98) and then passed on with the child as a kind of protection.

29–30 The first of many doubles in the narrative, the two knights and their two wives who are living joyfully until one wife, "envious," accuses the other of adultery.

42 The role of godparent was a serious one in the Middle Ages. See Joseph Lynch, *Godparents and Kinship in Early Medieval Europe* (Princeton: Princeton University Press, 1986), who found "more than three hundred references to baptismal kinship in Latin sources before A.D. 900" (p. 44) and who documents the rise of spiritual kinship and godsibbing throughout Western Europe in the twelfth and thirteenth centuries.

58 Giving gifts to the messenger who bears news of successful childbirth was common practice among the nobility in the late Middle Ages. Nicholas Orme, in his book *From Childhood to Chivalry: The Education of the English Kings and Aristocracy 1066-1530* (London: Methuen, 1984), reports "On 15 July 1273, St. Edith's Day, the wife of Nicholas, baron of Stafford, gave birth to a son in their home. Her joyful husband wrote at once to ask Roger de Pywelisdon, who lived at a distance, to come . . . to be the boy's godfather and lift him from the font" (p. 1). Orme also reports that when Edward III received news of the birth of his first son, the Black Prince, he rewarded the messenger (a yeoman) a life pension of forty marks a year. When he received news about the birth of his second son, he gave that messenger £100; and when informed of John of Gaunt's birth, he awarded the three ladies who bore the news £200 (p. 2).

60 Ellis renders *an envieous* as "malicious."

68 S translates: "And broadcast the disgrace everywhere."

69–72 The idea that twins were a sign of adultery was a popular belief in the Middle Ages, though it was condemned as ignorant by others. See Genesis 38:24 ff., which makes the superstition despicable.

77–82 The curse of the unnamed, undifferentiated "women" on Le Freine's mother is fulfilled quickly. Such curses occur often in the Breton lay. See Guenevere's self-destructive curse in *Launfal*; Emaré's "curse" of infertility on her husband for abandoning his child and his wife; the fairy king's command or *geis* on Heurodis in *Sir Orfeo*, and the *geis* Dame Triamour places on Launfal.

80 Seven Names for God were recognized in medieval Christianity. In her *Dictionary of Mythology, Folklore, and Symbols*, 3 vols. (New York: Scarecrow Press, 1962), vol. 2, pp. 1424–25, Gertrude Jobes mentions seven names for God which were particularly powerful in ancient Israel: "Adonai, Ehyeh-Asher-Ehyeh, El, Elohim, Shaddai, YHWH (in medieval Christianity, Jehovah), and Zebaot." Jobes writes, "In the Middle Ages, God sometimes was called The Seven."

91–92 Wb translates these lines as "I blame every woman as forbidden to speak harm of another." L reads *bite* as "bithe," meaning "is." V rejects both readings. H thinks *bite* is a scribal error for "be it" and translates: "may it be forbidden to each woman . . . ." W agrees with H. Jealousy was often depicted as a woman, as were gossip and envy. See the *Romance of the Rose* and its illuminations; see also notes to *Emaré* lines 535–40, and Christine de Pizan, *The Book of the City of Ladies* I.10.5–7. In another work, Christine writes: "Envy derives straight from the pride engendered in creatures who forget their poor fragility and their evolution from nothing. Overbearing from false arrogance, the pride in their hearts makes them forget their misery and their vices and consider themselves worthy of great honors and possessions. Because every creature so frequently deceives herself, each tends to want to outshine her neighbor and to rise above her not only in virtue but in worldly estate, esteem or possessions." On slander, she writes, "A person of great courage never slanders her enemy, because malicious words are the weapons of people with little power. To use them is to admit cowardice . . . . An apt illustration of the folly of slander is the person who wanted to make war on the heavens and pointed his bow toward the clouds. The arrows fell back on his head and wounded him severely. Likewise as these . . . show, the slander a hateful person speaks against her adversary turns against the slanderer, wounding both soul and honor." *A Medieval Woman's Mirror of Honor: The Treasury of the City of Ladies*, trans. Charity Cannon Willard (New York: Persea, 1989), pp. 158, 163.

95–104 The mother lays out three options for herself. Each is stressed by the repetition of grammatical forms beginning with "or" then, in lines 105–14, she explains the reasoning which takes her to her decision to "sle" her child. This lengthy representation of the internal thoughts of a character is somewhat rare in the Breton Lay. The fourth path is proposed, in Weber's reconstruction, by a noble lady-in-waiting who suggests leaving the one twin at a convent far away (lines 128–34 below).

109 *knaweleche.* V: *knaw lethe.*

112 *Leighster* would specify a female liar.

114 In canon law, abandoning children carried consequences only if the abandonment was known and then only for the father. In the *Decretals* of Pope Gregory IX, if a father gave up his child knowingly, he lost all legal control over the child (*patria potestas*). But on the issue of infanticide, the laws were much harsher, requiring penance (as the mother indicates here). The penance for infanticide, according to the *Decretals*, ranged from a lifetime of monastic

living to a year of bread and water fasting. Secular regulations prohibited infanticide, although it appears to have been practiced; see Boswell, esp. pp. 322–427, and Shulamith Shahar, *Childhood in the Middle Ages* (London: Routledge, 1990), esp. pp. 121–61. (For folklore, see Stith Thompson, pp. 300–95.)

115–18 See Shakespeare's *Winter's Tale* II, iii, 172–78:

> We enjoin thee . . . that thou carry
> This female bastard hence, and that thou bear it
> To some remote and desert place, quite out
> Of our dominions; and that there thou leave it,
> Without more mercy, to its own protection
> And favour of the climate.

See the echo in the falsified letter the mother-in-law writes which condemns Emaré and Segramour to the sea (*Emaré*, lines 587–97).

115–20 Because women assisted one another in childbirth, no one else, apparently, knows that the mother has delivered twins. For an actual case of the closeness that could develop between classes of women around childbirth, see the case of Agnes of Saleby, a barren woman who, to save her dying husband's estate from falling into his brother's hands, feigned pregnancy and birth. She allegedly did this under the tutelage of a poor woman who gave her own daughter, Grace, to be Agnes's "daughter." The case is recorded by Adam of Eynsham in his life of Hugh of Lincoln, *Magna vita Sancti Hugonis*, ed. Decima L. Douie and David Hugh Farmer, 2 vols., (Edinburgh: Thomas Nelson, 1961/62), vol. II, Ch. 5. The account is described quite thoroughly by Paulette L'Hermite-Leclerq, "The Feudal Order," in *A History of Women in the West II. Silences of the Middle Ages*, ed. Christine Klapisch-Zuber (Cambridge, Mass.: Harvard University Press, 1992), pp. 204–12.

121–33 These lines are missing from the MS. They were reconstructed by Wb and have commonly been included in modern editions of the lay. Wb's reconstruction is modelled on Marie de France's *Lai le Fresne* (lines 99–115).

137–38 The richly embroidered cloth never is described; however, the token has great power. Like Emaré's robe, it will accompany Le Freine everywhere she goes and will serve to solidify her identity. Also like the cloth in *Emaré*, this one is from Constantinople.

Lay le Freine

137–44 The *baudekine* and the ring become the tokens which precipitate the recognition scene at the end of the poem. Examining Talmudic regulations regarding abandoned children, Boswell writes, "Foundlings have limited marriage rights — i.e., cannot marry into the highest four genealogical classes . . . because their parents cannot be known and there is some danger of incest . . . . Yet a foundling was exempt from these restrictions if the mode of his or her abandonment offered evidence of parental concern, suggesting that a good family had given him or her up under duress: if he was found circumcised; with limbs set; massaged with oil and powdered, wearing beads, a tablet or an amulet, suspended from a tree out of reach of animals, left in a synagogue, in moving water, or near a public thoroughfare. The absence of such attentions would be indications that the child's parents did not care about him, or possibly that he was of undesirable ancestry . . ." (p. 151). The Christian tradition reiterated aspects of the Hebraic; so, for example, the Synod of Nimes in 1252 guaranteed that abandoned children who died near a church would be buried in sanctified ground unless "written evidence or some other sign should indicate that an abandoned child found dead had not been baptized." Le Freine's mother wants it known that the baby comes from "riche kende," and the maid who abandons the baby puts her in the hollow of an ash tree right next to the "chirche dore." Interestingly, Le Freine is not baptized before she is abandoned. See Boswell, pp. 322–94.

138 MS: *fram*.

142 MS: *pilt*. This is followed by Wb and V; E reads "plit" and glosses the word as "plaited, twisted." The manuscript, *pilt*, violates the rhyme scheme.

155 An ampersand has been inserted in MS.

159 MS: *steete*; Wb and V emend to *strete*.

167 MS: *he*.

174 W suggests, "the repetition of *bi hir* is probably an error."

197 MS: *betven*.

200 MS: *his* has been inserted.

224 The abbess gives Le Freine a certain amount of protection by claiming she is her "kinswoman." Boswell cites the German *Schwabenspiegel*, a civil code: "If any father or mother abandons a child, and someone else picks it up and rears it and feeds it until it is old enough to serve, it should serve the one who saved its life. And if the father or mother should wish to reclaim . . . they must first repay whatever cost [the finder] incurred . . ."(p. 326). However, finders who raised children as servants were the only ones who exerted parental powers over the child. A finder who raised the child as her own kin or as freeborn did not acquire legal rights over the child (p. 327).

231 V and E read *freyns* as "freyn" and read her "name." Wb and Z believe *freyns* means "freynsch," or "French."

233 A deleted thorn is visible before *le*. *Lay* has been rendered as *day* in Wb.

237–38 *eld* may be either a noun alongside "winter" or an adjective where "winter" is governed by "of."

241 *manhed* is rendered as "consanguinity" in E, and L agrees. W notes that there is little to support this reading, citing the *NED* (s.v. manhead). The *MED* cites this line from *Le Freine* in its entry for "manhed" under the first meaning listed which is "human condition, nature, or form."

260 *joliflich*. MS: *Iolifich*.

267 *swithe*. MS: *swhe*. This spelling is followed by Wb and V who read this as "so"; E and Z emend to "swithe," a reading W also prefers.

280 V: *y lovi* (I love); E: *I-lovi* (beloved); Wb: *y-lovi* (beloved). W writes, "It is easiest to suppose that a "d" has been forgotten and to read *ylouid*, meaning well-beloved in a virtuous way."

295 E: *swich*; Wb: *swithe*; V: *swi-Þorn-e*. The letters "c" and "t" are identical in MS. W prefers *swiche* which is also the reading by Z.

297–99 Le Freine's movements from one "world" to another happen in secrecy. Just as she was illicitly taken away from the childbed and abandoned in the tree, so here, she is illicitly taken from the convent to live as Guroun's mistress.

311–18 On the issue of class and its role here, see Harriet E. Hudson, "Construction of Class, Family, and Gender in Some Middle English Popular Romances," in Britton J. Harwood and Gillian R. Overing, eds., *Class and Gender in Early English Literature* (Bloomington: Indiana University Press, 1994), pp. 76–94. Hudson focuses on *Sir Eglamour of Artois*, *Torrent of Portengale*, *Paris and Vienne*, and *The Squire of Low Degree*, all late medieval romances. Compare the pressure placed on Arthur to marry at the beginning of *Sir Launfal*. Notice that Holy Chirche does not uphold consensual rights and instead supports a legitimate, arranged marriage of class solidarity. N.b. the Pope's dispensation granted to Syr Artyus in *Emaré*, lines 230–240.

327–34 The laws of consanguinity would identify Guroun's marriage to Le Freine's sister as an act of incest. Much written discussion surrounding the issue of abandoned children stresses the possibility that incest can result because bloodlines are not known. See the charts of consanguinity regularly appended to the *Decretum*. See also James Brundage, *Law, Sex, and Christian Society in Medieval Europe* (Chicago: University of Chicago Press, 1987); Georges Duby, *Medieval Marriage: Two Models from Twelfth-Century France*, trans. Elborg Forster (Baltimore: Johns Hopkins University Press, 1978). For a medieval audience, the threat of incest in *Le Freine* remains potential right up until Guroun's marriage to Le Codre is annulled. This also explains why the narrator reacts so emotionally at this point in the narrative and why the text emphasizes that the two are sisters, twins, with one father and one mother.

330 MS: *tvinnes.*

341–end Fol. 263 is cut out. The initial letters in the first column are left here and there. V provides these on pp. 422–33 in a footnote. Wb provided these lines in an imaginative re-creation of Middle English translated directly from Marie de France's lay.

342 If "Le Freine," the "ash tree," holds significance, so does "Le Codre," the "hazel tree." The sisters' names both derive from trees found in Celtic mythology. A tree frequently appears at the junction of two worlds — the human and the fairy Otherworld. See the discussion in Marie-Thérèse Brouland, *Sir Orfeo: le substrat celtique du lai breton anglais* (Paris: Didier Erudition, 1990), pp. 58–69. In the *Lai du Chevrefeuille* (lines 51–54), hazel (*le Coudrier*) is the wood Tristan uses to send his message to Yseut. See also notes to line 26 above.

345–46 The irony of these lines is clear given the fact that the two women are twins.

349 Whereas the narrative began with a celebration of new birth, the final social gathering celebrates a wedding, stressing the circularity and mirroring that is common in medieval romance.

355–58 The mother's empathetic response may suggest her preconscious reaction to the servant who will turn out to be her own daughter, but it may also show us a reformed mother. Where years before she could remain detached from her newborn and unempathetic, she now finds herself imagining Le Freine's internal experience. The three lines also continue the pattern of presenting the most poignant emotions of the protagonist through another character's eyes or through the narrator's voice.

362 Since Le Codre and Le Freine are twin sisters, Le Freine's belief that the "spousaile bed" is too shabby for "a may so bright" takes a reflexive turn. Without knowing it, when she values Le Codre and finds her deserving of the baudekyn, she values herself. The doubling here provides potentialities for psychological readings.

365 The origin of the cloth is mentioned a number of times, each time a partial truth, as no character knows the full story. See lines 137–38, 143–44, 190–94, 211–18, 241–49, 299–300, and 364–66. This information is followed by more, in lines 377, 379–84, 397–98. The last piece of information about the cloth is saved for lines 397–98 when we learn that the cloth was a gift of love, a "love-tokening," Le Freine's father had given to her mother. The cloth, like Le Freine, has a story which is not fully known, even to the audience, until the very last lines of the text, so where we know the tangle of human relationships that converge in the marriage bower, we don't know the full story of the cloth until the end of the poem. See *Emaré* for another text with a close connection between a beautiful cloth and the destiny and identity of the heroine.

395 Wb has *covent*.

399 The knight's courtesy is consistent throughout the poem. Just as he rejoiced in the births of his friend's sons, here he accepts and rejoices in the reunion with a long-lost daughter.

Sir Degaré

Introduction

Sir Degaré is extant in six manuscripts and three early printed editions.[1] In the Auchinleck MS the poem consists of 1065 lines and is incomplete; it lacks an introductory couplet, a few internal lines, and an ending.[2] Nonetheless, I have chosen Auchinleck as my base text for its general acceptance among scholars as the earliest example of the poem in Middle English.[3]

Much of the modern scholarship on *Sir Degaré* is concerned with aesthetics. While some scholars consider the poem to be imbued with positive attributes such as brevity and coherence without the usual digression of long romances,[4] others regard it with something approaching contempt. C. H. Slover, for instance, criticizes the poet for "hack-writing," suggesting in rather explicit terms that the poet's work is "inept" and lacks "literary quality." G. P. Faust, writing later than Slover but adopting a similar critical *ad hominem* position, notes the poet's predilection for creating "stock characters about whom we know at the end little more than we did at the beginning."[5] These two strongly negative valuations seem to have vitiated perceptions of

---

[1] See bibliography.

[2] Because of the incomplete state of the poem I have followed Gustav Schleich in creating a composite text using lines of Cambridge Ff. 2.38 to fill internal lacunae and the Rawlinson Poetry 34 MS to supply the conclusion. W. H. French and C. B. Hale also use the Auchinleck MS with insertions from Cambridge where needed, but have omitted both an opening couplet and the last thirty lines; they prefer instead to paraphrase the conclusion of the poem.

[3] See I. C. Cunningham and Derek Pearsall's introduction to the facsimile of the Auchinleck MS. "[Auchinleck's] significance is in its early date, in the range, variety and intrinsic interest of its contents, and in the evidence it provides for English poetry, of book production and readership in the period before Chaucer" (p. viii).

[4] See J. W. Hales and F. J. Furnivall, eds. *Bishop Percy's Folio Manuscript: Ballads and Romances* (London: N. Trübner, 1868); J. Burke Severs, *A Manual of the Writings in Middle English, 1050-1500* (New Haven: The Connecticut Academy of Arts & Sciences, 1967); William C. Stokoe, Jr., "The Double Problem of *Sir Degare*," *PMLA* 70 (1976), 518–34.

[5] Clark H. Slover, "*Sire Degarre*: A Study of a Medieval Hack Writer's Methods," *University of Texas Studies in English* 11 (1931), 6–23. See also George P. Faust, *Sire Degare*: A Study of the Texts and Narrative Structure (Princeton: Princeton University Press, 1935).

the poem; despite a positive review by Muriel Carr,[6] a non-controversial edition by Gustav Schleich,[7] and an equally neutral edition by French and Hale,[8] as William Stokoe notes, "the opinions of Slover and Faust seem to have prevailed."[9] Stokoe's attempt "to vindicate the judgment of the copyists, printers, modern editors, and critics who have admired *Sir Degaré*," reverses the *ad hominem* trend laudably, however, by refocusing attention on the poem's intrinsic worth and its crucial place in literary history. Bruce Rosenberg has followed suit by demonstrating the inherent value of the poem's folkloric material.[10]

While these scholars and critics concern themselves with aesthetics, others are concerned with traditional intertextual issues — sources, analogues and influences. Some scholars claim the poem to be based upon a lost Breton lai, *Lai d'Esgaré*, while others refute it; still others prefer to leave the question open to speculation or further study.[11] Mentioned most often in the scholarly discourse are the *Sohrab and Rustem* story which features a father/son combat, an important motif in *Degaré*,[12] an Irish tale, *The Second Battle of Moytura,* which may have contributed the sword motif,[13] *The Voyage of Maelduin*, and *Bricriu's Feast,* elements of which resonate in the enchanted castle scene.[14] The strong Oedipal theme may derive from the *Legend*

---

[6] Muriel Carr, *Modern Language Notes* 53 (1938), 153 ff.

[7] Gustav Schleich, ed., *Sire Degarre,* Englishche Textbibliothek, No. 19 (Heidelberg: C. Winter, 1929).

[8] W. H. French and C. B. Hale, eds., *Middle English Metrical Romances* (New York: Prentice-Hall, 1930), I, 287–320.

[9] William C. Stokoe, Jr., pp. 518–34. Stokoe's thesis is an attempt to overturn the negative valuations of the poem by pointing out the variations between the version found in the Auchinleck MS and that in a later MS significant enough to suggest two different versions rather than corrupt transmission and redaction.

[10] Bruce Rosenberg, "Medieval Popular Literature: Folkloric Sources," *The Popular Literature of Medieval England,* ed. Thomas J. Heffernan, *Tennessee Studies in Literature* 28 (Knoxville, 1985), 61–84.

[11] G. V. Smithers, "Story-Patterns in Some Breton Lays," *Medium Aevum* 22 (1953), 61–92.

[12] M. A. Potter, *Sohrab and Rustem: The Epic Theme of a Combat Between Father and Son,* Grimm Library, No. 14 (London: D. Nutt, 1902).

[13] Laura A. Hibbard [Loomis], p. 327.

[14] R. S. Loomis, *Arthurian Tradition & Chrétien de Troyes* (New York: Columbia University Press, 1949). Elements from *Bricriu's Feast* revolve around the scene in which Degaré stumbles upon a castle on an island inhabited only by women and a yellow-haired dwarf.

of Pope Gregory, contained in the *Gesta Romanorum* as well as in the Auchinleck MS. Whatever the sources or analogues or the pronouncements on the poet's ability, the integrity of the poem itself allows it to stand on its own merits. That fact is nearly lost in the critical and scholarly discourse swirling around it.

Sir Degaré, a heroic knight whose name at least one scholar associates with the lost Breton lay, announces the necessity of establishing an identity.[15] Like many medieval heroes he needs to prove himself worthy of knighthood by undertaking a quest and overcoming such obstacles as dragons and giants. Unlike many medieval heroes, Degaré's quest is complicated by the circumstances of his birth. Born illegitimately and abandoned by his mother in infancy, Degaré is marginalized both socially and politically. His status as an orphan and foundling early in the poem leaves him almost without an identity, almost without a name.[16] Degaré's quest, therefore, is twofold: not only must he undergo the ritualized testing that marks passage into the world of chivalry, but he needs to reestablish his kinship relations in order to legitimize his place in the social hierarchy. Degaré is thus compelled to seek out his natal parents and reclaim his patrimony, before he can then establish a life of his own. The resolution of Degaré's dilemma, as some scholars have noted, parallels the psychological development of any child.[17] The poem is family drama akin to fairytale where children under enchantment resolve psychological conflicts through quests and trials.

The family drama is immediately established by the bizarre relationship between the King of Brittany and his daughter. The narrative opens with the king's challenge to fight his daughter's potential suitors for the honor of her hand in marriage. The widowed king dotes on the princess overmuch, a situation that exceeds a father's protective instincts toward a daughter and points instead toward incest. Found more explicitly in the Catskin Cinderella folktales and Middle English narratives such as

---

[15] Nicolas Jacobs, "Old French *Degare* and Middle English *Degarre* and *Deswarre*," *Notes & Queries* n.s. 17 (1970), 164–65, suggests that Degaré's name may be related to the OF *esgare*, which means lost or destitute. It is related to the ME *deswarre*, which according to the *MED* is related to knight errancy, the *OED* defines the term *diswaryed* which means "strayed, gone astray or gotten lost."

[16] See Cheryl Colopy, "*Sir Degare:* A Fairy Tale Oedipus," *Pacific Coast Philology* 17 (1982), 31–39. She suggests that "the importance of a male heir is the central social problem in the story."

[17] See Bruno Bettelheim, *The Uses of Enchantment: The Meaning and Importance of Fairy Tales* (New York: Vintage Books, 1977) and Derek Brewer, *Symbolic Stories: Traditional Narratives of the Family Drama in English Literature* (Cambridge: D. S. Brewer, 1980).

Apollonius of Tyre and *Emaré*,[18] the incest motif involves the death of the beautiful queen and the substitution by the king of the only woman who matches the attributes of his lost spouse — their daughter.[19] Usually the daughter runs away to a different kingdom, meets a prince, marries him and lives happily ever after. In *Sir Degaré* the opportunity for escape is limited until the daughter is brought to the grave of her mother in the woods to commemorate her death. There the princess and her ladies-in-waiting separate from the king's entourage, and while the maids fall asleep under an enchanted chestnut tree the princess wanders away into the woods. At least one scholar reads this as the young woman's effort to escape the tacit sexual advances of her father;[20] others view it as the awakening of sexual desire.

Whatever the motivations for separating from the group the princess becomes suddenly aware that she is lost and vulnerable to "wilde bestes." At the moment of her greatest fear there suddenly appears a mysterious scarlet-robed stranger. Some scholars have likened this fairy knight to the angel in Joachim's garden or to the demon lover in *Tydorel*. Perhaps closer parallels may be found in *Sir Gowther* and *Sir Orfeo*. In *Gowther* a demon suddenly appears to the mother of the hero disguised as her husband; he rapes her and prophesies the birth of their child. In *Orfeo* the fairy king abducts the heroine to the Otherworld after first threatening her with bodily harm. *Degaré's* fairy knight, proclaiming to have loved her from afar for a long time, seems to combine the attributes of both the fairy king and the demonic "feltered [shaggy] fiend." He is threatening and takes what he wants:

> "Thou best mi lemman ar thou go, — *will be my lover before*
> Wether the liketh wel or wo." — *you like it much or hate it*
> Tho nothing ne coude do she
> But wep and criede and wolde fle;
> And he anon gan hire at holde, — *quickly seized her*
> And dide his wille, what he wolde.
> He binam hire here maidenhod . . . — *bereft her of her*
> (lines 107–13)

The fairy knight's rape of the nameless princess is clearly a violation of her body, but the poet seems to attenuate the crime by creating a portrayal that one scholar has described as "a curious mixture of benignity, almost solicitousness . . . an analogue

---

[18] See Laura A. Hibbard [Loomis], p. 302.

[19] The Catskin Cinderella motif, also known as Allerleirauh, involves a young woman who is forced to leave home because of her father's unwelcome sexual advances.

[20] See Colopy, p. 35.

of the Green Knight who wields his axe with a smile, laughing even as he strikes."[21] After the rape, the knight announces the impending birth of a "knave," gives the broken sword given as a token of recognition for their unborn son, and then he "kyst hys lemman and wentt." The rapist seems exonerated, the consequences of his violent act nullified at least from his viewpoint as he vanishes into the woods as quickly as he appeared. The consequences for the princess are much more severe, however, and create the dilemma that leads to Degaré's abandonment. How will she, a virgin, conceal the truth of her pregnancy from her doting father? And more importantly how will she deal with those who point to her father as the culprit?

Yif ani man hit underyete	*should attempt to explain it*
Men wolde sai bi sti and strete	*sty; path*
That mi fader the King hit wan	*begot*
(lines 167–69)	

The problem of incest, whatever form it takes — father/daughter, mother/son, brother/sister — is as old as the human family itself, but as John Boswell notes, the subject was particularly present in public consciousness in the late Middle Ages. Often associated with abandonment, incest became "a considerable preoccupation among medieval authors."[22] Boswell points to Pope Gregory whose legend rendered him "the most celebrated exposed child of the Middle Ages." Like Gregory, and so many other illegitimate medieval children, actual and literary, Degaré is abandoned by his mother, an act a modern audience may judge harshly.[23] But Degaré's mother attempts to make the best of the situation and orchestrates a careful plan. In the infant boy's cradle she includes four pounds of gold, ten of silver, a letter directing the finder to give the babe the tokens at age ten, and special gloves sent for the babe as a gift by her "lemman," his father. Degaré, the illegitimate child, is then spirited away by a maid servant and placed before the door of a hermitage.

The abandonment motif, particularly when linked to incest, is a component of the Oedipal legend scholars see so strongly represented in this poem. An ancient tale, it

---

[21]Colopy, pp. 32-33. The "Green Knight" refers to the villain in *Sir Gawain and the Green Knight*.

[22] John Boswell, *The Kindness of Strangers: The Abandonment of Children in Western Europe from Late Antiquity to the Renaissance* (New York: Pantheon Books, 1988), p. 373.

[23] In *Lay le Freine,* found in this volume, the mother fears allegations of adultery (twins were thought to be produced by separate fathers). In her anxiety she considers murdering one of the twin girls. Her maid talks her into abandoning the child in an ash tree near a monastery where she is subsequently raised to adulthood. Boswell notes that abandoned children were often suspended in trees to prevent wild animals from attacking them.

is most memorably defined by Sophocles in the second of the Theban plays — *Oedipus Rex* — where Oedipus, who is prophesied to grow up to kill his father and marry his mother, is bound by the feet and taken to Citheron to be abandoned (hence the derivation of Oedipus's name — "swollen foot"). Subsequently he is rescued by a sympathetic shepherd, raised by Polybus in Corinth, only to return to Thebes where he unwittingly fulfills the prophecy. In twelfth-century France the theme appears in the retelling of the story in the *Roman de Thebes* and becomes central to the medieval stories of Judas Iscariot and Pope Gregory.[24] But the legend is most familiar to modern audiences through Sigmund Freud's use of it to define the psychological complex he names Oedipal. According to Freud, it is the unconscious fantasy of every male child to "kill" his father in order to marry his mother.[25] The dilemma of Oedipus for Freud resides not in the dilemma of destiny and choice, as in Sophocles, but rather in the psychological tensions between parent and child.

Left at the door of a hermitage, Degaré is found the next morning and happily received by the kind hermit. This is no ordinary oblational abandonment, as the hermit soon discovers, but one accompanied by written instructions and the material means by which to raise the child.[26] The hermit christens the infant, names him appropriately "Degarre" (the "lost one"), and finds suitable foster parents until the boy is old enough to begin his education. Then just as so many other male mentors in literature — Chiron to Achilles, Merlin to Arthur, the hermit to Parsifal, Iron John to the golden-haired prince — the hermit prepares Degaré for his passage into the masculine world. At age ten Degaré begins his education; at age twenty, when the hermit has taught the boy everything he knows, Degaré is ready for the next stage of life. In releasing him the hermit returns to the youth his gold, the gloves, the pointless sword, and the letter from his mother which compels Degaré to find his parents. Lacking in horse and armor, still only a child in the chivalric world, he needs to prove himself worthy of knighthood by demonstrating his martial prowess. What better initiation into knighthood than to rescue an earl from a fire-breathing dragon, one of the most formidable enemies the medieval imagination could conjure up. One-to-one combat prepares Degaré psychologically for the greater battles of life. Degaré,

---

[24] See Lowell Edmunds, *Oedipus: The Ancient Legend and Its Later Analogues* (Baltimore: Johns Hopkins University Press, 1985). See also Thomas Hahn, "The Medieval Oedipus," *Comparative Literature* 32 (1980), 225–37.

[25] See Sigmund Freud, *The Interpretation of Dreams*, trans. James Strachey (London: George Allen, 1954), pp. 260–63.

[26] Oblation meant that abandoned children were offered to God vis-à-vis leaving them at the doorstep of a monastery.

who lacks both the training of a knight and a knight's arms, defeats the dragon with an oaken bat. His conquest marks his extraordinary strength and determination, qualities of mind and body necessary for the proper practice of chivalry. At this point in the narrative, "child" Degaré is dubbed "knight" by the Earl. But prowess alone does not guarantee greatness. Sir Degaré's next rite of passage is more complex as he prepares to fight for his patrimony and a legitimate place in society.

The battle between Sir Degaré and the king, his maternal grandfather, takes place when Degaré is twenty years old, and, although twenty years have passed, the situation of his mother in Brittany has remained unchanged, i.e., the apparently ageless princess is still being offered as the reward for the knight who can defeat the king in combat. It is an equal opportunity tournament open not only to knights but to barons, earls, burgesses, and churls. For a knight without a patrimony this is an attractive deal; the winner receives both princess and property. Sir Degaré answers the call, but it is only with great difficulty that he unhorses the stalwart king. For his strength and prowess in arms he wins the hand of the princess who is, of course, his mother. The consummation of their relation is thwarted in the nick of time, however, as Degaré remembers to try the enchanted gloves on the hands of his bride. Like Cinderella's slipper, they fit perfectly and recognition comes immediately to Degaré's mother as "Here viage wex ase red ase blod." Now her closely guarded secret of twenty years can no longer be kept and the revelation is made immediately. The consummation of mother/son incest so central to the Oedipal narratives is thus averted. Unlike Oedipus, the medieval Judas Iscariot, and Pope Gregory, Degaré discovers his error in time, flees his mother's home, and resumes the search for his father.

Although Sir Degaré is on a quest with a specific purpose, he is a practicing knight errant. His wanderings take him far and wide until finally the youthful knight chances upon an island castle with its bridge down and its gates ajar. Degaré, who has depended upon the kindness of strangers all his life, is attracted to the unusual place. Its open access encourages him to enter, stable his horse, and make himself comfortable at the hearth fire. From this point he is presented with sights worthy of any heterosexual male fantasy as it soon becomes clear that, aside from a male dwarf, Degaré has stumbled upon a community of women. And so begins another rite of passage. If the combats with dragon and grandfather test Degaré's martial prowess, then the lady of this castle will educate him in the finer points of chivalric love. Degaré begins to learn about local customs immediately when his comments are met at first with stony silence by four huntresses, then the yellow-haired dwarf, and the ladies-in-waiting.[27] But the silence is only a prelude to the sensorial delights to follow. Sumptuously wined and dined, serenaded by beautiful women and magical music, Degaré falls into an enchanted sleep.[28] He awakens to a knightly task which will ultimately prepare him for the most important battle of his life.

In a scenario one scholar has described as a "mirror" to earlier events, Degaré's mission is to rid the lady of an unwanted suitor, a "sterne knight" who has systematically slaughtered her protectors.[29] The lady, like Degaré's mother, is the only heir to her father's estate. Bound by codes of chivalry to defend the defenseless, Degaré must protect the lady and her household by defeating the marauding knight. The battle scene is as stellarly depicted as the two preceding it. Like the dragon and Degaré's grandfather, the knight proves a worthy opponent. But because the motif calls for the breaking of a magic spell, Degaré prevails and smites his opponent through the "helm, heved and bacinet." The lady is predictably grateful, but any readerly expectation of marriage is deferred until the last of Degaré's battles is fought. Instead of marriage, the lady provides him with new arms, a new horse and enough gold and silver to determine his own immediate future.

The culminating battle between father and son, often compared to the *Sohrab and Rustem* combat, satisfies all narrative expectations. It reunites the two errant kinsmen, resolves Degaré's desire to know who his father is, and brings his father and mother at last legitimately together. Neither father nor son recognizes the other at the outset of battle until both are unhorsed and begin hand-to-hand combat. When Degaré presents his pointless sword his father recognizes it immediately. The broken sword, which one scholar calls a "metonymy of maleness, signifying power and authority," suggests in its broken state the loss of that power.[30] The replacement of its point by a father, who has carried it around for twenty years, suggests a restoration of patrilinear authority. Unlike the illegitimate Mordred or Oedipus, both of whom mortally wound their fathers, the breech between father and son is dramatically healed:

---

[27] See David F. Johnson, "The Dwerff seyd neyther 'bow ne be': 'Ne bu ne ba' and 'Sir Degaré, Line 703," *Neuphilologische Mitteilungen* 93 (1992), 121–23. Johnson argues that the phrase means "to say neither one thing or another, nothing at all." Absent in the Auchinleck MS, the phrase is present in the later Rawlinson MS.

[28] The Celts were well known for their powers of enchantment.

[29] See Colopy, p. 36.

[30] Colopy, p. 35.

"What is thi name?" than saide he.
"Certes, men clepeth me Degarre." *call*
O Degarre, sone mine!
Certes ich am fader thine! *I am your father*
And bi thi swerd I knowe hit here:
The point is in min aumenere." *pouch*
He tok the point and set therto . . .
(lines 1056–62)

The end of the poem is missing in the Auchinleck MS, the leaves having been cut out, a near loss of the conclusion provided only by later manuscripts and printed editions. Degaré's marriage to his mother is undone, his parents are reunited, and he marries the lady of the island castle. The tragedy of Oedipus is thus transformed into comedy where difficult sociopolitical and psychological conflicts are resolved, crimes are forgiven, and all parties live happily ever after.

Select Bibliography

Manuscripts

Advocates Library of Scotland MS 19.2.1, called the Auchinleck MS. [Dated between 1330 and 1340, it is the earliest manuscript containing the poem. The poem consists of 1065 lines and lacks an ending, an introductory couplet, and a few internal lines.]

British Library MS Egerton 2862. [Dated the late fourteenth century; in this MS, the poem consists of two fragments totalling 161 lines.]

Cambridge University Library MS Ff. 2.38. [Dated approximately 1420–50; the poem begins at fol. 257b and extends to fol. 261b. Located at the end of the manuscript, it consists of 602 lines and is incomplete.]

MS Rawlinson Poetry 34 in the Bodleian Library. [Dated fifteenth century; the poem consists of 989 lines beginning at fol. 10b and ending at 17b. This version is "complete" and provides an ending to the Auchinleck text in this volume.]

MS Douce 261 in the Bodleian Library. [Dated 1561; *Sir Degaré*, found on leaves 8-14, consists of four fragments totaling 350 lines.]

Sir Degaré

Additional MS 27879 (Percy Folio) in the British Library. [Dated 1650; *Sir Degaré* (folio 183b–189a) consists of 900 lines including an ending.]

Early Printed (Black Letter) Editions

Wynkyn de Worde, 4to; J. Pierpont Morgan Library, New York. [George Patterson Faust suggests a possible date of 1502–34 (see *Sir Degare: The Texts and Their Relations*, p. 4). No other copy of this printing survives.]

Wyllyam Copland, 4to; in the British Library. [Possible date 1548–68 according to Faust. No other copy of this printing survives.]

John King, 4to; in the Bodleian Library. [Dated 1560 by Faust. No other copy of this printing survives.]

Editions

Laing, David, ed. *Sire Degarre, a Metrical Romance of the End of the Thirteenth Century*. Edinburgh: Abbotsford Club, 1849.

Carr, Muriel. *Sir Degarre, a Middle English Metrical Romance Edited from the Manuscript and Black Letter Texts.* Ph.D. dissertation, University of Chicago, 1923.

Rollow, Jack Wilcox. *The Text of Sire Degarre*. Ph.D. dissertation, Cornell University, 1950.

Schleich, Gustav. *Sire Degarre.* Englische Textbibliothek 19. Heidelberg: C. Winter, 1929. [Composite text using Auchinleck to line 1076 and Rawlinson for the conclusion.]

Collections

French, W. H., and C. B. Hale, eds. *The Middle English Metrical Romances.* 1930; rpt. New York: Russell & Russell, 1964. Pp. 287–320.

Rumble, Thomas C., ed., *Breton Lays in Middle English.* Detroit: Wayne State University Press, 1965. Pp. 44–78.

Utterson, E. V., ed. *Select Pieces of Early Popular Poetry*, 2 vols. London: Longman, Hurst, Rees, Orme, and Brown, 1817.

Related Studies

Colopy, Cheryl. "*Sir Degaré*: A Fairy Tale Oedipus." *Pacific Coast Philology* 17 (1982), 31–39. [Explores the connection between sexuality and identity.]

Faust, George Patterson. *Sir Degaré: A Study of the Texts and Narrative Structure*. Princeton: Princeton University Press, 1935.

Jacobs, Nicolas. "The Egerton Fragment of *Sir Degarre*." *Neuphilologische Mitteilungen* 72 (1971), 86–96. [Study of dialect, orthography, and transcription.]

——— ."Old French *Degaré* and Middle English *Degarre* and *Deswarre*." *Notes and Queries* n.s. 17 (1970), 164–65. [Relates OF *esgaré* to ME *deswarre* found in *Guy of Warwick*.]

———. "The Process of Scribal Substitution and Redaction: A Study of the Cambridge Fragment of *Sir Degarre*." *Medium Aevum* 53 (1984), 26–48. [Compares variant readings and discusses transmission.]

———. "Some Creative Misreadings in *Le Bone Florence of Rome*: An Experiment in Textual Criticism." In *Medieval English Studies Presented to George Kane*, eds. Edward Kennedy and Ronald Waldron. Woodbridge: Brewer, 1988. Pp. 279–84.

———."The Lost Conclusion of the Auchinleck *Sir Degarre*," *Notes and Queries*, n.s. 37 (1990), 154–58.

———."The Second Revision of *Sir Degarre*: The Egerton Fragment and Its Congeners." *Neuphilologische Mitteilungen* 85 (1984), 95–107. [Textual comparison of Egerton and Rawlinson MSS.]

Loomis, Laura Hibbard. *Medieval Romance in England*. London: Oxford University Press, 1924; rpt. New York: Burt Franklin, 1960. Pp. 301–05. [Study of sources and analogues.]

———. "The Auchinleck Manuscript and a Possible London Bookshop of 1330–1340." *PMLA* 57 (1942), 595–609.

Sir Degaré

Potter, M. A. *Sohrab and Rustem: The Epic Theme of a Combat Between Father and Son.* Grimm Library, No. 14. London: D. Nutt, 1902.

Rosenberg, Bruce A. "The Three Tales of *Sir Degaré.*" *Neuphilologische Mitteilungen* 76 (1975), 39–51. [Discusses the poem as a conflation of three folk motifs.]

Slover, Clark H. "*Sire Degarre*: A Study of a Medieval Hack Writer's Methods." *University of Texas Studies in English,* 11 (1931), 6–23. [Argues the poem's lack of aesthetic appeal.]

Stokoe, W. C., Jr. "The Double Problem of *Sir Degaré.*" *PMLA* 70 (1955), 518–34. [Argues that there are two distinct versions of the poem.]

——. "The Work of the Redacters of *Sir Launfal, Richard Coeur de Lion*, and *Sir Degaré.*" Ph. D. dissertation, Cornell University, 1946.

Sir Degaré

Lysteneth, lordinges, gente and fre, *gentle; noble*
Ich wille you telle of Sire Degarre:
Knightes that were sometyme in londe *were once*
Ferli fele wolde fonde *Wonderfully many; discover*
And sechen aventures bi night and dai,
Hou thai mighte here strengthe asai; *How they; their; try*
So dede a knyght, Sire Degarree:
Ich wille you telle wat man was he. *I; what*
In Litel Bretaygne was a kyng *Brittany*
Of gret poer in all thing, *power*
Stif in armes under sscheld, *Staunch; shield*
And mochel idouted in the feld. *feared*
Ther nas no man, verraiment, *was not any; truly*
That mighte in werre ne in tornament, *war nor*
Ne in justes for no thing, *jousts by any means*
Him out of his sadel bring,
Ne out of his stirop bringe his fot,
So strong he was of bon and blod.
This Kyng he hadde none hair *heir*
But a maidenchild, fre and fair; *noble*
Here gentiresse and here beauté *Her gentleness*
Was moche renound in ich countré. *each*
This maiden he loved als his lif, *as*
Of hire was ded the Quene his wif:
In travailing here lif she les. *childbirth; lost*
And tho the maiden of age wes *But when*
Kynges sones to him speke,
Emperours and Dukes eke,
To haven his doughter in mariage,
For love of here heritage;
Ac the Kyng answered ever *But*
That no man sschal here halden ever *shall ever have her*
But yif he mai in turneying *Unless; tournament*

Him out of his sadel bring,
And maken him lesen hise stiropes bayne. *lose; both*
Many assayed and myght not gayne. *tried; succeed*
That ryche Kynge every yere wolde *year*
A solempne feste make and holde
On hys wyvys mynnyng day, *wife's minding-day (memorial)*
That was beryed in an abbay *buried*
In a foreste there besyde.
With grete meyné he wolde ryde, *company of men*
Hire dirige do, and masse bothe, *requiem*
Poure men fede, and naked clothe,
Offring brenge, gret plenté,
And fede the covent with gret dayntè. *monastery*
Toward the abbai als he com ride, *abbey*
And mani knyghtes bi his side,
His doughter also bi him rod. *rode*
Amidde the forest hii abod. *they*
Here chaumberleyn she clepede hire to
And other dammaiseles two *maidens*
And seide that hii moste alighte *they must dismount*
To don here nedes and hire righte; *relieve themselves as they must do*
Thai alight adoun alle thre, *They dismounted*
Tweie damaiseles and ssche, *Two; she*
And longe while ther abiden,
Til al the folk was forht iriden. *had ridden forth*
Thai wolden up and after wolde,
And couthen nowt here way holde. *their*
The wode was rough and thikke, iwis, *wood; thick I imagine*
And thai token the wai amys. *took the wrong way*
Thai moste souht and riden west *should have gone south but rode*
Into the thikke of the forest.
Into a launde hii ben icome, *land they came*
And habbeth wel undernome *realized*
That thai were amis igon. *had gone amiss*
Thai light adoun everichon
And cleped and criede al ifere, *called; all together*
Ac no man aright hem ihere. *But; heard them at all*

Thai nist what hem was best to don; [1]
The weder was hot bifor the non; *weather; twelve o'clock*
Hii leien hem doun upon a grene, *They lay themselves*
Under a chastein tre, ich wene, *chestnut tree; think*
And fillen aslepe everichone *everyone*
Bote the damaisele alone. *Except*
She wente aboute and gaderede floures, *gathered flowers*
And herknede song of wilde foules. *listened to; birds*
So fer in the launde she goht, iwis, *far; goes; indeed*
That she ne wot nevere whare se is. *knows not where she is*
To hire maidenes she wolde anon. *her; would [return] quickly*
Ac hi ne wiste never wat wei to gon. *But she didn't know which way*
Whenne hi wende best to hem terne, *she thought; return to them*
Aweiward than hi goth wel yerne. *she; eagerly*
"Allas!" hi seide, "that I was boren!
Nou ich wot ich am forloren! *Now I know; lost*
Wilde bestes me willeth togrinde *beasts will eat me*
Or ani man me sschulle finde!" *Before any; shall find me*
Than segh hi swich a sight: *saw; such*
Toward hire comen a knight,
Gentil, yong, and jolif man; *handsome*
A robe of scarlet he hadde upon;
His visage was feir, his bodi ech weies; *face; in every way*
Of countenaunce right curteis; *courteous*
Wel farende legges, fot, and honde: *well-shaped*
Ther nas non in al the Kynges londe
More apert man than was he. *attractive*
"Damaisele, welcome mote thou be!
Be thou afered of none wihghte: *afraid of no man*
Iich am comen here a fairi knyghte;
Mi kynde is armes for to were, *nature*
On horse to ride with scheld and spere;
Forthi afered be thou nowt: *Therefore afraid*
I ne have nowt but mi swerd ibrout. *nothing; brought*
Iich have iloved the mani a yer, *I have loved you*
And now we beth us selve her, *are here by ourselves*

[1] *They didn't know what it would best be to do*

Thou best mi lemman ar thou go,	*You must become my lover before you go*
Wether the liketh wel or wo."	*Whether you like it or not*
Tho nothing ne coude do she	*Then nothing could she do*
But wep and criede and wolde fle;	
And he anon gan hire at holde,	*began to seize her*
And dide his wille, what he wolde.	*as he desired*
He binam hire here maidenhod,	*bereft*
And seththen up toforen hire stod.	*soon afterward*
"Lemman," he seide, "gent and fre,	
Mid schilde I wot that thou schalt be;	*With child I know*
Siker ich wot hit worht a knave;	*For sure I know it will be a boy*
Forthi mi swerd thou sschalt have,	
And whenne that he is of elde	*age*
That he mai himself biwelde,	*protect himself*
Tak him the swerd, and bidde him fonde	*Give; attempt*
To sechen his fader in eche londe.	*seek*
The swerd his god and avenaunt:	*is good; fitting*
Lo, as I faugt with a geaunt,	*giant*
I brak the point in his hed;	*broke; its head*
And siththen, when that he was ded,	*soon thereafter*
I tok hit out and have hit er,	*it [the point]; here*
Redi in min aumener.	*purse*
Yit paraventure time bith	*Yet sometime may come*
That mi sone mete me with:	
Be mi swerd I mai him kenne.	*By: know*
Have god dai! I mot gon henne."	*Have a good day; must go*
Thi knight passede as he cam.	*disappeared*
Al wepende the swerd she nam,	*weeping; she took*
And com hom sore sikend,	*came home sorely sighing*
And fond here maidenes al slepend.	*found her maidens all sleeping*
The swerd she hidde als she mighte,	
And awaked hem in highte,	*them in haste*
And doht hem to horse anon,	*ordered them*
And gonne to ride everichon.	
Thanne seghen hi ate last	*saw she at last*
Tweie squiers come prikend fast.	*Two; riding swiftly*
Fram the Kyng thai weren isent,	
To white whider his doughter went.	*To learn where*
Thai browt hire into the righte wai	

And comen faire to the abbay, *came gladly to the abbey*
And doth the servise in alle thingges, *did*
Mani masse and riche offringes;
And whanne the servise was al idone
And ipassed over the none, *nones was past*
The Kyng to his castel gan ride;
His doughter rod bi his side.
And he yemeth his kyngdom overal *rules*
Stoutliche, as a god king sschal. *Boldly; good*
Ac whan ech man was glad an blithe, *But; and joyful*
His doughter siked an sorewed swithe; *sickened and sorrowed greatly*
Here wombe greted more and more; *grew*
Therwhile she mighte, se hidde here sore. *she hid herself wretchedly*
On a dai, as hi wepende set, *she sat weeping*
On of hire maidenes hit underyet. *One; perceived*
"Madame," she seide, "par charité,
Whi wepe ye now, telleth hit me." *Why do you weep*
"A! gentil maiden, kinde icoren, *chosen one*
Help me, other ich am forloren! *otherwise; lost*
Ich have ever yete ben meke and milde:
Lo, now ich am with quike schilde! *living child (i.e., pregnant)*
Yif ani man hit underyete, *If any man should perceive it*
Men wolde sai bi sti and strete *sty; path*
That mi fader the King hit wan *begot*
And I ne was never aqueint with man! *intimate*
And yif he hit himselve wite, *learns of it*
Swich sorewe schal to him smite
That never blithe schal he be,
For al his joie is in me," *joy*
And tolde here al togeder ther *told*
Hou hit was bigete and wher. *How; begotten*
"Madame," quad the maide, "ne care thou nowt: *don't worry*
Stille awai hit sschal be browt. *Stealthily away*
No man schal wite in Godes riche *domain*
Whar hit bicometh, but thou and iche."
Her time come, she was unbounde,
And delivred al mid sounde; *with sound health*
A knaveschild ther was ibore:
Glad was the moder tharfore.

The maiden servede here at wille,
Wond that child in clothes stille, *Wrapped*
And laid hit in a cradel anon, *immediately*
And was al prest tharwith to gon. *ready*
Yhit is moder was him hold: *Yet his mother; faithful*
Four pound she tok of gold,
And ten of selver also;
Under his fote she laid hit tho, — *then*
For swich thing hit mighte hove; *be of aid*
And seththen she tok a paire glove *then*
That here lemman here sente of fairi londe, *her lover; from*
That nolde on no manne honde, *would not fit any human*
Ne on child ne on womman yhe nolde, *Neither; they would not [fit]*
But on hire selve wel yhe wolde. *she knew*
Tho gloven she put under his hade, *those gloves; head*
And siththen a letter she wrot and made,
And knit hit with a selkene thred *tied; silken*
Aboute his nekke wel god sped *quickly*
That who hit founde sscholde iwite. *know*
Than was in the lettre thous iwrite: *written*
"Par charité, yif ani god man *should any good*
This helples child finde can,
Lat cristen hit with prestes honde, *Let it be christened by a priest's hands*
And bringgen hit to live in londe, *rear it*
For hit is comen of gentil blod. *i.e., noble*
Helpeth hit with his owen god, *its own goods*
With tresor that under his fet lis; *treasure; lies*
And ten yer eld whan that he his, *when he is*
Taketh him this ilke gloven two, *Give him these*
And biddeth him, wharevere he go,
That he ne lovie no womman in londe *not love any*
But this gloves willen on hire honde; *Unless; [fit] her hands*
For siker on honde nelle thai nere *they will not ever fit*
But on his moder that him bere." *Except*
The maiden tok the child here mide, *with her*
Stille awai in aven tide, *evening*
Alle the winteres longe night.
The weder was cler, the mone light;
Than warhth she war anon *she became aware soon, (i.e., remembered)*

Of an hermitage in a ston:
An holi man had ther his woniyng. — *dwelling*
Thider she wente on heying, — *in haste*
An sette the cradel at his dore,
And durste abide no lengore, — *dared*
And passede forth anon right.
Hom she com in that other night, — *second*
And fond the levedi al drupni, — *downcast*
Sore wepinde, and was sori,
And tolde hire al togeder ther
Hou she had iben and wher.
The hermite aros erliche tho, — *early*
And his knave was uppe also,
An seide ifere here matines, — *together their matins*
And servede God and Hise seins. — *saints*
The litel child thai herde crie,
And clepede after help on hie; — *called; in haste*
The holi man his dore undede, — *door unlocked*
And fond the cradel in the stede; — *step*
He tok up the clothes anon
And biheld the litel grom; — *boy*
He tok the letter and radde wel sone — *read*
That tolde him that he scholde done. — *what he should do*
The heremite held up bothe his honde
An thonked God of al His sonde, — *blessings*
And bar that child in to his chapel, — *brought*
And for joie he rong his bel.
He dede up the gloven and the tresour — *put away; gloves*
And cristned the child with gret honour:
In the name of the Trinité,
He hit nemnede Degarre, — *named*
Degarre nowt elles ne is
But thing that not never what hit is, — *knows not ever*
Other thing that is neggh forlorn also; — *Or something; nearly lost*
Forthi the schild he nemnede thous tho. — *child; named*
The heremite that was holi of lif
Hadde a soster that was a wif; — *sister*
A riche marchaunt of that countré — *merchant*
Hadde hire ispoused into that cité. — *married her*

To hire that schild he sente tho *child*
Bi his knave, and the silver also,
And bad here take gode hede *bade her; heed*
Hit to foster and to fede,
And yif God Almighti wolde
Ten yer his lif holde, *Grant him ten years of life*
Ayen to him hi scholde hit wise: *Again; bring about*
He hit wolde tech of clergise. *doctrine*
The litel child Degarre
Was ibrout into that cité.
The wif and hire loverd ifere *her husband together*
Kept his ase hit here owen were. *as if it were their own*
Bi that hit was ten yer old, *By the time*
Hit was a fair child and a bold,
Wel inorissched, god and hende; *nourished; courteous*
Was non betere in al that ende. *region*
He wende wel that the gode man *thought; good*
Had ben his fader that him wan, *begot*
And the wif his moder also,
And the hermite his unkel bo; *uncle too*
And whan the ten yer was ispent,
To the hermitage he was sent,
And he was glad him to se,
He was so feir and so fre. *fair; noble*
He taughte him of clerkes lore
Other ten wynter other more; *Another ten winters or more*
And when he was of twenti yer,
Staleworth he was, of swich pouer *such power*
That ther ne wan man in that lond *no one*
That o breid him might astond. *Who could withstand one blow from him*
Tho the hermite seth, withouten les, *lying*
Man for himself that he wes, *That he was capable of being his own master*
Staleworht to don ech werk, *do each task*
And of his elde so god a clerk, *for his age*
He tok him his florines and his gloves *gave him*
That he had kept to hise bihoves. *fulfill his needs*
Ac the ten pound of starlings *But; sterling*
Were ispended in his fostrings. *spent in his fostering*
He tok him the letter to rede, *gave*

And biheld al the dede.
“O leve hem, par charité, *dear uncle*
Was this letter mad for me?” *made*
“Ye, bi oure Lord, us helpe sschal! *Who shall help us*
Thus hit was,” and told him al.
He knelede adoun al so swithe, *quickly*
And thonked the ermite of his live, *hermit for*
And swor he nolde stinte no stounde *would wait not a moment*
Til he his kinrede hadde ifounde. *kindred had found*
For in the lettre was thous iwrite, *written*
That bi the gloven he sscholde iwite *know*
Wich were his moder and who, *Who his mother was*
Yhif that sche livede tho, *If she still lived*
For on hire honden hii wolde, *would [fit]*
And on non other hii nolde. *would not*
Half the florines he gaf the hermite, *gave*
And halvendel he tok him mide, *half; with him*
And nam his leve an wolde go. *took*
“Nai,” seide the hermite, “schaltu no!
To seche thi ken mightou nowt dure *seek; kin; endure*
Withouten hors and god armure.” *Without a horse; good armor*
“Nai,” quad he, “bi Hevene Kyng, *by God*
Ich wil have first another thing!”
He hew adoun, bothe gret and grim, *cut down; massive; ugly*
To beren in his hond with him,
A god sapling of an ok; *stout; oak*
Whan he tharwith gaf a strok,
Ne wer he never so strong a man *Never was there*
Ne so gode armes hadde upon, *weaponry bore*
That he ne scholde falle to grounde;
Swich a bourdon to him he founde. *pilgrim's staff*
Tho thenne God he him bitawt, *commended to*
And aither fram other wepyng rawt. *weepingly departed*
   Child Degarre wente his wai
Thourgh the forest al that dai. *day*
No man he ne herd, ne non he segh, *saw*
Til hit was non ipassed hegh; *well past nones*
Thanne he herde a noise kete *heard; loud*
In o valai, an dintes grete. *a valley, one great blow*

Blive thider he gan to te: *Eagerly; hasten*
What hit ware he wolde ise. *observe*
An Herl of the countré, stout and fers, *Earl; strong; fierce*
With a knight and four squiers,
Hadde ihonted a der other two, *hunted a deer or two*
And al here houndes weren ago. *their; lost*
Than was thar a dragon grim, *fierce*
Ful of filth and of venim,
With wide throte and teth grete,
And wynges bitere with to bete. *bitterly*
As a lyoun he hadde fet, *i.e., feet like a lion*
And his tail was long and gret. *massive*
The smoke com of his nose awai
Ase fer out of a chimenai. *As fire out of a chimney*
The knyght and squiers he had torent, *mortally wounded*
Man and hors to dethe chent. *sent*
The dragon the Erl assaile gan,
And he defended him as a man, *himself*
And stoutliche leid on with his swerd,
And stronge strokes on him gerd; *struck*
Ac alle his dentes ne greved him nowt: *these blows*
His hide was hard so iren wrout. *as wrought iron*
Therl flei fram tre to tre — *The Earl fled*
Fein he wolde fram him be —
And the dragon him gan asail;
The doughti Erl in that batail
Ofsegh this child Degarre; *Saw*
"Ha! help!" he seide, "par charité!"
The dragoun seth the child com; *saw*
He laft the Erl and to him nom *left; went*
Blowinde and yeniend also *yawning*
Als he him wolde swolewe tho.
Ac Degarre was ful strong;
He tok his bat, gret and long, *cudgel*
And in the forehefd he him batereth *forehead; battered*
That al the forehefd he tospatereth. *shattered*
He fil adoun anon right, *soon fell down*
And frapte his tail with gret might *struck*
Upon Degarres side,

That up-so-doun he gan to glide; *upside down*
Ac he stert up ase a man *he [Degaré] lept*
And with his bat leide upan, *cudgel*
And al tofrusst him ech a bon, *smashed; each bone*
That he lai ded, stille as a ston.
Therl knelede adoun bilive *The Earl; humbly*
And thonked the child of his live, *for his life*
And maked him with him gon *made him go with him*
To his castel right anon,
And wel at hese he him made, *ease*
And proferd him al that he hade, *gave*
Rentes, tresor, an eke lond, *also land*
For to holden in his hond.
Thanne answerede Degarre,
"Lat come ferst bifor me
Thi levedi and other wimmen bold, *noble*
Maidenes and widues, yonge and olde,
And other damoiseles swete.
Yif mine gloven beth to hem mete *suitable*
For to done upon here honde, *put; their*
Thanne ich wil take thi londe;
And yif thai ben nowt so,
Iich wille take me leve and go." *say goodbye and leave*
Alle wimman were forht ibrowt *brought forth*
In wide cuntries and forth isowt: *sought*
Ech the gloven assaie bigan, *gloves to try on*
Ac non ne mighte don hem on. *But; put them on*
He tok his gloven and up hem dede, *picked them up*
And nam his leve in that stede. *took; from that place*
The Erl was gentil man of blod,
And gaf him a stede ful god *horse*
And noble armure, riche and fin,
When he wolde armen him therin,
And a palefrai to riden an, *palfrey*
And a knave to ben his man,
And yaf him a swerd bright,
And dubbed him ther to knyght,
And swor bi God Almighti
That he was better worthi

To usen hors and armes also
Than with his bat aboute to go.
  Sire Degarre was wel blithe,
And thanked the Erl mani a sithe, *time*
And lep upon hiis palefrai,
And doht him forth in his wai; *went forth*
Upon his stede righte his man, *suitably [rides]; squire*
And ledde his armes als he wel can;
Mani a jorné thai ride and sette. *journey; set upon*
So on a dai gret folk thei mette,
Erles and barouns of renoun,
That come fram a cité toun. *fortress*
He asked a seriaunt what tiding, *man-at-arms*
And whennes hii come and what is this thing? *from whence*
"Sire," he seide, "verraiment,
We come framward a parlement.
The King a gret counseil made
For nedes that he to don hade. *convened*
Whan the parlement was plener, *in full session*
He lette crie fer and ner,
Yif ani man were of armes so bold
That with the King justi wold, *would joust*
He sscholde have in mariage
His dowter and his heritage,
That is kingdom god and fair,
For he had non other hair. *heir*
Ac no man ne dar graunte therto, *consent*
For mani hit assaieth and mai nowt do: *attempted*
Mani erl and mani baroun,
Knightes and squiers of renoun;
Ac ech man, that him justeth with, tit *instantly*
Hath of him a foul despit: *humiliation*
Some he breketh the nekke anon,
And of some the rig-bon; *backbone*
Some thourgh the bodi he girt, *thrusts*
Ech is maimed other ihirt;
Ac no man mai don him no thing *cause him any harm*
Swich wonder chaunce hath the King. *good fortune*
Sire Degarre thous thenche gan: *began to reflect*

"Ich am a staleworht man,
And of min owen ich have a stede,
Swerd and spere and riche wede; *armor*
And yif ich felle the Kyng adoun,
Evere ich have wonnen renoun;
And thei that he me herte sore, *hurt sorely*
No man wot wer ich was bore. *knows where; born*
Whether deth other lif me bitide, *befall*
Agen the King ich wille ride!" *Against*
In the cité his in he taketh, *lodging*
And resteth him and meri maketh.
On a dai with the King he mette,
And knelede adoun and him grette: *greeted*
"Sire King," he saide, "of muchel might,
Mi loverd me sende hider anon right *lord; now*
For to warne you that he
Bi thi leve wolde juste with the, *permission*
And winne thi dowter, yif he mai;
As the cri was this ender dai, *other*
Justes he had to the inome." *He would undertake to joust with you*
"De par Deus!" quath the King, "he is welcome. *By God*
Be he baroun, be he erl,
Be he burgeis, be he cherl, *burgess; churl*
No man wil I forsake.
He that winneth al sschal take."
  Amorewe the justes was iset;
The King him purveid wel the bet, *himself purveyed*
And Degarre ne knew no man,
Ac al his trust is God upon.
Erliche to churche than wente he;
The masse he herde of the Trinité.
To the Fader he offreth hon florine, *one florin*
And to the Sone another al so fine,
And to the Holi Gost the thridde;
The prest for him ful yerne gan bidde. *eagerly did pray*
And tho the servise was idon, *when; done*
To his in he wente wel son *To his inn*
And let him armi wel afin, *presently*
In god armes to justi in. *joust*

His gode stede he gan bistride;
His squier bar his sschaft biside; *carried his lance*
In the feld the King he abide gan,
As he com ridend with mani a man,
Stoutliche out of the cité toun,
With mani a lord of gret renoun;
Ac al that in the felde beth
That the justes iseth *saw*
Seide that hi never yit iseghe *they; saw*
So pert a man with here egye *distinguished; their eyes*
As was this gentil Degarre,
Ac no man wiste whennes was he. *knew where he came from*
Bothe thai gonne to justi than,
Ac Degarre can nowt theron. *knew nothing*
The King hath the gretter schaft *lance*
And kan inowgh of the craft. *knew enough*
To breke his nekke he had iment: *intended*
In the helm he set his dent, *helmet; landed; blow*
That the schaft al tosprong; *splintered*
Ac Degarre was so strong
That in the sadel stille he set,
And in the stiropes held his fet;
For sothe I seie, withoute lesing,
He ne couthe nammore of justing.
"Allas!" quath the King, "allas! *knew*
Me ne fil nevere swich a cas, *experienced; situation*
That man that ich mighte hitte
After mi strok mighte sitte!"
He taketh a wel gretter tre *lance*
And swor so he moste ithe, *prosper*
"Yif his nekke nel nowt atwo, *will not*
His rigg schal, ar ich hennes go!" *backbone; before*
He rod eft with gret raundoun *once more; violence*
And thought to beren him adoun,
And girt Degarre anon *struck*
Right agein the brest-bon *against*
The schaft was stef and wonder god, *strong*
And Degarre stede astod, *reared*
And al biforen he ros on heghth, *as before*

And tho was he ifallen neghth; — *nearly*
But as God Almighti wold,
The schaft brak and might nowt hold,
And Degarre his cours out ritte, — *altered*
And was agramed out of his witte. — *enraged*
"Allas!" quath he, "for vilaynie!
The King me hath ismiten twie, — *twice*
And I ne touchede him nowt yete. — *yet*
Nou I schal avise me bette!" — *advise myself better*
He turned his stede with herte grim, — *fierce*
And rod to the King, and he to him,
And togider thai gert ful right, — *thrust*
And in the scheldes here strokes pight — *were placed*
That the speres al toriveth — *broke to pieces*
And up right to here honde sliveth, — *split*
That alle the lordings that ther ben
That the justing mighte sen
Seiden hi ne seghe never with egye — *Said they never saw; eyes*
Man that mighte so longe dreghye, — *continue*
In wraththe for nothing, — *Even in serious combat*
Sitten a strok of here King; — *Endure; from their*
"Ac he his doughti for the nones, — *But he is valiant certainly*
A strong man of bodi and bones."
The King with egre mod gan speke: — *eager mood (anger)*
"Do bring me a schaft that wil nowt breke!
A, be mi trewthe, he sschal adoun! — *Ah! By my*
Thai he be strengere than Sampson; — *Even though*
And thei he be the bare qued, — *though; devil himself*
He sschal adoun, maugré his heved!" — *despite all his strength*
He tok a schaft was gret and long,
The schild another al so strong; — *child (Degaré); equally*
And to the King wel evene he rit; — *met him in mid-course*
The King faileth, and he him smit; — *faltered; smote*
His schaft was strong and god withal,
And wel scharped the coronal. — *sharpened; spear head*
He smot the Kyng in the lainer: — *shield strap*
He might flit nother fer ne ner. — *escape*
The King was strong and harde sat; — *firmly*
The stede ros up biforn with that, — *reared*

And Sire Degarre so thriste him than *thrust*
That, maugré whoso grochche bigan, *grudge*
Out of the sadel he him cast,
Tail over top, right ate last.
Than was ther long houting and cri; *shouting*
The King was sor asschamed forthi;
The lordinges comen with might and mein
And broughte the King on horse agein,
An seide with o criing, iwis, *one shout indeed*
"Child Degarre hath wonne the pris!" *prize*
Than was the damaisele sori,
For hi wist wel forwhi: *she knew*
That hi scholde ispoused ben
To a knight that sche never had sen,
And lede here lif with swich a man
That sche ne wot who him wan, *begot*
No in what londe he was ibore; *Nor; born*
Carful was the levedi therefore. *Sorrowful; lady*

Than seide the King to Degarre,
"Min hende sone, com hider to me: *noble*
And thou were al so gentil a man *If*
As thou semest with sight upan,
And ase wel couthest wisdomes do *i.e., good deeds*
As thou art staleworht man therto, *Since*
Me thouwte mi kingdoms wel biset: *would be well served*
Ac be thou werse, be thou bet,
Covenaunt ich wille the holde.
Lo, her biforn mi barons bolde, *here*
Mi douwter I take the bi the hond, *give you*
And seise the her in al mi lond. *endow her to you with*
King thou scalt ben after me:
God graunte the god man for to be!" *you be a good man*
Than was the child glad and blithe,
And thonked the Kyng mani a sithe. *time*
Gret perveaunce than was ther iwrout: *preparations; wrought*
To churche thai were togidere ibrout,
And spoused that levedi verraiment, *married; lady truly*
Under Holi Sacrement.
Lo, what chaunse and wonder strong *chance; great marvel*

Bitideth mani a man with wrong, — *misfortune*
That cometh into an uncouthe thede — *ignorant people*
And spouseth wif for ani mede — *whatever reward*
And knowes nothing of hire kin,
Ne sche of his, neither more ne min, — *less*
And beth iwedded togider to libbe — *live*
Par aventoure, and beth neghth sibbe! — *close kinsmen*
So dede Sire Degarre the bold
Spoused ther is moder — *Marry there his mother*
And that hende levedi also — *noble lady*
Here owene sone was spoused to,
That sche upon here bodi bar. — *bore*
Lo, what aventoure fil hem thar! — *befell*
But God, that alle thingge mai stere, — *guide*
Wolde nowt that thai sinned ifere: — *together*
To chirche thai wente with barouns bolde;
A riche feste thai gonne to holde;
And wan was wel ipassed non — *when; i.e., late afternoon*
And the dai was al idon,
To bedde thai sscholde wende, that fre,
The dammaisele and Sire Degarre.
He stod stille and bithouwte him than — *remembered*
Hou the hermite, the holi man,
Bad he scholde no womman take
For faired ne for riches sake — *fairness*
But she mighte this gloves two
Lightliche on hire hondes do.
"Allas, allas!" than saide he,
"What meschaunce is comen to me?
A wai! witles wrechche ich am! — *Ah woe!*
Iich hadde levere than this kingdam — *rather*
That is iseised into min hond — *given*
That ich ware faire out of this lond!" — *departed*
He wrang his hondes and was sori,
Ac no man wiste therefore wi. — *no man knew why*
The King parceyved and saide tho, — *perceived*
"Sire Degarre, wi farest thou so? — *why do you behave*
Is ther ani thing don ille,
Spoken or seid agen thi wille?"

"Ya, sire," he saide, "bi Hevene King!"
"I chal never, for no spousing,   *shall*
Therwhiles I live, with wimman dele,
Widue ne wif ne dammeisele,   *widow*
But she this gloves mai take and fonde   *try on*
And lightlich drawen upon hire honde."
His yonge bride that gan here,
And al for thout chaunged hire chere   *remembrance; countenance*
And ate laste gan to turne here mod: *mood*
Here visage wex ase red ase blod: *blood*
She knew tho gloves that were hire.   *hers*
"Schewe hem hider, leve sire."   *dear*
Sche tok the gloves in that stede   *place*
And lightliche on hire hondes dede,
And fil adoun, with revli crie,   *revellous*
And seide, "God, mercy, mercie!
Thou art mi sone hast spoused me her,
And ich am, sone, thi moder der.
Ich hadde the loren, ich have the founde;   *lost you; found you*
Blessed be Jhesu Crist that stounde!"   *moment*
  Sire Degarre tok his moder tho   *then*
And helde here in his armes two.
Keste and clepte here mani a sithe;   *Kissed; embraced; time*
That hit was sche, he was ful blithe.   *blissful*
Than the Kyng gret wonder hadde
Why that noise that thai made,
And mervailed of hire crying,
And seide, "Doughter, what is this thing?"
"Fader," she seide, "thou schalt ihere: *hear*
Thou wenest that ich a maiden were,   *thought*
Ac certes, nay, sire, ich am non: *not*
Twenti winter nou hit is gon
That mi maidenhed I les
In a forest as I wes,
And this is mi sone, God hit wot: *God knows*
Bi this gloves wel ich wot."   *By these gloves: I know*
She told him al that sothe ther,   *truth*
Hou the child was geten and wher;   *begotten*
And hou that he was boren also,

To the hermitage yhe sente him tho,
And seththen herd of him nothing; *since then*
"But thanked be Jhesu, Hevene King,
Iich have ifounde him alive!
Ich am his moder and ek his wive!" *also*
"Leve moder," seide Sire Degarre, *Dear*
"Telle me the sothe, par charité: *truth; please*
Into what londe I mai terne
To seke mi fader, swithe and yerne?" *quickly; eagerly*
"Sone," she saide, "bi Hevene Kyng,
I can the of him telle nothing
But tho that he fram me raught, *when; departed*
His owen swerd he me bitaught, *bestowed on me*
And bad ich sholde take hit the forthan *give it to you then*
Yif thou livedest and were a man."
The swerd sche fet forht anon right, *fetched right away*
And Degarre hit out plight. *plucked*
Brod and long and hevi hit wes:
In that kyngdom no swich nes. *such [sword was] known*
Than seide Degarre forthan, *consequently*
"Whoso hit aught, he was a man! *Whoever owned it*
Nou ich have that ikepe, *kept [in my possession]*
Night ne dai nel ich slepe *I will not*
Til that I mi fader see,
Yif God wile that hit so be."
In the cité he reste al night.
Amorewe, whan hit was dai-lit, *daylight*
He aros and herde his masse;
He dighte him and forth gan passe. *prepared himself*
Of al that cité than moste non
Neither with him riden ne gon
But his knave, to take hede *squire*
To his armour and his stede.
Forth he rod in his wai
Mani a pas and mani jurnai; *step; a journey*
So longe he passede into west *Before long*
That he com into theld forest *the ancient*
Ther he was bigeten som while. *Where he was begotten*
Therinne he rideth mani a mile;

Mani a dai he ride gan;
No quik best he fond of man, *living [domestic] beast*
Ac mani wilde bestes he seghth *saw*
And foules singen on heghth. *birds singing; high*
So longe hit drouwth to the night, *continues until*
The sonne was adoune right.
Toward toun he wolde ride,
But he nist never bi wiche side. *never knew by which direction*
  Thenne he segh a water cler,
And amidde a river,
A fair castel of lim and ston: *mortar*
Other wonying was ther non. *dwelling*
To his knave he seide, "Tide wat tide, *Happen what will happen*
O fote forther nel I ride, *One step; will not*
Ac here abide wille we, *But*
And aske herberewe par charité, *shelter*
Yif ani quik man be here on live." *living*
To the water thai come als swithe;
The bregge was adoune tho, *bridge*
And the gate open also,
And into the castel he gan spede. *hasten*
First he stabled up his stede;
He taiede up his palefrai. *tied*
Inough he fond of hote and hai; *oats; hay*
He bad his grom on heying *knave in safe keeping*
Kepen wel al here thing. *their*
He passed up into the halle,
Biheld aboute, and gan to calle;
Ac neither on lond ne on hegh *on ground floor or above*
No quik man he ne segh. *living person; saw*
Amidde the halle flore
A fir was bet, stark an store, *fire; kindled, strong and vigorous*
"Par fai," he saide, "ich am al sure
He that bette that fure *kindled; fire*
Wil comen hom yit tonight;
Abiden ich wille a litel wight." *while*
He sat adoun upon the dais, *at the high table*
And warmed him wel eche wais, *every way*
And he biheld and undernam *perceived*

Hou in at the dore cam
Four dammaiseles, gent and fre;
Ech was itakked to the kne. — *bare-legged (tacked up)*
The two bowen an arewen bere, — *carried bows and arrows*
The other two icharged were — *laden*
With venesoun, riche and god.
And Sire Degarre upstod — *stood up*
And gret hem wel fair aplight, — *greeted them politely*
Ac thai answerede no wight, — *not at all*
But yede into chaumbre anon — *proceeded*
And barred the dore after son. — *soon afterwards*
Sone therafter withalle
Ther com a dwerw into the halle. — *dwarf*
Four fet of lengthe was in him;
His visage was stout and grim;
Bothe his berd and his fax — *hair*
Was crisp an yhalew as wax; — *and yellow*
Grete sscholdres and quarré; — *shoulders; square*
Right stoutliche loked he;
Mochele were hise fet and honde — *Large*
Ase the meste man of the londe; — *biggest men*
He was iclothed wel aright, — *well-clothed*
His sschon icouped as a knight; — *shoes slashed*
He hadde on a sorcot overt, — *an open surcoat*
Iforred with blaundeuer apert. — *Trimmed with white fur*
Sire Degarre him biheld and lowggh, — *laughed*
And gret him fair inowggh, — *hailed*
Ac he ne answerede nevere a word,
But sette trestles and laid the bord, — *set; table*
And torches in the halle he lighte,
And redi to the soper dighte. — *prepared*
Than ther com out of the bour — *bedchamber*
A dammeisele of gret honour;
In the lond non fairer nas;
In a diapre clothed she was — *fabric with patterned figures*
With hire come maidenes tene, — *ten*
Some in scarlet, some in grene,
Gent of bodi, of semblaunt swete,
And Degarre hem gan grete;

Ac hi ne answerede no wight, *no one*
But yede to the soper anon right. *went*
"Certes," quath Sire Degarre,
"Ich have hem gret, and hi nowt me; *they*
But thai be domb, bi and bi *Unless; mute*
Thai schul speke first ar I."
The levedi that was of rode so bright, *complexion*
Amidde she sat anon right,
And on aither half maidenes five.
The dwerw hem servede al so blive *dwarf; swiftly*
With riche metes and wel idight; *adorned*
The coppe he filleth with alle his might. *cup*
Sire Degarre couthe of curteisie:
He set a chaier bifore the levedie, *chair; lady*
And therin himselve set,
And tok a knif and carf his met;
At the soper litel at he, *ate*
But biheld the levedi fre,
And segh ase feir a wimman *saw; woman*
Als he hevere loked an, *ever looked upon*
That al his herte and his thout *thought*
Hire to love was ibrowt.
And tho thai hadde souped anowgh, *when*
The drew com, and the cloth he drough; *dwarf; withdrew*
The levedis wessche everichon *washed everyone*
And yede to chaumbre quik anon. *went; right away*
Into the chaumbre he com ful sone.
The levedi on here bed set,
And a maide at here fet,
And harpede notes gode and fine;
Another broughte spices and wine.
Upon the bedde he set adoun
To here of the harpe soun.
For murthe of notes so sschille, *pleasure; agreeable*
He fel adoun on slepe stille;
So he slep al that night.
The levedi wreith him warm aplight, *wrapped; warmly I assure you*
And a pilewe under his heved dede, *head placed*
And yede to bedde in that stede. *went; in that place*

Amorewe whan hit was dai-light,
Sche was uppe and redi dight.
Faire sche waked him tho:
"Aris!" she seide, "graith the, an go!" *dress yourself and depart*
And saide thus in here game:
"Thou art worth to suffri schame, *suffer*
That al night as a best sleptest, *beast*
And non of mine maidenes ne keptest." *guarded*
"O gentil levedi," seide Degarre,
"For Godes love, forgif hit me!
Certes the murie harpe hit made, *caused [the sleep]*
Elles misdo nowt I ne hade;
Ac tel me, levedi so hende, *gentle*
Ar ich out of thi chaumber wende, *Before; depart*
Who is louerd of this lond? *lord*
And who this castel hath in hond?
Wether thou be widue or wif, *Whether; widow*
Or maiden yit of clene lif? *virgin*
And whi her be so fele wimman *there; many women*
Allone, withouten ani man?"
The dameisele sore sighte, *sorely sighed*
And bigan to wepen anon righte,
"Sire, wel fain ich telle the wolde, *gladly*
Yif evere the better be me sscholde. *If it should do me any good*
Mi fader was a riche baroun,
And hadde mani a tour and toun. *tower*
He ne hadde no child but me;
Ich was his air of his cuntré. *heir*
In mené ich hadde mani a knight *For company (suitors)*
And squiers that were gode and light, *active*
An staleworht men of mester, *skill*
To serve in court fer and ner;
Ac thanne is thar here biside *But*
A sterne knight, iknawe ful wide. *powerful; known*
Ich wene in Bretaine ther be non *I know; none*
So strong a man so he is on. *as; one*
He had ilove me ful yore; *for a long time*
Ac in herte nevere more
Ne mighte ich lovie him agein; *in return*

But whenne he seghye ther was no gein, *saw; gain*
He was aboute with maistri *force*
For to ravisse me awai. *ravish, i.e., abduct*
Mine knightes wolde defende me,
And ofte fowghten hi an he; *they and*
The beste he slowgh the firste dai,
And sethen an other, par ma fai, *a second*
And sethen the thridde and the ferthe, —
The beste that mighte gon on erthe!
Mine squiers that weren so stoute,
Bi foure, bi five, thai riden oute,
On hors armed wel anowgh:
His houen bodi he hem slough. *[By] his own hand*
Mine men of mester he slough alle, *skill; slew*
And other pages of mine halle.
Therfore ich am sore agast
Lest he wynne me ate last."
With this word sche fil to grounde,
And lai aswone a wel gret stounde. *in a faint; while*
Hire maidenes to hire come
And in hire armes up hire nome. *took*
He beheld the levedi with gret pité.
"Loveli madame," quath he,
"On of thine ich am here: *One*
Ich wille the help, be mi pouere." *power*
"Yhe, sire," she saide, "than al mi lond *Yes*
Ich wil the give into thin hond,
And at thi wille bodi mine, *desire*
Yif thou might wreke me of hine." *rid; him*
Tho was he glad al for to fighte, *Then*
And wel gladere that he mighte
Have the levedi so bright
Yif he slough that other knight. *If*
  And als thai stod and spak ifere, *spoke together*
A maiden cried, with reuful chere,
"Her cometh oure enemi, faste us ate! *quickly toward us*
Drauwe the bregge and sschet the gate, *bridge; shut*
Or he wil slen ous everichone!" *slay every one of us*
Sire Degarre stirt up anon

And at a window him segh,
Wel i-armed on hors hegh;
A fairer bodi than he was on
In armes ne segh he never non.
Sire Degarre armed him blive *himself quickly*
And on a stede gan out drive.
With a spere gret of gayn, *worth*
To the knight he rit agein. *rode*
The knighte spere al tosprong, *broke into pieces*
Ac Degarre was so strong
And so harde to him thrast, *thrust*
But the knight sat so fast,
That the stede rigge tobrek *horse's backbone broke in two*
And fel to grounde, and he ek;
But anon stirt up the knight
And drough out his swerd bright. *drew*
"Alight," he saide, "adoun anon;
To fight thou sschalt afote gon. *on foot, i.e., hand-to-hand*
For thou hast slawe mi stede, *slain*
Deth-dint schal be thi mede; *Death blow; reward*
Ac thine stede sle I nille, *horse; will not*
Ac on fote fighte ich wille."
Than on fote thai toke the fight,
And hewe togidere with brondes bright. *clashed; swords*
The knight gaf Sire Degarre
Sterne strokes gret plenté, *Fierce*
And he him agen also, *in return*
That helm and scheld cleve atwo. *cut in two*
The knight was agreved sore
That his armour toburste thore: *broke to pieces there*
A strok he gaf Sire Degarre,
That to grounde fallen is he;
But he stirt up anon right,
And swich a strok he gaf the knight
Upon his heved so harde iset *head so vigorously brought down*
Thurh helm and heved and bacinet
That ate brest stod the dent; *at the breast the blow stopped*
Ded he fil doun, verraiment. *truly*
The levedi lai in o kernel, *battlement*

And biheld the batail everi del.
She ne was never er so blithe:
Sche thankede God fele sithe. *many times*
Sire Degarre com into castel;
Agein him com the dammaisel, *To him*
And thonked him swithe of that dede. *swiftly for*
Into chaumber sche gan him lede,
And unarmed him anon,
And set him hire bed upon,
And saide, "Sire, par charité,
I the prai dwel with me,
And al mi lond ich wil the give,
And miselve, whil that I live." *myself*
"Grant merci, dame," saide Degarre,
"Of the gode thou bedest me: *For; offer*
Wende ich wille into other londe,
More of haventours for to fonde; *adventures; attempt*
And be this twelve moneth be go, *after twelve months*
Agein ich wil come the to."
The levedi made moche mourning
For the knightes departing,
And gaf him a stede, god and sur, *steady*
Gold and silver an god armur,
And bitaught him Jhesu, Hevene King. *commended him to*
And sore thei wepen at here parting.
  Forht wente Sire Degarre *Forth*
Thurh mani a divers cuntré; *Through; diverse*
Ever mor he rod west.
So in a dale of o forest
He mette with a doughti knight *doughty, i.e., strong*
Upon a stede, god and light, *active*
In armes that were riche and sur,
With the sscheld of asur *azure*
And thre bor-hevedes therin *boars' heads*
Wel ipainted with gold fin. *costly*
Sire Degarre anon right
Hendeliche grette the knight, *Graciously greeted*
And saide, "Sire, God with the be;"
And thous agein answered he:

“Velaun, wat dost thou here, *Villain*
In mi forest to chase mi dere?”
Degarre answerede with wordes meke:
“Sire, thine der nougt I ne seke: *I seek none of your deer*
Iich am an aunterous knight, *dutiful*
For to seche werre and fight.” *seek war*
The knight saide, withouten fail,
“Yif thou comest to seke batail,
Here thou hast thi per ifounde: *you've found your match*
Arme the swithe in this stounde!” *Arm yourself swiftly; place*
Sire Degarre and his squier
Armed him in riche atir, *attire*
With an helm riche for the nones, *splendid helmet*
Was ful of precious stones
That the maide him gaf, saun fail, *without*
For whom he did rather batail. *earlier*
A sscheld he kest aboute his swere *cast around; neck*
That was of armes riche and dere, *heraldic ornament; precious*
With thre maidenes hevedes of silver bright, *heads*
With crounes of gold precious of sight.
A sschaft he tok that was nowt smal, *lance*
With a kene coronal. *sharp head*
His squier tok another spere;
Bi his louerd he gan hit bere. *lord*
Lo, swich aventoure ther gan bitide —
The sone agein the fader gan ride,
And noither ne knew other no wight![2]
Nou biginneth the firste fight.
  Sire Degarre tok his cours thare;
Agen his fader a sschaft he bare; *Against*
To bere him doun he hadde imint. *intended*
Right in the sscheld he set his dint; *blow*
The sschaft brak to peces al, *pieces*
And in the sscheld lat the coronal. *left; point*
Another cours thai gonne take;
The fader tok, for the sones sake,

---

[2] *But neither knew who the other person was*

A sschaft that was gret and long,
And he another also strong. — *even as*
Togider thai riden with gret raundoun, — *force*
And aither bar other adoun. — *neither bore*
With dintes that thai smiten there,
Here stede rigges toborsten were. — *horses' backs*
Afote thai gonne fight ifere — *together*
And laiden on with swerdes clere. — *bright*
The fader amerveiled wes — *was astonished*
Whi his swerd was pointles, — *When he realized that*
And seide to his sone aplight, — *emphatically*
"Herkne to me a litel wight: — *Listen; for a moment*
Wher were thou boren, in what lond?"
"In Litel Bretaigne, ich understond: — *Brittany*
Kingges doughter sone, witouten les, — *Son of a king's daughter; lie*
Ac I not wo mi fader wes." — *But I don't know who*
"What is thi name?" than saide he.
"Certes, men clepeth me Degarre." — *Deservedly; call*
"O Degarre, sone mine!
Certes ich am fader thine! — *Truly*
And bi thi swerd I knowe hit here:
The point is in min aumenere." — *pouch*
He tok the point and set therto;
Degarre fel iswone tho, — *into a swoon*
And his fader, sikerli, — *surely*
Also he gan swony; — *began to swoon*
And whan he of swone arisen were, — *arose from his swoon*
The sone cride merci there — *begged forgiveness*
His owen fader of his misdede, — *for*
And he him to his castel gan lede,
And bad him dwelle with him ai. — *forever*
"Certes, sire," he saide, "nai;
Ac yif hit youre wille were, — *if you are willing*
To mi moder we wende ifere,
For she is in gret mourning."
"Blethelich," quath he, "bi Hevene Kyng." — *Gladly*
Syr Degaré and hys father dere,
Into Ynglond they went in fere. — *together*
They were armyd and well dyghtt. — *decorously appointed*

As sone as the lady saw that knyght,
Wonther wel sche knew the knyght; *Wondrously*
Anon sche chaungyd hur colowr aryght,
And seyd, "My dere sun, Degaré, *son*
Now thou hast broughtt thy father wyth the!"
"Ye, madame, sekyr thow be! *right you are*
Now well y wot that yt ys he."
"I thank, by God," seyd the kyng,
"Now y wot, wythowtt lesyng, *without a doubt*
Who Syr Degaré his father was!"
The lady swounyd in that plass. *place*
Then afterward, now sykyrly,
The knyghtt weddyd the lady.
Sche and hur sun were partyd atwynn, *divorced*
For they were to nyghe off kyn. *too close of*
Now went forth Syr Degaré;
Wyth the kyng and his meyné, *retinue*
His father and his mother dere.
Unto that castel thei went infere *together*
Wher that wonnyd that lady bryght
That he hadd wonne in gret fyght,
And weddyd hur wyth gret solempnité
Byfor all the lordis in that cuntré.
Thus cam the knyght outt of his care;
God yff us grace well to fare. *give*
Amen

The lyff of Syr Degaré
Both curteys and fre.

Notes

Abbreviations: A: Auchinleck; C: Cambridge; R: Rawlinson; F&H: French and Hale; Ru: Rumble; S: Schleich; L: Laing.

1–3 The upper corner of fol. 78 has been cut out. Thus the first two lines and any designation of title are missing along with lines 36–42 on the verso of the leaf. C provides the first three lines of the opening. George P. Faust contends that C stands closer to A than any of the other MSS *(Sir Degaré*, p. 15) and is the primary text used to fill lacunae in L, S, and F&H. "Lysteneth, lordinges" constitutes a conventional exhortation to the audience.

3 C reads *some tyme in land.*

6 *thai.* MS: *ȝhe.* The scribe frequently uses ȝ for the initial sound in pronouns, whether *th*, *s*, or *y*. It also serves as a sign for back gutteral consonants where we would supply *g* or *gh*. I have transcribed all such uses with letters of the modern alphabet indicative of the sound used by the scribe elsewhere in the MS, whether *th-* as in *thei*, *s-* as in *she* or *sche*, or *y-* as in *you* or *yow*.

18 *strong.* A: *stron.* L's emendation, followed universally.

19–20 A smudge on the MS obscures the latter halves of these lines. L supplies *he hadde none* (line 19) and *fre and* (line 20), which F&H accept. S reads: *the kyng he hadde none [other] hair* (line 19).

23–24 Several scholars have noted the Catskin Cinderella motif in these lines, i.e., the death of the Queen and the suggestion of father/daughter incest. See lines 168–176 for a more explicit indication of the motif.

25 *she.* The A scribe occasionally uses ȝ for the sibilant, where elsewhere he uses *s-*, *sc-*, *ss-*. I have silently transcribed all such uses as *s*.

36–42 These lines are supplied by C. See note to lines 1–2.

39 F&H note that "a *minding day* is one set apart for prayers and penances for the

soul of a dead person. Giving to the poor was thought an act of merit; and maintaining religious houses insured constant prayers toward any desirable object" (p. 289). See lines 147–49. Almsgiving is an important feature of a number of Middle English romances particularly those with penitential themes.

43–46 The initial letters of these four lines have been obliterated in A, but are clear in C.

47 *toward*. A: *towar.*

54 *To don here nedes and hire righte*. The poet considers "nature's call" to be a natural right whereby the woman can stop the entourage according to her will and privilege.

58 *forht*. The scribe reverses the usual order of *h* and *t*. I have followed F&H in retaining the idiosyncracy.

60 S follows C and emends to: *and couþen nowt here riȝt way holde*.

63 *souht*. S emends to *south*. See note 58.

66 S follows C and inserts *riȝt* after *habbeth* to improve the meter.

70 *aright*. S follows C with *mighte*.

74 *chastein tre*. The chestnut tree has particular significance in the Breton lay; not only does it constitute a liminal area between the Celtic Otherworld and fictional reality, but in Christian iconography represents chastity; the chestnut in its husk is surrounded by thorns but remains unharmed by them. See notes on *Sir Orfeo, Sir Gowther,* and *Sir Launfal.*

75 F&H suggest that "sleep signals enchantment." Quite literally it marks the movement into the symbolic realm. Many scholars have noted that the language of the poem, much like that of dream, myth, and fairytale, encourages psychoanalytic readings. See Derek Brewer, "Medieval Literature, Folk Tale, and Traditional Literature," *Dutch Quarterly Review of Anglo-American Letters* 11.4 (1981), 243–56, and Cheryl Colopy, "*Sir Degaré*: A Fairy Tale Oedipus," cited above; also note to line 855, below.

85 The scribe often uses yoghs for thorns and vice versa. I have followed S by replacing one with the other where sense is otherwise impeded.

85–86 This passage finds a close analogue in *Lay le Freine*, a companion text in A. In that poem Freine's mother laments woefully after having given birth to twin girls, for it implicates her as an adulterer. Some believed that each child born required separate paternity; twins, therefore, would result from two separate fathers. The *Degaré* poet uses the passage to describe the king's daughter's fear of being lost in the woods and eaten by wild beasts.

> "Allas," sche seyd, "that y was born!
> Withouten ende ich am forlorn!
> (*Lay le Freine*, lines 95–96)

91–97 Superlative descriptions of appearance are usually reserved for the romance heroine. The description of the fairy knight is the first in the poem following the introduction of the king's daughter, who is left undescribed.

101–02 Knights often rode unarmed, arming themselves (with the help of a squire) only in preparation for battle.

108 *wel or wo*: "in gladness or grief," i.e., "under any circumstances."

109–14 The rape of a woman by a supernatural being, according to Clark H. Slover, belongs to the *Sohrab and Rustem* tale type, which includes a theme of combat between father and son. See note for line 1032. Many Middle English romances depict seductions of mortal women by supernatural beings usually in the guise of the husband, e.g., *Sir Gowther*, or, as in *Sir Orfeo*, where "ravishment" by the fairy king simply means "abduction," but rape seems to be a rare occurrence. For this reason, the similarity between this episode and the rape in the Wife of Bath's Tale is worth noting:

> In th' olde dayes of Kyng Arthour,
> Of which that Britons speken greet honour,
> Al was this land fulfild of fayerye . . . .
> And so bifel it that this kyng Arthour
> Hadde in his hous a lusty bacheler,
> That on a day cam ridynge fro ryver;
> And happed that, allone as she was born,
> He saugh a mayde walkynge hym biforn,
> Of which mayde anon, maugree hir heed,

> By verray force, he rafte hir maydenhed.
> (lines 857–59; 882–88)

Laura A. Hibbard [Loomis], in "Chaucer and the Breton Lays of the Auchinleck MS," suggests that, though *Degaré* is not an Arthurian tale, Chaucer had it in mind when he wrote the Wife's story:

> In these two preliminary episodes in the Wife's Tale and in *Degaré*, each serving as the incidental opening to a more important main story, we have the same association of "Britoun land" with fairy folk, the same emphasis on a king's noble knight, and the same situation, a helpless maiden ravished by this "noble" knight. When we reflect that no other known version of the Loathly Lady story has the rape incident for its introduction, that this was again, so far as we know anything about it, Chaucer's private and peculiar contribution, the probability that he borrowed it from something already associated in his mind with Britoun fairy tale is heightened (p. 31).

116 *schilde*. S emends to *child* here and elsewhere in the text.

117 The prophecy of the child's birth is a motif also present in other medieval romances, e.g., *Yonec, Sir Gowther, Arthour and Merlin,* etc. Some critics have noted an allusion to the apocryphal story of Joachim and Anna who, at an advanced age, became the parents of the Virgin Mary. See note on line 56 in *Sir Gowther*.

125 F&H note that the headless spear functions as the means of identification in *Voyage of Bran*. Here the fairy knight has killed a giant, the very act that Degaré will perform later.

128 *aumener*. A purse or pouch, usually possessing magical qualities, as in *Sir Launfal*. Here it functions as the container for the sword point, the object by which the son is identified by the father (see line 1062).

135 S follows C and emends to read: *And went away, sore sikend.*

155 Indentation here and subsequently in the text indicate rubricated capitals in A.

168–76 The earlier suggestion of father/daughter incest is made more explicit in this passage. Similar situations occur in *Apollonius of Tyre*, a popular narrative extant in several versions, e.g., Greek, Latin, Old English, Middle English, and Modern English (see Elizabeth Archibald's *Apollonius of Tyre: Medieval and Renaissance Themes and Variations* [Cambridge: D. S. Brewer, 1991]), and *Emaré*, though the daughter here is not cast out of the kingdom. Alan Dundes in "To Love My Father All: A Psychoanalytic Study of the Folktale Source of *King Lear*," cites the Catskin Cinderella narrative as the source for the father/daughter incest motif in Shakespeare's *King Lear*. The motif also appears in *Pericles*, Shakespeare's retelling of Gower's *Apollonius of Tyre* story, where it helps to distinguish good kingship from tyranny. The tyrant is consumed by unnatural love for his daughter while the good king avoids the temptation.

172 S follows R and emends to: *Swich sorewe to his herte wil smite.*

173 *blithe*. A: *bliȝe*.

177 S follows C to read: *Gode madame, ne care þou nowt!*

181–82 This passage has a close analogue in *Lai le Freine*. It may be significant that the births in both poems are described as sound or healthy, i.e. both mother and child survive:

> When God wild, sche was unbounde,
> And deliverd al with sounde:
> (*Lay le Freine*, lines 85–86)

193 *mighte hove*. A: *my houe*. S: *behove*. I follow F&H's emendation.

194 The gloves sent from fairy land constitute the garment of recognition for the mother/son relation. Cheryl Colopy suggests that "the gloves — like Cinderella's slipper — would appear to be a female symbol, betokening a particular sexual *fit* and insuring recognition of the proper mate" (p. 31). Here, of course, Degaré's mate is not "proper," and the function of the gloves is more protective than conjugal, though still a means of identifying the right woman, in this case, his mother. George P. Faust suggests that the glove motif is a late addition to the narrative; its lack of integration seems an afterthought (p. 81). Perhaps this is the case; however, Degaré's

recognition of his mother by a feminine garment so effectively balances the equation of the recognition of his father by a "phallic" device (i.e., the sword point) that the motif seems appropriate.

219–22 This passage finds a close parallel in *Lay le Freine*. Because of the salacious implications of her birth to twins, Freine's mother decides to send her away. Degaré's birth is illegitimate, but it is the implication of incest that compels his mother to send him away:

> The maide toke the childe hir mide,
> And stale oway in an eventide,
> And passed over a wild heth;
> Thurch feld and thurch wode hye geth
> Al the winterlong night.
> The weder was clere, the mone was light.
> (lines 145–50)

219 *child.* A: *chil.*

231 A: *drupni*; F&H emend to *drupi.*

232 S emends *was* to *swithe.*

254 The name given to the child by the hermit is significant. Meaning "almost lost" it describes the situation of the hero whose task is to find his parents, establish his inheritance, and attain an individual identity. It is probably no accident that Emaré's chosen name, Egaré, resembles Degaré. Meaning "outcast" Emaré conceives the name for herself when, cast out of her own kingdom, she arrives in a new land. *Sir Degaré*, written before *Emaré,* may also be related to the lost French poem *L'Egaré*.

257 *Other.* A: *Othe.*

265 S follows C to read: *And bad, she scholde take gode hede.*

266 *foster.* A: *forster*; F&H's emendation.

268 S emends the short line to read: *Ten yer his lif she scholde holde.*

269 *hi.* A: *i.*

274 *here.* A: *ere;* S: *here*; F&H: *there.*

277 A: *inorisscher*; F&H have emended to *innorissched.*

282 *bo.* S emends to *too.*

284 *hermitage.* S emends to *hermite.*

290 A: *Sstaleworth*; F&H have emended to *Stalworht.*

291 *wan.* S emend to *was.*

297 *florines.* According to the *OED* a florin is "the English name of a gold coin weighing about 54 grams, first issued at Florence in 1252. From the Latin *florem, flos,* or 'flower,' the coin originally was so called because it was imprinted with a lily." The English florin was first issued by Edward III.

302 S supplies a subject: *And he biheld* . . . .

303 *hem.* The scribe frequently aspirates vowels, as *his* for *is*, *hit* for *it*, *Herl* for *Erl*, and *hem* for *em*.

327 It may be significant that Degaré chooses the oak as his weapon. According to George Ferguson in *Signs & Symbols in Christian Art*, the oak tree resonates symbolic value in both Celtic and Christian traditions:

> Long before the Christian era, the ancient Celtic cult of Druids worshipped the oak. As was often the case with pagan superstitions, the veneration of the oak tree was absorbed into Christian symbolism and its meaning changed into a symbol of Christ or the Virgin Mary. The oak was one of the several species of trees that were looked upon as the tree from which the Cross was made. Because of its solidity and endurance, the oak is also a symbol of the strength of faith and virtue, and of the endurance of the Christian against adversity (p. 35).

329 *Ne.* S read *Ac.*

335 S inserts *forþ* for *wente.*

347 For an interesting discussion of dragon lore, see Anne Clark's *Beasts & Bawdy* (New York: Taplinger, 1975).

347–56 It has been noted by Muriel Carr, George Faust, and others, that the description of the dragon is closely related to that in *Bevis of Hampton* in some of the *Degaré* MSS. For a complete discussion of the borrowing see Faust's study, p. 22, or Carr's dissertation.

359 F&H note that "monsters usually could not be injured with manmade weapons; they had to be fought with their own (see also the sword in *Beowulf*) or with primitive things like the club here, or even with bare hands" (p. 299). The Earl cannot penetrate the tough hide of the dragon with his sword, yet Degaré accomplishes the killing of the mighty beast with his oak "bat."

369 A: *dagroun*; S and F&H emend to *dragoun*.

374 S inserts *was* after *bat*.

384 F&H add *a* to maintain the meter.

401 S inserts *þat* before *þai* to maintain meter.

403–06 The brideshow is another possible Cinderella motif and refers to a custom whereby emperors or kings seeking a bride would order a number of eligible women to be assembled for perusal and selection. See Photeine Bourboulis, "The Bride-show Custom and the Fairy-Story of Cinderella," *Cinderella: A Casebook*, ed. Alan Dundes (Madison: University of Wisconsin Press, 1982), pp. 98–109.

404 A: *wide cuntries and forth isowt*; C: *In that cuntre that myght be sowt*. F&H and S replace this line with line 398 of C, but I have retained the original line because it suggests a more extensive pool of potential candidates than C.

416 Degaré is dubbed a knight by the Earl thereby marking his progression toward legitimation and manhood. To this point in the narrative he has only been referred to as Degaré or child Degaré.

418 S emends to: *was wel bet*.

Sir Degaré

423 A: *palefrai hiis*; F&H emend to *hiis palefrai,* thus maintaining the rhyme.

436 S inserts *þer* after *counseil.*

458 S heads the line with *And seide* to complete the octosyllabic line.

465 *bitide*. S emends to *tide*.

470 S inserts *feir* before *him*.

471 The *OED* defines *sire* as a term signifying both knighthood and paternity, particularly as *grandsire*.

472 *anon*. A: *non*. F&H's emendation.

478 S deletes *quath the King*.

489–91 F&H note that a knight's offering to the Trinity before a battle or a test of his prowess is also present in *Havelok, Squire of Low Degree, The Song of Roland, Sir Gawain & the Green Knight*, and *Pelerinage of Charlemagne*.

493 A: *And to*; S and F&H emend to *And tho*.

504 S inserts *þer* before *iset*.

511 S inserts *wel* after *hath*.

523 S inserts *Þe* before *man*.

542 *twie*. A: *þrie*. S's emendation followed by F&H. The third stroke results in the king's unhorsing and occurs later.

544 A: *vise me*; S emends to *avise me* to save the meter. F&H suggest *me vise* to improve the meter (see note, p. 304).

555 S begins the line with *Nor*.

563 *bare qued.* The term, literally translated, means "naked evil." Here it is a euphemism for the devil who, it was believed, could not be called by his "real" name for fear of attracting him.

575 S omits *Sire.*

584 Degaré's designation as a "child" is commonplace and simply means knight; he is beyond childhood chronologically, but has much to learn about chivalric codes of conduct and the vicissitudes of life.

588–91 The motif of marriage to a spouse of unknown genealogy is also present in *Lay le Freine*. See also line 618.

590 *wot.* S emends to *wiste.*

599 *kingdoms.* S reads an ellision with *is* and transcribes *kingdom's wel.*

601 A: *Covonaunt*; F&H emend to *Covenaunt.*

611 *And.* S emends to *He.*

619–25 Though the Oedipal myth is suggested here, another likely source for this situation derives from *The Legend of Pope Gregory,* a companion text in A. There are many similarities between the two poems. Gregory, born of an incestuous union between brother and sister, cast out in a small boat, found and subsequently educated by a cleric, returns to his homeland by chance and unknowingly marries his mother. The recognition does not occur before the consummation of the marriage. However, once the fact is discovered both mother and son perform a protracted penance to atone for their sin. Gregory exiles himself for seventeen years exposed to harsh weather conditions; later he is elected Pope. Thomas Mann's *The Holy Sinner* is based upon the German version of the story, *Gregorius.*

622 L adds *to hold* to fill the lacuna in the MS and meet the rhyme requirements. S reads *his* for *is* and adds *to have and hold*, F&H add *hold*, which they gloss as "gracious." Conceivably the rhyme word was *old.* C breaks off at line 615 and is no help is solving the omission.

628 *thai.* A: *tha.*

643 S emends to read: *Awai! A witles wrechche ich am.*

659 The *yonge bride* here is about 35 years old, rather mature by medieval standards.

660 S inserts *sche* before *chaunged.*

676 *was*. A: *wa*.

677 *Than the*. A: *The*. S's emendation.

678 A: *What*; F&H emend to *Why*. The motivations behind the noises Degaré and his mother make would be of interest to the king, since they would deviate from the kinds of noises he might expect to hear on his daughter's wedding night.

679 *mervailed*. A: *mervaile.*

680 S heads the line with *Hou*.

685–86 In A these two lines are copied as a single line.

690 A: *Hou*; F&H emend to *When*. I have returned to the original question.

695 Discovery of the lost or abandoned child is an important motif in medieval romance, both facilitating narrative progression and fulfilling the basic romance paradigm of separation and reunion. See also *Octavian, Emaré, Lay le Freine*, etc.

710 A: *hyngdom*; L emends to *kyngdom*; followed by S and F&H.

713 *ikepe*. L and S read: *I kepe*; F&H: *in kepe.*

722–3 F&H note that this was practiced "so that the hero could encounter the enemy unaided — the only terms on which success was possible" (p. 564). Degaré's need to attain his own identity may also be a factor (see the introduction).

735 A: *longe he*; F&H emend to *longe hit*. S emends to: *So longe he rode, hit drouwȝ*.

755 A: *heþing*; F&H emend to *heying*. The scribe of A did not consistently distinguish between yoghs and thorns.

762–64 The enchanted castle motif is also present in *Sir Gawain and the Green Knight, Perceval, Voyage of Maelduin, Guingamor*, etc. Laura A. Hibbard [Loomis] suggests that the "special reference to a great fire burning in the hall, seem[s] closer to the text of *Libeaus [Desconus]*" (*Medieval Romance in England*, p. 305).

772 A: *itakked*. F&H emend to *nakked*; S to *itukked*. L follows A.

773 The motif of a land ruled by women may be linked to a tradition associated with Morgan le Fay and the Isle of Avalon. In this tradition, Morgan, who lives with nine sisters, brings Arthur to Avalon and heals his wounds. Laura A. Hibbard [Loomis] suggests that allusions to the tradition exist in narratives such as *Fergus,* Malory's *Book of Gareth*, Chrétien's *Yvain*, the French *Lanzelet*, and the Middle English *Sir Launfal*, among others. See *Chaucer and His Contemporaries: Essays on Medieval Literature and Thought*, ed. Helaine Newstead (Greenwich, Conn.: Fawcett Publications, 1968), p. 292. Often the community of women, under siege by a fierce knight, necessitates their lady's request for the aid of the hero whom she has healed or harbored. In return she gives him splendid gifts and profound promises of love.

776 *Sire*. Omitted in A. S's emendation.

783–87 The dwarf closely parallels that in *Libeaus Desconus*.

792 The shoe style worn by the dwarf, as noted by Ru and F&H, is that of a knight. F&H explain that the "upper part of the shoes was pierced in regular patterns so that the bright color of the stocking would show through" (p. 311). L notes that early editors of the poem used the shoe style as an aid in dating it to the first half of the fourteenth century.

797 The line indicates the dwarf's silence. For an interesting discussion of this line as it appears in R and its subsequent misunderstanding, see David F.

Johnson, "The Dwerff seyd neyther 'bow ne be': 'Ne bu ne ba' and 'Sir Degaré,' Line 703," *Neuphilologische Mitteilungen* 93 (1992), 121–23.

809 S inserts *him* before *no*.

835 F&H suggest that there is a lacuna after this line. *Sone* seems to be left without a rhyme, the couplet incomplete, but the sense of the scene is not disrupted by the omission. S adds a line to fill the lacuna with a false rhyme: *Up at the gres his wai he nom*.

838 Celtic harpers were known for their ability to induce an enchanted sleep.

840 *the bedde he*. A: *Upon the he set adoun*. F&H add *bedde*.

846 A: *pilewer*; F&H emend to *pilewe*. L and S follow A.

855 The gloss that F&H offer on this line, which I have retained, suggests that the lady is chastising Degaré for not having performed his professional duties as a protector of women. Derek Brewer, in his essay cited at line 75, asserts that the lady "mocks him for having slept like a beast all night and paid no attention to the ladies" (p. 253). Brewer seems to suggest that Degaré is neglecting his duties as a lover rather than as a knight.

859 *nowt I ne hade*. A: *nowt ne hade*. S and F&H add *I* thus providing a subject for the verb. Headless clauses are frequent in A, however; e.g., lines 926, 1017, 1066.

899 *His houen.* S emends to *Here owen.*

917 A: *A wel*; F&H emend to *And wel*. S emends to *Ac wel*.

926 S inserts *he* before *him.*

937 *But the*. F&H emend to *And the*.

938 Equine backbreaking is a common motif in medieval romance. Though the slaying of the knight's mount leaves the rider profoundly unhorsed, his loss does not imply his lack of jousting skill, but simply promotes hand-to-hand combat.

940 *stirt*. A: *stir*

961 A: *That*; F&H emend to *Thurh*. A *bacinet* is a steel skull cap worn underneath the chain-mail hood.

1004 A: *Velaun*; R: *belamy*. The distinction between the two terms may be significant. While the first means "villain" rather straightforwardly; the second could be used ironically as "rascal" or "knave." The latter term was often used in direct address to enemies or inferiors held in contempt.

1005 S begins the line *And saide*, for meter's sake.

1017 S begins the line with *Hit* to remedy the meter.

1032 See M. A. Potter, *Sohrab & Rustem: The Epic Theme of a Combat Between Father and Son*, for the literary significance of this confrontation, and Sigmund Freud on the psychological implications of this phase of the Oedipal complex. Derek Brewer suggests that *Sir Degaré* is more appropriately termed "anti-Oedipal," presumably because Degaré does not kill his father.

1065 A: *swouþ*; S reads *swony*; followed by F&H.

1066 A: *whanne of*; F&H add the subject *when he of*. S emends to place the subject before *were*: *And whanne of swone arisen hi were*. L leaves the verb headless.

1076–1109 The last page of *Degaré* in A has been cut out, except for some of the initial letters (fol. 84a). The ending is provided by R. I have followed S who also uses R to conclude the poem in his edition. L follows the black letter edition, which is somewhat different from R in wording.

1082 *My dere* is omitted in R. Ru supplies the phrase from Utterson who uses the Copland early print and the Percy Folio. S supplies the same phrase.

1088 *Degaré his father*. *His* functions as a sign of possession: Degaré's father.

1092 The marriage between Degaré and his mother is nullified (*parted atwynn*), which clears the way for the remarriage of Degaré to his lady and the marital consummation of his long-separated parents. See *Lay le Freine* where the annulment of the marriage between Guroun and Codre allows his remarriage to Freine, the twin he truly loves.

1093 *were*. R: *we*; Ru and S emend to *were*.

1095 S: *With the kyng and his meyne*.

1100 *weddyd*. S: *wedd*.

1103 R: *yff*; Ru and S emend to *gyff*. The benediction in L is more elaborate by two lines, adding *and that we, upon Domes day, / come to the blysse that lasteth aye*!

Emaré

Introduction

The Middle English *Emaré* is extant in only one manuscript, Cotton Caligula A. ii, which dates from the early fifteenth-century. The manuscript also contains Thomas Chestre's *Sir Launfal* (a lay included in this volume) as well as eight other metrical narratives. Although the MS dates from the early fifteenth century, the dialect features in *Emaré* indicate a late fourteenth-century Northeast Midlands or East Anglian dialect.[1] The song-like qualities of the Breton lay genre are quite noticeable in *Emaré* where phrases and whole lines are frequently repeated. The poem consists of eighty-six twelve-line stanzas in tail-rhyme. The rhythm is somewhat bumpy, and the iambic pattern is frequently broken. The anonymous author's repetitions, word choices, rhymes, and rhythms attest to the popular origin of the lay. Edith Rickert notes "the limitations of the author's vocabulary are best shown by a comparison with Gower's and Chaucer's versions of the same story. *Emaré* in 1035 lines uses 802 words; Gower in 1014 lines, 945 words; Chaucer in 1029 lines, 1265 words — showing half again as large a vocabulary" (p. xxii). Rickert concludes from this, and from numerous other textual features, that *Emaré* is a "popular poem by a market-place minstrel" (p. xxvii). Though it is doubtful that such a poem was ever recited in the "market-place," certainly its bourgeoise origins seem likely, perhaps among the great wool merchant houses of East Anglia.

This lay preserves a version of what is known as the "Constance-saga," a narrative which was quite popular in late medieval literature. The story appears in a twelfth-century English document written in Latin, the *Vitae Offae Primi,* as well as in several fourteenth-century English texts: Nicholas Trivet's *Anglo-Norman Chronicle* (c. 1335), the *Gesta Romanorum* (c. 1350), Chaucer's Man of Law's Tale (c. 1385–92), and John Gower's *Confessio Amantis* (prior to 1390).[2] The tale enjoyed popularity well beyond

[1] Rickert, in her critical edition of the poem, claims a Northeast Midlands dialect; Trounce declares it East Anglian. See Edith Rickert, *The Romance of Emare*, EETS e.s. 99 (London: Kegan Paul, Trench, Trübner, 1908); A. McI. Trounce, "The English Tail-rhyme Romances," *Medium Aevum* 1 (1932), 87–108, 168–82; 2 (1933), 34–57; 3 (1934), 30–50.

[2] The *Vita Offae Primi*, edited and translated, is available in *Originals and Analogues of Some of Chaucer's Canterbury Tales*, ed. F. J. Furnivall, Edmund Brock, and W. A. Clouston (London: N. Trübner for The Chaucer Society, 1872–87), pp. 73–84. Trivet's narrative is also in *Originals and*

England, occurring in French, Spanish, German, Italian, Arabic, Persian, and Latin renditions in genres as diverse as chronicle, romance, gest cycles, and drama. The Old French *La Belle Helene de Constantinople* and *La Manekine* by Phillipe de Beaumanoir, as well as the German romance, *Mai und Beaflor*, and a large number of other non-English texts bear striking resemblance to the Middle English *Emaré*. Additionally, elements of the tale can be found in the Middle English *Sir Degaré*, *Lay le Freine*, *Octavian*, *Torrent of Portyngale*, *Eglamour of Artois*, *Le Bone Florence of Rome*, *Generides*, the *Chevalere Assigne*, and others.[3] The folklore motifs in *Emaré* are shared with folktales from throughout the world. Here we find an accused queen, the monstrous birth (in this case, alleged), magic clothes, exchanged letters, an incestuous father, a persecuting mother-in-law, and a child who redeems its parents.

In the "Constance-Saga," an innocent girl is accosted by her own father, is exiled or flees from him, travels *incognito* across the sea (or into a forest), and eventually marries a prince of another land in accordance with one of the basic Cinderella tropes. While her husband is away, she is accused of a crime connected to the birth of her child: infanticide, birthing a monster, adultery, or birthing an animal. The accuser is often a relative, in this case, the mother-in-law. The story frequently features an exchange of letters which harm the protagonist. Exiled, imprisoned, or mutilated, the Constance figure is eventually redeemed from her persecution, often by her own child. Stemming from the Eros of folktale rather than from the Thanatos of mythic tragedy, the conclusion of the Constance narrative is usually an affirmation of love, a reunion of the family, and a reaffirmation of community. The suffering in the narrative does not go unrewarded; it is what Tolkien has called the "good catastrophe."[4]

Analogues, pp. 2–70. This volume also contains other analogues for the Man of Law's Tale, many of which share similarities with *Emaré*. See pp. 221–50; 367–414. For Chaucer, see *The Riverside Chaucer*, ed. Larry D. Benson (Boston: Houghton Mifflin, 1987) or F. N. Robinson, ed., *The Works of Geoffrey Chaucer* 2nd ed. (Boston: Houghton Mifflin, 1957). For Gower, see G. C. Macauley's *Confessio Amantis*, *The English Works of John Gower*, EETS e.s. 81, 82 (London: Kegan Paul, Trench, Trübner, 1900-01; rpt. Oxford University Press, 1957).

[3] For the relationship between *Emaré* and analogues, see Hermann Suchier, *Oeuvres poetiques de Philippe de Remi, sire de Beaumanoir*, Sociétè des Anciens Textes Francais (Paris: Firmin Didot, 1884/85), vol. 1, xxiii–xcvi; clix–clx; A. B. Gough, *The Constance Saga*, Palaestra 23 (Berlin: Mayer & Muller, 1902); and most especially, Margaret Schlauch, *Chaucer's Constance and Accused Queens* (New York: New York University Press, 1927), esp. pp. 62–114.

[4] J. R. R. Tolkien, "On Fairy-Stories," in *Essays Presented to Charles Williams* (Grand Rapids: William R. Eerdmans, 1966), p. 81.

The tale is constructed within a simple moral matrix: there are good characters and bad characters, good actions and evil actions. Moral complexity or confusion only exists in relation to an object: the elegant robe that Emaré wears. Characters are two dimensional, character development nearly non-existent. The lengthy prayer which introduces the narrative suggests that the poem's purpose is primarily religious or, at least, didactic. The tale denies the finality of evil, reminding us that the realm of magic is still accessible, that the ugly may be transformed, the lonely be found, the victimized, redeemed. Furthermore, the happy ending is achieved "thorow grace of God in Trinité" (line 944), and it depends, as endings do in many other English lays, on faith or persistence, on the protagonist's restraint, on his or her willingness to wait for the propitious moment, and on his or her willingness to be helped or to help someone else.

Here — as in *Le Freine*, also included in this volume — the narrative focuses on a female protagonist. Emaré offers what Hanspeter Schelp calls, "ein modell christlich-beispielhafte," a model of Christ-like virtues: she suffers for her allegiance to divine law in the face of pressures from human powers.[5] In its emphasis on "passio" (suffering and acceptance stemming from faith and its consequences in a fallen world), *Emaré* shares qualities with legends of women's saints' lives. As Dieter Mehl notes, "the significance of her pitiable fate depends on its being completely unmerited," and "she comes very near to being a kind of secularized Saint."[6] As a tale of extreme female sacrifice, *Emaré* also shares a common theme with classical tales such as the legend of Alceste, who was willing to die in her husband's place, and who, in classical legends bequeathed to the Middle Ages, descended into Hades in exchange for her husband's life. The link between suffering women and weaving or embroidery which is established in *Emaré* can also be found in a number of classical figures: Penelope, who suffers silently as a hostage on Ithaca, weaving and unweaving a shroud, trying to hold off the suitors until Odysseus returns; Ariadne, who helps Theseus escape from the labyrinth by giving him a ball of thread to unroll and then follow back out; and Philomela, raped and mutilated, left speechless, who weaves her story into a tapestry to communicate the crime. Stories like these which feature suffering women were quite popular and can be found in hagiography and in secular texts like Chaucer's *Legend of Good Women*, Christine de Pizan's *Le Livre de la Cité des Dames*, and in various tales by Ovid, and Gower.

---

[5] Hanspeter Schelp, *Exemplarische Romanzen im Mittelenglischen*, Palaestra 246 (Göttingen: Vandenhoeck & Ruprecht, 1967), p. 113.

[6] Dieter Mehl, *The Middle English Romances of the Thirteenth and Fourteenth Centuries* (New York: Barnes and Noble, 1969), p. 139.

Emaré

Like many medieval tales which feature a female protagonist, *Emaré* reinscribes the tradition of domestic romance with its focus on the family and on the heroine's personal relationships. Within the domestic romance, her role is to suffer adversity relatively passively. Typically, her only departure from passivity is resisting rape, in this case, incest. Actively refusing her father's advances also marks the beginning of Emaré's trials. Her extreme suffering and her endurance of that suffering form the plot. Even when she is exiled on the sea, left to die in an open boat, she does not curse those who mistreat her; instead, she speaks harshly to the sea: "Wele owth y to warye the, see, / I have myche shame yn the!" (lines 667–68). In his book, *Chivalric Romances*, Lee Ramsey notes that "in the romances peril and distress come increasingly to stand as central images of the woman's relationship to her society."[7] The lay of *Emaré* represents the threats against the heroine as almost always sexual: the initial threat is of incest; the subsequent threat on her life occurs after she marries and bears a child. Emaré's extreme suffering takes the form of exile, of isolation from society. Whereas the wilderness certainly offers hardships for male protagonists in medieval romance, it can also offer the arena for heroism, usually in the form of combat even if linked to religious faith. For the female protagonist in this English lay, the wilderness offers an arena only for acts of faith; in her second sojourn on the sea, she suffers through her trial with her face hidden in her cloak, lying face down on the keel of the boat. Her journeys are not actively chosen; instead, she is the object set to sea by others' active choices. Ramsey suggests that this kind of punishment (ostracism) "perhaps represent[s] the life to which the medieval woman saw herself condemned: emotional but inactive, accepting what happened because there was no other choice, isolated from the . . . centers of society" (p. 177). And yet, Emaré, weaving her words together, weaves people and different worlds together as well, and finds ways, albeit restricted ways, to influence her world. As Joan Ferrante comments, "With limited opportunities to exercise real power over their own or others' lives, women in medieval literature and sometimes in real life find subtle or hidden ways to exercise such power, to manipulate people and situations, and to spin out fictions which suit them better than their reality, fictions by which they can, or hope to, control reality."[8] Emaré's disguises, her adoption of lower class status, and her off-stage directions which create the reunion scenes

---

7 Lee C. Ramsey, *Chivalric Romances: Popular Literature in Medieval England* (Bloomington: Indiana University Press, 1983), pp. 176-77.

8 Joan Ferrante, "Public Postures and Private Maneuvers: Roles Medieval Women Play," in Mary Erler and Maryanne Kowaleski, eds. *Women and Power in the Middle Ages* (Athens: University of Georgia Press, 1988), p. 213.

between Segramour and his father and Segramour and his grandfather, are all, then, efforts Emaré makes to control her world. Besides her direct resistance to her father's incestuous advances, she demonstrates throughout the text that she is not completely helpless in the face of adversity. Her words take on considerable power. She refuses her father's sexual advances successfully; she shames the ocean into calming; she prays to God and Mary to preserve her on the open sea, and they do; she keeps her infant son alive; she makes her way in foreign lands by teaching, sewing, and embroidering; and she successfully reunites the fragments of her family, thereby insuring that her son will assume the imperial throne.

Although the text generally builds itself around a simple morality, some elements in the tale are left ambiguous, particularly the nature of Emaré's robe. Like Le Freine's fine cloth or Orfeo's harp, the robe is the one object which accompanies Emaré as she moves from one country to another, from one identity to another. The "glysteryng" garment receives a description of ninety-eight lines (lines 82–180) in a poem that is, itself, only 1035 lines, so that the lengthy description calls attention to the importance of the object. It is exotic, enchanting, and foreign. Consisting of four embroidered and bejeweled panels which depict lovers, the cloth was sewn by the Amerayle's daughter for her beloved, the Sultan's son. It is, then, woven by a woman as a wedding gift to be worn by a man, an interesting detail which is duplicated in the narrative itself when Emaré steps into the garment and, thereby, simultaneously steps into the protagonist's role. She assumes the man's garment just as she takes on the subject position within the narrative. But if wearing the robe marks Emaré's assumption of the hero's role, it simultaneously marks her subjugation as a beautiful female creature within a patriarchal social order. The cloth, originally given in love, is taken by force from the Sultan by Sir Tergaunte's father who, in an act of love, gives it to his son, who, in turn, in an act of devotion gives it to his lord, the emperor Syr Artyus. The emperor, in an act of love which turns sexually coercive, then has a robe made of it for Emaré. Thus, the link between the cloth and Emaré, established throughout the narrative, may also reinforce her status as more like an object exchanged than as an active subject. The history of the robe interweaves love and violence, again echoing the plot surrounding Emaré herself.

In examining the robe, scholars have interpreted its meaning in various ways. Mortimer Donovan finds its images of true lovers to represent a "gallery of ideals."[9] For Deiter Mehl, the cloth emphasizes Emaré's beauty "because her robe is always

---

[9] Mortimer J. Donovan, "Middle English *Emare* and the Cloth Worthily Wrought," in Larry D. Benson, ed., *The Learned and the Lewed: Studies in Chaucer and Medieval Literature*, Harvard English Studies 5 (Cambridge: Harvard University Press, 1974), p. 339. See also Hanspeter Schelp, pp. 105–16.

mentioned whenever her beauty impresses the beholders" (p. 139). Maldwyn Mills calls attention to the secular nature of the lovers depicted on the garment and argues that the robe reflects the king's sexual attraction to Emaré or her sexual attractiveness any time she puts it on.[10] Indeed, many have noticed these images of love embroidered on the cloth and have interpreted the garment as a symbol for the power of female puberty and the temptations of the flesh, especially since the cloth's presence in the narrative can be read as connected in some way with Artyus's incestuous desires for his pubescent daughter. The text records the Emperor's initial reaction to the cloth: "Sertes, thys ys a fayry, / Or ellys a vanyté!" (lines 104–05), suggesting that the robe may be enchanted (a judgment which still remains ambiguous). French and Hale read the cloth as "a love-charm — originally given to the fairy Emaré by supernatural well-wishers."[11] Like Mills, they assume that the Emperor's attraction to Emaré and later the King of Galys are charmed reactions, solicited magically by the cloth itself. Indeed, in the text, Emaré appears to be "non erthely wommon" when she dons the robe (lines 245, 396, 439–450, 697–702). Ramsey suggests that the robe's dual function, highlighting romantic love and spawning incestuous and murderous violence, illustrates ways "*Emaré* . . . seems to be almost an antilove romance, accepting the major conventions of the genre but portraying the love advocated in romances as potentially a shocking evil" (p. 184). Yet another reading of the enchanted robe is possible: the cloth begins as an unformed potentiality and is made into a robe, an image of order, a symbol of civilization. Reading the garment this way connects it with the incest taboo which, likewise, has been identified as a cornerstone for the development of civilization and order. Ross Arthur adds another reading: "the poet directs us toward considering the cloak . . . as a sign." The challenge of the poem and of the gem-cloak in particular is the problem of interpretation: "There are no thieves who wish to possess it. . . ; no one who gives an authoritative explication of its meaning; . . . it stays with [Emaré] throughout the poem without any rational reflective choice on her part . . . . Without knowing [the robe's] 'meaning' all [the characters] 'interpret' the cloak as a sign."[12] The gem-cloak is, for Arthur, "a touchstone for determining the spiritual state and charting the spiritual progress of those who behold and respond to it" (p. 91).

---

[10] Maldwyn Mills, *Six Middle English Romances* (London: Dent, 1973), pp. xxv–xxvi.

[11] Walter Hoyt French and Charles B. Hale, eds. *The Middle English Metrical Romances* (New York: Russell & Russell, 1964), p. 428, note.

[12] Ross G. Arthur, "Emaré's Cloak and Audience Response," in Julian N. Wasserman and Lois Roney, eds. *Sign, Sentence, Discourse: Language in Medieval Thought and Literature* (Syracuse: Syracuse University Press, 1989), p. 90.

Select Bibliography

Manuscript

British Library MS Cotton Caligula A.ii, fols. 71–76. [The early fifteenth-century manuscript consists of two paper quartos, the first of which contains *Emaré* and other English verse texts as well as a treatise on pestilence, a prose treatise on the rite of confession, a short Latin chronicle and a few prescriptions. The second quarto contains statutes of the Carthusian order dating from 1411 to 1504.]

Critical Editions

Gough, A. B., ed., *Emaré.* In *Old and Middle English Texts,* L. Morsbach and F. Holthausen, eds., vol. II, London: Sampson Low Marston; New York: G. E. Stechert; Heidelberg: C. Winter, 1901.

Rickert, Edith, ed. *The Romance of Emare.* EETS e.s. 99. London: Kegan Paul, Trench, Trübner, 1908; rpt. 1958.

Collections

French, Walter Hoyt, and Charles Brockway Hale, eds. *The Middle English Metrical Romances.* 2 vols. New York: Russell & Russell, 1964. I, 423–55.

Mills, Maldwyn, ed. *Six Middle English Romances.* London: Dent, 1973. Pp. 46–74.

Ritson, Joseph, ed. *Ancient Engleish Metrical Romanceë.* 3 vols. Rev. ed. Edinburgh: E. Goldsmid, 1802. II, 204–47.

Rumble, Thomas C., ed. *The Breton Lays in Middle English.* Detroit: Wayne State University Press, 1965. Pp. 97–133.

Related Studies

Arthur, Ross G. "Emaré's Cloak and Audience Response." In Julian N. Wasserman and Lois Roney, eds., *Sign, Sentence, Discourse: Language in Medieval Thought and Culture.* Syracuse: Syracuse University Press, 1989. Pp. 80–92. [Uses Augustine's discussion of signs in *De Doctrina Christiana* to read character's names, character's reactions to Emaré and her cloak, as well as the gemmed cloak itself in connection with interpretation and spirituality.]

Donovan, Mortimer J. "Middle English *Emare* and the Cloth Worthily Wrought." In Larry D. Benson, ed., *The Learned and the Lewed: Studies in Chaucer and Medieval Literature*. Harvard English Studies 5. Cambridge: Harvard University Press, 1974. Pp. 337–42. [Notes the tendency of Breton lays to highlight one central object which carries symbolic meaning — here, the cloth robe. Donovan briefly discusses the function and symbolism of the cloth and the robe made out of it.]

Gough, A. B. *The Constance Saga*, Palaestra 23. Berlin: Mayer and Müller, 1902.

Isaacs, Neil D. "Constance in Fourteenth-Century England." *Neuphilologische Mitteilungen* 59 (1958), 260–77. [Provides descriptions and compares Chaucer's Man of Law's Tale, Gower's version of the Constance story in his *Confessio Amantis*, and the Middle English *Emaré*.]

Rickert, Edith. "The Old English Offa Saga." *Modern Philology* 2 (1904–05), 29–76; 321–76. [Examines the *Vitae Duorum Offarum* (MS Cotton Nero D I, folios 2–25) for the purposes of identifying separate threads and sources of the *Offa* narrative and its relationship to history and legend. Compares this version of the Offa narrative with both *Emaré* and Trivet's *Constance*. Examines sources and variations on the *Offa* legend pointing to Emaré's participation in a powerful and recurring cultural narrative which focused on the plight and sorrow of besieged queens.]

Schelp, Hanspeter. *Exemplarische Romanzen im Mittelenglischen,* Palaestra 246. Göttingen: Vandenhoeck & Ruprecht, 1967. Pp. 97–113. [Explores Christian symbols and themes in *Emaré*, focusing particularly on those themes which arise out of characterization, narrative structures, and the symbol of the cloth robe. In German.]

Schlauch, Margaret. *Chaucer's Constance and Accused Queens*. New York: New York University Press, 1927. [Examines figures of innocent queens who are besieged or exiled in medieval literature. Includes discussion of folktale elements common to these narratives, including themes of infanticide, animal birth, various persecutions meted out to heroines, and typical plot endings. Identifies numerous analogues for Chaucer's Man of Law's Tale, analogues which include and are useful for a study of *Emaré*.]

Emaré

Jhesu, that ys kyng in trone, *on throne*
As Thou shoope bothe sonne and mone, *created*
  And all that shalle dele and dyghte, *dispense and rule*
Now lene us grace such dedus to done, *lend*
In Thy blys that we may wone — *dwell*
  Men calle hyt heven lyghte; *heavenly*
And Thy modur Mary, hevyn qwene, *mother*
Bere our arunde so bytwene,[1]
  That semely ys of syght, *Who [Mary] is beautiful to see*
To thy Sone that ys so fre, *noble (generous)*
In heven wyth Hym that we may be,
  That lord ys most of myght.

Menstrelles that walken fer and wyde, *far and wide*
Her and ther in every a syde, *Here; all regions*
  In mony a dyverse londe, *many*
Sholde, at her bygynnyng, *at the beginning of their lays*
Speke of that ryghtwes kyng *righteous*
  That made both see and sonde. *sea and sand*
Whoso wyll a stounde dwelle,[2]
Of mykyll myrght y may you telle, *much mirth*
  And mornyng ther amonge; *mourning intermingled with it*
Of a lady fayr and fre,
Her name was called Emaré,
  As I here synge in songe.

Her fadyr was an emperour
Of castell and of ryche towre; *splendid*
  Syr Artyus was hys nome. *name*

---

[1] *Bear our errand (prayer) between heaven and earth*

[2] *Whoever will, for a time, stay (to listen to me)*

He hadde bothe hallys and bowrys, *halls and private chambers*
Frythes fayr, forestes wyth flowrys; *Woodlands*
So gret a lord was none.
Weddedde he had a lady
That was both fayr and semely,
Whyte as whales bone:
Dame Erayne hette that emperes; *was named*
She was full of love and goodnesse;
So curtays lady was none. *courteous*

Syr Artyus was the best manne
In the worlde that lyvede thanne, *lived then*
Both hardy and therto wyght; *brave*
He was curtays in all thyng,
Bothe to olde and to yynge, *the young*
And well kowth dele and dyght.[1]
He hadde but on chyld in hys lyve *one; life*
Begeten on hys weddedde wyfe,
And that was fayr and bryght; *that [child]*
For sothe, as y may telle the, *truth; thee*
They called that chyld Emaré,
That semely was of syght. *fair*

When she was of her modur born,
She was the fayrest creature borne
That yn the lond was thoo. *then*
The emperes, that fayr ladye,
Fro her lord gan she dye,
Or hyt kowthe speke or goo. *Before it [the child] could talk or walk*
The chyld, that was fayr and gent, *noble*
To a lady was hyt sente, *sent*
That men kalled Abro. *called*
She thawghth hyt curtesye and thewe, *taught; courtesy; good manners*
Golde and sylke for to sewe, *silk*
Amonge maydenes moo. *more*

[1] *And knew well how to distribute [wealth] and govern*

Abro tawghte thys mayden small,
Nortur that men useden in sale, — *Manners; in hall*
Whyle she was in her bowre. — *bower*
She was curtays in all thynge,
Bothe to olde and to yynge,
And whyte as lylye-flowre.
Of her hondes she was slye; — *skillful*
All her loved that her sye, — *saw*
Wyth menske and mychyl honour. — *reverence; much*
At the mayden leve we, — *Let's leave the maiden for now*
And at the lady fayr and fre, — *The lovely and noble lady*
And speke we of the Emperour.

The Emperour of gentyll blode — *noble lineage*
Was a curteys lorde and a gode, — *good [lord]*
In all maner of thynge. — *every way*
Aftur, when hys wyf was dede, — *dead*
And ledde hys lyf yn weddewede, — *as a widower*
And myche loved playnge. — *playing (amusement or music)*
Sone aftur, yn a whyle,
The ryche Kynge of Cesyle — *Sicily*
To the Emperour gan wende; — *did visit*
A ryche present wyth hym he browght,
A cloth that was wordylye wroght. — *worthily made*
He wellcomed hym as the hende. — *courteously*

Syr Tergaunte, that nobyll knyght,
He presented the Emperour ryght, — *presented [himself to]*
And sette hym on hys kne,
Wyth that cloth rychyly dyght, — *spendidly adorned*
Full of stones ther hyt was pyght, — *it was studded*
As thykke as hyt myght be: — *thick*
Off topaze and rubyes — *Of*
And othur stones of myche prys, — *great price*
That semely wer to se;
Of crapowtes and nakette, — *toad-stones and agates*
As thykke ar they sette,
For sothe, as y say the. — *Truly; tell you*

The cloth was dysplayed sone; *unfurled quickly*
The Emperour lokede therupone
And myght hyt not se,
For glysteryng of the ryche ston; *glistening*
Redy syght had he non,
And sayde, "How may thys be?"
The Emperour sayde on hygh, *in haste*
"Sertes, thys ys a fayry, *Surely; from*
Or ellys a vanyté!" *else an illusion*
The Kyng of Cysyle answered than,
"So ryche a jwell ys ther non *jewel; none*
In all Crystyanté." *Christianity*

The Emerayle dowghter of hethenes *daughter of the Emir of heathendom*
Made thys cloth wythouten lees, *lies*
And wrowghte hyt all wyth pryde; *wrought*
And purtreyed hyt wyth gret honour, *portrayed (painted) on it*
Wyth ryche golde and asowr *azure*
And stones on ylke a syde. *each side*
And, as the story telles in honde, *at hand*
The stones that yn thys cloth stonde,
Sowghte they wer full wyde. *Sought; far and wide*
Seven wynter hyt was yn makynge, *Seven winters*
Or hyt was browght to endynge, *Ere; an ending*
In herte ys not to hyde.

In that on korner made was *one corner*
Ydoyne and Amadas, *(see note)*
Wyth love that was so trewe;
For they loveden hem wyth honour, *loved each other*
Portrayed they wer wyth trewe-love-flour,
Of stones bryght of hewe: *[Made] of; hue*
Wyth carbunkull and safere, *saffire*
Kassydonys and onyx so clere *Chalcedony*
Sette in golde newe,
Deamondes and rubyes, *Diamonds*
And othur stones of mychyll pryse,
And menstrellys wyth her glewe. *their song*

In that othur corner was dyght *made*
Trystram and Isowde so bryght,
That semely wer to se;
And for they loved hem ryght, *because; each other truly*
As full of stones ar they dyght, *adorned*
As thykke as they may be:
Of topase and of rubyes,
And othur stones of myche pryse,
That semely wer to se;
Wyth crapawtes and nakette, *toadstones; agates*
Thykke of stones ar they sette,
For sothe, as y say the.

In the thyrdde korner, wyth gret honour, *third*
Was Florys and Dam Blawncheflour,
As love was hem betwene;
For they loved wyth honour, *Because*
Purtrayed they wer wyth trewe-love-flour,
Wyth stones bryght and shene: *shining*
Ther wer knyghtus and senatowres,
Emerawdes of gret vertues, *virtues (powers or value)*
To wyte wythouten wene; *To know; doubt*
Deamoundes and koralle, *coral*
Perydotes and crystall, *Chrysolite*
And gode garnettes bytwene. *good garnets*

In the fowrthe korner was oon, *fourth; one*
Of Babylone the Sowdan sonne, *Babylonian Sultan's son*
The Amerayles dowghtyr hym by. *Emir's daughter beside him*
For hys sake the cloth was wrowght; *made*
She loved hym in hert and thowght,
As testymoyeth thys storye. *testifies*
The fayr mayden her byforn *before*
Was portrayed an unykorn, *unicorn*
Wyth hys horn so hye;
Flowres and bryddes on ylke a syde, *birds; each*
Wyth stones that wer sowght wyde,
Stuffed wyth ymagerye. *imagery*

When the cloth to ende was wrowght, *was finished*
To the Sowdan sone hyt was browght, *soon*
That semely was of syghte.
"My fadyr was a nobyll man;
Of the Sowdan he hyt wan *From; Sultan; won*
Wyth maystrye and wyth myghth. *force; might*
For gret love he gaf hyt me; *gave it to me*
I brynge hyt the in specyalté; *to you as a rare gift*
Thys cloth ys rychely dyght." *splendidly made*
He gaf hyt the emperour; *gave it [to]*
He receyved hyt wyth gret honour,
And thonkede hym fayr and ryght.

The Kyng of Cesyle dwelled ther
As long as hys wyll wer, *he wished*
Wyth the Emperour for to play;
And when he wolde wende, *would go*
He toke hys leve at the hende, *leave courteously*
And wente forth on hys way.
Now remeveth thys nobyll kyng. *departs*
The Emperour aftur hys dowghtur hadde longyng,
To speke wyth that may. *maiden*
Messengeres forth he sent
Aftyr the mayde fayr and gent,
That was bryght as someres day. *summer's*

Messengeres dyghte hem in hye; *took themselves hastily*
Wyth myche myrthe and melodye,
Forth gon they fare,
Both by stretes and by stye, *streets; path[s]*
Aftur that fayr lady,
Was godely unthur gare. *appropriately dressed (under cloth)*
Her norysse, that hyghte Abro, *nurse; was called*
Wyth her she goth forth also,
And wer sette in a chare. *carriage or litter*
To the Emperour gan they go;
He come ayeyn hem a myle or two; *toward them*
A fayr metyng was there.

The mayden, whyte as lylye flour,   *flower*
Lyghte ayeyn her fadyr the Emperour;   *Alighted opposite*
Two knyghtes gan her lede.
Her fadyr that was of gret renowne,
That of golde wered the crowne,   *wore*
Lyghte of hys stede.   *Alighted from*
When they wer bothe on her fete,   *their*
He klypped her and kyssed her swete,   *embraced*
And bothe on fote they yede.   *together; went*
They wer glad and made good chere;
To the palys they yede in fere,   *went together*
In romans as we rede.   *romance (story)*

Then the lordes that wer grete,   *great lords*
They wesh and seten doun to mete,   *washed; sat down to food*
And folk hem served swythe.   *quickly*
The mayden that was of sembelant swete,   *appearance*
Byfore her owene fadur sete,   *sat*
The fayrest wommon on lyfe;   *alive*
That all hys hert and all hys thowghth
Her to love was yn browght:
He byhelde her ofte sythe.   *oftentimes*
So he was anamored hys thowghtur tyll,   *daughter*
Wyth her he thowghth to worche hys wyll,
And wedde her to hys wyfe.

And when the metewhyle was don,   *meal; done*
Into hys chambur he wente son   *immediately*
And called hys counseyle nere.
He bad they shulde sone go and come,   *bade; soon*
And gete leve of the Pope of Rome   *permission*
To wedde that mayden clere.   *pure*
Messengeres forth they wente.
They durste not breke hys commandement,   *dared; break*
And erles wyth hem yn fere.   *earls; together*
They wente to the courte of Rome,
And browghte the Popus bullus sone,   *Pope's bulls quickly*
To wedde hys dowghter dere.   *To [permit him to]*

Then was the Emperour gladde and blythe,
And lette shape a robe swythe *had a robe made quickly*
  Of that cloth of golde;
And when hyt was don her upon, *put*
She semed non erthely wommon, *earthly*
  That marked was of molde. *clay (earth or mortality)*
Then seyde the Emperour so fre,
"Dowghtyr, y woll wedde the, *will*
  Thow art so fresh to beholde."
Then sayde that wordy unthur wede, *worthy woman clothed in the robe*
"Nay syr, God of heven hyt forbede, *forbade*
  That ever do so we shulde!

"Yyf hyt so betydde that ye me wedde *If; befell*
And we shulde play togedur in bedde, *have sexual intercourse*
  Bothe we were forlorne! *Both of us would be lost*
The worde shulde sprynge fer and wyde; *news*
In all the worlde on every syde
  The worde shulde be borne. *would be carried*
Ye ben a lorde of gret pryce, *are; renown*
Lorde, lette nevur such sorow aryce: *arise*
  Take God you beforne! *Hold God's law before you*
That my fadur shulde wedde me,
God forbede that I hyt so se, *should ever see it*
  That wered the crowne of thorne!" *wore*

The Emperour was ryght wrothe, *angry*
And swore many a gret othe, *oath*
  That deed shulde she be. *dead*
He lette make a nobull boot, *boat*
And dede her theryn, God wote, *put herself; knows*
  In the robe of nobull ble. *bright color*
She moste have wyth her no spendyng, *might; money*
Nothur mete ne drynke, *Neither food*
  But shate her ynto the se. *pushed herself*
Now the lady dwelled thore, *there*
Wythowte anker or ore,
  And that was gret pyté!

Ther come a wynd, y unthurstonde,
And blewe the boot fro the londe,
Of her they lost the syght.
The Emperour hym bethowght
That he hadde all myswrowht, *done amiss*
And was a sory knyghte.
And as he stode yn studyynge, *meditating*
He fell down in sowenynge, *swooning*
To the erthe was he dyght. *fallen (doomed)*
Grete lordes stode therby,
And toke yn the Emperour hastyly,
And comforted hym fayr and ryght.

When he of sownyng kovered was, *of his swoon recovered*
Sore he wepte and sayde, "Alas, *Grievously*
For my dowhter dere!
Alas, that y was made man,
Wrecched kaytyf that I hyt am!" *villian*
The teres ronne by hys lere. *down; face*
"I wrowght ayeyn Goddes lay *acted against; law*
To her that was so trewe of fay. *faith*
Alas, why ner she here!" *why isn't*
The teres lasshed out of hys yghen; *splashed; eyes*
The grete lordes that hyt syghen *saw*
Wepte and made yll chere.

Ther was nothur olde ny yynge *neither; nor*
That kowthe stynte of wepynge, *could stop*
For that comely unthur kelle. *[one who was]; cloak*
Into shypys faste gan they thrynge, *throng*
Forto seke that mayden yynge,
That was so fayr of flesh and fell. *skin*
They her sowght ovurall yn the see
And myghte not fynde that lady fre,
Ayeyn they come full snell. *quickly*
At the Emperour now leve we,
And of the lady yn the see,
I shall begynne to tell.

The lady fleted forth alone; *floated*
To God of heven she made her mone, *complaint*
And to Hys modyr also.
She was dryven wyth wynde and rayn,
Wyth stronge stormes her agayn, *against her*
Of the watur so blo. *dark (stormy)*
As y have herd menstrelles syng yn sawe, *story*
Hows ny lond myghth she non knowe, *House; see*
Aferd she was to go. *Afraid*
She was so dryven fro wawe to wawe, *wave*
She hyd her hede and lay full lowe,
For watyr she was full woo. *Of; terrified*

Now thys lady dwelled thore *there*
A good seven nyghth and more, *seven nights*
As hyt was Goddys wylle;
Wyth carefull herte and sykyng sore, *sighing sorrowful*
Such sorow was here yarked yore, *ordained long before*
And ever lay she styll.
She was dryven ynto a lond,
Thorow the grace of Goddes sond, *mercy*
That all thyng may fulfylle.
She was on the see so harde bestadde, *harshly beset*
For hungur and thurste almost madde.
Woo worth wederus yll! *Woe come to all evil weathers (storms)*

She was dryven into a lond
That hyghth Galys, y unthurstond, *is called*
That was a fayr countré.
The kyngus steward dwelled ther bysyde, *(beside the sea)*
In a kastell of mykyll pryde;
Syr Kadore hyght he.
Every day wolde he go,
And take wyth hym a sqwyer or two,
And play hym by the see.
On a tyme he toke the eyr *air*
Wyth two knyghtus gode and fayr;
The wedur was lythe of le. *quietly pleasant*

A boot he fond by the brym, *boat; shore*
And a glysteryng thyng theryn, *glittering*
  Therof they hadde ferly. *were amazed*
They went forth on the sond *shore*
To the boot, y unthurstond,
  And fond theryn that lady.
She hadde so longe meteles be *without food been*
That hym thowht gret dele to se; *he thought it a great sorrow to see*
  She was yn poynt to dye. *at the point of death*
They askede her what was her name:
She chaunged hyt ther anone, *immediately*
  And sayde she hette Egaré. *was called*

Syr Kadore hadde gret pyté;
He toke up the lady of the see,
  And hom gan her lede.
She hadde so longe meteles be, *been without food*
She was wax lene as a tre, *had grown lean; stick*
  That worthy unthur wede. *robe*
Into hys castell when she came,
Into a chawmbyr they her namm, *took*
  And fayr they gan her fede,
Wyth all delycyus mete and drynke *delicious*
That they myghth hem on thynke, *could devise*
  That was yn all that stede. *place*

When that lady, fayr of face,
Wyth mete and drynke kevered was, *recovered*
  And had colour agayne,
She tawghte hem to sewe and marke *embroider*
All maner of sylkyn werke;
  Of her they wer full fayne. *pleased*
She was curteys yn all thyng,
Bothe to olde and to yynge,
  I say yow for certeyne.
She kowghthe werke all maner thyng *knew how to fashion; of thing[s]*
That fell to emperour or to kyng, *were worn by*
  Erle, barown or swayne. *countryman*

Syr Kadore lette make a feste
That was fayr and honeste,
Wyth hys lorde, the kynge.
Ther was myche menstralsé,
Trommpus, tabours and sawtré, — *Trumpets, drums; psaltery*
Bothe harpe and fydyllyng. — *fiddling*
The lady that was gentyll and small — *slender*
In kurtull alone served yn hall, — *robe*
Byfore that nobull kyng.
The cloth upon her shone so bryghth — *bright*
When she was theryn ydyghth, — *dressed*
She semed non erthly thyng.

The kyng loked her upon,
So fayr a lady he sygh nevur non: — *saw*
Hys herte she hadde yn wolde. — *[her] power*
He was so anamered of that syghth, — *enamoured*
Of the mete non he myghth, — *food; [eat]*
But faste gan her beholde. — *fixedly*
She was so fayr and gent, — *gracious*
The kynges love on her was lent, — *bestowed*
In tale as hyt ys tolde.
And when the metewhyle was don, — *meal*
Into the chambur he wente son,
And called hys barouns bolde.

Fyrst he called Syr Kadore,
And othur knyghtes that ther wore, — *were*
Hastely come hym tyll.
Dukes and erles, wyse of lore, — *wise; learning*
Hastely come the kyng before
And askede what was hys wyll.
Then spakke the ryche yn ray, — *array*
To Syr Kadore gan he say
Wordes fayr and stylle: — *quietly*
"Syr, whenns ys that lovely may — *[from] whence; maid*
That yn the halle served thys day?
Tell my yyf hyt be thy wyll."

Then sayde syr Kadore, y unthurstonde,
"Hyt ys an erles thowghtur of ferre londe, *she; daughter; distant*
That semely ys to sene.
I sente aftur her certeynlye
To teche my chylderen curtesye, *teach*
In chambur wyth hem to bene. *them*
She ys the konnyngest wommon, *most skillful*
I trowe, that be yn Crystendom,
Of werke that y have sene." *embroidery*
Then sayde that ryche raye, *splendid king*
"I wyll have that fayr may *maid*
And wedde her to my quene." *as*

The nobull kyng, verament, *truly*
Aftyr hys modyr he sent
To wyte what she wolde say. *know*
They browght forth hastely
That fayr mayde Egarye;
She was bryghth as someres day.
The cloth on her shon so bryght
When she was theryn dyght, *dressed*
And herself a gentell may,
The olde qwene sayde anon,
"I sawe never wommon
Halvendell so gay!" *Half so beautiful*

The olde qwene spakke wordus unhende *spoke; discourteous*
And sayde, "Sone, thys ys a fende, *Son; fiend*
In thys wordy wede! *noble robe*
As thou lovest my blessynge, *If*
Make thou nevur thys weddynge,
Cryst hyt the forbede!"
Then spakke the ryche ray, *king*
"Modyr, y wyll have thys may!" *maiden*
And forth gan her lede.
The olde qwene, for certayne,
Turnede wyth ire hom agayne,
And wolde not be at that dede. *ceremony*

The kyng wedded that lady bryght;
Grete purvyance ther was dyghth, *preparations; made*
In that semely sale. *hall*
Grete lordes wer served aryght, *appropriately*
Duke, erle, baron and knyghth,
Both of grete and smale.
Myche folke, forsothe, ther was,
And therto an huge prese, *press (throng)*
As hyt ys tolde yn tale.
Ther was all maner thyng
That fell to a kyngus weddyng, *belonged*
And mony a ryche menstralle. *many a splendid*

When the mangery was done, *feasting*
Grete lordes departed sone,
That semely were to se.
The kynge belafte wyth the qwene; *remained*
Moch love was hem betwene,
And also game and gle. *sport; pleasure*
She was curteys and swete,
Such a lady herde y nevur of yete;
They loved both wyth herte fre. *(both loved); heart*
The lady that was both meke and mylde
Conceyved and wente wyth chylde, *conceived*
As God wolde hyt sholde be. *willed*

The kyng of France yn that tyme
Was besette wyth many a Sarezyne, *beseiged by; Saracen*
And cumbered all in tene; *oppressed; distress*
And sente aftur the kyng of Galys,
And othur lordys of myche prys,
That semely were to sene.
The kyng of Galys, in that tyde,
Gedered men on every syde, *gathered*
In armour bryght and shene. *shining*
Then sayde the kyng to Syr Kadore
And othur lordes that ther wore,
"Take good hede to my qwene." *care of*

The kyng of Fraunce spared none,
But sent for hem everychone,
Both kyng, knyghth and clerke.
The steward bylaft at home — *remained*
To kepe the qwene whyte as fome, — *care for; (sea) foam*
He come not at that werke. — *did not take part in that [military] action*
She wente wyth chylde yn place,
As longe as Goddus wyll was,
That semely unthur serke; — *lovely one under smock*
Thyll ther was of her body — *Until; from*
A fayr chyld borne and a godele; — *good-looking (one)*
Hadde a dowbyll kyngus marke. — *[And he] had a double king's [birth]mark*

They hyt crystened wyth grete honour — *christened*
And called hym Segramour:
Frely was that fode. — *Noble; child*
Then the steward, Syr Kadore,
A nobull lettur made he thore, — *then*
And wrowghte hyt all wyth gode. — *wrote; good (news)*
He wrowghte hyt yn hyghynge — *haste*
And sente hyt to hys lorde the kynge,
That gentyll was of blode. — *lineage*
The messenger forth gan wende, — *go*
And wyth the kyngus modur gan lende, — *tarry*
And ynto the castell he yode. — *went*

He was resseyved rychely, — *received handsomely*
And she hym askede hastyly
How the qwene hadde spedde. — *fared*
"Madame, ther ys of her yborne
A fayr man-chylde, y tell you beforne, — *now*
And she lyth in her bedde."
She gaf hym for that tydynge — *gave; tiding*
A robe and fowrty shylynge, — *forty shilling(s)*
And rychely hym cladde.
She made hym dronken of ale and wyne, — *drunk*
And when she sawe that hyt was tyme,
Tho chambur she wolde hym lede. — *To*

And when he was on slepe browght,
The qwene that was of wykked thowght, *wicked intention*
Tho chambur gan she wende. *To*
Hys letter she toke hym fro,
In a fyre she brente hyt tho; *burned it then*
Of werkes she was unhende. *actions; malicious*
Another lettur she made wyth evyll, *wrote; evil*
And sayde the qwene had born a devyll;
Durste no mon come her hende. *dared; man; near*
Thre heddes hadde he there, *three heads*
A lyon, a dragon, and a beere: *bear*
A fowll feltred fende. *foul matted-haired fiend*

On the morn when hyt was day,
The messenger wente on hys way,
Bothe by stye and strete; *path*
In trwe story as y say,
Tyll he come theras the kynge laye, *where; was*
And speke wordus swete.
He toke the kyng the lettur yn honde,
And he hyt redde, y unthurstonde,
The teres downe gan he lete. *shed*
And as he stode yn redyng, *reading*
Downe he fell yn sowenyng,
For sorow hys herte gan blede.

Grete lordes that stode hym by
Toke up the kyng hastely;
In herte he was full woo.
Sore he grette and sayde, "Alas, *wept*
That y evur man born was!
That hyt evur shullde be so. *should*
Alas, that y was made a kynge,
And sygh wedded the fayrest thyng *then*
That on erthe myght go.
That evur Jesu hymself wolde sende
Such a fowle, lothly fende *fiend*
To come bytwene us too."

When he sawe hyt myght no bettur be,
Anothur lettur then made he,
And seled hyt wyth hys sele. *sealed*
He commanded yn all thynge *respects*
To kepe well that lady yynge *care for*
Tyll she hadde her hele; *health*
Bothe gode men and ylle
To serve her at her wylle,
Bothe yn wo and wele. *woe; joy*
He toke thys lettur of hys honde, *[The messenger]; from*
And rode thorow the same londe, *through*
By the kyngus modur castell. *mother's*

And then he dwelled ther all nyght;
He was resseyved and rychely dyght *attended*
And wyst of no treson. *knew; treason*
He made hym well at ese and fyne,
Bothe of brede, ale and wyne,
And that berafte hym hys reson. *took away from him his reason*
When he was on slepe browght,
The false qwene hys lettur sowghte. *examined*
Into the fyre she kaste hyt downe:
Another lettur she lette make, *had made*
That men sholde the lady take, *[Indicating] that*
And lede her owt of towne,

And putte her ynto the see,
In that robe of ryche ble, *color*
The lytyll chylde her wyth;
And lette her have no spendyng, *money*
For no mete ny for drynke,
But lede her out of that kyth. *land*
"Upon payn of chylde and wyfe
And also upon your owene lyfe,[1]
Lette her have no gryght!" *shelter*
The messenger knewe no gyle, *guile*

---

[1] *On sentence of death for the child and wife / And for fear of your own life*

But rode hom mony a myle,   *many*
  By forest and by fryght.   *wilderness*

And when the messenger come home,   *came*
The steward toke the lettur sone,
  And bygan to rede.
Sore he syght and sayde, "Alas,   *sighed*
Sertes thys ys a fowle case,   *Surely; wicked situation*
  And a delfull dede!"   *cruel*
And as he stode yn redyng,
He fell downe yn swonygne;
  For sorow hys hert gan blede.
Ther was nothur olde ny yynge,   *neither*
That myghte forbere of wepynge   *forbear*
  For that worthy unthur wede.

The lady herde gret dele yn halle;   *dole (lamentation)*
On the steward gan she calle,
  And sayde, "What may thys be?"
Yyf anythyng be amys,   *amiss*
Tell me what that hyt ys,
  And lette not for me."   *withhold nothing from*
Then sayde the steward, verament,   *truly*
"Lo, her a lettur my lord hath sente,   *here*
  And therfore woo ys me!"
She toke the lettur and bygan to rede;
Then fonde she wryten all the dede,
  How she moste ynto the see.   *must [be put]*

"Be stylle, syr," sayde the qwene,
"Lette syche mornynge bene;   *mourning*
  For me have thou no kare.   *care*
Loke thou be not shente,   *dishonored*
But do my lordes commaundement,   *obey*
  God forbede thou spare.
For he weddede so porely
On me, a sympull lady,   *simple (humble)*
  He ys ashamed sore.
Grete well my lord fro me,   *Greet*

So gentyll of blode yn Cristyanté, — *a child*
  Gete he nevur more!" — *Beget*

Then was ther sorow and myche woo,
When the lady to shype shulde go; — *had to go*
  They wepte and wronge her hondus. — *their hands*
The lady that was meke and mylde,
In her arme she bar her chylde,
  And toke leve of the londe.
When she wente ynto the see
In that robe of ryche ble,
  Men sowened on the sonde. — *swooned; shore*
Sore they wepte and sayde, "Alas, — *Sorrowfully*
Certys thys ys a wykked kase! — *Surely; case*
  Wo worth dedes wronge!" — *Woe come to evil deeds*

The lady and the lytyll chylde
Fleted forth on the watur wylde, — *Floated*
  Wyth full harde happes. — *harsh fortunes*
Her surkote that was large and wyde, — *overcoat*
Therwyth her vysage she gan hyde, — *face*
  Wyth the hynthur lappes; — *outer folds*
She was aferde of the see,
And layde her gruf uponn a tre, — *face down; plank*
  The chylde to her pappes. — *breasts*
The wawes that were grete and strong,
On the bote faste they thonge, — *struck*
  Wyth mony unsemely rappes. — *hard blows*

And when the chyld gan to wepe,
Wyth sory herte she songe hyt aslepe, — *sang*
  And putte the pappe yn hys mowth,
And sayde, "Myghth y onus gete lond, — *once get to*
Of the watur that ys so stronge, — *Off*
  By northe or by sowthe,
Wele owth y to warye the, see, — *ought; curse you sea*
I have myche shame yn the!"
  And evur she lay and growht; — *grieved*
Then she made her prayer

To Jhesu and Hys modur dere,
In all that she kowthe. — *all [ways]; knew*

Now thys lady dwelled thore
A full sevene nyght and more,
As hyt was Goddys wylle;
Wyth karefull herte and sykyng sore, — *sighing*
Such sorow was her yarked yore, — *destined for her long ago*
And she lay full stylle.
She was dryven toward Rome,
Thorow the grace of God yn trone, — *Through; on throne*
That all thyng may fulfylle.
On the see she was so harde bestadde,
For hungur and thurste allmost madde,
Wo worth chawnses ylle! — *Accursed be such bad luck*

A marchaunte dwelled yn that cyté,
A ryche mon of golde and fee, — *property*
Jurdan was hys name.
Every day wolde he
Go to playe hym by the see,
The eyer forto tane. — *air; take*
He wente forth yn that tyde,
Walkynge by the see syde,
All hymselfe alone.
A bote he fonde by the brymme — *boat; shore*
And a fayr lady therynne,
That was ryght wo-bygone.

The cloth on her shon so bryght,
He was aferde of that syght,
For glysteryng of that wede; — *glittering; robe*
And yn hys herte he thowghth ryght — *directly*
That she was non erthyly wyght; — *earthly*
He sawe nevur non such yn leede.[1]
He sayde, "What hette ye, fayr ladye?" — *are you called*

---

[1] *He had never seen such [a beautiful one] among the people*

"Lord," she sayde, "y hette Egarye,
That lye her, yn drede."   *Who lies here in dread*
Up he toke that fayre ladye
And the yonge chylde her by,
And hom he gan hem lede.

When he come to hys byggynge,   *dwelling*
He welcomed fayr that lady yynge
That was fayr and bryght;
And badde hys wyf yn all thynge,
Mete and drynke forto brynge
To the lady ryght.
"What that she wyll crave,   *Whatever*
And her mowth wyll hyt have,
Loke hyt be redy dyght.   *prepared*
She hath so longe meteles be,
That me thynketh grette pyté;
Conforte her yyf thou myght."   *Restore*

Now the lady dwelles ther,
Wyth alle metes that gode were,   *foods; good*
She hedde at her wylle.   *had*
She was curteys yn all thyng,
Bothe to olde and to yynge;
Her loved bothe gode and ylle.
The chylde bygan forto thryfe;   *thrive*
He wax the fayrest chyld on lyfe,
Whyte as flour on hylle.
And she sewed sylke werk yn bour,   *bower*
And tawghte her sone nortowre,   *son; manners*
But evyr she mornede stylle.   *always; mourned*

When the chylde was seven yer olde,
He was bothe wyse and bolde,
And wele made of flesh and bone;
He was worthy unthur wede
And ryght well kowthe pryke a stede;   *ride*
So curtays a chylde was none.
All men lovede Segramowre,

Bothe yn halle and yn bowre,
Whersoevur he gan gone.
Leve we at the lady clere of vyce,
And speke of the kyng of Galys,
Fro the sege when he come home. *seige*

Now the sege broken ys,
The kyng come home to Galys,
Wyth mykyll myrthe and pryde;
Dukes and erles of ryche asyce, *assize (estate)*
Barones and knyghtes of mykyll pryse, *great esteem*
Come rydynge be hys syde. *by*
Syr Kadore, hys steward thanne,
Ayeyn hym rode wyth mony a man, *Toward*
As faste as he myght ryde.
He tolde the kyng aventowres *adventures*
Of hys halles and hys bowres,
And of hys londys wyde. *lands*

The kyng sayde, "By Goddys name,
Syr Kadore, thou art to blame
For thy fyrst tellynge! *For telling me these things first*
Thow sholdest fyrst have tolde me *should*
Of my lady Egaré,
I love most of all thyng!"
Then was the stewardes herte wo, *woeful*
And sayde, "Lorde, why sayst thou so?
Art not thou a trewe kynge?
Lo her, the lettur ye sente me, *here*
Yowr owene self the sothe may se;
I have don your byddynge." *done; bidding*

The kyng toke the lettur to rede,
And when he sawe that ylke dede, *same*
He wax all pale and wanne.
Sore he grette and sayde, "Alas, *grieved*
That evur born y was,
Or evur was made manne!
Syr Kadore, so mot y the, *so might I thrive*

Thys lettur come nevur fro me; *came*
I telle the her anone!" *you here at once*
Bothe they wepte and yaf hem ylle. *lamented; berated themselves*
"Alas!" he sayde, "Saf Goddys wylle!" *save*
And both they sowened then. *of them swooned*

Grete lordes stode by,
And toke up the kyng hastyly;
Of hem was grete pyté;
And when they both kevered were, *recovered*
The kyng toke hym the letter ther
Of the heddys thre. *[Which told] of*
"A, lord," he sayde, "be Goddus grace,
I sawe nevur thys lettur yn place!
Alas, how may thys be?"
Aftur the messenger ther they sente,
The kyng askede what way he went:
"Lord, be your modur fre." *by*

"Alas!" then sayde the kynge,
"Whethur my modur wer so unhende *was so malicious*
To make thys treson?
By my krowne she shall be brent, *burned*
Wythowten any othur jugement; *further trial*
That thenketh me best reson!"
Grete lordes toke hem betwene *decided between them*
That they wolde exyle the qwene
And berefe her hyr renowne. *deprive; honors (rank)*
Thus they exiled the false qwene
And byrafte her hyr lyflothe clene: *deprived; livelihood completely*
Castell, towre and towne.

When she was fled ovur the see fome,
The nobull kyng dwelled at hom,
Wyth full hevy chere;
Wyth karefull hert and drury mone, *sorrowful moan*
Sykynges made he many on *Sighings*
For Egarye the clere. *fair*
And when he sawe chylderen play,

He wepte and sayde, "Wellawey,
  For my sone so dere!"
Such lyf he lyved mony a day,
That no mon hym stynte may, *could stop him (from mourning)*
  Fully seven yere.

Tyll a thowght yn hys herte come,
How hys lady whyte as fome,
  Was drowned for hys sake.
"Thorow the grace of God yn trone,
I woll to the Pope of Rome,
  My penans for to take!" *penance*
He lette ordeyne shypus fele *He ordered many ships to be readied*
And fylled hem full of wordes wele, *worldly wealth*
  Hys men mery wyth to make.
Dolys he lette dyghth and dele, *Alms he had prepared and distributed*
For to wynnen hym sowles hele; *soul's health*
  To the shyp he toke the gate. *took his way*

Shypmen that wer so mykyll of pryce, *much*
Dyght her takull on ryche acyse, *Prepared their tackle; manner*
  That was fayr and fre.
They drowgh up sayl and leyd out ore; *drew*
The wynde stode as her lust wore, *The wind blew just as they desired*
  The wethur was lythe on le. *fair and calm*
They sayled over the salt fome,
Thorow the grace of God in trone,
  That most ys of powsté. *power*
To that cyté, when they come,
At the burgeys hous hys yn he nome, *he took his lodging*
  Theras woned Emarye. *Where dwelled*

Emaré called her sone
Hastely to here come
  Wythoute ony lettynge, *delay*
And sayde, "My dere sone so fre,
Do a lytull aftur me, *Do [just] as I shall tell you for a little while*
  And thou shalt have my blessynge.
Tomorowe thou shall serve yn halle,

In a kurtyll of ryche palle, *tunic; fabric*
Byfore thys nobull kyng.
Loke, sone, so curtays thou be, *See to it*
That no mon fynde chalange to the *fault with you*
In no manere thynge! *any way*

When the kyng ys served of spycerye, *dessert*
Knele thou downe hastylye,
And take hys hond yn thyn.
And when thou hast so done,
Take the kuppe of golde sone, *quickly*
And serve hym of the wyne.
And what that he speketh to the, *what[ever]*
Cum anon and tell me,
On Goddus blessyng and myne!"
The chylde wente ynto the hall,
Among the lordes grete and small,
That lufsumme wer unthur lyne. *handsome; linen*

Then the lordes that wer grete,
Wysh and wente to her mete; *Washed; their*
Menstrelles browght yn the kowrs. *course*
The chylde hem served so curteysly, *them*
All hym loved that hym sy, *saw*
And spake hym gret honowres.
Then sayde all that loked hym upon,
So curteys a chylde sawe they nevur non,
In halle ny yn bowres. *nor*
The kynge sayde to hym yn game, *joyfully*
"Swete sone, what ys thy name?"
"Lorde," he seyd, "y hyghth Segramowres." *I am called*

Then that nobull kyng
Toke up a grete sykynge, *Began; sighing*
For hys sone hyght so; *was named the same*
Certys, wythowten lesynge, *lying*
The teres out of hys yen gan wryng; *eyes*
In herte he was full woo.
Neverthelese, he lette be, *controlled himself*

And loked on the chylde so fre,
  And mykell he lovede hym thoo. — *greatly; then*
The kyng sayde to the burgeys anon, — *burgess*
"Swete syr, ys thys thy sone?"
  The burgeys sayde, "Yoo." — *Yes*

Then the lordes that wer grete
Whesshen ayeyn aftyr mete, — *Washed again*
  And then come spycerye. — *came the sweets*
The chylde that was of chere swete, — *sweet face*
On hys kne downe he sete, — *knee*
  And served hym curteyslye.
The kynge called the burgeys hym tyll,
And sayde, "Syr, yf hyt be thy wyll,
  Yyf me thys lytyll body! — *give; fellow*
I shall hym make lorde of town and towr;
Of hye halles and of bowre,
  I love hym specyally." — *specially*

When he had served the kyng at wylle, — *willingly*
Fayr he wente hys modyr tyll — *went; to*
  And tellys her how hyt ys.
"Soone, when he shall to chambur wende,
Take hys hond at the grete ende, — *(see note)*
  For he ys thy fadur, ywysse; — *most certainly*
And byd hym come speke wyth Emaré,
That changed her name to Egaré,
  In the londe of Galys."
The chylde wente ayeyn to halle,
Amonge the grete lordes alle,
  And served on ryche asyse. — *in splendid manner*

When they wer well at ese afyne, — *finally*
Bothe of brede, ale and wyne,
  They rose up, more and myn. — *less*
When the kyng shulde to chambur wende,
He toke hys hond at the grete ende,
  And fayre he helpe hym yn; — *courteously*
And sayde, "Syr, yf your wyll be,

Take me your honde and go wyth me, *Give me*
For y am of yowr kynne! *kin*
Ye shull come speke wyth Emaré
That chaunged her nome to Egaré,
That berys the whyte chynne." *bears*

The kyng yn herte was full woo
When he herd mynge tho *mention then*
Of her that was hys qwene;
And sayde, "Sone, why sayst thou so?
Wherto umbraydest thou me of my wo? *Why reproach*
That may never bene!" *(What you say)*
Nevurtheles wyth hym he wente;
Ayeyn hem come the lady gent, *Toward*
In the robe bryght and shene. *shining*
He toke her yn hys armes two,
For joye they sowened, both to, *swooned; two*
Such love was hem bytwene.

A joyfull metyng was ther thore,
Of that lady, goodly unthur gore, *gown*
Frely in armes to folde. *Gently; embrace*
Lorde, gladde was Syr Kadore,
And othur lordes that ther wore, *were*
Semely to beholde.
Of the lady that was put yn the see,
Thorow grace of God in Trinité,
That was kevered of cares colde. *recovered*
Leve we at the lady whyte as flour,
And speke we of her fadur the emperour,
That fyrste thys tale of ytolde.

The Emperour her fadyr then
Was woxen an olde man, *Had grown into*
And thowght on hys synne:
Of hys thowghtyr Emaré *daughter*
That was putte ynto the see,
That was so bryght of skynne.
He thowght that he wolde go,

For hys penance to the Pope tho *then*
  And heven for to wynne. *salvation*
Messengeres he sente forth sone,
And they come to the kowrt of Rome *court*
  To take her lordes inne. *prepare their; lodging*

Emaré prayde her lord, the kyng, *asked*
"Syr, abyde that lordys komyng *await; coming*
  That ys so fayr and fre.
And, swete syr, yn all thyng,
Aqweynte you wyth that lordyng, *acquaint*
  Hyt ys worshyp to the." *honor*
The kyng of Galys seyde than,
"So grete a lord ys ther non,
  Yn all Crystyanté."
"Now, swete syr, whatevur betyde,
Ayayn that grete lord ye ryde,
  And all thy knyghtys wyth the."

Emaré tawghte her sone yynge,
Ayeyn the Emperour komynge, *coming (his arrival)*
  How that he sholde done: *behave*
"Swete sone, yn all thyng
Be redy wyth my lord the kyng,
  And be my swete sone!
When the Emperour kysseth thy fadur so fre,
Loke yyf he wyll kysse the,
  Abowe the to hym sone; *Bow*
And bydde hym come speke wyth Emaré,
That was putte ynto the see,
  Hymself yaf the dome." *gave; command*

Now kometh the Emperour of pryse; *most excellent*
Ayeyn hym rode the kyng of Galys,
  Wyth full mykull pryde.
The chyld was worthy unthur wede, *clothes*
A satte upon a nobyll stede, *He*
  By hys fadyr syde;
And when he mette the Emperour,

He valed hys hode wyth gret honour *lowered; hood*
And kyssed hym yn that tyde; *time*
And othur lordys of gret valowre, *valor*
They also kessed Segramowre;
In herte ys not to hyde.

The Emperours hert anamered gretlye *greatly*
Of the chylde that rode hym by
Wyth so lovely chere. *face*
Segramowre he stayde hys stede; *reined in*
Hys owene fadur toke good hede,
And othur lordys that ther were.
The chylde spake to the Emperour,
And sayde, "Lord, for thyn honour,
My worde that thou wyll here:
Ye shull come speke wyth Emaré
That changede her name to Egaré,
That was thy thowghthur dere." *daughter*

The Emperour wax all pale,
And sayde, "Sone, why umbraydest me of bale, *reproach; [my] evil*
And thou may se no bote?" *If; see no remedy*
"Syr, and ye wyll go wyth me, *if you*
I shall the brynge wyth that lady fre, *gentle*
That ys lovesom on to loke." *lovely*
Nevurthelesse, wyth hym he wente;
Ayeyn hym come that lady gent,
Walkynge on her fote.
And the Emperour alyghte tho,
And toke her yn hys armes two,
And clypte and kyssed her sote. *embraced; sweet*

Ther was a joyfull metynge *meeting*
Of the Emperour and of the Kynge,
And also of Emaré;
And so ther was of Syr Segramour,
That aftyr was emperour:
A full gode man was he.
A grette feste ther was holde, *held*

Of erles and barones bolde,
As testymonyeth thys story. *testifies*
Thys ys on of Brytayne layes *one*
That was used by olde dayes,
Men callys "Playn d'Egarye."
Jhesus, that settes yn Thy trone,
So graunte us wyth The to wone *dwell*
In thy perpetuall glorye! Amen.

Explicit Emaré.

Notes

Abbreviations: MS: Cotton Caligula A.ii; Kö: Kölbing; G: Gough; M: Mills; F&H: French & Hale; R: Rickert; Ri: Ritson; Ru: Rumble; S: Sands. See Select Bibliography for full references.

1–12 Although most romances begin with a prayer or invocation, this one is somewhat longer than most. R claims that it is "the longest introductory prayer in any English romance" (p. 33).

2 The images of light which inform the opening prayer are pervasive throughout the tale. Emaré herself is frequently described as "fayr and bryght" and her robe is dazzling.

4 The narrator asks God for an act of "grace" which will inform the actions of both narrator and listener. The narrative that follows illustrates the grace given for virtuous action.

7–8 The poet appeals to the Virgin, praying that she will intercede to secure a place for humanity in heaven. This same intercession is sought by Emaré in lines 315, 671. Emaré, as the long-suffering mother of the next Holy Roman Emperor, is modeled after the Virgin: the Virgin is intercessor between humanity and heaven, so Emaré is the intercessor between the various worlds of the poem, eventually uniting three generations of men.

23 R discusses the derivation of the name "Emaré," assuming it is meant to contrast with "Egaré," a name Emaré adopts in line 360. "Egaré" comes from the OF *esgaree*, meaning "outcast." The word "Emaré," stems from OF *esmeree*, meaning "refined" or "excellent"; although it also could come from OF *esmarie*, meaning "afflicted or troubled" (*Emare*, p. xxix).

24 The narrator calls attention to his source quite frequently throughout the poem, though no direct source is known. See lines 115, 162, 216, 319.

52–54 See Beaumanoir's *La Manekine*, in which the queen, on her deathbed, urges the king to marry his own daughter. She insists on this only if the barons refuse to recognize the daughter as heir to the throne. If he takes a second wife, she charges him that she must look exactly like his first wife; obviously, the only woman who will resemble the queen will be her own daughter. Here, the death of Queen Erayne begins Emaré's series of misfortunes. See also Perrault's rendition of the popular folk narrative *Peau d'Ane* (Donkey Skin), which adheres to these same stipulations which impel the king toward incest. The child without one or both parents is a common feature in medieval romance and folklore. See Chaucer's Clerk's Tale, Physician's Tale, Knight's Tale, and *Perceval*, various *Tristrem* romances, tales of the young Arthur, *Le Freine*, *King Horn*, *Havelok*, and *Le Bone Florence of Rome*.

56 The nurse figure who nurtures and/or trains the young protagonist can also be found in the OF *La Belle Helene de Constantinople*. R (in her line note) makes several suggestions about the name "Abro." Probably it comes from the medieval Latin "Abra," meaning "female servant," though a corruption from Arabic might also be possible.

58–62 The narrator emphasizes Emaré's ability to embroider throughout the text. See lines 67, 376–84, 427–29, 730. Embroidery is also the Amerayle's daughter's forte. In Nicholas Trivet's *Anglo-Norman Chronicle*, Constance learns the seven liberal arts and numerous foreign languages. See also *Le Bone Florence of Rome* (lines 58–63): "He set to scole that damsyell, / Tyll sche cowde of the boke telle, / And all thynge dyscrye, / Be that she was xv yere olde, / Wel she cowde as men me tolde, / Of harpe and sawtyre."

66 *whyte*. MS: *whythe*.

68 MS: *All he*.

77 A: *And*. R and M emend to read *A ledde*, meaning "he led," as in line 989.

78 *Playnge* may well carry sexual connotations here; see line 254.

83 The earliest medieval silks came from Sicily where schools of silk weavers were famous from the mid-twelfth century onward. Arab invasion and occupation of the island from 827 to 1091 placed skilled weavers and designers from the Middle East on the island. Later, under the Norman kings who conquered the island in 1091, the weaving industry continued to thrive, especially in Palermo. Palermo silks were highly prized in cathedrals and courts throughout Europe.

Rickert notes that the cloth is similar to actual cloths woven in Palermo; she cites Michel, *Recherches sur le Commerce, la Fabrication et l'Usage des Etoffes de Soie, d'Or, et d'Argent* (Paris: Impr. de Crapelet, 1852-54), esp. vol. II, 354–55. She also speculates on potential connections between characters in the text and historical personages (Introduction, pp. xxxi-xxxii). The wealth associated with the cloth can be ascertained in comparison with statistics available on the cloth industry in medieval Europe. A fine piece of cloth from Brussels could easily be worth 800 grams of gold or one diamond, five rubies, and five emeralds.

83–180 The robe described in this passage is a key image in the poem (see introduction). The long description of the parade of fairy ladies in *Sir Launfal* has a similar effect, though placed toward the end of the narrative. *Galeran de Bretagne*, lines 509–51, presents a description of an elegant cloth. In that romance, the female child is abandoned wrapped in a cloth on which are embroidered two couples: Paris and Helen, and Floris and Blancheflor (see notes to *Le Freine)*. For actual elegant fabrics, embroidery, and garments worn during the period, whether European or Byzantine, see Eunice R. Goddard, *Women's Costume in French Texts of the Eleventh and Twelfth Centuries*, The Johns Hopkins Studies in Romance Literatures and Languages, vol. 7 (Baltimore: Johns Hopkins University Press, 1927; rpt. New York: Johnson, 1973); Mary G. Houston, *Medieval Costume in England & France, the 13th, 14th and 15th Centuries*, A Technical History of Costume, vol. 3 (London: Adam & Charles Black, 1939); Mary G. Houston, *Ancient Greek, Roman and Byzantine Costume and Decoration*, 2nd ed., A Technical History of Costume, vol. 2 (London: Adam & Charles Black, 1947; rpt. New York: Barnes & Noble, 1965); Joan Evans, *Dress in Medieval France* (Oxford: Clarendon, 1952); *Opus Anglicanum: English Medieval Embroidery* (London: Victoria and Albert Museum, 1963); Blanche Payne, *History of Costume* (New York: Harper & Row, 1965), especially her chapters on the twelfth, thirteenth, and fourteenth centuries, pp. 157–97; Pauline Johnstone, *The Byzantine Tradition in Church Embroidery* (London: Tiranti, 1967); Cyril G. E. Bunt, *Byzantine Fabrics* (Leigh-on-Sea: F. Lewis, 1967); Maurice Lombard, *Les Textiles dans le monde musulman du VIIe au XIIe siecle* (Paris: Mouton, 1978); Stella M. Newton, *Fashion in the Age of the Black Prince: A Study of the Years 1340–1365* (Woodbridge: Boydell Press, 1980); Kay Staniland, *Embroiderers* (Toronto: University of Toronto, 1991). Mary Houston's texts are especially useful because they identify the MSS which contain the visual images. She notes that ornamental woven and embroidered textiles reached "their finest and fullest development . . . [in] the last half of the thirteenth century and the beginning of the fourteenth" (*Medieval Costume*, p. 62). In her study of Byzantine costume, Houston discusses the shroud of Byzantine Emperor Honorius' wife, Maria, which, when it was melted down, yielded 36 lbs. of pure gold (*Ancient,* p. 134). Houston notes that the extant examples of royal Byzantine costume, from the tenth to the thirteenth centuries were dignified in construction and elegant to an extreme. Gem studdings are not uncommon. Cloaks of the Byzantine royal household often contained embroidered panels, called *tablion* "which was an important feature of men's court dress from the fifth to the tenth century, and even later. On it was lavished the most sumptuous decoration of the whole costume. As a rule, it was a cloth of gold embroidered in jewels. The Empresses wore it also from the eighth to the eleventh century, but otherwise it was confined to the Emperor and his nobles" (p. 136). The use of embroidery for illustration in cloth can be seen in the depiction of the adoration of the Magi which forms the substantial border of Empress Theodora's cloak, represented in a sixth-century mosaic in the church of S. Vitali, Ravenna. (It is represented by Houston's figs. 148a and 148b on p. 137.) Houston also discusses a carved ivory panel depicting the bejewelled and embroidered court costumes of Emperor Romanus and Empress Eudocia who reigned in Constantinople from 1068 to 1071 (*Ancient*, pp. 150–51). She notes that Byzantine costume influenced the Western courts and ecclesiastical dress considerably; Western Europe imitated the elegance, design, and expense of Byzantine clothings. See, for example, her fig. 167a (p. 157) depicting the German emperor which demonstrates this line of influence. In the *Rotuli litterarum clausarum in turri londinensi asservati* by Thomas D. Hardy (London: Eyre and Spottiswoode, 1833–44), vol. 1, 54, King John is reported (in an inventory from 1205) as having a royal robe made of Eastern silk which was studded with sapphires, cameos, pearls, emeralds, rubies, and turquoise. And in Henry Thomas Riley's *Memorials of London and London Life in the 13th, 14th, and 15th Centuries* (London: Longmans, Green & Co. 1868), p. 44, Richard II in 1377 is reported to have used hats and hoods as security for a loan. One was made of scarlet, embroidered with rubies, balasses, diamonds, sapphires, and large pearls; the others were cloth or fur studded with embroidered gems. Magic clothes are a feature of the Cinderella folktale. *Emaré* shares several features of the widespread Cinderella tradition. See Alan Dundes, *Cinderella: A Folklore Casebook* (New York: Garland, 1982); Marian Roalfe Cox, *Cinderella* (London: David Nutt, 1893); Anna Birgitta Rooth, *The Cinderella Cycle* (Lund: C. W. K. Gleerup, 1951). Also compare her cloak with the pilgrim's sclavin in Langland where it is covered with protective metals (*Piers Plowman*, B text V, 527–31, ed., W. W. Skeat [London: Oxford University Press, 1886], I, 180):

> An hundreth of ampulles · on his hatt seten,
> Signes of Synay · and shelles of Galice;
> And many a cruche on his cloke · and keyes of Rome,
> And the vernicle bifore · for men shulde knowe,
> And se bi his signes whom he soughte hadde.

85 The MS includes the word *hyght* at the end of the line. The word is blotted and, since it disrupts the meter, Kö and G considered it erased. Ru, M, and F&H all leave the word out; R leaves it in.

91 Gems, "stuffed with ymagerye" (line 168), were thought to possess virtues (or powers). Lapidaries, or guides to stones and their qualities, were popular in the Middle Ages. The *Peterborough Lapidary* (*PbL*) and several others mentioned in subsequent notes are gathered in a collection called *English Mediaeval Lapidaries*, ed. Joan Evans and Mary S. Serjeantson EETS o.s. 190 (London: Oxford University Press, 1933). The correspondence between the stones on Emaré's robe and the virtue of the gems is discussed by Hanspeter Schelp; however, he selects only those qualities of the stones which are consistent with his religious/moral reading of *Emaré*. On the virtues of stones, see Chaucer's *Romaunt of the Rose*:

> Rychesse a girdell hadde upon,
> The bokel of it was of a stoon
> Of vertu gret and mochel of myght,
>
> . . . .
>
> The mourdaunt wrought in noble wise,
> Was of a stoon full precious,
> That was so fyn and vertuous,
> That hol a man it coude make
> Of palasie, and of toth-ake.
> (lines 1085–87, 1094–98)

And Langland's *Piers Plowman*: "Fetislich hir fyngres · were fretted with golde wyre / And there-on red rubyes · as red as any glede / And diamantz of derrest pris · and double manere safferes, / Orientales and ewages · enuenymes to destroye" (B text, II, 11–14). For *topaze*, see notes to line 139; for *rubies*, see line note 130.

94 *Crapowtes* were believed to originate in a toad's head. Toad-stones, in the *Peterborough Lapidary* (Evans and Serjeantson, p. 79), are "gode for medecyne and for venym, and ther as he is may no yvel be done. And he maketh a man and

woman myghty; also he maketh a man to incres fro day to day, and abounde in worthinnes. And some seyne that ther is one of the colour of wax, and he is gode to conquer batayls." *Nakette* is "agate," with the n from the definite article allided to the initial vowel. The "Achate," or agate in the *PbL* "temporeth softly and comforteth old men . . . . All the maner of achates ben god ayens venymm and ayens bighting of serpentes and he kepeth A man fro evell thinges; and he encresite strengthe and maketh god spekyng togeder and creable and of goode colour; he geveth gode consayl and he maketh good beleve, he holpeth the plesauns to god and to the wordell." Of another color of Agate, the writer claims "Men trowen that the fyft maner ther-of helpith wich-crafte, for ther-with thei changen tempest and stauncheth ryvers and stremes" (pp. 64-65). R suggests that this stone is "nacre," meaning mother-of-pearl. In this and subsequent notes, I have provided fuller quotations from the lapidaries (I have regularizing u/v, i/j, þ, and writing out abbreviations).

104 The Emperor's comment points to the possibility of reading the effect of the cloth as an enchantment.

111 The fact that the Saracen princess makes the cloth "wyth pryde" opens up the possibility for reading the cloth as sinful or as inappropriately powerful, although it also attests to the perfection of craft in the garment. See introduction.

113 Azure was a highly esteemed color for cloth in the Middle Ages.

121–56 R notes similarities between this description and a passage in *Mai und Beaflor* where a young woman wears a marvelous robe.

122 Ydoyne and Amadas are well-known lovers. Amadas is not of the same rank as his beloved Ydoyne; he goes through a long series of sufferings and trials before he wins her. The similarity with Emaré only occurs in the extreme trials that must be endured and in Emaré's statement that she is "symple" and lowborn (although this is not true at all). Her rank and lineage are what confer upon her son the title of emperor. The tale of Ydoyne and Amadas, also woven in a cloth, is described in *Sir Degrevant* (lines 1477–78).

125 The "trewe-love-flour" is an herb whose four leaves resemble a love knot. It is mentioned in *Sir Gawain and the Green Knight* (line 612).

127 *Carbunkull*, "schineth as feyre whose schynyng is not overcom by nyght" (*PbL*, 82). *Saffere*, or sapphire, "distrowen fowlnes and envy, and comforteth the body and membres, and letteth the man fro enprisonyng; and he that with the saphir towcheth the iiij places of the prison or of the cheynes, if he have gode beleve he schal be delyverd by vertu of the ston . . . The bok tellen us that the saphir is wel good to acord men togidder, and to brek wyche-craft; and it is mych worthe to hele byles and swellyng; if it be geven to him that have byles or swellyng within the body, anon he schall be hole by vertu that gode hathe gyven therto; and it schall kele the body of hot syknes, and do away the sorow of the hede, and it helpeth the seknes of goomes, and it chaseth owte the ange of yene . . . it maketh a man to have wyte and myght . . . Also this ston was of gret autorite in old tyme, that men seyd that they wold holowgh it to hir god, and so it was syngulerly holowed to her god appolyne. For when nacioun̄s axedet consel of appolyn in tyme of sacrifice, they hope to be certefy and to have answer the rather if saphir ston wer present" (*PbL*, 101–02).

128 *Kassydonys* is Chalcedony: "Calcidonice is a ston of white pale coler . . . and it cometh owt of the est, and it is lik to cristal; and he that bereth him schall be wel spekyng and ful of gret eloquens; and if he have eny ple or cause, schwe the stone to his adversary, and it schall helpe him in his cause . . . and if a man be juged thorow fals jugement this wol nat leve fro him that he schall not be lost from him; and he schall love the service of god whiles he bereth him clen" (*PbL*, 75). *Onyx* can "kepeth him saaf and encreseth his bewte. The onycle is blak of color . . . . He doeth away fantasies, and maketh a man to hawe gret dremes, and he maketh a man hardy in fyght, and he helpeth a man in plee, and so to conquer his ryght. . . . He that bereth it schal have many gode graces" (*PbL*, 115–16). In the *London Lapidary*, its blackness "signifieth the synne of man and also the tendrenesse of . . . the flesshe that is alwey freele to falle"(*PbL*, 27).

130 *Deamondes*: "The lapidare seyth us that god gave many fayre vertues and grace to the diamond, that if a man bere it in strenth and vertu, it kepith him fro grevance, metinges and temtacions, and fro venym . . . it defendeth him fro his enemyis; . . . also it kepth the sed of man wythinne the wombe of his wyfe, and it helpeth the child and kepeth the childis membres hole" (*PbL*, 83). And the *London Lapidary* observes: "holy he shal be that this vertuouse ston berith in clennesse"(p. 31). On *Rubyes*, the *London Lapidary* says: "the gentil rubie fyne and clene is lorde of stones and is also of water of waters" (pp. 21–22).

132 *glewe.* MS: *Gle.* Emended by G, R, F&H, Ru, and M to maintain the rhyme scheme.

134 Tristrem and Isowde is a famous story of adulterous love; in some versions of their story, however, the magic potion is emphasized. The fated nature of the two lovers' suffering and their separations are similar to Emaré's fate; however, adultery is never an issue here.

139 *Topase*: "He that bereth this ston schall love to lede his body chastly, and then mor to loke hevenly wayes . . . In the tresor of kyngges no thyng is mor cler nor mor preciose then this preciose ston is . . . he helpeth ayens the passioun of lynatik folke . . . . Also he stancheth blode, and he helpeth hem that han the emoroides and swageth him. And he wold not suffre fervent water for to boile, as it is seyd in bokes. Dias seythe that it asswageth bothe wrath and sorowgh, and it helpeth ayens yvel thowghtes and frenesesy, and ayens soden dethe" (*PbL*, pp. 106–07).

146 Florys and Blawncheflour's idyllic courting takes place in a Middle Eastern setting, exotic for medieval English listeners. The story was popular. See F. C. de Vries, ed., *Floris and Blanchefleur* (Dissertation, 1930; rpt. Groningen Drukkerijv Press, 1966); A. B. Taylor, ed., *Floire et Blancheflor* (Oxford: Clarendon Press, 1927). It is also available in S and F&H.

151 *knyghtus and senatowres.* These nouns seem out of place in a list of gems. R suggests "Ther were onyx and centaureus."

152 *Emerawde* "is a ston that overpasseth al the grennesse of grenhede; . . .and the esmeraude cometh owte of the lond of tyre by a water of paradis. Nero hathe a myrrour of this ston wherein he loked, and he wyst by the vertu of this stone al that he wole seke or deseyre. It encresseth ryches and maketh word of man dredfull. Also is myche worthe ayens the gowte and ayens tempest and ayenes lechery. . . "(*PbL*, 85). The *Sloane Lapidary* says: "it mendeth the sight of a man, and doth away great tempests of wethers" (p. 121); and the *North Midlands Lapidary* claims: "Emeraud helpys a man is eyn and kepes the syght" (p. 40).

vertues. M emends to *v[alowr]es* to preserve the rhyme scheme. See line 994.

154 *Coral*: "a ston that growcth in the red see as an erbe that is gren, and when it is owte in the eyr it wexyth hard and red and recembleth to a branche . . . it

kepeth away tempest and . . . delyverith a man fro fantaseys; ane it geveth a gode begynnyng and a gode endyng . . . . Also whoso bereth this stone upone him or one his fynger, he schal get love . . . . Wycches tellen that this stone withstondith lyghtynge; and Ised [Isidore of Seville] sayth the same, that it putteth away tempest and whirlewyndes" (*PbL* p. 77).

155 *Perydotes* may well be the "deadotes" described in the *PbL*: "He that bereth this ston, ther schall no fantasie overcom him. Also yf this ston towche a ded body thris, this body schall aryse and mowe by vertu of this ston, but he schall not speke neyther doe . . . a man schal never dye whiles this ston is upon him" (p. 84). *Crystall*: "a stone that conceyveth wel fyre of the sone bem. Also make pouder ther-of, gif it to the nurse to drynke, and it schal increse her mylke. . . Also he kepeth a man chast . . ."(*PbL*, 76).

156 *garnettes* are not listed in the English lapidaries. Anselmus Boetius de Boot published his *Gemmarum et Lapidum Historia* in Lyons in 1636, and it claims that the garnet protects against melancholia. See Joan Evans, *Magical Jewels of the Middle Ages and the Renaissance* (Oxford: Clarendon Press, 1922), pp. 152–53.

158 The Sultan of Babylon appears in a number of other Middle English texts; see *The Romaunce of the Sowdone of Babylone and of Ferumbras*, ed. Emil Hausknecht, EETS e.s. 38 (London: Trübner, 1881) and the *Sultan of Babylon* in *Three Middle English Charlemagne Romances*, ed. Alan Lupack (Kalamazoo: Medieval Institute Publications, 1990), pp. 1–103.

164 The unicorn is a symbol of virginity. It was, according to legend, notoriously vicious and wild; it could only be tamed by a virgin, and would lay its head in her lap. See John Williamson, *The Oak King, the Holly King and the Unicorn: The Myths and Symbolism of the Unicorn Tapestries* (New York: Harper and Row, 1986); Jurgen W. Einhorn, *Spiritalis unicornis: das Einhorn als Bedeutungstrager in Literatur und Kunst des Mittelalters* (Munchen: W. Fink, 1976).

168 *ymagerye*. See *Launfal* line 951 and Gower's *Confessio Amantis,* 5. 5771.

198 The idea of Emaré (and later Segramour) being "worthy under clothing" is emphasized and repeated throughout the lay. See Chaucer's Sir Thopas, line 2107: "So worthy under wede"; Second Nun's Tale, lines 132–33: "She, ful

devout and humble in hir corage, / Under hir robe of gold, that sat ful faire "; and the *Romaunce of the Rose*, lines 2684, 4754, and 6359.

202 *they go*. MS: *gan the go*.

218 *doun*. MS: *dou*.

223–28 Here, Syr Artyus's incestuous desires are revealed to the audience. See Elizabeth Archibald, "Incest in Medieval Literature and Society," *Forum for Modern Language Studies* 25 (1989), 1–15; James A. Brundage, *Law, Sex, and Christian Society in Medieval Europe* (Chicago: University of Chicago Press, 1987); David Herlihy, *Medieval Households* (Cambridge: Harvard University Press, 1985). See the theme developed in *Sir Degaré* and in Gower's "Apollonius of Tyre," "Canace and Machaire," and "Tale of Constance." The possessiveness of the father is also echoed in Chaucer's Physician's Tale. As with the Oedipal myth which featured mother-son incest, the Middle Ages' most well-known incest narrative featured a victimized male: St. Gregorius. See Hartmann von Aue, *Gregorius* (Tubingen: M. Niemeyer, 1984). See also the OF *La Belle Helene de Constantinople* and *La Manekine*.

219 *swythe*. MS: *swyde*. Ru's emendation.

239 A papal bull is, in this case, a dispensation from the laws of consanguinity.

245 This may be a hint of the fairy origins of Emaré. See also lines 396, 443, and 701.

247–49 The king now reveals his sexual desire for his daughter to her. It has been hinted in lines 188–89 and made clear to the audience in 223–28.

264 MS: *þorne*.

268 See Chaucer's Man of Law's Tale, line 439.

273 M emends *shate* to *shote*.

280 This sudden reversal in emotion, without any explanatory development or representation of internal debate, is common in the action-oriented romance or

lay. M (p. 199) points to *La Manekine*, lines 6697–714, as a text which represents a more gradual change of heart.

287 *yn*. MS: *vn*. R emends to *vp*, followed by M and F&H. G reconstructs the line to read: *And toke [hym] up [full] hastyly*.

303 *kelle* is usually glossed as "headdress" but could also mean "cloak," "garment," or "shroud," thus befitting the King rather than Emaré. M (p. 199) argues for the latter interpretation, noting also lines 612 and 938.

310 *Now* is inserted in the margin at the end of the line.

313–27 The image of the rudderless ship is a powerful one, both in Christian iconography of the Middle Ages and in the English literary tradition. Within the Christian tradition, the ship has often been used as an image of faith or of Holy Church. An extensive and excellent discussion of the iconography is available, with illustrations, in V. A. Kolve's chapter, "The Man of Law's Tale: The Rudderless Ship and the Sea," pp. 297–358 in his book, *Chaucer and the Imagery of Narrative: The First Five Canterbury Tales* (Stanford: Stanford University Press, 1984). Within the literary tradition of northern Europe, the image of Tristan and Isolde on their various ship journeys, the ship of faith and various other boats found in the Holy Grail quest narratives, the ships that carry souls from one world to another in dream visions and romances, and the image of the sorrowful mariner in the Old English "Song of the Wayfarer," are just a few well-known examples. See also Guillaume de Deguileville, *Pilgrimage of the Lyf of the Manhode*, ed. William A. Wright. (London: Roxburghe Club, 1869), pp. 190–92. See also the psychological-religiosity of the "at sea" image found, for example, in Hugh of St. Victor's treatise on Noah's Flood (*De arca Noe morali*): "let a man return to his own heart, and he will find there a stormy ocean lashed by the fierce billows of overwhelming passions and desires, which swamp the soul as often as by consent they bring it into subjection. For there is this flood in every man, as long as he lives in this corruptible life, where the flesh lusts against the spirit. Or rather, every man is in this flood, but the good are in it as those borne in ships upon the sea, whereas the bad are in it as shipwrecked persons at the mercy of the waves" (cited in Kolve, pp. 336–37); Hugh of St. Victor's text is available in his *Selected Spiritual Writings* (London: Faber, 1962).

314–15 See the Man of Law's Tale, lines 832–33: "In hym triste I, and in his mooder deere, / That is to me my seyl and eek my steere." See also lines 670–72 below.

Emaré

331 In the MS, this line is followed by line 338 which is crossed out and then repeated in the correct position.

357 *poynt.* MS: *poyn.* Universally emended to *poynt.*

366 *worthy.* MS: *wordy.*

377 MS: *sylky* is partially erased; I have emended to *sylkyn* following M, F&H, and Ru.

396 MS: *erdly.*

409 MS: *calle.*

411 This line was omitted and added in the margin of the MS.

415 M emends the line to *Then spakke the ryche ray* to parallel line 430.

441–50 This unearthly characteristic of Emaré is emphasized in the poem: see lines 245 and 396. Since the Queen considers Emaré a cast-off from her own land, possibly from the fairy world, and possibly a "fiend," note the complication added here if we consider Galatians 4:30 "What saith the scripture? Cast out the bondwoman and her son; for the son of the bondwoman shall not be heir with the son of the free woman."

445 M (p. 199) finds the word "unhende" to be consistent with "the deliberately low-keyed style" of the poem.

450 *the.* MS: *de.* Ru emends as I do.

481–95 R suggests that the passage may reflect "the last great Saracenic attempt upon Europe" which was conducted in 1212. Then, the King of Castile summoned help from other European countries to repel the Ottoman Empire's territorial advancements.

496 MS: *stward.*

499 *yn place* has been variously interpreted. In her notes, R suggests that the line be emended to "yn thylke place" meaning "as it was her place to do." Ru

interpolates place so that it becomes *palace*: "She wente wyth chylde yn palace." F&H gloss "place" as "there."

504 The birthmark in many romances, like *Havelok*, can serve to identify children who are separated somehow from their parents. Here, however, Segramowre is always with Emaré. It may indicate his later ascendence to the imperial throne, or it may be a hold-over from other folk materials where the birthmark identifies a lost child. See *Havelok*, line 604: "On his right shuldre a kine-merk," and lines 2139–47:

> So weren he war of a croiz full gent
> On his right shuldre swithe bright,
> Brighter than gold again the light
> So that he wiste, heye and lowe,
> That it was kunrick that he sawe.
> It sparkede and full brighte shon
> So doth the gode charbuncle ston
> That men see moughte by the light
> A penny chesen so was it bright.

F&H (p. 439) read this mark as indicating that both father and mother were of royal blood.

529 *he.* MS: *she.*

533 *tho.* MS: *do.* M leaves *do* with the gloss of "then." In fact, the scribe repeatedly interchanges *þ*, *d*, and *t*.

535–40 Although the motive for the evil mother-in-law is not certain here, Gower places his version of the story in a section on "Envy." In Chaucer's translation of the *Romaunt of the Rose*, Envy is portrayed as follows:

> And by that ymage, nygh ynough,
> Was peynted Envye, that never lough,
> Nor never wel in hir herte ferde,
> But if she outher saugh or herde
> Som gret myschaunce or gret disese.
> Nothyng may so moch hir plese
> As myschef and mysaventure;
> Or whan she seeth discomfiture
> Upon ony worthy man falle,

Than likith hir wel withalle.
She is ful glad in hir corage,
If she se any gret lynage
Be brought to nought in shamful wise.
. . . .
Envie is of such crueltee
That feith ne trouthe holdith she
To freend ne felawe, bad or good.
Ne she hath kyn noon of hir blood,
That she nys ful her enemy . . .
. . . .
I trowe that if Envie, iwis,
Knewe the beste man that is
On this side or biyonde the see,
Yit somwhat lakken hym wolde she;
And if he were so hende and wis
That she ne myght al abate his pris,
Yit wolde she blame his worthynesse,
Or by hir wordis make it lesse.
(lines 247–59, 265–69, 281–88)

540 See *Sir Gowther*, line 71: "a felturd fende."

558 MS: *That hyt euur so shullde be*. I have followed R's emendation which maintains the rhyme scheme. M, Ru, and F&H emend likewise.

580 R notes that *fyne* should probably be emended to *afyne* as in line 913.

587–97 See Shakespeare's *Winter's Tale* II, iii, 170-83. Leontes instructs Antigonus to abandon Perdita:

Mark and perform it — seest thou? for the fail
Of any point in't shall not only be
Death to thyself but to thy lewd-tongu'd wife
. . . . We enjoin thee,
As thou art liegeman to us, that thou carry
This female bastard hence, and that thou bear it
To some remote and desert place, quite out
Of our dominions; and that there thou leave it,
Without more mercy, to its own protection
And favour of the climate. As by strange fortune
It came to us, I do in justice charge thee,

> On thy soul's peril, and thy body's torture,
> That thou commend it strangely to some place
> Where chance may nurse or end it. Take it up.

594 *kith*. MS: *kygh*. G and Ru also emend to *kith*. The scribe frequently interchanges yoghs and thornes.

606 *delfull*. MS: *defull*. G's emendation, followed by others.

629 MS: *commaunndement*.

631–33 See Chaucer's Clerk's Tale, lines 463–83.

635 *blode*. MS: *blolde*.

667–68 Emaré asserts herself. See also Clerk's Tale, lines 1037–43.

684 *chawnses ylle*. M glosses as "tribulations," which is perhaps best.

685 MS: *dw led*. A blemish in the MS obliterates the "el."

685–87 Emaré winds up in the house of a merchant. In most versions of the narrative, the long-suffering wife is put to sea and then taken in by a Roman Senator. M argues that "the substitution of the merchant for the senator . . . makes very little difference, since he is a quite colourless character"(p. 200). But Ramsey notes that the lower aristocracy in the figure of Syr Kadore and the middle class in the figure of the burgess here indicates some criticism levelled at the aristocracy. If so, it is consistent with material found in most of the other English Breton lays which suggests that virtue often resides or can reside in those outside the centers of power or outside the court worlds.

688 MS: *Eeuery*.

692 *syde*. MS: *sythe*.

701 *erthyly*. MS: *erdyly*.

702 *such*. MS: *shuch*.

722 *metes.* MS: *mete.*

730 *sewed.* MS: *shewed.*

733–41 See Florent in *Octavian*. Mills writes, "here, as at other points in *Emaré*, vividness is sacrificed to the celebration of well-bred courtesy" (p. 200).

751 MS: *Kodore.*

780 *they.* MS: *the.*

792 *Lord.* MS: *Lor.*

799–804 M notes again that the sentence on the mother-in-law is softened. In other texts she is commonly killed. See *Octavian* and Chaucer's Man of Law's Tale.

820–22 M notes that "the king's wish to do penance is rather unexpected, as he had never, even in his thoughts, been guilty of his wife's death, but it enhances the parallelism between his situation and that of his father-in-law. In the Man of Law's Tale, it is remorse at having slain his own mother that brings the husband to Rome as a penitent" (lines 988–94).

838 *they.* MS: *the.*

839 In the MS, line 837 gets repeated after this one, but is then crossed out.

841 *her.* MS: *he.*

846 *shalt.* MS: *shat.*

867 *Menstrelles.* MS: *Mentrelles.*

897 In the MS, *chylde* is written and crossed out after the word *lytyll.*

905, 917 *grete ende.* The meaning of the phrase is obscure. R notes: "The 'great end' of the hand would naturally be the thumb (see also Italian *dito grosso*, Catalan *dit gros*, English *great toe*)" (p. 46). G, F&H, and M read *grece ende.* G glosses *grece* as stairs (from OF *gres*), thus, according to R, "top of the stairs." F&H gloss as "foot of the (dais) steps," and M as "foot of the steps." Ru reads *grete end* and observes: "possibly what is intended is the hall or stairway, leading from the central part of the building to the sleeping chambers, the 'great end' being that end nearest the central rooms" (p. 128).

943 *that.* MS: *wat.*

950 *was.* MS: *wax.* So emended by G, R, Ru and M.

973 *tawghte.* MS: *thawghte.*

989 Ri and G both emend *A* to *And*. R, Ru and M gloss the *A* as "he."

1000 *stayde*. MS: *sayde*. R's emendation. G emends to *say[s]de* (seized).

1024 *Segramour*. MS: *egramour.*

1030 See *Le Freine* where the evidence of the beautiful cloth confirms identity.

1032 MS: *playn þ garye*. The thorn can be interpreted as "the" or the French "de." "Complaint" is a verse form common in Celtic and Middle English literature. F&H (p. 455) suggest that "stories were often written around [complaints] to explain their existence and provide a setting."

1033 *Jhesus.* MS: *Ihe*. R transcribes *Ihero*; G, *Jesu*; F&H, *Ihesus*; M, *Jesus.*

1034 *wone*. MS: *wene*. I follow R's emendation, as does M.

Sir Launfal

Introduction

Thomas Chestre's *Sir Launfal*, written in the late fourteenth century, is preserved in only one early fifteenth-century manuscript: British Library MS Cotton Caligula A. ii. The Launfal narrative can be found in several medieval versions, however, the earliest of which is Marie de France's twelfth-century *Lanval*. *Sir Launfal* and *Lay le Freine* are the only two Middle English Breton Lays which can be traced directly back to Marie de France's collection. Marie claimed that her "lais" were translations of ancient Celtic tales of love and magic which she heard the Bretons sing. Her collection was written for an aristocratic audience and is preserved complete in one mid-thirteenth-century manuscript: British Library MS Harley 978. Selections and fragments of her lays are also preserved in at least four other manuscripts dating from the thirteenth and fourteenth centuries. Extant translations of Marie de France's *Lanval* can be found in Middle English and Old Norse; a Middle Dutch version (now lost) has also been posited.[1]

When Thomas Chestre composed his version of the narrative, he drew on three earlier texts, two of which survive. The immediate and primary source for Chestre is the 538-line Middle English *Sir Landevale*, which is an adaptation from Marie de France. It has been preserved in a number of manuscripts and early printed books. Verbal echoes of *Sir Landevale* are pronounced in Chestre's text; in fact, Chestre borrowed whole lines from it. The Old French lay of *Graelent* forms the other known source for *Sir Launfal*. This anonymous text, or some version of it, appears to be the source for four passages in *Sir Launfal*: Guenevere's conflict with Arthur's knights, Launfal's conversation with the mayor's daughter, the episode in which gifts are brought to Launfal's abode, and the disappearance of Gyfre and Blaunchard immedi-

[1] For the Old Norse see *Strengleikar eda Liodabok*, eds. R. Keyser and C. R. Unger (Feilberg & Landmark, 1850), and more recently, *Strengleikar: An Old Norse Translation of Twenty-One Old French Lais*, ed. Robert Cook and Mattias Tveitane (Oslo: Norsk historisk kjeldeskrift-institutt, 1979). The Middle Dutch version is posited by Wilhelm Hertz, *Spielmannsbuch* (Stuttgart: J. G. Cotta, 1900). *Lanval* has also been claimed to have influenced Italian and Middle High German narrative poems. For a critical edition of Marie de France's text, see *Le Lai de Lanval*, ed. Jean Rychner (Genéve: Droz, 1958).

ately after Launfal speaks of his fairy-lover.[2] Most scholars assume that Chestre used at least one other source (now lost) which probably contained the tournament at Carlisle and the Sir Valentyne episode. An analogue of this lengthy episode can be found in Andreas Capellanus's *The Art of Courtly Love* (*De Amore*).[3]

The dialect features of Chestre's *Launfal* suggest that its scribe may have been Kentish, although the problems presented in the language of the text are considerable.[4] The scribal hand of the manuscript is clear but the orthography is problematic, and, as A. J. Bliss has commented, it presents "peculiarities" which record the effects of phonological and orthographic changes occurring in language sound and written hand in the early fifteenth century.[5] *Sir Launfal* is a tail-rhyme romance and shares the form with at least twenty-three other tail-rhyme romances written in the fourteenth century.[6] It is, thus, a more popular and less aristocratic poem than the highly crafted *Lanval* by Marie de France. A. C. Spearing has recently labelled Chestre's poem "a fascinating disaster."[7] Chaucer's parody of tail-rhyme romances in the Tale of Sir Thopas presents a courtly and educated parody of the more popular form.[8]

---

[2] See *Graelent and Guingamor: Two Breton Lays*, ed. and trans. Russell Weingartner (New York: Garland, 1985). For a critical edition, see E. Margaret Grimes, ed., *The Lays of Desiré, Graelent and Melion* (New York: Institute of French Studies, 1928), pp. 76–101.

[3] See *Andreas Capellanus on Love*, trans. P. G. Walsh (London: Duckworth, 1982), pp. 271–85, or *The Art of Courtly Love*, trans. John Jay Parry (New York: Norton, 1969), pp. 177–86. Another analogue, identified by Roger Sherman Loomis in his *Arthurian Tradition & Chrétien de Troyes* (New York: Columbia University Press, 1949) and discussed by A. J. Bliss in his critical edition of *Sir Launfal* (London: Thomas Nelson, 1960), is Wauchier de Denain's continuation of *Perceval le Gallois*.

[4] See Bliss, pp. 5–12. See also Erna Fischer, *Der Lautbestand des sudmittelenglischen Octavian: verglichen mit seinen Entsprechungen im Lybeaus Desconus und im Launfal* (Heidelberg: C. Winter, 1927).

[5] See Bliss, pp. 10–12; also his article, "The Spelling of *Sir Launfal*," *Anglia* 75 (1957), 275–89.

[6] See Mortimer J. Donovan, *The Breton Lay: A Guide to Varieties* (Notre Dame, IN: University of Notre Dame Press, 1969).

[7] A. C. Spearing, "The *Lanval* Story," in *The Medieval Poet as Voyeur: Looking and Listening in Medieval Love-Narratives* (Cambridge: Cambridge University Press, 1993), p. 106.

[8] Sir Thopas also contains some narrative features similar to *Sir Launfal*; see Laura Hibbard Loomis, "Sir Thopas," in *Sources and Analogues of Chaucer's Canterbury Tales*, eds. W. F. Bryan and Germaine Dempster (1941; rpt. New York: Humanities Press, 1958), pp. 486–559.

Sir Launfal is one of only a few Middle English romances or lays which record the author's name. In line 1039, the author writes, "Thomas Chestre made thys tale." Nothing definitive is known of him. For quite some time, scholars assumed that he was also the author of *Octavian* and *Libeaus Desconus*, romances which reside on either side of *Sir Launfal* in the Cotton Caligula manuscript. The exact relationship of the three tales is highly disputed, and it cannot be assumed that Chestre wrote any except the one he "signed"; however, the three texts bear some correspondence.[9] The tail-rhyme form coupled with the narrative simplicity and the blunt criticism of the court world suggest that he lived outside the aristocratic world. Bliss assumes that Chestre wrote for a peasant audience, but if we consider how and where the text itself might have been performed, read, or copied into a manuscript, we would likely establish a potentially wider and somewhat more varied audience, perhaps not peasant, but certainly mercantile. Bliss and Donovan criticize the poem for its lack of courtly sophistication. But Spearing offers the more likely view that the poem rather masterfully satirizes a bourgeois mentality. From this point of view the poem becomes a commentary on medieval popular culture.[10]

The poem, apparently written in the same period as the Peasants' Revolt, treats the court world and wealthy urban society with a certain amount of mockery, although the established order of a powerful, manly, and aristocratic world is affirmed at the beginning of the poem. Arthur's authority is never questioned, less so even than it was in Marie de France's version, but, as in a number of fourteenth-century romances including the very courtly *Sir Gawain and the Green Knight*, the King appears to be inept. Here he has a hasty temper and is quite easily manipulated by Guenevere. Despite the fact that Launfal had been Arthur's faithful steward for ten years, Arthur believes Guenevere when she, seeking revenge against Launfal, claims that Launfal propositioned her. Impetuously and in anger, Arthur swears "by God . . . that Launfal schuld be sclawe" (lines 722–23). Only the intervention of other kindly knights gives Launfal a reprieve of one year to find his fairy-lover. There is also a certain coldness implied in the court's invitation for Launfal to return once he's known to be wealthy again, since they hadn't sought after him before. The poem also includes what Bliss calls an uncourtly and "unpleasant streak of bloodthirstiness" (p. 43). When Launfal defeats Sir Valentyne, he not only slays his downed opponent, he also kills all the lords of Atalye and expresses satisfaction about the slaughter;

---

[9] For a discussion of correspondences see Bliss's critical edition of *Sir Launfal*, pp. 12–14. He includes references to a number of other scholars' work on this issue.

[10] See A. C. Spearing, *The Medieval Poet as Voyeur: Looking and Listening in Medieval Love-Narratives* (Cambridge: Cambridge University Press, 1993), 97–119.

neither character nor narrator appears concerned about negotiating fourteenth-century chivalric codes governing combat or tournament. Launfal's vengeful response to both the mayor and Guenevere is hardly courtly, although both antagonists deserve punishment. The blinding of Guenevere as a fulfillment of the queen's casual remark, though consistent with folkloric patterns, is severe. In a more courtly narrative, shame might well have been sufficient punishment. The criticism of the court is certainly suggested by the conclusion of the narrative as well. The court does not reward Launfal or give him any restitution for his ordeal; instead, Launfal rides off into the Otherworld with Dame Tryamour. Subsequently, the unmanly or "soft" court is repeatedly challenged by Launfal's spirit which crosses into this world once a year to joust with any man who wants "to kepe hys armes fro the rustus" (1028).

Contributing to the fund of medieval Arthurian material, *Sir Launfal* sustains the late Middle Ages' represention of Arthur as a passive figure around whom the active knights revolve. Queen Guenevere, as usual, deceives her husband and is promiscuous with her husband's knights. Although other late medieval writers frequently treated her more sympathetically, Chestre's representation of Guenevere harks back to an earlier period in Arthurian romance when she was frequently despised. As many scholars have noted, her rash oath and her blinding have no known parallels in Arthurian materials, though the gestures of the rash oath and blinding can be found in other narratives influenced by folklore and mythology.

Sir Launfal contains a number of narrative elements which proclaim its connections to folktale tradition: the spendthrift knight, the fairy lover, a journey to the Otherworld, combat with a giant, the magical dwarf-servant, magical gifts, a beauty contest, the offended fay, a secret oath that is broken, and the cyclic return of the mounted warrior's spirit to this world once a year. Such folktale material led B. K. Martin to argue against scholars who tried to read the text through codes of chivalry ("*Sir Launfal* and the Folktale," *Medium Aevum* 35 [1966], 199–210). If the Middle English Breton Lay has connections with Celtic folktale, the connections can be easily perceived in *Launfal*. Celtic tales often revolve around the motif of an offended fay. In these tales, a mortal man either visits the Otherworld and is chosen by, or wins the love of, a fairy maiden; or the supernatural female figure visits the mortal world and takes him as her human lover. All is well until the mortal disobeys the fay's commands and suffers. Sometimes he loses everything, including his life; sometimes he is restored to his fairy lover.[11] Numerous medieval texts inscribe tales

[11] See Elizabeth Willson, *The Middle English Legends of Visits to the Other World and Their Relation to the Metrical Romances.* Diss., University of Chicago, 1917; and Tom Peete Cross, "The Celtic Elements in the Lays of *Lanval* and *Graelent*," *Modern Philology* 12 (1915), 585–644.

of fantastic female lovers, perhaps the most familiar of these being the Swan maiden tales with their corollary in the well-known Tchaikovsky ballet, Swan Lake.[12]

Besides, Chestre's sources, the lays of *Guingamor*, *Tydorel*, and *Desiré* (as well as others) bear striking resemblance to *Sir Launfal*. In *Desiré*, for example, the lover is guided by a beautiful maiden to meet his fay. The meeting apparently occurs in the mortal world, but Desiré finds the fay lying on a beautiful bed and, chasing after her, seizes her. After they make love, the fay gives Desiré a ring and commands him never to speak of her. He is sent away to another country to fight the King's enemy whom he defeats. On his arrival home, he mentions his beloved fay at confession; she abandons him for a year. She finally relents and, appearing at the King's court, reclaims her lover and carries him off to her Otherworld. The lay of *Desiré* introduces other materials into the narrative design, but the correspondence with *Launfal* is pronounced.[13]

In his *Chivalric Romances: Popular Literature in Medieval England*, Lee C. Ramsey argues that the conflict between individual and community forms a central meaning in *Sir Launfal* and many other medieval lays and romances. On the one hand civilization, the community and its conventions, protects and provides; on the other hand, it subjects its citizens to its prejudices and judges their successes and failures within its own assumptions and frame. The narrative of *Launfal*, Ramsey claims, expresses a fantasy solution to the tension between community and individual drives and desires: "By a natural extension of the family-romance myth, this could be achieved by rejecting (slaying) the civilization emblemized as father and uniting oneself with it as emblemized by the mother-lover" (p. 147). The giant Sir Valentine embodies the power of civilization to dominate, overwhelm, and subject; the fairy-lover, Dame Tryamour embodies the power of a civilization to comfort, protect and delight.

The poem contains other tensions as well. Issues of generosity, vows and moral obligation (*geis*), mercy and sexuality are powerfully present in this poem. The feudal world in which generosity is prized, in which Launfal can earn the high rank of steward because of his largesse, gives way to a courtly world when Arthur marries

---

[12] See G. V. Smithers, "Story-Patterns in Some Breton Lays," *Medium Aevum* 22 (1953), 61–92. Stith Thompson discusses the supernatural wife/swan maiden narrative in the context of folktale types in his book, *The Folktale* (New York: Holt, Rinehart and Winston, 1946), pp. 87–93. He cites the Launfal narrative as belonging to this fairytale type (p. 92). See also William Henry Schofield, "The Lays of *Graelent* and *Lanval* and the *Story of Wayland*," *PMLA* 15 (1900), 121–80. Tom Peete Cross argues that the swan maiden narrative is further afield from the Launfal narrative than Celtic precursors: "The Celtic Fée in *Launfal*," in *Anniversary Papers by Colleagues and Pupils of George Lyman Kittredge* (Boston: Ginn, 1913; rpt. New York: Russell & Russell, 1967), pp. 377–87.

[13] See E. Margaret Grimes, ed. *The Lays of Desiré, Graelent and Melion*, pp. 76–101.

Guenevere. And when Launfal, former benefactor to the mayor of Caerleon, seeks a haven in the urban world, he is rebuffed. In his "excessive" gift-giving, Launfal is reminiscent of the epic hero whose reputation rests, in part, on his ability to give gifts to his comitatus. But moved into this romance world, the same actions cause misery. Stripped of everything, even his horse, Launfal falls into poverty and despair. Noticeably, he cannot, on his own, achieve his restoration; he is reestablished in wealth by the fairy-lover acting as a *deus ex machina*. Whereas Sir Cleges turns to prayer and to God to relieve his poverty, Sir Launfal is simply chosen by the fairy world. This very secular narrative gives no direct explanation for why Launfal is chosen to be the lover of the most beautiful woman alive, although his moral indignation about Guenevere's promiscuity may imply, indirectly, that his ethical standards are rewarded. Since he is praised for his liberality, that too, may be the reason he is rewarded. The lay sets sexual liberality against pecuniary liberality, punishing one and rewarding the other. If Guenevere is the main obstacle, the one who disrupts the manly idealized world pictured in the opening of the lay, Dame Tryamour becomes the agent of salvation by the end of the poem. Exercising mercy, she forgives Launfal for violating the *geis* and rides into Arthur's court parading in after her retinue of beautiful ladies. Proving that she is, indeed, the most beautiful woman alive — more beautiful than the indignant queen — she breathes on Guenevere, blinds her, and avenges her beloved Launfal. Unlike most medieval lays and romances, Launfal does not conclude with a reintegration of the hero back into the court world; instead, he rides off into the fairy otherworld as soon as he is restored to Dame Tryamour.

Select Bibliography

Manuscript

British Library MS Cotton Caligula A.ii, fols. 35v–42v. [Dating from the first half of the fifteenth century, this paper manuscript contains thirty-eight items, including poems by Lydgate, anonymous poems, and ten romances. *Sir Launfal* is the seventh item in the manuscript. It is preceded by *Octavian* and followed by *Libeaus Desconus*, both of which have been, at times, attributed to Thomas Chestre. The text is organized in two columns per page, each column containing about forty lines, and the hand is clear. *Landevale*, the earlier Middle English version of the lay which Thomas Chestre apparently knew, is preserved in three manuscripts and two fragments of early printed books. The best manuscript of *Landevale* is MS Rawlinson C 86 found in the Bodleian Library (a late fifteenth-century text). *Landevale* can also be found in Cambridge University MS Kk.v.30, a seventeenth-century paper manuscript inscribed by James Murray of Tibbermuir. This MS version of *Landevale* is incomplete and fragmentary. The third manuscript of *Landevale* is MS Additional 27897, also called the "Percy Folio Manuscript" (c. 1650), which is housed in the British Library. *Landevale* in this paper manuscript is very corrupt and includes interesting additions. For full descriptions of this manuscript see J. W. Halls and F. J. Furnivall, *Bishop Percy's Folio Manuscript* (1867) I, xii-xiv. The two early printed texts of *Landevale* offer quite incomplete versions of the poem, and both contain additions. Bliss dates these texts to the early sixteenth century. G. L. Kittredge has studied the manuscript affiliation: see his article "Launfal," *American Journal of Philology* 10 (1889), 4-17. Manuscript readings, where emended, are contained in the notes. I am much indebted to the work of A. J. Bliss, both in textual decisions and commentary.]

Critical Editions

Bliss, A. J., ed. *Sir Launfal*, London: Nelson, 1960.

Johnson, Lesley, and Elizabeth Williams, eds. *Sir Orfeo and Sir Launfal.* Leeds: University of Leeds Press, 1984.

Ritson, Joseph, ed. *Launfal, An Ancient Metrical Romance by Thomas Chestre to Which Is Appended the Still Older Romance of Lybeaus Disconus.* Edinburgh: E. and G. Goldsmid, 1891. Pp. 1–33.

Collections

Fellows, Jennifer, ed. *Of Love and Chivalry: An Anthology of Middle English Romance* London: Dent, 1993. Pp. xviii–xx; 199–229.

French, Walter Hoyt, and Charles Brockway Hale, eds. *Middle English Metrical Romances.* New York: Prentice-Hall, 1930. Pp. 345–80.

Rickert, Edith, trans. & ed. *Early English Romances in Verse: Done into Modern English.* London: Chatto and Windus, 1908. Pp. 57–80.

Rumble, Thomas C., ed. *The Breton Lays in Middle English.* Detroit: Wayne State University Press, 1965. Pp. 3–43.

Sands, Donald B., ed. *Middle English Verse Romances.* New York: Holt, Rinehart & Winston, 1966. Pp. 201–32.

Sir Launfal

Related Studies

Anderson, Earl R. "The Structure of *Sir Launfal*." *Papers on Language and Literature*, 13 (1977), 115–24. [Provides a reading of the lay, emphasizing its thematic and structural components. Argues that the testing of Launfal's manhood is the poem's central theme with accompanying parallels and contrasts. "The congruence of structure and theme is Chestre's major contribution to the Lanval story, and represents a credible claim to significant artistry" (p. 124).]

Bliss, A. J. "The Hero's Name in the Middle English Versions of Lanval." *Medium Aevum* 27 (1958), 80–85.

Cross, Tom Peete. "The Celtic Fée in *Launfal*." In *Anniversary Papers by Colleagues and Pupils of George Lyman Kittredge* (Boston: Ginn, 1913). Pp. 377-87. [Discusses *Lanval, Desiré, Graelent*, and *Guingamor* to uncover Celtic symbols underlying each poem.]

——. "The Celtic Elements in the Lays of *Lanval* and *Graelent*." *Modern Philology* 12 (1915), 585–644. [A thorough study of Celtic affinities in the narrative: the fée, her assertiveness, her gifts, her *geis* or taboo command, and her withdrawal into the Otherworld. Identifies parallels between *Launfal* and other texts influenced by Celtic myth and folklore.]

Martin, B. K. "*Sir Launfal* and the Folktale." *Medium Aevum* 35 (1966), 199–210. [Cautions against over-reading the tale, expecting to find the complexity of a Chaucer in the work of lesser poets. Identifies features of the tale as folkloric, not for purposes of defending the aesthetics of *Launfal*, but for purposes of understanding the tale. Differs from Cross's studies of the Celtic elements in *Launfal*, instead discusses the European folktale genre more generally and its influence on the lay.]

Nappholz, Carol J. "Launfal's 'Largesse': Word-Play in Thomas Chestre's *Sir Launfal*." *English Language Notes* 25.3 (1988), 4–9. [Argues that Chestre's *Launfal* uses the word "largesse" for the purposes of sexual innuendo and pun. Maintains that "Chestre consciously set out to write a humorous piece rather than a serious romance" (p. 9).]

Ramsey, Lee C. *Chivalric Romances: Popular Literature in Medieval England* (Bloomington: Indiana University Press, 1983). Especially Chapter 6: "The Fairy

Princess," pp. 132–56. [Reads *Launfal* thematically in terms of general social and political contexts and in terms of generalized psychological frameworks.]

Spearing, A. C. "The Lanval Story." In *The Medieval Poet as Voyeur: Looking and Listening in Medieval Love-Narratives.* Cambridge: Cambridge University Press, 1993), pp. 97–119. [Compares Marie de France's *Lanval* with Chestre's, emphasizing wish-fulfillment, the erotic, and Freudian readings alongside the authors' gender differences and ways the authors' differences are written into the texts: "If Marie has a role in the *Lanval* story, it is not as Lanval but as the fairy lady who confines him to the world of fiction. He may imagine that he is devouring her; actually she, as storyteller if not as mother, is devouring him" (p. 106). "Chestre's own social insecurity may reveal itself in the way his hero (Launfal) is more concerned with avoiding shame in others' eyes than with gaining honour" (p. 112); "Chestre so exclusively identifies with his hero that his narrative becomes an open invitation to diagnosis" (p. 114).

Willson, Elizabeth. *The Middle English Legends of Visits to the Other World and Their Relation to the Metrical Romances*. Ph. D. dissertation, University of Chicago, 1917. [I have not examined this document.]

Sir Launfal

Be doughty Artours dawes — *In mighty Arthur's days*
That helde Engelond yn good lawes, — *Who*
Ther fell a wondyr cas — *befell a wondrous event*
Of a ley that was ysette, — *Of which a lay was composed*
That hyght "Launval" and hatte yette. — *was named; is called yet*
Now herkeneth how hyt was! — *listen*
Doughty Artour som whyle — *at one time*
Sojournede yn Kardevyle, — *Dwelt*
Wyth joye and greet solas, — *satisfaction*
And knyghtes that wer profitable — *worthy*
Wyth Artour of the Rounde Table —
Never noon better ther nas! — *was not*

Sere Persevall and Syr Gawayn,
Syr Gyheryes and Syr Agrafrayn,
And Launcelet du Lake;
Syr Kay and Syr Ewayn,
That well couthe fyghte yn playn, — *knew how to; on the field*
Bateles for to take. — *Battles to win*
Kyng Banbooght and Kyng Bos
(Of ham ther was a greet los — — *them; fame*
Men sawe tho nowher her make), — *then; their equal*
Syr Galafre and Syr Launfale,
Wherof a noble tale
Among us schall awake.

Wyth Artour ther was a bacheler,
And hadde ybe well many a yer: — *had been*
Launfal, forsoth he hyght. — *was called*
He gaf gyftys largelyche, — *gave; generously*
Gold and sylver and clothes ryche,
To squyer and to knyght. — *squire*
For hys largesse and hys bounté — *generosity*
The kynges stuward made was he — *steward*

Ten yer, I you plyght; *year; assure*
Of alle the knyghtes of the Table Rounde,
So large ther nas noon yfounde *generous; none*
Be dayes ne be nyght.

So hyt befyll, yn the tenthe yer *it befell; year*
Marlyn was Artours counsalere; *Merlin; counselor*
He radde hym forto wende *advised; go*
To Kyng Ryon of Irlond, right, *right away*
And fette hym ther a lady bright, *fetch*
Gwennere, hys doughtyr hende. *daughter courtly*
So he dede, and hom her brought, *did; home*
But Syr Launfal lykede her noght,
Ne other knyghtes that wer hende; *were well-bred*
For the lady bar los of swych word *bore reputation; renown*
That sche hadde lemmannys under her lord, *lovers besides*
So fele ther nas noon ende. *many; was not ever an end*

They wer ywedded, as I you say, *tell*
Upon a Wytsonday, *Whitsunday*
Before princes of moch pryde.
No man ne may telle yn tale
What folk ther was at that bredale *All the; bridal feast*
Of countreys fer and wyde! *From; far*
No nother man was yn halle ysette *seated*
But he wer prelat other baronette *Unless; prelate or*
(In herte ys naght to hyde). *No reason to hide anything*
Yf they satte noght all ylyke, *Even if; equally*
Har servyse was good and ryche, *Their service*
Certeyn yn ech a syde. *Truly on all sides*

And whan the lordes hadde ete yn the halle, *eaten*
And the clothes wer drawen alle, *table clothes; removed*
As ye mowe her and lythe, *may hear; listen*
The botelers sentyn wyn *wine servants served wine*
To alle the lordes that wer theryn, *therein*
Wyth chere bothe glad and blythe. *blithe*
The Quene yaf yftes for the nones, *gave gifts believe me*
Gold and selver and precyous stonys *stones*

Her curtasye to kythe. — *to make known*
Everych knyght sche gaf broche other ryng, — *gave brooch or*
But Syr Launfal sche yaf nothyng — — *gave*
That grevede hym many a sythe. — *saddened; time*

And whan the bredale was at ende, — *wedding feast*
Launfal tok hys leve to wende — *asked permission to depart*
At Artour the kyng, — *From*
And seyde a lettere was to hym come
That deth hadde hys fadyr ynome — — *his father taken*
He most to hys beryynge. — *must [go]; burying*
Tho seyde Kyng Artour, that was hende, — *gracious*
"Launfal, yf thou wylt fro me wende, — *depart*
Tak wyth the greet spendyng, — *you costly gifts*
And my suster sones two — — *sons*
Bothe they schull wyth the go
At hom the for to bryng." — *To accompany you home*

Launfal tok leve, wythoute fable, — *a lie*
Wyth knightes of the Rounde Table, — *From*
And wente forth yn hys journé — *on*
Tyl he come to Karlyoun,
To the meyrys hous of the toune, — *mayor's*
Hys servaunt that hadde ybe. — *Who had been his servant*
The meyr stod, as ye may here, — *mayor; hear*
And sawe hym come ryde up anblere, — *ambling*
Wyth two knightes and other mayné. — *retinue*
Agayns hym he hath wey ynome, — *[The mayor] went to meet him*
And seyde, "Syr, thou art well come!
How faryth our Kyng? — tel me!" — *fares*

Launfal answerede and seyde than,
"He faryth as well as any man
Ane elles greet ruthe hyt wore. — *Or else it were great pity*
But, Syr Meyr, without lesyng, — *deceit*
I am departyd fram the Kyng, — *estranged*
And that rewyth me sore. — *aggrieves me sorely*
Ne ther thar no man, benethe ne above, — *Nor; need; low born or high*
For the Kyng Artours love

Onowre me never more. *Honor; anymore*
But, Syr Meyr, I pray the, par amour, *for friendship's sake*
May y take wyth the sojoure? *lodging*
Som tyme we knewe us, yore." *Once; knew each other, long ago*

The Meyr stod and bethoghte hym there *contemplated*
What might be hys answere,
And to hym than gan he sayn, *did he speak*
"Syr, seven knyghtes han her har in ynome *have taken lodging here*
And ever y wayte whan they wyl come, *until*
That arn of Lytyll Bretayne." *Who are*
Launfal turnede hymself and lowgh, *laughed*
Therof he hadde scorn inowgh, *enough*
And seyde to hys knyghtes tweyne, *two*
"Now may ye se, swych ys service *such*
Under a lord of lytyll pryse! — *value*
How he may therof be fayn!" *be appreciative*

Launfal awayward gan to ryde.
The Meyr bad he schuld abyde *bade*
And seyde yn thys manere:
"Syr, yn a chamber by my orchardsyde,
Ther may ye dwelle wyth joye and pryde,
Yyf hyt your wyll were."
Launfal anoon ryghtes, *immediately*
He and hys two knytes,
Sojournede ther yn fere; *Lodged; together*
So savegelych hys good he besette *wealth; spent*
That he ward yn greet dette *fell*
Ryght yn the ferst yere. *first*

So hyt befell at Pentecost,
Swych tyme as the Holy Gost
Among mankend gan lyght, *alight*
That Syr Huwe and Syr Jon
Tok her leve for to gon *their*
At Syr Launfal the knight. *From*
They seyd, "Syr, our robes beth torent, *are torn*
And your tresour ys all yspent,

And we goth ewyll ydyght."   *badly clothed*
Thanne seyde Syr Launfal to the knightes fre,
"Tellyth no man of my poverté,
For the love of God Almyght!"

The knyghtes answerede and seyde tho   *then*
That they nolde hym wreye never mo,   *would not betray him ever*
All thys world to wynne.   *Even to gain the whole world*
Wyth that word they wente hym fro
To Glastyngbery, bothe two,
Ther Kyng Artour was inne.   *Where; residing*
The kyng sawe the knyghtes hende,
And agens ham he gan wende,   *to them; hastened*
For they wer of hys keene.   *kin*
Noon other robes they ne hadde
Than they owt wyth ham ladde,   *them had taken*
And thò wer totore and thynne.   *those; all torn*

Than seyde Quene Gwenore, that was fel,   *cruel*
"How faryth the prowde knyght Launfal?
May he hys armes welde?"   *Can he still bear arms*
"Ye, madame," sayde the knytes than,
"He faryth as well as any man,
And ellys God hyt schelde!"   *If otherwise; prevent*
Moche worchyp and greet honour
To Gwenore the Quene and Kyng Artour
Of Syr Launfal they telde,   *told*
And seyde, "He lovede us so
That he wold us evermo   *desired us forever*
At wyll have yhelde.   *To have stayed freely*

But upon a rayny day hyt befel
An huntynge wente Syr Launfel
To chasy yn holtes hore;   *To hunt in ancient woods*
In our old robes we yede that day,   *went*
And thus we beth ywent away,   *have come*
As we before hym wore."   *In what we previously wore*
Glad was Artour the kyng
That Launfal was yn good lykyng —   *comfort*

The Quene hyt rew well sore, *regretted sorely*
For sche wold wyth all her myght *wished*
That he hadde be bothe day and nyght
In paynys mor and more. *pains*

Upon a day of the Trinité
A feste of greet solempnité
In Carlyoun was holde;
Erles and barones of the countré
Ladyes and borjaes of that cité, *burgesses*
Thyder come, bothe yongh and old. *young*
But Launfal, for hys poverté,
Was not bede to that semblé — *invited; gathering*
Lyte men of hym tolde. *Little [did]; think*
The meyr to the feste was ofsent; *invited*
The meyry's doughter to Launfal went
And axede yf he wolde *asked*

In halle dyne wyth her that day. *dine*
"Damesele," he sayde, "nay!
To dyne have I no herte.
Thre dayes ther ben agon, *passed*
Mete ne drynke eet y noon, *Food*
And all was for povert. *because of*
Today to cherche I wolde have gon, *wanted to*
But me fawtede hosyn and schon, *lacked hose; shoes*
Clenly brech and scherte; *Clean breeches*
And for defawte of clothynge, *lack*
Ne myghte y yn the peple thrynge. *among; make my way*
No wonder though me smerte! *that I smart (am hurt)*

But o thyng, damesele, y pray the:
Sadel and brydel lene thou me *loan*
A whyle forto ryde,
That I myghte confortede be
By a launde under thys cyté, *In a clearing near*
Al yn thys underntyde." *morning time*
Launfal dyghte hys courser, *harnassed; charger*
Wythoute knave other squyer. *or*

He rood wyth lytyll pryde;
Hys hors slod, and fel yn the fen, *slipped; mud*
Wherefore hym scornede many men
Abowte hym fer and wyde.

Poverly the knyght to hors gan sprynge. *Wretchedly*
For to dryve away lokynge, *To stop [their] staring*
He rood toward the west.
The wether was hot the underntyde; *that morning*
He lyghte adoun, and gan abyde *dismounted; rest*
Under a fayr forest. *Beside*
And, for hete of the wedere, *because of; weather*
Hys mantell he feld togydere, *folded*
And sette hym doun to reste.
Thus sat the knyght yn symplyté, *simplicity*
In the schadwe under a tre, *shadow*
Ther that hym lykede beste. *it pleased him*

As he sat yn sorow and sore *grief*
He sawe come out of holtes hore *ancient forest*
Gentyll maydenes two:
Har kerteles wer of Indesandel, *Their gowns; Indian silk*
Ylased smalle, jolif, and well — *Laced tightly; neatly*
Ther myght noon gayer go.
Har manteles wer of grene felvet, *Their; velvet*
Ybordured wyth gold, ryght well ysette, *Embroidered; adorned*
Ypelured wyth grys and gro. *Furred; grey; white*
Har heddys wer dyght well wythalle: *Their; coifed*
Everych hadde oon a jolyf coronall *coronet*
Wyth syxty gemmys and mo. *gems*

Har faces wer whyt as snow on downe; *Their; [a] hill*
Har rode was red, her eyn wer browne. *complexion; eyes*
I sawe nevir non swyche!
That oon bar of gold a basyn, *carried; basin*
That other a towayle, whyt and fyn, *towel*
Of selk that was good and ryche. *silk; expensive*
Har kercheves wer well schyre, *head-dresses; very bright*
Arayd wyth ryche gold wyre. *wire*

Launfal began to syche; *sigh*
They com to hym over the hoth; *heath*
He was curteys, and agens hem goth, *toward them goes*
And greette hem myldelyche. *greets them politely*

"Damesels," he seyde, "God yow se!" *protect*
"Syr Knyght," they seyde, "well the be!
Our lady, Dame Tryamour,
Bad thou schuldest com speke wyth here *Bade; her*
Yyf hyt wer thy wylle, sere, *If it; sir*
Wythoute more sojour." *delay*
Launfal hem grauntede curteyslyche, *to them consented*
And went wyth hem myldelyche.
They wheryn whyt as flour. *were; a flower*
And when they come in the forest an hygh, *above*
A pavyloun yteld he sygh, *tent pitched; saw*
Wyth merthe and mochell honour. *great*

The pavyloun was wrouth, forsothe, ywys, *wrought, truly indeed*
All of werk of Sarsynys, *work; Saracens*
The pomelles of crystall; *pole knobs*
Upon the toppe an ern ther stod *top; eagle*
Of bournede golde, ryche and good, *burnished*
Ylorysched wyth ryche amall. *Decorated; costly enamel*
Hys eyn wer carbonkeles bryght — *eyes; rubies*
As the mone they schon anyght, *moon; by night*
That spreteth out ovyr all. *spreads; over*
Alysaundre the conquerour,
Ne Kyng Artour yn hys most honour, *pomp*
Ne hadde noon scwych juell! *such jewel*

He fond yn the pavyloun *found*
The kynges doughter of Olyroun,
Dame Tryamour that hyghte; *who was called*
Her fadyr was Kyng of Fayrye, *Fairyland*
Of Occient, fer and nyghe, *far; near*
A man of mochell myghte.
In the pavyloun he fond a bed of prys *sumptuous*
Yheled wyth purpur bys, *Covered; linen*

That semyle was of syghte.	*seemly*
Therinne lay that lady gent	*gracious*
That after Syr Launfal hedde ysent,	
That lefsom lemede bryght.	*lovely one glittered brightly*

For hete her clothes down sche dede	*Because of the heat; undid*
Almest to her gerdylstede	*Almost; waist*
Than lay sche uncovert.	*uncovered*
Sche was as whyt as lylye yn May,	*lily*
Or snow that sneweth yn wynterys day —	
He seygh never non so pert.	*saw; beautiful*
The rede rose, whan sche ys newe,	
Agens her rode nes naught of hewe,[1]	
I dar well say, yn sert.	*with certainty*
Her here schon as gold wyre;	*hair*
May no man rede here atyre,	*describe her attire*
Ne naught wel thenke yn hert.	*Nor; imagine in [his] heart*

Sche seyde, "Launfal, my lemman swete,	*darling*
Al my joye for the y lete,	*renounce*
Swetyng paramour!	*Sweet lover*
Ther nys no man yn Cristenté	*Christendom*
That y love so moche as the,	
Kyng neyther emperour!"	
Launfal beheld that swete wyghth —	*creature (wight)*
All hys love yn her was lyghth, —	*upon her had settled*
And keste that swete flour	*kissed*
And sat adoun her bysyde,	
And seyde, "Swetyng, whatso betyde,	*whatever happens*
I am to thyn honour!"	*at; service*

She seyde, "Syr Knyght, gentyl and hende,	*gracious*
I wot thy stat, ord and ende;[2]	
Be naught aschamed of me!	*in my presence*
Yf thou wylt truly to me take	*devote [yourself]*

[1] *The red rose, when it first blooms, / Is, in comparison with her complexion, of insignificant color*

[2] *I know thy situation, beginning and end*

And alle wemen for me forsake,
Ryche I wyll make the.
I wyll the yeve an alner *give a purse*
Ymad of sylk and of gold cler,
Wyth fayre ymages thre. *shining*
As oft thou puttest the hond therinne, *thy hand*
A mark of gold thou schalt wynne
In wat place that thou be. *whatever*

"Also," sche seyde, "Syr Launfal,
I yeve the Blaunchard, my stede lel, *loyal steed*
And Gyfre, my owen knave. *servant*
And of my armes oo pensel *coat-of-arms a banner*
Wyth thre ermyns ypeynted well, *ermines*
Also thou schalt have.
In werre ne yn turnement
Ne schall the greve no knyghtes dent, *harm; blow*
So well y schall the save."
Than answerede the gantyl knyght *gentle*
And seyde, "Gramarcy, my swete wyght! *thank you; thing*
No bettere kepte y have!" *provision have I received (see note)*

The damesell gan here up sette, *did sit herself up*
And bad her maydenes her fette *fetch*
To hyr hondys watyr clere — *hands*
Hyt was ydo wythout lette. *done; delay*
The cloth was spred, the bord was sette, *table*
They wente to hare sopere. *their supper*
Mete and drynk they hadde afyn, *plenty*
Pyement, clare, and Reynysch wyn, *Spiced wines; Rheinish*
And elles greet wondyr hyt wer.
Whan they had sowpeth, and the day was gon,
They wente to bedde, and that anoon, *immediately*
Launfal and sche yn fere. *together*

For play, lytyll they sclepte that nyght, *lovemaking; slept*
Tyll on morn hyt was daylyght.
Sche badd hym aryse anoon; *bade*
Hy seyde to hym, "Syr gentyl knyght, *She*

And thou wylt speke wyth me any wyght, *If; wish to; any time*
To a derne stede thou gon. *secret place*
Well privyly I woll come to the *secretly; will*
(No man alyve ne schall me se)
As stylle as any ston." *still; stone*
Tho was Launfal glad and blythe, *Then*
He cowde no man hys joye kythe *could [to]; make known*
And keste her well good won. *kissed; many times*

"But of o thyng, Syr Knyght, I warne the,
That thou make no bost of me *boast*
For no kennes mede! *no kind of reward*
And yf thou doost, I warny the before, *[as] before*
All my love thou hast forlore!" *utterly lost*
And thus to hym she seyde.
Launfal tok hys leve to wende. *leave to go*
Gyfre kedde that he was hende, *showed; helpful*
And brought Launfal hys stede;
Launfal lepte ynto the arsoun *saddle*
And rood hom to Karlyoun
In hys pover wede. *clothes*

Tho was the knyght yn herte at wylle; *at ease*
In hys chaunber he hyld hym stylle *held himself at peace*
All that underntyde. *afternoon*
Than come ther, thorwgh the cité, ten
Well yharneysyth men *armored*
Upon ten somers ryde; *pack-horses riding*
Some wyth sylver, some wyth gold —
All to Syr Launfal hyt schold; *it should [go]*
To presente hym, wyth pryde,
Wyth ryche clothes and armure bryght,
They axede aftyr Launfal the knyght, *asked about*
Whar he gan abyde.

The yong men wer clothed yn ynde; *indigo*
Gyfre, he rood all behynde
Up Blaunchard whyt as flour. *Upon*
Tho seyde a boy that yn the market stod, *Then*

"How fere schall all thys good?	*far; these treasures go*
Tell us, par amour!"	*for friendship's sake*
Tho seyde Gyfre, "Hyt ys ysent	*It*
To Syr Launfal, yn present,	*as a*
That hath leved yn greet dolour."	*Who; lived; misery*
Than seyde the boy, "Nys he but a wrecche!	*He is nothing but*
What thar any man of hym recche?	*What need has any man to heed him*
At the Meyrys hous he taketh sojour."	*lodging*
At the Merys hous they gon alyghte,	
And presented the noble knyghte	
Wyth swych good as hym was sent;	*to him*
And whan the Meyr seygh that rychesse	*saw*
And Syr Launfales noblenesse,	
He held hymself foule yschent.	*considered; sorely abused*
Tho seyde the Meyr, "Syr, par charyté,	*for*
In halle today that thou wylt ete wyth me!	
Yesterday y hadde yment	*intended*
At the feste we wold han be yn same,	*have been together*
And yhadde solas and game,	
And erst thou were ywent!"	*But before [I could invite you], you were gone*
"Sir Meyr, God foryelde the!	*reward*
Whyles y was yn my poverté,	
Thou bede me never dyne.	*never invited me to dine [with you]*
Now y have more gold and fe,	*[But] now; wealth*
That myne frendes han sent me,	
Than thou and alle thyne!"	
The Meyr for schame away yede.	*went*
Launfal yn purpure gan hym schrede,	*purple dressed himself*
Ypelured wyth whyt ermyne.	*Trimmed*
All that Launfal hadde borwyth before,	*borrowed*
Gyfre, be tayle and be score,	*by tally; by account*
Yald hyt well and fyne.	*Repaid*
Launfal helde ryche festes.	
Fyfty fedde povere gestes,	*He fed fifty poor guests*
That yn myschef wer.	*Who were in distress*
Fyfty boughte stronge stedes;	*Bought fifty steeds*

Fyfty yaf ryche wedes	*[And] gave fifty sets of fine clothing*
To knyghtes and squyere.	
Fyfty rewardede relygyons;	*Rewarded fifty clerics*
Fyfty delyverede povere prysouns,	*prisoners*
And made ham quyt and schere;	*them free; clear*
Fyfty clodede gestours.	*Clothed fifty minstrels*
To many men he dede honours	
In countreys fer and nere.	*far; near*
Alle the lordes of Karlyoun	
Lette crye a turnement yn the toun	*Announced*
For love of Syr Launfel,	
And for Blaunchard, hys good stede,	
To wyte how hym wold spede	*know; he would succeed*
That was ymade so well.	*Who; built*
And whan the day was ycome	
That the justes were yn ynome,	*jousts; [to be] held*
They ryde out also snell.	*quickly*
Trompours gan har bemes blowe.	*began to blow their horns*
The lordes ryden out arowe	*in a row*
That were yn that castell.	
Ther began the turnement,	
And ech knyght leyd on other good dent,	*inflicted on the others*
Wyth mases and wyth swerdes bothe.	*maces*
Me myghte ysé some therfore	*A person might see*
Stedes ywonne and some ylore,	*lost*
And knyghtes wonder wroghth.	*enraged*
Syth the Rounde Table was,	*[Ever] since*
A bettere turnement ther nas,	*never was*
Y dare well say, forsothe!	
Many a lord of Karlyoun	
That day were ybore adoun,	
Certayn wythouten othe.	*Surely; oath*
Of Karlyoun the ryche constable	*governor*
Rod to Launfal, wythout fable,	*a lie*
He nolde no lengere abyde.	*would not; endure [Launfal's success]*
He smot to Launfal, and he to hym;	*hit at*

Well sterne strokes and well grym	*serious blows; fierce*
Ther wer yn eche a syde.	*on both sides*
Launfal was of hym yware:	*aware*
Out of hys sadell he hym bar	
To grounde that ylke tyde;	*very moment*
And whan the constable was bore adoun,	
Gyfre lepte ynto the arsoun	*saddle*
And awey he gan to ryde.	
The Erl of Chestere therof segh;	*saw all this*
For wrethe yn herte he was wod negh,	*wrath; nearly mad*
And rood to Syr Launfale	
And smot him yn the helm on hegh	*on the top*
That the crest adoun flegh —	*[So] that; fly*
Thus seyd the Frenssch tale.	
Launfal was mochel of myght:	*of great strength*
Of hys stede he dede hym lyght,	*Off; knocked him*
And bar hym doun yn the dale.	*threw; on the ground*
Than come ther Syr Launfal abowte	*There clustered all around Launfal*
Of Walssche knyghtes a greet rowte,	*company*
The numbre y not how fale.	*I [know] not how many*
Than myghte me se scheldes ryve	*one see shields split*
Speres tobreste and todryve,	*broken and splintered to pieces*
Behinde and ek before.	
Thorugh Launfal and hys stedes dent	*Through; blow[s]*
Many a knyght verement	*truly*
To ground was ybore.	
So the prys of that turnay	*prize; tournament*
Was delyvered to Launfal that day,	
Wythout oth yswore.	*oath*
Launfal rod to Karlyoun,	
To the meyrys hous of the toun,	*mayor's*
And many a lord hym before.	
And than the noble knyght Launfal	
Held a feste ryche and ryall	*royal*
That leste fourtenyght.	*lasted [a]*
Erles and barouns fale	*many*

Semely wer sette yn sale	*Seemly; hall*
And ryaly wer adyght.	*royally; adorned*
And every day Dame Triamour,	
Sche com to Syr Launfal bour	*bower*
Aday whan hyt was nyght.	*Each day*
Of all that ever wer ther tho	*then*
Segh her non but they two,	*Saw; none*
Gyfre and Launfal the knyght.	
A knyght ther was yn Lumbardye;	
To Syr Launfal hadde he greet envye —	*envy*
Syr Valentyne he hyghte.	*was called*
He herde speke of Syr Launfal,	*heard; tell*
How that he couth justy well	*knew how to joust*
And was a man of mochel myghte.	
Syr Valentyne was wonder strong;	
Fyftene feet he was longe.	*tall*
Hym thoughte he brente bryghte	
But he myghte wyth Launfal pleye [1]	
In the feld, betwene ham tweye	*field; them two*
To justy other to fyghte.	*or*
Syr Valentyne sat yn hys halle;	
Hys massengere he let ycalle,	*had called*
And seyde he moste wende	*must go*
To Syr Launfal, the noble knyght	
That was yholde so mychel of myght.	
To Bretayne he wolde hym sende:	*himself*
"And sey hym, for love of his lemman,	*beloved*
Yf sche be any gantyle woman,	*gentle*
Courteys, fre, other hende,	*or polite*
That he come wyth me to juste,	*joust*
To kepe his harneys from the ruste,	*harness*
And elles hys manhod schende."	*Or else; shame*

[1] *It seemed to him that he would completely consume himself (with envy or enmity) / Unless he could play (i. e. compete) with Launfal*

The messengere ys forth ywent
To do hys lordys commaundement.
He hadde wynde at wylle — *favorable wind*
Whan he was over the water ycome;
The way to Syr Launfal he hath ynome,
And grette hym wyth wordes stylle, — *quiet*
And seyd, "Syr, my lord Syr Valentyne,
A noble werrour and queynte of gynne, — *skillful; ingenuity*
Hath me sent the tylle, — *to you*
And prayth the, for thy lemmanes sake, — *lover's*
Thou schuldest wyth hym justes take."
Tho lough Launfal full stylle, — *Then laughed; quietly*

And seyde, as he was gentyl knyght,
Thylke day a fourtenyght, — *[On] this; [in]*
He wold wyth hym play. — *joust*
He yaf the messenger, for that tydyng, — *gave; occasion*
A noble courser, and a ryng,
And a robe of ray. — *striped robe*
Launfal tok leve at Triamour, — *from*
That was the bryght berde yn bour, — *radiant lady; bower*
And keste that swete may. — *kissed; maid*
Thanne seyde that swete wyght, — *creature*
"Dreed the nothyng, Syr gentyl knyght, — *Dread*
Thou schalt hym sle that day!" — *slay*

Launfal nolde nothyng wyth hym have — *would not take anything*
But Blaunchard hys stede and Gyfre hys knave — *Except*
Of all hys fayr mayné. — *retinue*
He schypede, and hadde wynd well good, — *shipped*
And wente over the salte flod — *flood*
Into Lumbardye.
Whan he was over the water ycome
Ther the justes schulde be nome — *To where; held*
In the cyté of Atalye, — *city*
Syr Valentyn hadde a greet ost, — *host*
And Syr Launfal abatede her bost — *quashed their arrogance*
Wyth lytyll companye. — *few companions*

And whan Syr Launfal was ydyght *seated*
Upon Blaunchard, hys stede lyght, *agile (eager, swift)*
Wyth helm and spere and schelde,
All that sawe hym yn armes bryght
Seyde they sawe never swych a knyght,
That hym wyth eyen beheld.
Tho ryde togydere thes knyghtes two, *toward one another*
That har schaftes tobroste bo *So that their spears both shattered*
And toschyverede yn the felde; *splintered; field*
Another cours todgedere they rod, *charge*
That Syr Launfal helm of glod, *Launfal's helmet was knocked off*
In tale as hyt ys telde. *it; told*

Syr Valentyn logh, and hadde good game: *laughed; was delighted*
Hadde Launfal never so moche schame *Launfal had*
Beforhond, yn no fyght.
Gyfre kedde he was good at nede *knew; greatly in need*
And lepte upon hys maystrys stede — *master's*
No man ne segh wyth syght; *saw*
And er than thay togedere mette, *before*
Hys lordes helm he on sette,
Fayre and well adyght.
Tho was Launfal glad and blythe,
And thonkede Gyfre many sythe *thanked; times*
For hys dede so mochel of myght.

Syr Valentyne smot Launfal soo *smote; so [hard]*
That hys scheld fel hym fro, *fell; from*
Anoon ryght yn that stounde. *immediately; moment*
And Gyfre the scheld up hente *seized*
And broghte hyt hys lord, to presente, *[to]; to present*
Er hyt cam doune to grounde. *before; came*
Tho was Launfal glad and blythe,
And rode ayen the thrydde sythe, *again; third time*
As a knyght of mochell mounde. *great valour*
Syr Valentyne he smot so dere *fiercely*
That hors and man bothe deed were, *dead*
Gronyng wyth grysly wounde. *grisly*

Alle the lordes of Atalye
To Syr Launfal hadde greet envye
That Valentyne was yslawe, *Because; slain*
And swore that he schold dye *he [Launfal]*
Er he wente out of Lumbardye, *Before*
And be hongede and todrawe. *hanged; drawn*
Syr Launfal brayde out hys fachon, *drew; sword*
And as lyght as dew he leyde hem doune *laid them down*
In a lytyll drawe; *time*
And whan he hadde the lordes slayn,
He wente ayen yn to Bretayn
Wyth solas and wyth plawe. *solace; joy*

The tydyng com to Artour the Kyng *came*
Anoon, wythout lesyng, *lying*
Of Syr Launfales noblesse. *noble deeds*
Anoon he let to hym sende *had*
That Launfall schuld to hym wende *come*
At Seynt Jonnys Masse, *Saint John's Mass*
For Kyng Artour wold a feste holde *feast*
Of erles and of barouns bolde,
Of lordynges more and lesse.
Syr Launfal schud be stward of halle
For to agye hys gestes alle, *control; guests*
For cowthe of largesse. *knowledge; generosity*

Launfal toke leve at Triamour *leave*
For to wende to Kyng Artour,
Hys feste forto agye. *manage*
Ther he fond merthe and moch honour, *found mirth*
Ladyes that wer well bryght yn bour,
Of knyghtes greet companye.
Fourty dayes leste the feste, *lasted*
Ryche, ryall, and honeste
(What help hyt forto lye?),
And at the fourty dayes ende,
The lordes toke har leve to wende,
Everych yn hys partye. *in his [own] direction*

And aftyr mete Syr Gaweyn, — *meat (dinner)*
Syr Gyeryes and Agrafayn,
  And Syr Launfal also
Went to daunce upon the grene — *green*
Under the tour ther lay the Quene — *tower where*
  Wyth syxty ladyes and mo.
To lede the daunce Launfal was set. — *appointed*
For hys largesse he was lovede the bet — *best*
  Sertayn, of alle tho. — *those*
The Quene lay out and beheld hem alle: — *leaned*
"I se," sche seyde, "daunce large Launfalle; — *generous*
  To hym than wyll y go."

"Of alle the knyghtes that y se there,
He ys the fayreste bachelere. — *fairest*
  He ne hadde never no wyf; — *wife*
Tyde me good other ylle,
I wyll go and wyte hys wylle: — *discover*
  Y love hym as my lyf!"
Sche tok wyth her a companye,
The fayrest that sche myghte aspye —
  Syxty ladyes and fyf — — *five*
And wente hem doun anoon ryghtes, — *them*
Ham to pley among the knyghtes, — *Them; play (dance)*
  Well stylle wythouten stryf. — *still (peacefully)*

The Quene yede to the formeste ende — *went; beginning*
Betwene Launfal and Gauweyn the hende,
  And after her ladyes bryght;
To daunce they wente, alle yn same: — *together*
To se hem play, hyt was fayr game,
  A lady and a knyght.
They hadde menstrales of moch honours, — *minstrels*
Fydelers, sytolyrs, and trompours, — *citole players*
  And elles hyt were unryght; — *wrong*
Ther they playde, forsothe to say,
After mete, the somerys day — *dinner; summer's*
  All what hyt was neygh nyght. — *Until; nearly*

And whanne the daunce began to slake,
The Quene gan Launfal to counsell take, — *spoke privately with Launfal*
And seyde yn thys manere: — *manner*
"Sertaynlyche, Syr Knyght, — *Certainly*
I have the lovyd wyth all my myght — *loved*
More than thys seven yere! — *[For] more than these*
But that thou lovye me, — *Unless*
Sertes y dye fore love of the, — *Surely; die*
Launfal, my lemman dere!" — *darling*
Than answerede the gentyll knyght,
"I nell be traytour day ne nyght, — *will not*
Be God, that all may stere!" — *By; should rule*

Sche seyde, "Fy on the, thou coward! — *Fie*
Anhongeth worth thou hye and hard! — *A hanging you deserve high*
That thou ever were ybore! — *[Alas] that*
That thou lyvest, hyt ys pyté! — *livest; pity*
Thou lovyst no woman, ne no woman the —
Thou were worthy forlore!" — *fit to be destroyed*
The knyght was sore aschamed tho; — *sorely*
To speke ne myghte he forgo — *He couldn't keep himself from speaking*
And seyde the Quene before,
"I have loved a fayryr woman — *fairer*
Than thou ever leydest thyn ey upon — *laid; eye*
Thys seven yer and more!

"Hyr lothlokest mayde, wythoute wene, — *most loathly; doubt*
Myghte bet be a Quene — *better*
Than thou, yn all thy lyve!" — *life*
Therefore the Quene was swythe wroghth; — *very angry*
Sche taketh hyre maydenes and forth hy goth — *her; they*
Into her tour, also blyve. — *quickly*
And anon sche ley doun yn her bedde. — *lay*
For wrethe, syk sche hyr bredde — *she made herself sick*
And swore, so moste sche thryve,
Sche wold of Launfal be so awreke — *would; avenged*
That all the lond schuld of hym speke
Wythinne the dayes fyfe. — *five*

Kyng Artour com fro huntynge,
Blythe and glad yn all thyng.
To hys chamber than wente he.
Anoon the Quene on hym gan crye,
"But y be awreke, y schall dye! *Unless; avenged*
Myn herte wyll breke athre! *in three*
I spak to Launfal yn my game,
And he besofte me of schame — *propositioned me shamefully*
My lemman for to be; *lover*
And of a lemman hys yelp he made, *boast*
That the lothlokest mayde that sche hadde *most loathly*
Myght be a Quene above me!"

Kyng Artour was well wroth, *very angry*
And by God he swor hys oth *oath*
That Launfal schuld be sclawe. *slain*
He wente aftyr doughty knyghtes *valiant*
To brynge Launfal anoonryghtes
To be hongeth and todrawe. *hanged and drawn*
The knyghtes softe hym anoon, *sought*
But Launfal was to hys chaumber gon
To han hadde solas and plawe. *enjoyment; pleasure*
He softe hys leef, but sche was lore *sought; lover; lost*
As sche hadde warnede hym before.
Tho was Launfal unfawe! *Then; wretched*

He lokede yn hys alner, *looked; purse*
That fond hym spendyng all plener,[1]
Whan that he hadde nede, *whenever*
And ther nas noon, for soth to say; *was none*
And Gyfre was yryde away *had ridden*
Up Blaunchard, hys stede. *Upon*
All that he hadde before ywonne, *won (earned)*
Hyt malt as snow ayens the sunne, *melted; under*
In romaunce as we rede;
Hys armur, that was whyt as flour,

---

[1] *Where he [usually] found spending money plentiful*

Hyt becom of blak colour. *became*
And thus than Launfal seyde:

"Alas!" he seyde, "my creature, *beloved*
How schall I from the endure, *survive [away] from you*
Swetyng Tryamour? *Beloved*
All my joye I have forelore, *lost*
And the — that me ys worst fore — [1]
Thou blysfull berde yn bour!" *lady*
He bet hys body and hys hedde ek, *beat; head also*
And cursede the mouth that he wyth spek,
Wyth care and greet dolour;
And for sorow yn that stounde *moment*
Anon he fell aswowe to grounde. *in a swoon*
Wyth that come knyghtes four

And bond hym and ladde hym tho *bound; led*
(Tho was the knyghte yn doble wo!) *double woe*
Before Artour the kyng;
Than seyde Kyng Artour,
"Fyle ataynte traytour, *Vile filthy traitor*
Why madest thou swyche yelpyng? *boasting*
That thy lemmannes lothlokest mayde *most loathsome attendant*
Was fayrer than my wyf, thou seyde!
That was a fowll lesynge! *foul lie*
And thou besoftest her, befor than, *asked; then*
That sche schold be thy lemman —
That was mysprowd lykynge!" *an arrogant desire*

The knyght answerede wyth egre mode, *angry mood*
Before the kyng ther he stode, *where; stood*
The Quene on hym gan lye: *against him did slander*
"Sethe that y ever was yborn, *Since*
I besofte her herebeforn *sought from her*
Never of no folye! — *any foolishness*
But sche seyde y nas no man,

[1] *And the losing of you — that, for me, is the worst trial*

Ne that me lovede no woman
   Ne no womannes companye.
And I answerede her, and sayde
That my lemmannes lothlekest mayde
   To be a Quene was better worthye.

"Sertes, lordynges, hyt ys so!
I am aredy for to do   *ready*
   All that the court wyll loke."   *command*
To say the soth, wythout les,   *tell the truth; lies*
All togedere how hyt was,   *What really happened*
   Twelf knyghtes wer dryve to boke. [1]
All they seyde ham betwene,   *among themselves*
That knewe the maners of the Quene   *Who; ways (behavior)*
And the queste toke,   *And undertook consideration of the question*
The Quene bar los of swych a word   *deserved such accusation*
That sche lovede lemmannes wythout her lord —   *besides her husband*
   Har never on hyt forsoke.   *Not one of them denied it*

Therfor they seyden alle
Hyt was long on the Quene, and not on Launfal —   *the fault of*
   Therof they gonne hym skere;   *Of that [first charge]; acquit*
And yf he myghte hys lemman brynge   *could; beloved bring (to court)*
That he made of swych yelpynge,   *Of whom; boasting*
   Other the maydenes were
Bryghtere than the Quene of hewe,
Launfal schuld be holde trewe   *judged innocent*
   Of that, yn all manere;   *that (second charge)*
And yf he myghte not brynge hys lef,   *could not; lover*
He schud be hongede as a thef,   *should; hanged*
   They seyden all yn fere.   *in agreement*

Alle yn fere they made proferynge   *As one; proposal*
That Launfal schuld hys lemman brynge.
   Hys heed he gan to laye;   *head; gave as pledge*
Than seyde the Quene, wythout lesynge,

---

[1] *Twelve knights were brought to the book (sworn in as jurors)*

"Yyf he bryngeth a fayrer thynge,
Put out my eeyn gray!" *lovely eyes*
Whan that wajowr was take on honde, *wager; agreed upon*
Launfal therto two borwes fonde, *sureties (hostages) found*
Noble knyghtes twayn: *two*
Syr Percevall and Syr Gawayn,
They wer hys borwes, soth to sayn,
Tyll a certayn day.

The certayn day, I yow plyght, *promise*
Was twelfe moneth and fourtenyght, *months; two weeks*
That he schuld hys lemman brynge.
Syr Launfal, that noble knyght,
Greet sorow and care yn hym was lyght — *on; had settled*
Hys hondys he gan wrynge; *hands; wring*
So greet sorowe hym was upan,
Gladlyche hys lyf he wold a forgon *Gladly; have forgone*
In care and yn marnynge; *mourning*
Gladlyche he wold hys hed forgo. *head*
Everych man therfore was wo *woeful*
That wyste of that tydynge. *knew; tiding*

The certayn day was nyghyng: *appointed; nearing*
Hys borowes hym brought befor the kyng; *guarantees*
The kyng recordede tho,
And bad hym bryng hys lef yn syght. *bade; beloved*
Syr Launfal seyde that he ne myght —
Therfore hym was well wo.
The kyng commaundede the barouns alle
To yeve jugement on Launfal *pronounce*
And dampny hym to sclo. *condemn him to be slain*
Than sayde the Erl of Cornewayle,
That was wyth ham at that counceyle, *them; council*
"We wyllyd naght do so.

Greet schame hyt wer us alle upon
For to dampny that gantylman, *condemn*
That hath be hende and fre;
Therfor, lordynges, doth be my reed! *do according to my advice*

Our kyng we wyllyth another wey lede: *wish to go another way*
  Out of lond Launfal schall fle." *[this] land; flee (be exiled)*
And as they stod thus spekynge,
The barouns sawe come rydynge
  Ten maydenes, bryght of ble. *fair of face*
Ham thoghte they wer so bryght and schene *It seemed they [the maidens]*
That the lodlokest, wythout wene, *most loathly; doubt*
  Har Quene than myghte be. *Their; then*

Tho seyde Gawayn, that corteys knyght, *courteous*
"Launfal, brodyr, drede the no wyght! *fear; man*
  Her cometh thy lemman hende." *Here; gracious loved one*
Launfal answerede and seyde, "Ywys, *Indeed*
Non of ham my lemman nys, *None; them; is*
  Gawayn, my lefly frende!" *beloved friend*
To that castell they wente ryght: *they [the maidens]*
At the gate they gonne alyght;
  Befor Kyng Artour gonne they wende,
And bede hym make aredy hastyly *ready immediately*
A fayr chamber, for her lady *their*
  That was come of kynges kende. *from; kin (lineage)*

"Ho ys your lady?" Artour seyde. *Who*
"Ye schull ywyte," seyde the mayde,
  "For sche cometh ryde." *riding*
The kyng commaundede, for her sake,
The fayryst chaunber for to take
  In hys palys that tyde. *palace; time*
And anon to hys barouns he sente
For to yeve jugemente *give*
  Upon that traytour full of pryde:
The barouns answerede anoon ryght, *swiftly*
"Have we seyn the madenes bryght, *seen*
  We schull not longe abyde." *delay*

A newe tale they gonne tho, *discussion; began*
Some of wele and some of wo, *good; bad*
  Har lord the Kyng to queme: *Their; please*
Some dampnede Launfal there, *condemned*

And some made hym quyt and skere — *acquitted; blameless*
Har tales wer well breme. *arguments; quite heated*
Tho saw they other ten maydenes bryght, *another*
Fayryr than the other ten of syght, *in appearance*
As they gone hym deme. *judged them*
They ryd upon joly moyles of Spayne, *mules*
Wyth sadell and brydell of Champayne,
Har lorayns lyght gonne leme. *harness brightly glittered*

They wer yclodeth yn samyt tyre; *samite attire*
Ech man hadde greet desyre
To se har clothynge. *their*
Tho seyde Gaweyn, that curtayse knyght,
"Launfal, her cometh thy swete wyght,
That may thy bote brynge." *remedy*
Launfal answerede wyth drery thoght *wretched*
And seyde, "Alas! y knowe hem noght, *them*
Ne non of all the ofsprynge." *Nor none; those youth*
Forth they wente to that palys *palace*
And lyghte at the hye deys *dismounted; high dais*
Before Artour the Kynge,

And grette the Kyng and Quene ek, *also*
And oo mayde thys wordes spak *one*
To the Kyng Artour:
"Thyn halle agrayde, and hele the walles *prepare; cover*
Wyth clothes and wyth ryche palles, *rich drapes*
Ayens my lady Tryamour." *To greet*
The kyng answerede bedene, *at once*
"Well come, ye maydenes schene, *beautiful*
Be Our Lord the Savyour!" *By*
He commaundede Launcelot du Lake to brynge hem yn fere *together*
In the chamber ther har felawes were, *where their*
Wyth merthe and moche honour.

Anoon the Quene supposed gyle: *suspected guile*
That Launfal schulld, yn a whyle,
Be ymade quyt and skere *Be acquitted; free*

Thorugh hys lemman, that was commynge. *coming*
Anon sche seyde to Artour the kyng,
"Syre, curtays yf thou were,
Or yf thou lovedest thyn honour,
I schuld be awreke of that traytour *avenged on*
That doth me changy chere. *gets me so riled up*
To Launfal thou schuldest not spare,
Thy barouns dryveth the to bysmare — *humiliation*
He ys hem lef and dere!" *beloved of them; dear*

And as the Quene spak to the Kyng,
The barouns seygh come rydynge *saw*
A damesele alone
Upoon a whyt comely palfrey.
They saw never non so gay
Upon the grounde gone: *earth*
Gentyll, jolyf as bryd on bowe, *bird; bough*
In all manere fayr ynowe *extremely fair*
To wonye yn wordly wone. *dwell; worldly dwelling*
The lady was bryght as blosme on brere; *briar*
Wyth eyen gray, wyth lovelych chere, *countenance*
Her leyre lyght schoone. *complexion shone radiantly*

As rose on rys her rode was red; *twig; complexion*
The her schon upon her hed *hair*
As gold wyre that schynyth bryght; *wire; shines*
Sche hadde a crounne upon her molde *crown; head*
Of ryche stones, and of golde,
That lofsom lemede lyght. *lovely gleamed*
The lady was clad yn purpere palle, *purple cloth*
Wyth gentyll body and myddyll small, *slender*
That semely was of syght; *pleasant*
Her matyll was furryd wyth whyt ermyn, *mantle; trimmed; ermine*
Yreversyd jolyf and fyn — *Lined splendidly; fine*
No rychere be ne myght. *richer*

Her sadell was semyly set: *seemly adorned*
The sambus wer grene felvet *saddle blankets; velvet*
Ypaynted wyth ymagerye. *Painted; images*

The bordure was of belles — *borders*
Of ryche gold, and nothyng elles
  That any man myghte aspye.
In the arsouns, before and behynde, — *saddle bows*
Were twey stones of Ynde, — *two jewels; India*
  Gay for the maystrye. — *Exceedingly brilliant*
The paytrelle of her palfraye — *breast-plate; palfrey*
Was worth an erldome, stoute and gay, — *stately; magnificent*
  The best yn Lumbardye.

A gerfawcon sche bar on her hond; — *gyrfalcon; bore*
A softe pas her palfray fond, — *slow pace; went*
  That men her schuld beholde.
Thorugh Karlyon rood that lady;
Twey whyte grehoundys ronne hyr by — — *Two; ran*
  Har colers were of golde. — *Their collars*
And whan Launfal sawe that lady,
To alle the folk he gon crye an hy, — *aloud (eagerly)*
  Bothe to yonge and olde:
"Her," he seyde, "comyth my lemman swete! — *Here*
Sche myghte me of my balys bete, — *misfortunes relieve*
  Yef that lady wolde." — *If*

Forth sche wente ynto the halle
Ther was the Quene and the ladyes alle, — *There where*
  And also Kyng Artour.
Her maydenes come ayens her, right, — *toward her decorously*
To take her styrop whan sche lyght, — *stirrup; dismounted*
  Of the lady Dame Tryamour.
Sche dede of her mantyll on the flet, — *took off; floor*
That men schuld her beholde the bet, — *better*
  Wythoute a more sojour. — *any more delay*
Kyng Artour gan her fayre grete,
And sche hym agayn, wyth wordes swete
  That were of greet valour.

Up stod the Quene and ladyes stoute, — *stately*
Her for to beholde all aboute, — *on every side*
  How evene sche stod upryght; — *straight (tall, proudly)*

Than wer they wyth her also donne *[compared] with her as dim*
As ys the mone ayen the sonne *moon against; sun*
Aday whan hyt ys lyght. *By day; it*
Than seyde sche to Artour the Kyng,
"Syr, hydyr I com for swych a thyng:
To skere Launfal the knyght; *liberate*
That he never, yn no folye, *madness*
Besofte the quene of no drurye, *Besought; illicit love*
By dayes ne be nyght.

"Therfor, Syr Kyng, good kepe thou nyme! *take good heed*
He bad naght her, but sche bad hym *bade*
Here lemman for to be; *her*
And he answerede her and seyde *he [Launfal]*
That hys lemmannes lothlokest mayde
Was fayryre than was sche." *fairer*
Kyng Artour seyde wythouten othe, *doubt*
"Ech man may ysé that ys sothe, *see what is truth*
Bryghtere that ye be." *More beautiful*
Wyth that Dame Tryamour to the quene geth, *goeth*
And blew on her swych a breth *such*
That never eft myght sche se. *again*

The lady lep an hyr palfray *lept onto*
And bad hem alle have good day —
Sche nolde no lengere abyde. *would; longer*
Wyth that com Gyfre all so prest, *immediately*
Wyth Launfalys stede, out of the forest,
And stod Launfal besyde.
The knyght to horse began to sprynge
Anoon, wythout any lettynge, *delay*
Wyth hys lemman away to ryde;
The lady tok her maydenys achon *each one*
And wente the way that sche hadde er gon, *previously taken*
Wyth solas and wyth pryde.

The lady rod thorth Cardevyle *through*
Fer ynto a jolyf ile, *Far; pleasant isle*
Olyroun that hyghte. *is called*

Every yer, upon a certayn day, *year*
Me may here Launfales stede nay, *One; hear; neigh*
  And hym se wyth syght.
Ho that wyll ther axsy justus, *Who; ask to joust*
To kepe hys armes fro the rustus, *rust*
  In turnement other fyght, *tournament or combat*
Dar he never forther gon; *Need; further go*
Ther he may fynde justes anoon
  Wyth Syr Launfal the knyght.

Thus Launfal, wythouten fable, *without a doubt*
That noble knyght of the Rounde Table,
  Was take ynto Fayrye; *taken; the land of faery*
Seththe saw hym yn thys lond noman, *Since then; this land no one*
Ne no more of hym telle y ne can,
  For sothe, wythoute lye.
Thomas Chestre made thys tale
Of the noble knyght Syr Launfale,
  Good of chyvalrye.
Jhesus, that ys hevene kyng,
Yeve us alle Hys blessyng, *Give*
  And Hys modyr Marye! *mother*
  AMEN

  Explicit Launfal

Notes

Abbreviations: MS: Cotton Caligula A.ii; Bl: Bliss; F: Fellows; F&H: French and Hale; J&W: Johnson and Williams; M: Mills; R: Rickert; Ri: Ritson; Ru: Rumble; S: Sand. See bibliography for complete references. The title occurs in the MS as *Launfal Miles*.

1 In early Arthurian literature, King Arthur played an active role; he still does so in Malory's opening books of the *Morte d'Arthur* as well as in the fourteenth-century *Alliterative Morte Arthure* and *Stanzaic Morte Arthur*, but he also takes on a passive role in many romance narratives of the later Middle Ages, remaining at court while his knights take up the active roles as warriors and wanderers.

1–2 These lines anticipate the power of law to constrain Arthur's rage toward Launfal later in the tale.

2 The nostalgic opening is typical, not only of romances and Breton lays, but of many late fourteenth-century texts. The need for "good lawes" is echoed by Thomas Chestre's contemporaries. See Langland's *Piers Plowman*, Chaucer's "Ballad for a Former Age," the works of John Gower, and such romances and diatribes as *Athelston* and *Piers Plowman's Creed*.

5 Bl suggests: "In many of the Breton lays the name of the lay is mentioned with some emphasis, as if to recall to the reader (or listener) the tune to which the original lyrical lay was sung" (p. 83).

6 The presence of both performer and audience is articulated in this line, as well as many others. See lines 49, 817, 1036–37. See also *Erle of Tolous*, lines 7–8, 23, 173, 478–79; *Emaré*, lines 19–20, 70–72, 96, 144, 310–12, 381, 946–948; and similar lines in *Sir Gowther* and other lays and romances.

7 *Kardevyle*: Carlisle as a place associated with Arthuriana is rendered "Kaerdubalum" in Geoffrey of Monmouth (c. 1136). Wace (c. 1155) uses the form "Kaerleil" but never situates Arthur's court there. In their book, *The Place-Names of Cumberland* (Cambridge: Cambridge University Press, 1950–52), pp. 40–42, A. M. Armstrong *et al* provide an etymology for the word "Carlisle": in

Latin, the place-name was "Luguvalium, [from] Modern Welsh *Caer Liwelydd* 'belonging to *Luguvallos*,' a personal name meaning 'strong as *Lugus*' [a Celtic god]." In her *Lanval* Marie de France places Arthur's court at Kardoel. And the Middle English *Landevale* places it at "Carlile." It certainly can be confused with Caerleon near the river Usk in Wales, a city long associated with Arthur. *Caerleon* means "Fort of the Legions." Malory situates Guenevere's trial and her subsequent rescue from the stake in Carlisle, in contrast to Chestre's condemnation and blinding of Guenevere here in the *Launfal* poem. It appears that Caerleon and Carlisle have a confused and interwoven role to play in the late medieval Arthurian records.

13–24 This list of knights does not occur in either Marie de France's *Lanval* or in the Middle English *Landevale*, but *Libeaus Desconus* does contain a list like this (see lines 218–21) as does the OF *Le Bel Inconnu*. In the introduction to his critical edition, Bl calls attention to Chestre's ordering. Notably, the list proceeds from the most important knight, Perceval (who achieves the Holy Grail) to the least important: Galafre and Launfal, both otherwise unknown as Round Table knights. The ordering may suggest a hierarchy of worth, or it could simply be determined by meter or be a way of placing Launfal in the ultimate position among the company of the best and greatest of Arthur's knights. In Malory's *Morte d'Arthur*, Gawain, Gaheres and Agravayn are all brothers, sons of King Lot and Arthur's half-sister, Morgawse. They are mentioned again in *Launfal*, lines 637–38. This group is followed by Lancelot, then Sir Kay (Arthur's stepbrother), Ywayn (Arthur's nephew and son of Morgan la Fay), then King Ban and King Bors (father and uncle to Lancelot and allies of Arthur), and finally Galafre and Launfal. Perceval is hero of numerous romances, particularly Chrétien's twelfth-century metrical romance and the early fifteenth-century English *Percevall of Galles*. Yvain is the main hero of Chrétien's *Chevalier au Lion* as well as the Middle English *Ywain and Gawain*. Gawain's inclusion in the Arthurian retinue has a long history. Found in William of Malmesbury (c. 1125) as Arthur's most distinguished knight, he is also a powerful figure in Geoffrey of Monmouth (c. 1136), Wace (c. 1155), and Layamon (c. 1190). In a number of continental romances, he becomes degenerate — hence, his brutishness in Malory's *Morte d'Arthur*. But he remained a noble figure in English popular literature and within texts like *Sir Gawain and the Green Knight* and *The Awntyrs of Arthur*. In *Sir Launfal*, he is the picture of courtesy (see lines 853, 892, 662) and one of the hero's best friends. Gawain stands next to Launfal during the dance (line 662), does surety for him (line 814), and announces the arrival of the maidens (lines 853, 892). See Chaucer's Squire's Tale (line 95): "Gawain, with his olde curteisye. . . ." Bl notes, "the substitution of [Lancelot's] name in *Launfal* (line 910) for the 'Gawayn' of *Landevale* (line 413), at the cost of ruining the metre, must be the work of a late scribe more familiar with the continental than with the English tradition" (p. 40). Galafre is not known as an Arthurian knight. On the origins of Launfal's name see Bl. Spearing (p. 107) argues that the list illustrates Chestre's desire "to 'epicize' Launfal's role" and render him more heroic than he appears in *Sir Landevale*.

19 King Banbooght and King Bos are most likely King Ban and King Bors found elsewhere in Arthurian literature. They are father and uncle of Lancelot and fight as allies with Arthur against kings who resist Arthur's kingship and thus help solidify the kingdom. The word "booght" is obscure. Bl notes: "Possibly Booght is a duplication of Bos. The Old French form of Bors is nominative Bo(h)ors, oblique Bo(h)ort; in many fifteenth-century hands the letter 'r' after 'o' has exactly the form of the upper part of yough, so that an ill-written 'Boort' could easily be read as 'booght'" (1958, p. 84).

22 The name "Galafre" is not found elsewhere as a knight of the Round Table; see note to lines 13–24 above.

25 *bacheler*. Here means a novice or young knight who would lack the retinue of experienced and more wealthy established knights.

28–30 Largesse or generosity is a knightly virtue. See *Sir Isumbras,* lines 25–30. See also *Sir Cleges*, lines 13–23. For medieval codes of chivalry, see Ramón Lull, *Le libre del orde de cauayleria* (c. 1276), available in Caxton's 1484 translation; Honoré Bonet, *Arbre des Batailles* (c. 1387), trans. G. W. Coopland: *The Tree of Battles of Honoré Bonet* (Liverpool: University of Liverpool Press, 1949); and John of Salisbury, *Policraticus* (c. 1159), ed. and trans. Cary J. Nederman (Cambridge: Cambridge University Press, 1990).

29 *clothes*. MS: *clodes*.

30 The word "squyer" can designate someone who is in training for knighthood, a personal servant who attends a knight's needs, or a soldier below the rank of "knight."

32 A frequent figure of romances and lays, the loyal steward was in charge of his master's household. He would supervise all domestic servants, oversee the

master's table, and regulate the household's expenditures. A steward held considerable power within the domestic world of high ranking aristocrats. See *Sir Orfeo*, lines 204–08, 554–79, 593–96, and *Amis and Amiloun*, lines 191, 205–16.

37–72 This material does not appear in *Landevale* or *Lanval* (see appendices).

38 Merlin appears here briefly and then never again. He does not appear at all in either Marie de France's *Lanval* or *Landevale*. Chestre's Merlin advises Arthur to marry Guenevere; elsewhere, Merlin commonly counsels Arthur against marrying Guenevere. Although it can be found in many Arthurian romances, the marriage episode was apparently added to *Sir Launfal* by Chestre; it does not occur in either *Lanval* or *Landevale*.

40 King Ryon is, most likely, King Ryence who appears in other romances where he is usually ruler of North Wales. In other texts central to the Arthurian canon, Ryence is an enemy to Arthur and Lodegryaunce. Lodegryaunce, or Leodegraunce, is commonly Guenevere's father. Perhaps Lodeg "ryaunce" has become "Ryon" here.

41 *fette*. Ri rcads *sette*.

42 *Gwennere*: Contracted forms of Guenevere's name are common in ME (see lines 157, 164). In the Welsh tradition, references to her extend back to the *Triads*, collections of Welsh myth, history, and legend; there, her name is "Gwenhwyfar" meaning "White Phantom." The standard edition of the *Triads*, including a discussion of the texts, is *Trioedd ynys Prydein: The Welsh Triads*, ed. and trans. Rachel Bromwich (Cardiff: University of Wales Press, 1961; 2nd. ed., 1978; 1991).

44 *lykede*. The implication is that Gwennere was displeased with Launfal and other Round Table knights, since "lykede" is usually impersonal in ME; however, like modern English "liked," it would mean that Launfal and the other knights disapproved of Gwennere because of her promiscuity (lines 46–48).

46–47 Early Welsh tradition, preserved within the *Triads*, ascribes "Gwenhwyfar" with a reputation of being adulterous. She is listed as more treacherous than any notorious woman named in the triad of "Three Faithless Wives": "and one was more faithless than those three: Gwenhwyfar, wife of Arthur, since she shamed a better man than any of them" (Triad #80 in Bromwich; also translated by John K. Bollard, "Arthur in the Early Welsh Tradition," in *The Romance of Arthur*, ed. James J. Wilhelm and Laila Z. Gross (New York: Garland, 1984), p. 25. Although Chrétien de Troyes and other high and late medieval authors frequently idealized Guenevere, the portrait of her in Chestre's poem is consistent with the earliest written records of her character; that is, Guenevere's affair with Lancelot is not mentioned in *Sir Launfal*.

50 Whitsunday, meaning literally "White Sunday," is another name for Pentecost, a high feast of the Christian calendar; it is often the day adventures begin in Arthurian romances.

56 *baronette*. A lesser noble, a diminuitive of "baron." R suggests "knight-landowner," *Early English Romances* (London: Chatto and Windus, 1908), p. 59.

57 A tag phrase. Bl translates: "There is no reason for concealment."

64 A *boteler* is a wine servant or cupbearer.

67–72 See *Graelent,* lines 151–62. In this source, Guenevere's motive for not giving Launfal a gift or payment is, perhaps, made clear. The queen advises the king not to pay Graelent so that he cannot leave the court. It may, then, be intended to make Launfal more vulnerable to Guenevere's promiscuity or punish him for his aloofness, although the text never explicitly explains the queen's move. See also lines 676–80 below. Spearing interprets Guenevere in Freudian terms "as a stepmother figure, an intruder into the family" (p. 108).

82 Sir Hugh and Sir John are not found elsewhere in the extant Arthuriana as nephews of Arthur. Bl suggests that these names may be corruptions of Ywain and Gawain, who were Arthur's nephews (1958, p. 86).

85–216 No parallels for this material exist in *Landevale* or *Lanval*, but *Graelent* contains some likenesses.

88 *Karlyoun*. Often identified with Camelot: see Derek Brewer, *Arthur's Britain: The Land and the Legend* (Cambridge: Pevensey Press, 1985), p. 109.

89 The romance of *Graelent* (lines 172–80) does not describe him as a mayor.

101 *departyd*. MS: *þe party*. Ri and Bl read *thepartyth*; so too F&H, with the gloss "departed."

103 *Ne ther thar*. Bl combines the first two words; so too F&H with *thar* glossed as "need." S reads *Nether thare*, with the gloss "nor/need."

112 MS: *vij*. The final *-e* in *ynome* has been trimmed from the MS.

118–20 Bl (p. 86) translates these lines: "Now you can see what it is like to be in the service of a lord of little importance, and how grateful the lord will be for your service." Launfal speaks with bitter sarcasm.

119 *Under*. MS: *Unþer*. The scribe often writes *d* for *þ*. E.g., 29, 202, 204, 209, 414, 450, 511, 530, 587, 594, 596, 598, 641 (unþer), 683, 763, 779, 780, 891, 905, 1021.

133 This marks one full year that Launfal has been away from court.

136 Syr Huwe and Syr John are Arthur's nephews mentioned in line 82 who accompanied Launfal "hom." See note to line 82.

137–49 See also *Sir Amadas*, lines 351–75.

140 *tresour*. MS: *tosour*. Ri emends to *tresour*. Emendation followed by F&H, Bl, Ru, and S.

142 MS: the *-e* on *fre* has been trimmed from the MS.

143 MS: *Tellyd*. Ri reads *Tell yd*; Ru emends to *tellyth*.

149 Glastonbury has long been associated with the island of Avalon. See Brewer, *Arthur's Britain*, pp. 60–62.

154–55 Retainers and servants were regularly provided with clothes and food by their lords. When Sir Hugh and Sir John return to Arthur's court wearing the same clothes they had on a year before, it would be immediately noticeable and evoke questions; these clothes are tattered and torn.

160 *knytes*. S emends to *knightes*.

162 See *Lay le Freine*, line 101.

164 MS, F&H, Ru, and Bl read: *Gonnore*; Ri, *Gonere*; S, *Gwenere*.

171 *holtes hore* is a common description found in romances (see line 230). It usually suggests grey, bare branches of a winter forest or lichen-covered trees. Here, however, the action is set in summer, where *hore* suggests shadowy.

174 *wore*. S: "A disputed line whose crux is '*wore*,' either '*wore*,' or '*were*,' either interpretation being possible. The sense is probably '[dressed just] as we were in his presence'" (p. 208).

181 Trinity Sunday is the first Sunday after Whitsun and celebrates the Holy Trinity. In the time frame of the narrative, this happens one week after Sir Hugh and Sir John leave him.

185 *borjaes*. Bl reads *boriaes*; S, *borieies*.

191–216 See *Graelent*, lines 176–94.

202 MS: *clodynge*.

204 *Though*. MS: *dough*. See note to line 119.

211 A courser is a powerful horse used by knights in battle.

214 The image of a young dashing courtier riding a horse was a common iconographic image for the month of May. Consequently, the image of Launfal and his horse falling into the mud is potentially comic. This is a detail apparently added by Chestre. In *Graelent* 201–02, the onlookers stare because the knight's clothes are old and tattered. William J. Stokoe, "The Sources of *Sir Launfal*: *Lanval* and *Graelent*," *PMLA* 58 (1948), 398: "[In Marie de France's version,] the horse trembles because it feels the presence of the supernatural." Here, however, it falls in the "fen." Bl writes, "it illustrates the general lack of respect for the upper classes which is a feature of the poem" (p. 88).

222 Chestre's extant sources, *Landevale* and *Graelent*, both situate this scene near a river, as is consistent with Celtic mythology. William H. Schofield assumes a river is implied in lines 244–45 and that the maidens carrying the basin and

towel are fetching water for bathing, "The Lays of *Graelent* and *Lanval*, and the Story of Wayland," *PMLA,* 15 (1900), 145. Here it seems the maidens have been sent to fetch Launfal, and, since he's hot and muddy, he would need washing.

227 Sitting under the shadow of a tree often leads to an adventure in the English lays: see *Sir Orfeo* lines 67–68. Constance Bullock-Davies, "Ympe Tre and Nemeton," *Notes and Queries* n.s. 9 (1962), 6–9; John Block Friedman, "Eurydice, Heurodis, and the Noon-day Demon," *Speculum* 41 (1966), 22–29. See notes to *Orfeo,* line 70 in this volume. See *The Pistel of Swete Susan* (also found partially in Cotton Caligula A.ii, fols. 3a-5a) where Susan, undressing to bathe, relaxes under a laurel tree at midday before she is trapped by the elders.

235 MS: *felwet*. S emends to *felvett*. The maidens are dressed in green, connecting this summons with Celtic folk materials. See Cross, "Celtic Elements" (p. 595 and fn. 3 on the same page). See also *Sir Gawain and the Green Knight* and Child, *Ballad* #37.

249 Just why Launfal would sigh isn't clear. Is he struck by the maidens' beauty? Is he embarrassed by his poverty and filth? Does he simply want to be left alone?

250 Instead of glossing *hoth* as "heath," as I have done, Bl (p. 89) assumes it designates an actual place. He cites A. Mawer and F. M. Stenton, *The Place-Names of Sussex* (Cambridge: Cambridge University Press, 1929/30), p. 270, to support his reading.

255 *Tryamour*. The lady is not named in *Lanval* or *Landevale*. A number of meanings are suggested by this name. Obviously "try-amour" meaning "to test or try love" is one. But the first syllable also contains echoes of the prefix, "tri" meaning three. This association could be reminiscent of "Tir" or "Tyr" which in Saxon and ancient Cimbric was the name for Odin and sometimes other deities. Ri's notes on the name are informative: "Tyr," he claims, could be used for any great leader, prince, lord, emperor, and occasionally meant Creator or God. In *Libeaus Desconus*, found in the same manuscript as *Launfal*, "Termagaunt" refers to the God of the Saracens. The syllable "ter" also carries meanings of "very" as well as "three." The word "three" had, as Ri notes, mythic signification well before Christianity's Trinity. He cites

Virgil's *Aeneid* IV: "*Tergeminamque Hecaten, tria virginia ora Dianae.*" Closer to our fourteenth-century text, the name is given to a knight in the medieval romance, *Sir Tryamour*. In *Sir Launfal* the number "three" recurs in the three fairy images which adorn the magic purse Dame Tryamour gives to Launfal and the three ermines which are, apparently, her heraldric signs: see lines 328–30. Bl (p. 89) prefers a simpler explanation: in his notes to the line, he suggests it means "choice love." Although the fairy lover's name is Tryamour, she may have connections to Morgan le Fay. Bl (p. 20) argues for this connection by citing the association in Old French between Graelent, Guingamor, and Lanval, and by recalling that Morgan le Fay is the lover of both Graelent (a.k.a. Graillemuers) and Guingamor in Chrétien de Troyes' *Erec*. See also Laurence Harf-Lancner, *Les Fées au Moyen Age: Morgane et Mélusine, La naissance des fées* (Paris: Champion, 1984).

266 *werk of Sarsynys*. Romances often contain references to Middle Eastern, non-Christian characters, places, cultures, and objects. After Sicily was conquered by the Normans, the silk weavers found there traded their goods throughout Europe more easily.

271 *carbonkeles*: R (1908, p. 63) notes that in the lapidaries, carbuncles are noted for their light-giving qualities. F (1993, p. 286) notes: "A belief prevailed in the Middle Ages that precious stones, particularly carbuncles, shone with a light of their own. It has been suggested that descriptions of buildings surmounted by such refulgent gems may represent an attempt to interpret the lighthouse of Alexandria: see E. Faral, *Recherches sur les sources latines des contes et romans courtois du moyen age* (Paris: E. Champion, 1913), pp. 81–85. Descriptions of brilliant bejewelled cities and palaces occur frequently in Middle English romance." Compare castles in *Libeaus Desconus* line 1789ff.; *Huon of Burdeaux* XXV, p. 75, CXVII, 424; *Sir Degrevant*, lines 1425, 1473; and *Reinbroun*, stanza 79ff.; *Le Bel Inconnu*, lines 1877–1919; esp. lines 1913–16.

272 *they schon.* MS: *the schon.*

274 Alexander the Great, one of the nine worthies, a well-known hero of romances.

278 *Olyroun*. Perhaps the island d'Oleron off the coast of Brittany. *Lanval,* line 641, reads "Aualun" and *Landevale* (line 92) reads "Amylion." See *Huon of Burdeux* (EETS e.s. 40, 41, 43, 50) where Oberon's palace is across the sea and

next to a large body of water (p. 597; see also pp. 358, 379, 439, 584). In *Le Bel Inconnu*, the caste of the Ile d'Or is also situated across water. Ri (p. 12) notes that maritime laws were called "la ley Olyron" and notes that Richard I revised the maritime laws on the island of Olyroun on his way back to England from the Holy Lands.

280 The consensus among scholars studying fairy lore is that the word *fairy* comes from Latin and French origins. Lewis Spence, *Fairy Tradition in Britain* (London: Rider, 1948), links "fairy" with *Fata* which is itself linked to both the Fates of classical mythology and the nymphic *Fatuae*. His opinion has been sustained more or less by subsequent scholars. See Laurence Harf-Lancner, *Les Fées au Moyen Age* (Paris: Champion, 1984). See also Jack Zipes, *Breaking the Magic Spell: Radical Theories of Folk and Fairy Tales* (New York: Methuen, 1984) and James Roy King, *Old Tales and New Truths: Charting the Bright-Shadow World* (Albany: State University of New York Press, 1992), consider the fairytale's cultural role in the contemporary West. Their analyses of the fairytale raise some provocative issues to consider in relation to *Sir Launfal*, particularly since it belongs to "popular culture." See also the notes to *Sir Orfeo*, line 10.

281 *Occient.* May mean "west" or "ocean," perhaps a reference to Avalon, a land or island associated with faery or the Otherworld.

292–300 The description of Dame Tryamour conforms to myriads of other medieval catalogue descriptions of women's faces and bodies. See D. S. Brewer, "The Ideal of Feminine Beauty in Medieval Literature," *Modern Language Review* 50 (1955), 257–69. See also *Launfal*, lines 934–45.

301–16 The wooing woman is a motif common in Celtic folklore. See Howard R. Patch, "The Adaptation of Otherworld Motifs to Medieval Romance," in *Philologica: The Malone Anniversary Studies*, eds. Thomas A. Kirby and Henry Bosley Woolf (Baltimore: Johns Hopkins University Press, 1949), pp. 115–23. See also Judith Weiss, "The Wooing Woman in Anglo-Norman Romance," in *Romance in Medieval England*, ed. Mills, Fellows, and Meale, pp. 149–61.

316–17 These words are close to contemporary betrothal vows. Vows spoken between two people, even when not witnessed, could constitute a valid marriage. The solemnization of marriage includes the following lines "wilt thou have this woman to thy wedded wife, wilt thou love her, honour her, keep her and guard her, in health and in sickness, as a husband should a wife, and forsaking all others on account of her, keep thee only unto her, so long as ye both shall live?" *The Sarum Missal in English* trans. Frederick E. Warren (London: Alexander Moring, 1911) and found conveniently in *Chaucer Sources and Backgrounds,* ed. Robert P. Miller (New York: Oxford University Press, 1977), pp. 373–84. Compare Chaucer's Tale of Sir Thopas, lines 794–95: "Alle othere wommen I forsake, / And to an elf-queen I me take."

319–33 The gifts Dame Tryamour gives to Launfal parallel quite closely the gifts Graelent receives. (See *Graelent*, lines 350–92.)

329 Ri's edition misnumbers the text hereafter, with line 329 as 330.

323 A mark is quite a sum of money. In the late fourteenth century, it signifies about eight ounces of gold.

326 *Blaunchard* is a white horse (OF: *blanche*). The white horse appears frequently as a fairy horse. See *Sir Orfeo*, line 146, *Graelent,* line 354, and the supernatural horse in *Sir Amadas*, line 427. Roger S. Loomis, in his book, *Celtic Myth and Arthurian Romance* (New York: Columbia University Press, 1927), pp. 88–89, 106–07, identifies many tales in which Morgan le Fay gives a knight a horse, particularly a white one. The correspondence may suggest a connection between Dame Tryamour and Morgan le Fay, although the gift of the white horse can be easily found occurring elsewhere as well. See Cross, "Celtic Elements," pp. 628–35.

327 Gyfre is not found in *Landevale* or *Lanval*, but the hero in *Graelent* (line 351) is given a servant, his "chambellanc."

328 *pensel*. A small pennon, a "favor" worn to signify allegiance to his lady.

336 *kepte*. Bl (p. 91) suggests the word is the past participle "embraced." Ru emends to *klepte* meaning "embraced." S glosses the line: "No better have I received," noting an obsolete sense of "to receive" for *keep* attested to here. F&H emend to *chepe*, which they gloss as "bargain." I have glossed the term as a form of *keeping*, with the implication of "provision" or "offering" being received.

343 Fairy food is often dangerous for mortals to eat. A number of medieval texts include in their descriptions of the Otherworld the imprisoning capacity of fairy food. In Chrétien de Troyes' *Erec*, for example, humans who eat fruit from King Evrain's garden are unable to find their way out of that kingdom. In the Irish romance of *Connla the Fair*, Connla eats a fairy apple and, from that moment on, wants no mortal food, and, for another taste of that magic fruit, follows the fairy away into the Otherworld. Although there is nothing in this text to suggest that the fairy food is dangerous, Launfal does, at the end of the text, follow his lemman into her otherworld.

344 *Pyement* and *clare* are both red wines mixed with honey and spices. *Reynysch wyn* is, apparently, Rhine wine. The *MED* gives the example from the *Alliterative Morte d'Arthur*, line 203: "Rynisch wyne," which indicates a rarer and more costly wine.

362 The fairy-lover puts a *geis*, or magic taboo, on Launfal, whereby he must never mention her name. This motif derives from folk materials though its origin is disputed. J. G. Frazer, in his volume on "Taboo," writes that in some cultures "persons most intimately connected by blood and especially by marriage . . . are often forbidden, not only to pronounce each other's names, but even to utter ordinary words which resemble or have a single syllable in common with these names," *The Golden Bough: A Study in Magic and Religion,* 3rd. ed., 12 vols. (New York: Macmillan, 1911–15), II, 335. The name taboo suggests that anyone who possesses an individual's name may exert power over that individual. Thus, in some cultures, individuals have two names: one, the sacred name, known only to her/himself, and the other, the common name, used by the community.

373–420 Material not found in either *Lanval* or *Landevale*. Chestre draws, apparently, on *Graelent* to construct this episode.

394–95 This exchange between a boy of the town and Gyfre helps to reinforce the theme of generosity which is prominent in the poem.

409–14 Compare Chaucer's Parson's Tale X (I) 443: "Pride of the table appeereth eek ful ofte; for certes, riche men been cleped to festes, and povre folk been put awey and rebuked."

414 *thyne*. MS: *dyne*.

416 Wearing purple is a common sign of wealth in medieval literature.

417 Ermine fur, like purple cloth, indicates wealth.

419 It is amusing that Launfal is now so wealthy that Gyfre serves not only as his squire but as his accountant as well. Bl (p. 92) notes that the two nouns "tayle" and "score" are "identical in meaning." Each originally meant a notch in a stick, and each came to mean the stick that bears the notches. The reference is to the medieval system of book-keeping whereby the amount of debt was recorded by a number of notches cut into a stick; the stick was then split longitudinally; one half was kept by the creditor, the other by the debtor, so that neither could falsify the record.

421–32 David Carlson has examined these lines closely, identifying the way they echo Matthew 25: 34–40 and James I: 27. St. Augustine and St. Thomas Aquinas cite these passages as the origin of the Seven Corporal Acts of Mercy. The passage from Matthew reads, "Then shall the king [Christ] say to them that shall be on his right hand: Come, ye blessed of my Father, possess you the kingdom prepared for you from the foundation of the world. For I was hungry, and you gave me to eat; I was thirsty, and you gave me to drink; I was a stranger, and you took me in: naked, and you covered me: sick, and you visited me: I was in prison, and you came to me. Then shall the just answer him, saying: Lord, when did we see thee hungry, and fed thee; thirsty, and gave thee drink? And when did we see thee a stranger, and took thee in? or naked, and covered thee? Or when did we see thee sick or in prison and came to thee? And the king answering, shall say to them: Amen I say to you, as long as you did it to one of these my least brethren, you did it to me" (Douai translation). The passage from James reads, "Religion clean and undefiled before God and the Father, is this: to visit the fatherless and widows in their tribulation: and to keep one's self unspotted from this world." Carlson uses lines 421–32 in *Sir Launfal* and the corresponding lines in the other English versions to argue that the Middle English redactions derive, not directly from the Old French, but from another intermediate text, now lost. Marie de France's *Lanval* names only one act of Corporal Mercy – visiting the imprisoned:

> Lanval donnoit les riches dons,
> Lanval aquitoit les prisons.
> Lanval vestoit les jugleors,

> Lanval feoit les granz honnors . . .
> (*Lanval*, lines 209–12)

See David Carlson, "The Middle English *Lanval*, the Corporal Works of Mercy, and Bibliotheque Nationale, Nouv. Acq. FR. 1104," *Neophilologus* 72 (1988), 97–106. Interestingly, Dame Tryamour also accomplishes works of corporal mercy, although no one has commented upon this, using the material rather to discuss Launfal. And, interestingly, Launfal may well create widows and orphans when he slaughters all the Lords of Atalye (lines 607–12); and, obviously, neither Launfal nor Dame Tryamour is chaste.

422–32 The repetition of the word "Fyfty" where Marie de France's *Lanval* repeats the hero's name has led Julian Harris, in "A Note on Thomas Chestre," *Modern Language Notes* 46 (1930), 24–25, to argue that Chestre "was apparently using a MS which contained the abbreviation L. for Lanval in lines 209-216 of Marie de France's *Lanval*." Harris speculates that Chestre mistook the "£" for "L" meaning fifty. Marie de France's lines read:

> Lanval donnoit les riches dons,
> Lanval aquitoit les prisons
> Lanval vestoit les jugleors,
> Lanval feoit les granz honnors,
> Lanval despendoit largement,
> Lanval donnoit or et argent.
> N'i ot estrange ne prive
> A cui Lanval n'eust donne.

430 Here, as in other romances, the narrator calls attention to the generosity given by aristocrats to minstrels, perhaps a plea for the immediate audience to give generously to the minstrel performing or reciting the lay. Perhaps it is a topos which marks the texts' original oral performance and need for patronage. See also *Sir Orfeo* (lines 25–38; 430–52; 515–18), and *Sir Cleges* (lines 49–54).

433–504 This material is unique in Chestre's version of the narrative. However, in line 474, he makes reference to "the Frenssch tale," which may be a now-lost source or it may be the conventional claim to authority. Bl suggests (p. 25) an analogue in Andreas Capellanus's *Art of Courtly Love*, trans. John J. Parry (New York: Norton, 1969), pp. 177-86.

450 MS: *kyghtes wonþer*.

467 The clever squire Gyfre claims the constable's horse.

470 MS: *wreththe.*

484 Notice that Blaunchard delivers blows alongside Launfal. The motif of the helpful animal-guide figure is common in folklore. See Roger S. Loomis, *Arthurian Tradition and Chrétien de Troyes* (New York: Columbia University Press, 1949), pp. 315–16. However, a well-accoutred war horse might wound men with spiked armor as it moved.

505–06 MS indents these two lines, as if to leave space for a rubricated A. Ri marks his text here as Part II.

505–612 Chestre's Valentine episode is paralleled in *Graelent*. It is also a tale told by Andreas Capellanus. Bl discusses the relationships between these versions of the story in his notes to lines 505-612 (pp. 93–94) and on page 25 of his critical edition. *Eger and Grime* locates Greysteel, the knights' supernatural combatant-adversary, in another land across a river, and Arthur, in the *Alliterative Morte Arthure*, must fight a giant who lives across the channel atop Mont St. Michael. The journey across water to fight a giant adversary on an island has a long tradition; see *Tristan* and *Beowulf*, for example. Spearing considers this episode "absurd" and evidence of the poem's failure (p. 106).

509 *How that.* MS: *That that.* S's emendation. Bl, Ru, F&H follow MS.

511 *wonder.* MS: *wonther.* Ru's emendation, followed by S.

527–28 See lines 1027–28. These lines are obviously intended to be insulting. The challenge is multivalent: challenging the knight's masculinity and challenging the court's "effeminacy."

530 *do.* MS: *tho.* Ru's emendation.

536 Bl glosses the line: "'skillful in every device,' or, in a free translation, 'up to all the tricks'"(p. 94).

541–43 Notice that Launfal does not reveal his lover's identity; he simply said "He wold wyth hym play."

561 *Atalye*. Bl (p. 94) notes: "according to the OF romance of *Otinel*, lines 190–92, the city of Atille was built by the 'pagans' in Lombardy, between two rivers."

569 Ri heads the line with *And*.

582 Gyfre apparently can make himself invisible as he helps Launfal out.

587 *thonkede . . . sythe*. MS: *donkede . . . syde*.

594 *doune*. MS: *þoune*.

596 *sythe*. MS: *syde*.

598 *dere*. MS: *þhere*.

606 To be "drawn" means to be torn apart by horses pulling in opposite directions. Arthur will threaten Launfal with the same punishment later in the poem (line 726).

610 MS: *sclayn*.

616 *he let*. MS: *alet*. Ri emends *let* to read "letter." I follow Bl who reads the *a* as the pronoun "he."

618 The feast of St. John the Baptist (June 24), yet another summer festival.

624 F&H add a pronoun to the line so it reads: "For he cowthe of largesse."

636 *partye* also means "country."

656 *sche*. MS: *sch*.

668 The citole is a flat-backed stringed instrument which is plucked like a guitar or lute.

669 MS: *un rryght*.

676–81 The inconsistency between these lines and Guenevere's treatment of Launfal earlier in the lay suggests that these lines are not to be understood as coy and disingenuous, but seductive. However, we could also read them back into the beginning of the poem as a reason why Launfal left the court and why Guenevere passed him over at the gift-giving. See notes to lines 67–72. Spearing (p. 108) argues: "I suspect that . . . Guenevere's promiscuity has come to symbolize the general problem of the mother's sexuality, which makes her both desirable and frightening to the son; and [this] encounter between her and Launfal, in which he perceives her as having attempted to seduce him while her story is that he has attempted to seduce her, is another way of treating the ambivalence of the son's desire for the mother."

683 *day*. MS: *þay*. Bl (p. 96) notes the similarity of this refusal to *Amis and Amiloun,* lines 598–609.

689 In this line Guenevere accuses the hero of homosexuality. Marie de France's *Lanval* (281–82) is more explicit: Guenevere accuses Launval of preferring boys to women; *Laundevale* (line 226) has the exact same line as Chestre's version here.

696 Nothing in the poem indicates the passing of seven years, until we reach this line. Of course, when Launfal visits the fairy Otherworld, time slows for him even though it has gone on as usual in this world.

697 MS: *lothlokste*.

705–08 The dynamic of the powerful woman who accuses a lower-ranking man of rape or of desiring her sexually can be found along a continuum of incest tales like the *Seven Sages*. In that text, the queen, desiring sex with her own step-son, is so outraged that he won't comply that she accuses him of rape and has him thrown in prison. The text records the debate in the court between the empress, who seeks her own step-son's execution, and the seven sages (councilors) who defend her step-son's life.

714 Although the usual phrase is "my heart will break in two," Bl (p. 96) notes "this rather ludicrous modification is necessitated by the rhyme."

715 Gwenevere accuses Launfal of two crimes: trying to seduce her and insulting her beauty. The ensuing trial actually revolves around the insult, since it is conventionally taken to be an attack on the king.

719 MS: *lodlokest.*

721 *wroth.* MS: *worth.* Bl's emendation.

724 F&H emend *wente* to *sente.*

730 The apparent dissolution of the fairy world happens suddenly. Compare Perceval who, falling asleep at the castle of maidens, wakes next morning to find himself under a tree, the castle completely vanished in Chrétien's *Conte du Graal.* It is a common motif in folktales and legends.

733–44 This material is not in *Lanval* or *Landevale.* It is present in *Graelent* (lines 529–30). M discusses possible sources for the episode in "A Note on *Sir Launfal*, 733–744," *Medium Aevum* 35 (1966), 122–24.

738 *Up.* Ri emends to *Upon*, to improve meter and sense.

741 Romances often make reference to sources (real or imagined), as if to lend credence to the tale. The device is also found in early English hagiography and late classical literature. See H. L. Levy "As myn auctor seyth," *Medium Aevum* 12 (1943), 25–39. Most likely, it means a "French book" (see line 474). In this instance the tag is perhaps triggered by the veiled literary allusion to the *ubi sunt* trope — the "where are they now" — in line 740, which puts the narrator in mind of literary conventions, and thus the tag acknowledging such tropes.

755 Launfal suffers from conventional lovesickness which afflicts many lovers in medieval literature.

760 The trial scene occurs in Marie de France with an emphasis on the legal maneuvers. Both Rychner, in his critical edition of *Lanval,* and E. A. Francis in her article, "The Trial in *Lanval,*" in *Studies in French Language and Mediaeval Literature Presented to Mildred K. Pope* (Manchester: Manchester University Press, 1939), pp. 115–24, assume that Marie de France based her representation of Lanval's trial on a real trial. Here, Chestre follows

Landevale, thereby rendering the episode quite briefly. His interest seems, rather, on the passages describing the entrance of the maidens.

761 Bl translates "ataynte" as "convicted," stressing Arthur's hasty and angry judgment on Launfal (p. 97).

763 MS: *lodlokest*.

772 *Sethe*. The first word of the line has been deleted by the scribe; *sethe* is the second word.

772–83 Launfal denies the first charge Gwenevere has brought against him and, faced with the second charge, he stands by his word, leaving the court to decide.

779 MS: *lodlokest*.

780 MS: *wordye*.

783 The word "loke" resonates with several meanings: it can mean command and it can mean look. Just as Launfal "fell" under the scorn of many men in lines 209–19 and sprang to his horse, riding toward the west to escape their "lokynge," here, at the end of the poem, he falls under many men's "lokynge," and will eventually "sprynge" to his horse and ride "ynto a jolif ile" (lines 1015, 1022).

784–86 F&H translate: "They were forced to consult books to say what was law" (I, p. 371). Bl: "Twelve knights were compelled . . . to swear a Bible-oath . . . to judge truly what the position was in all respects" (p. 98).

790 Literally "bore repute (fame) of such a charge of infidelity."

800 MS: *scluld*.

811–16 Perceval and Gawain agree to serve as hostages or sureties for Launfal. They guarantee he will be present for his trial; it is a serious pledge of support, for if Launfal fails to uphold his word, the sureties could be executed.

831 Because *recordede* carries legal meaning far beyond what Chestre inscribes here, Bl (pp. 98–99) notes that an accurate translation of the line would be

"The king had the charge and the defence read out from the record." Chestre's text, however, seems to omit much of the legality which Marie de France found interesting; consequently, the line could read "His [Launfal's] sureties brought him before the king; the king recorded that, and bade him [Launfal] to produce his beloved." Since sureties can guarantee the "word" or "truth" of the accused, their lives are on the line.

838 The Earl of Cornwall is mentioned in *Landevale* (line 335) and in *Lanval* (line 433), but the other three MSS call him a duke. Earlier Arthuriana refer to the "Duke of Cornwall," even though the Dukedom of Cornwall didn't formally exist until 1337. Consequently, Bl (p. 99) assumes that the scribe of *Landevale* wanted to reflect historical accuracy in his text and that Thomas Chestre simply followed suit. The last Earl of Cornwall died in 1237. The title Duke of Cornwall was revived in the fourteenth century and conferred on the Black Prince and his son, the future Richard II.

840–46 Bl (p. 99) notes, "Both *Launfal* and *Landevale* abridge, or rather omit the greater part of the long and reasoned judgment delivered by the Earl of Cornwall in *Lanval*." See *Lanval*, lines 433–60.

846 The threat of banishment is ironic, considering both Launfal's earlier choice to avoid Guenevere's advances by leaving the court and his later choice, at the end of the poem, to "flee" with his lemman into another world.

863 As Bl (p. 99) notes, only extremely high ranking guests would be housed in more private quarters; most would simply share the great hall.

876 *We*. MS: *Whe*.

877 Ru suggests that *tale* may mean "tally," in which case the sense would be "A new tally they took then."

891 MS: *clodynge*.

905 MS: *clodes*.

918 *thou*. Omitted in MS; supplied by Ri, F&H, Bl, and S.

925–72 Compare *Libeaus Desconus* (lines 925–48), *Erle of Tolous*, (lines 343–60), and notes to lines 292–300 above.

958 *Paytrelle* (or *peitrel*) is a word which can indicate either decorative trappings worn across the breast of the horse or an armor which protects the horse in battle. The image works either way. As ornament, it adds to the opulence of the fee; as armor, it adds to the image of the woman as a warrior coming to rescue her lemman. See Chaucer's Parson's Tale X (I) 431–33: "Also the synne of aornement or of apparaille is in thynges that apertenen to ridynge, as in to manye delicat horses that been hoolden for delit, that been so faire, fatte, and costlewe; / and also in many a vicious knave that is sustened by cause of hem; and in to curious harneys, as in sadeles, in crouperes, peytrels, and bridles covered with precious clothyng, and riche barres and plates of gold and of silver. / For which God seith by Zakarie the prophete, 'I wol confounde the rideres of swiche horses.'"

961 The *gerfawcon* was usually carried by a king; the *MED* identifies it as a large falcon. Both *Lanval* and *Landevale* have Dame Tryamour carrying a sparrowhawk, a smaller hawk more commonly carried by priests or ladies. Chestre's iconography here may simply indicate Dame Tryamour's aristocratic rank as a king's daughter, but it may also add to the powerful warrior imagery already established in the description of Dame Tryamour's horse. See John Cummins, *The Hound and the Hawk: The Art of Medieval Hunting* (New York: St. Martins, 1988), pp. 188, 194.

970–72 Compare *Landevale*, lines 459–60: "Now I have her seyn with myn ee, / I ne reke when that I dye."

989 Cross, in "Celtic Elements," comments that "the dropping of the mantle as a sign of respect was common both among men and women in medieval courtly circles." He also notes, however, that the action can be meant to stun the onlookers with the power of the body's exhibition, in this case, because Dame Tryamour is so beautiful (p. 639).

997 MS: *myne*. F&H retain *myne* and gloss the idiom: "take good heed." S retains the MS spelling, but provides no gloss on the line. I follow Bl in emending to "nyme," as does Ru. Ri reads *myne*.

999 MS: *lemmam*.

1006–08 The blinding of Guenevere is unique to *Launfal*. It is foreshadowed in line 810 by Guenevere herself. Despite its uniqueness, Stith Thompson comments, "Medieval storybooks are filled with tales of persons who are deceived into humiliating positions. Such stories are usually purely literary and often go back to much older sources. Many of them . . . concern exposed adultery" [*The Folktale* (New York: Holt, Rinehart, and Winston, 1949), p. 202]. A number of romances record narratives wherein the hero humiliates someone or a number of people. *Sir Ipomadon* tells the story of a knight who pretends not to joust (in fact, he jousts and wins each tournament *incognito*). The courtiers who laugh at Ipomadon are, themselves, the fools of the story. Guenevere and the mayor play similar parts here where they treat Launfal poorly, only to be repaid with a vengeance for their foolishness and for their attack on, or neglect of, the hero.

1015–17 In *Landevale*, the hero receives the lady's forgiveness only after she scolds him thoroughly (lines 503–28).

1021 *Thorth*. MS: *dorþ*.

1024 *yer*. MS: *er*. F&H's emendation, followed by Ru and S.

1025 See *Graelent*, lines 735–40, where the hero's horse is heard neighing in mourning for its master who, while riding across the river, was swept in and lost. Cross notes that the Irish *Each Labhra* (Speaking Horse) "was wont to issue from a mound on every midsummer eve, and answer questions regarding the events of the coming year" ("Celtic Elements," p. 634, fn. 3). Cross also cites Gervais of Tilbury's *Otia Imperialia* and the *Gesta Romanorum* for instances in the Cambridge region of "a supernatural warrior on horseback [who] meets all who challenge him on moonlight nights" (*ibid.*, p. 635).

1027–28 An echo of lines 526–27 which were an insult to Launfal's manhood. Since they are first Sir Valentyne's challenge to Launfal and here Launfal's challenge to any other men, they suggest the possibility that Launfal has replaced Valentyne in the scheme of things as the one who tests mortal men. Compare Sir Bertilak, the Green Knight, in *Sir Gawain and the Green Knight* and his subservience to Morgan le Fay. The mythic yearly return of the knight on horseback, the icon for the month of May, suggests correspondences between Launfal and season mythology like the Persephone myth. See Mircea Eliade,

The Myth of the Eternal Return or, Cosmos and History, trans. W. R. Trask, Bollingen Series XLVI (Princeton: Princeton University Press, 1954; rpt. 1964).

1042–44 As Bl (p. 102) notes, "the invocation of the Blessed Virgin . . . is surprisingly rare in the romances." Here at the end, Chestre provides the Christian prayer which conventionally closes literary works. The text is, however, overwhelmingly secular in its concerns and in its language.

Sir Gowther

Introduction

Sir Gowther is found in two late fifteenth-century manuscripts, British Library Royal MS 17.B.43 and National Library of Scotland MS Advocates 19.3.1. Both versions of the poem are in twelve-line tail rhyme stanzas and, though there are dialectic variations, scholars concur that both derive from the Northeast Midlands.[1] Stylistic differences between the two versions suggest, however, that the Royal MS is later and probably intended for a more cultured and refined audience.[2] One of the most striking differences is Royal's omission of the passage in which the preconversion hero, together with his cohorts, commits a heinous crime — the raping and pillaging of a convent of nuns. Perhaps the redactor of Royal determined this action to be too explicit for his refined audience. Whatever the reasons for the omission, there is additional internal evidence to suggest a gentler overall treatment of the story by the Royal scribe. The Advocates version, in contrast, tells the story in a more vigorous and decidedly more explicit manner, replete with graphic descriptions for the sake of truth (see line 189). Although their styles and approaches vary, both manuscript versions present Gowther's criminal acts in such a way that his rehabilitation, the subject of the narrative, is extraordinarily memorable.

The differences between the Royal and Advocates versions extend to the contents of the manuscripts themselves. While the Royal seems to emphasize a more visionary theme combining items such as *Sir John Maundeville's Travels,* William Staunton's *Vision of St. Patrick's Purgatory*, the *Vision of Tundale* and a short religious poem beginning "*Com home agayne / com home agayne / Mi nowine swet hart*," the Advocates does not. Rather Advocates, which contains John Lydgate's *Stans Puer ad Mensam,* a didactic work on table manners,[3] *The Life of Our Lady*, a hagiographical piece, which includes the birth and youth of Christ, and *Sir Isumbras*, a romance

---

[1] In his unpublished critical edition, Cornelius Novelli suggests that there are variations which indicate that the Royal is from the West Midlands, while the Advocates is more easterly.

[2] See Shirley Marchalonis, "*Sir Gowther*: The Process of a Romance," *Chaucer Review* 6 (1971/2), 24, 27.

[3] See Walter F. Schirmer, *John Lydgate: A Study in the Culture of the XVth Century* (London: Methuen & Co., 1952), p. 110.

about a knight who suffers the loss of his family only to regain them in the end, seems to express an interest in domestic life, familial relationships, and a didactic shaping of personal conduct. That *Sir Gowther* complements both manuscript themes equally well indicates the poem's ability to conform to diverse categories, an adaptability evident again when scholars attempt to situate the poem within a definitive genre. Defined variously as a tale of trial and faith, a penitential romance, a hagiographical romance, secular hagiography, a Breton lay, and simply a "process" of romance, *Sir Gowther* resists singular designations, but rather complies to a variety of possibilities.[4]

The source narrative most often cited in relation to *Sir Gowther* is a French poem entitled *Robert le Diable*, a five-thousand line *roman d'aventure* composed in the late twelfth century. Extant in only two manuscripts the poem, based upon legend, nonetheless generated versions in diverse forms – chronicle, exemplum, miracle play, romance, lai, dit – as well as several languages – French, Latin, English, Dutch, Spanish, Portuguese – as it was disseminated across Europe during the course of the next few centuries.[5] Although most scholars accept the legend as Gowther's source, a literary genealogy that includes an eleventh-century Irish tale, a twelfth-century Breton lai (*Tydorel*), the *Legend of Gregorius* and the *Life of St. Alexius*, has been mapped out.[6] Such source studies are useful to establish the complicated intertext-

---

[4] See Laura A. Hibbard [Loomis], *Medieval Romance in England* (London: Oxford University Press, 1924), pp. 49–57; E. M. Bradstock, "The Penitential Pattern in *Sir Gowther*," *Parergon* 20 (1978), 3–10; Andrea Hopkins, *The Sinful Knights: A Study of Middle English Penitential Romance* (Oxford: Clarendon Press, 1990), pp. 144–78; Margaret Bradstock, "*Sir Gowther*: Secular Hagiography or Hagiographical Romance or Neither?," *AUMLA* 59 (1983), 26–47; Florence Leftwich Ravenel, "*Tydorel* and *Sir Gowther*," *PMLA* 20 (1905), 152–78; M. B. Ogle, "The Orchard Scene in *Tydorel* and *Sir Gowther*," *Romanic Review* 13 (1922), 37–43.

[5] See Laura A. Hibbard [Loomis], pp. 49–51. The legend's influence on the fifteenth-century Middle English *Sir Gowther*, as well as the fourteenth-century *Roberd of Cesile*, marks the acknowledgment of the tale in England. The legend grows in popularity after its translation and printing in the sixteenth century.

[6] See Ronald S. Crane, "An Irish Analogue of the Legend of Robert the Devil," *Romanic Review* 5 (1914), 55–67. As his title suggests Crane argues for an earlier Irish analogue for the Robert legend. Florence Leftwich Ravenel contends that *Tydorel* is the lost Breton lai indicated by the Gowther poet while Andrea Hopkins claims a close resemblance to the legend of Gregorius, a story about the life of a boy born of incest, who leaves home, grows up and inadvertently marries his mother. He discovers the error, undertakes seventeen years of penance on a rock in the sea, after which time he is elected to the papacy and becomes Pope Gregory. See also Margaret Bradstock, "*Sir Gowther*: Secular Hagiography?" for a discussion of the relation of the poem to the *Life of St. Alexius*.

uality connecting the poem to other places, times, and literary genres, but, because they are often one-to-one comparisons, they fail to illuminate the contribution of extraliterary factors. Like many other lays and romances, *Sir Gowther* derives much of its inspiration from a rich and vastly underappreciated folk tradition. Popular ideology, particularly as it is expressed in folk narrative and fairytale, often places enormous emphasis on familial relations and the politics of domestic life, as well as the concerns of the larger community.

The motif that initiates the poem and creates the narrative dilemma involves the paternity of the hero. Gowther's mother, unable to conceive a child with her husband, prays in desperation for a child:

Scho preyd to God and Maré mylde
Schuld gyffe hur grace to have a chyld,
  On what maner scho ne roghth. *she didn't care*
In hur orchard apon a day
Ho meyt a mon, tho sothe to say, *She met a man; truth*
  That hur of luffe besoghth.
As lyke hur lorde as he myght be,
He leyd hur down undur a tre,
  With hur is wyll he wroghtth. *his will*
  (lines 64–72)

The Wish Child motif, as it is known by folklorists, calls for a woman to make a wish for a child while alone in an orchard or wooded area at a certain time of day. There she meets a stranger, a supernatural being in disguise, who becomes the agent of her pregnancy. Found in the apocryphal legend of St. Anne and reinscribed in the events of the Annunciation, the motif expresses the sanctity of a union between the divine and the mortal; the child born from such a union is destined to be extraordinary and exhibits a precocity of virtue and maturity beyond his/her years. Within the constellation of stories just mentioned examples are St. Anne, the Virgin Mary, and Christ himself. But in narratives in which the motif foreshadows an ominous event of some sort, i.e., a promise to the devil, it is referred to as the Devil's Contract.[7] One of the most famous instances of this type and relevant to *Sir Gowther* is that of Merlin, the famed counselor to King Arthur, whose circumstances of conception are similar to

[7] See Jennifer Fellows, "Mothers in Middle English Romance," in *Women and Literature in Britain 1150-1500*, ed. Carol M. Meale (Cambridge: Cambridge University Press, 1993), pp. 41–60. Fellows cites *Octavian* and *Sir Gowther* and traditional narratives such as *Rapunzel, Thumbelina, Little Prince Ivan*, *The Witch Baby*, and the *Little Sister of the Sun*. To the list of narratives which feature this motif we might add Marie de France's *Yonec* and the Middle English *Sir Orfeo*, though there is no evidence of pregnancy in the latter.

Gowther's: a lone woman is approached by a demon disguised as a handsome youth who seduces her and then announces the impending birth of a wondrous child. Merlin is precocious from the start and grows up to inspire a range of portrayals, some more positive than others. For many writers he is the preternatural prophet and trusted mentor of King Arthur; for others he is a wild man sired by a demon. Demonologists in the late Middle Ages considered him a figure for the Antichrist, prophesied in the *Book of Revelation* to signal the end of the world.[8] Given Gowther's "wylde" antics in the first half of the poem, his genealogical relation to the demonic Merlin seems to be born of necessity. Not only is Gowther conceived in a similar way, but an explicit relation is established between the two. Born of different mothers, they are sired by the same father:

> This chyld within hur was no nodur, *none other*
> Bot eyvon Marlyon halfe brodur
> For won fynd gatte hom bothe. *one fiend begot them*
> (lines 97–99)

The fraternal relation between Gowther and Merlin and their shared paternity with the fiend would most certainly presage disaster for a medieval audience.[9]

Gowther's demonic paternity is proven not only by his precocious growth and development,

> In a twelmond more he wex *twelve months*
> Then odur chyldur in seyvon or sex, *children of seven or six*
> (lines 145–46)

---

[8] See J. A. MacCulloch, *Medieval Faith & Fable* (London: Harrap, 1932): "In Nennius' *Historia Brittonum* his mother has no idea how her child was conceived. Geoffrey of Monmouth (d. 1154) makes Merlin's father a beautiful youth who talked with the girl invisibly . . . In Layamon's *Brut* (end of the twelfth century) Merlin's mother says, 'The fairest thing that ever was born, as it were a tall knight arrayed in gold; oft it kissed me and oft it me embraced. I know not whether it were evil thing or on God's behalf dight'" (p. 54).

[9] See J. A. MacCulloch in *Medieval Faith & Fable*, who claims that writers such as Caesarius of Heisterbach, Gervase of Tilbury, Giraldus of Cambrensis, Matthew of Paris, and others took the belief seriously enough to consider its theological implications. Caesarius of Heisterbach posited the theory that demons collected *crementum humanum, quod contra naturam funditur*, and from this formed bodies for themselves, either male or female. Their offspring were therefore human. Thomas Aquinas comes to a similar conclusion, determining that demons stole the semen from mortal men and impregnated women with it (see note for line 17).

but by his early dentition. As an infant he suckles nine wet nurses to death and when his mother attempts to take over the job he bites off her nipple. According to folk belief the presence of teeth at an early age functioned as proof of demonic paternity. Matthew Paris, for instance, records the existence of a child begotten by an incubus on a Hertfordshire woman, who, "at six months had teeth and was like a child of seven years old."[10] Such accelerated physical development in Gowther is accompanied by his uncontrollable aggression. In a short time his appetite for food assumes a predatory form — hunting becomes his favorite pastime — but not as practiced by other members of the aristocracy. Rather he becomes the raptor, a sharp-taloned, aggressive predator of the disempowered: religious women, a widow, a newlywed couple, hermits, and clerics, those supposed to be protected by knights and chivalric codes of honor. Dubbed a knight by his "father" the Duke in a fruitless attempt to control his behavior, Gowther disregards the precepts of chivalry and subverts the system that he has been entrusted to uphold.

Gowther's wild behavior and rough appearance associate him with a tradition of wild folks known throughout Europe during the Middle Ages. Depicted frequently in medieval iconography, the margins of medieval romances, Books of Hours, misericords, and cathedral architecture, wild folk engaged in a variety of human activities — hunting, jousting, dancing, etc. Sometimes represented as hybrid, half-human creatures,[11] they could silently challenge or mock established social and religious institutions from their frozen marginal positions.[12] Inscribed with a range of representations that could and often did correlate to human potentiality — the perpetual struggle with destructive impulses such as anger, violence, and unbridled sexuality as well as the promise of achieving human perfection by divine grace — wild folk inspired both fear and hope.[13] Often wild folk became synonymous with insanity.

---

[10]See J. A. MacCulloch, *Medieval Faith & Fable*, p. 56.

[11]Another facet of this tradition derives from the exotic descriptions and illustrations of hybrid creatures in the Alexander Romances, *Sir John Mandeville's Travels, Wonders of the East*, and the letters from Alexander the Great to Aristotle. See Andrea Rossi-Reder, "Wonders of the Beast: Medieval Monsters and Xenophobes," *Medieval Feminist Newsletter*, No. 16 (Fall 1993), 24–27.

[12] For an interesting discussion of marginal images see Michael Camille, *Image on the Edge: The Margins of Medieval Art* (Cambridge: Harvard University Press, 1992).

[13] See David A. Sprunger, "Wild Folk and Lunatics in Medieval Romance," in *The Medieval World of Nature: A Book of Essays*, ed. Joyce E. Salisbury (New York: Garland, 1933), pp. 145–63.

In a literary convention Penelope Doob calls the "unholy wild man," the bestial body functions as a metaphor for sin.[14] The Scriptural prototype is Nebuchadnezzar who, in the *Book of Daniel*, is transformed into a four-legged hybrid beast and exiled in the wild. Punished by God for persecuting the Hebrews, his madness acquires a moral component curable only by the satisfaction of his assigned penance. In contrast to this prototype of the "unholy wild man," which, for Doob includes Merlin, wild people could belong to an alternate category which Doob calls "holy wild men." In this group reside such luminaries as John the Baptist, Mary Magdalene, and numerous other Christian saints and ascetics, those who voluntarily removed themselves from human society, donned roughly cut animal skins, and retreated into the woods or wilderness to live a solitary life. Occasionally these holy wild folks assumed the position of the lowest in the social order – usually beggars or fools – and donned hairshirts or beggars' garb to signify their adoption of the holy life. Their motive was to establish a closer relation to God, reform themselves, and proclaim by word and example the possibility of redemption for all. Overcome by what Plato might call "divine madness" they were frequently perceived by others as fools for God.[15]

In secular literature wild folk and madmen are linked by puns on the Middle English term "wode" (wood, mad) and by their reputation for gravitating to wooded or wilderness areas.[16] In Geoffrey of Monmouth's *Vita Merlini*, for instance, Merlin is portrayed as an insane wildman driven to the woods when his "fury" seizes him.[17] In Chrétien de Troyes' *Yvain*, the hero is driven to the woods by a madness equated with lovesickness, and in Sir Thomas Malory's *Morte D'Arthur*, Lancelot and Tristan

---

[14] Penelope B. R. Doob, *Nebuchadnezzar's Children: Conventions of Madness in Middle English Literature* (New Haven: Yale University Press, 1974).

[15] One such graphic example is St. Francis who is depicted iconographically as talking to birds, stripping naked in public, and engaging in various activities thought crazy by other people.

[16] Richard Bernheimer, *Wild Men in the Middle Ages: A Study in Art, Sentiment, and Demonology*, (Cambridge, MA: Harvard University Press, 1952): "We may suspect that the category of wildness had its corrollary in contemporary reality, even though the writers may have forced the facts into a pattern of their own. It was a habit in the Middle Ages to let many lunatics go free unless they were believed to be obsessed and subject to the exorcism appropriate to their case. Such insane persons were thus at liberty to follow their irrational urges and desires. If we are to believe the romances, they commonly chose to retire into the woods thus laying a barrier of distance between themselves and their fellow men" (p. 12).

[17] Brocéliande Forest in Brittany was a frequent retreat for those experiencing the effects of love in these narratives. Its reputation as a place of enchantment no doubt encouraged the association between madness and a wooded locale.

experience a similar fate. In the Middle English *Sir Orfeo*, the hero's grief-stricken wilderness sojourn is initiated by the abduction of his beloved Heurodis to the Otherworld. The causes of medieval madness, at least in its literary forms, are brought about by a loss of reason that, as Doob's categories suggest, could be positively or negatively construed. The *Sir Gowther* poet, as if defying categories, locates his hero on the threshold between sanity and insanity, the unholy and the holy, the sacred and the profane in a symbolic position that seems to subvert these traditional binary oppositions, creating a narrative dilemma that can only be resolved by a miracle.[18]

Although the attempts of the Duke to reverse Gowther's irrational behavior by baptizing and knighting him fail, Gowther's redemption remains possible because he retains his ability to reason. Activated by the observation of the old Earl, "We howpe [think] thu come never of Cryston stryn, / Bot art sum fendys son, we weyn" (lines 208–09), Gowther is startled into a course of action. Just as so many other young orphans of myth and legend he demands to know who his real father is. But Gowther's approach is far more violent and threatening than that of others; he holds his mother at knifepoint until she answers the question:

> He seyd, "Dame, tell me in hye,
> Who was my fadur, withowt lye,
>   Or this schall thoro the glyde";
> He sette his fachon to hur hart:
> "Have done, yf thu lufe thi qwart!" *Speak; health*
> (lines 220–24)

Accompanied by a threat with such a formidable weapon, the question becomes a verbal assault reminiscent of Gowther's earlier physical assault on his mother's body. Perhaps not so ironically the action here compels a quest for penance that will erase his demonic paternity, the essence of his identity to this point. But when ordered to give up his falchion by the Pope Gowther refuses. No ordinary sword carried by

---

[18] See Michel Foucault, *Madness and Civilization: A History of Insanity in the Age of Reason* (New York: Vintage Books, 1973): "The madman's voyage is at once a rigorous division and an absolute Passage. In one sense, it simply develops, across a half-real, half-imaginary geography, the madman's liminal position on the horizon of medieval concern — a position symbolized and made real at the same time by the madman's privilege of being confined within the city gates: his exclusion must enclose him; if he cannot and must not have another prison than the threshold itself, he is kept at the point of passage" (p. 11).

knights, it symbolizes his identity as a wild man.[19] As necessary to him as Orfeo's harp is to Sir Orfeo, the falchion, which is the weapon of so much destruction in the first half of the poem, functions as the instrument of Gowther's final rehabilitation and return to legitimate knighthood. With it he defeats the Saracen enemy, and, in this sense, overcomes the wild man in himself.

Penance is one part of a penitential system intended to discipline and punish the transgressor in a manner often commensurate with the sin.[20] Because Gowther has committed harmful speech acts as well as acts of physical violence his penance seems appropriate. His muteness addresses the injuries done by his mouth in speech and action. Like Nebuchadnezzar Gowther is punished by his inability to communicate with other people; separated from society he is forced to contemplate what he has done. Ordered to eat only the food brought to him by dogs Gowther experiences life at the bottom of the social hierarchy. In his newly humbled state, he is forced to rely upon creatures that would ordinarily rely upon him. The greyhounds that minister to Gowther in the wilderness too are mute, a quality that according to Albertus Magnus lends them a certain nobility among dogs; the legend of the Holy Greyhound accorded them a sanctity no other breed could claim.[21] Here their mute presence creates a nexus between the silent Gowther and the mute princess who aids in his final redemption. Gowther's sojourn in the wilderness, much like that of the grief-stricken Orfeo, is followed by a process of reintegration into human society. He does not immediately acquire the position of knight in the Emperor's court, but rather maintains his muteness, assumes the role of fool and positions himself under the table with the dogs.

The Emperor's mute daughter becomes crucial to the narrative at this point; it is she who attends to Gowther's needs watching over him and providing food for him at court; it is she who, in a mock eucharistic ceremony, washes the mouths of the greyhounds who then administer bread and wine to him. It is she who ultimately

---

[19] Some scholars have argued that Gowther's falchion is associated with the Orient and has symbolic value particularly when it is used to kill the Sultan and his Saracen troops. See E. M. Bradstock, "The Penitential Pattern in *Sir Gowther*," *Parergon* 20 (April 1978), 3–10.

[20] The four-part system includes: contrition, confession, satisfaction, and absolution.

[21] See Jean-Claude Schmitt, *The Holy Greyhound: Guinefort, Healer of Children Since the Thirteenth Century*, trans. Martin Thom (Cambridge: Cambridge University Press, 1983). See also Dante, *Inferno* I, line 101. According to Charles Singleton, the Hound represents the temporal monarch Dante so fervently hoped would save the world.

mediates between Gowther and God, she who signals the miracle that ends his penance.[22]

The war between the Sultan and the Emperor, sometimes referred to as the three-day tournament, is the narrative event that leads to Gowther's final expiation.[23] On three successive days he prays for the accoutrements of chivalry – armor, shield, and horse – so that he might better fight the enemy. On each day his prayers are miraculously answered, evidence that his voice, however silent to those around him, is being heard by God. On each day his colors change, from black, to red, to white representing what some scholars believe to be a purification process.[24] During each battle Gowther fights successfully, but returns afterward to his assigned place under the table and his role of Hobbe the Fool; his identity as the rescuing knight is unknown to all but the maiden. On the third, culminating day Gowther receives a shoulder wound, a symbolic injury which initiates the final transformative event. As the sympathetic mediatrix falls out of her tower to what seems to be sure death, hope for Gowther's redemption fades.[25] But her comatose body becomes the locus of a miracle that transforms both her and Gowther. When, after three days, the maiden finally awakens, resurrected from seeming death, her muted voice has been miraculously restored and she speaks Gowther's absolution:

> Ho seyd, "My lord of heyvon gretys the well, *She*
> And forgyffeus the thi syn yche a dell *every bit*
> And grantys the tho blys;
> And byddus the speyke on hardely,

---

[22] Some scholars have noted a male Cinderella motif for this portion of the poem. Common to many medieval heroes, including some of Malory's knights, it requires a young man, assigned to domestic drudgery, to prove himself worthy of knighthood in some extraordinary way, i.e., by championing a lady, defeating a formidable enemy (giant or dragon), or proving his proficiency in battle. See Donald L. Hoffman, "Malory's 'Cinderella Knights' and the Notion of Adventure," *Philological Quarterly* 67 (1988), 145–56.

[23] It is sometimes difficult to differentiate between actual life and fiction even in the Middle Ages. Laura A. Hibbard [Loomis] in *Medieval Romance in England* notes that Malory's patron, Richard Beauchamp, Earl of Warwick, "during his governorship of Calais, under such names as the Chevalier Vert, for three days challenged French knights to a tourney" (p. 55).

[24] See Jessie Laidlay Weston, *The Three Days' Tournament: A Study in Romance and Folklore* (London: D. Nutt, 1902).

[25] Like Beowulf to Hrothgar, or Roland to Charlemagne, Gowther serves his lord without regard for his own life.

Eyte and drynke and make mery;
Thu schallt be won of His."
(lines 661–66)

Gowther is liberated from his position under the table and the silent prison of his body. But most significantly Gowther's paternity is transferred from one father to another:

"Now art thu Goddus chyld;
The thar not dowt tho warlocke wyld, *You need not fear; devil*
Ther waryd mot he bee." *vanquished must*
(lines 673–75)

The remainder of the poem functions as satisfaction in its own right as Gowther's restoration is delineated: he marries the miraculous maiden, inherits the German Empire, and arranges the marriage of the old Earl to his mother. But most importantly he builds an abbey to atone for his devastating crime against the nuns. Herein lies an important difference between the Royal and Advocates MSS. Whereas Advocates retains Gowther's identity, Royal identifies him with Saint Guthlac, the founder of Croyland Abbey in England in the early eighth century. At least one scholar finds the correlation unconvincing arguing that Guthlac's life "does not provide as suitable an example of salvation from sin as Gowther does."[26] This may be true and there are undoubtedly political motives behind the omission that warrant further study. What is clear from the Advocates version presented here is that Gowther, madman and criminal, achieves personal salvation and becomes at his death the locus of miracles for the poor, the dissolute, and the insane.

Select Bibliography

Manuscripts

British Library Royal MS 17.B.43. Fols. 116a–131b.

National Library of Scotland MS Advocates 19.3.1. Fols. 11a–28a.

[26] See Margaret Bradstock, "*Sir Gowther*: Secular Hagiography?," p. 40.

Introduction

Critical Editions

Breul, Karl. *Sir Gowther.* Oppeln: E. Frank, 1886.

Novelli, Cornelius. *Sir Gowther.* Ph. D. dissertation, University of Notre Dame, 1963. [Offers side-by-side versions of Royal and Advocates MSS and includes textual and explanatory notes.]

Collections

Utterson, Edward Vernon, ed. *Select Pieces of Early Popular Poetry.* London: Longman, Hurst, Lees, Orme and Brown, 1817.

Mills, Maldwyn, ed. *Six Middle English Romances.* London: Dent, 1973. Pp. 148–68.

Rumble, Thomas C., ed. *The Breton Lays in Middle English.* Detroit: Wayne State University Press, 1965. Pp. 179–204 [Uses the Royal MS.]

Related Studies

Bradstock, E. M. "The Penitential Pattern in *Sir Gowther.*" *Parergon* 20 (1974), 3–10. [Explores interconnecting themes of heroic prowess and the penitential process.]

——."*Sir Gowther*: Secular Hagiography or Hagiographical Romance or Neither?" *Journal of the Australasian Universities Language and Literature Association* 59 (1983), 26–47. [Reviews problems of generic classification and concludes that 'secular hagiography' may be a useful term to apply to some narratives.]

Hopkins, Andrea. *The Sinful Knights: A Study of Middle English Penitential Romances.* Oxford: Clarendon Press, 1990, pp. 144–78. [Sees the penitential theme in the poem to be its generic determination.]

Marchalonis, Shirley. "*Sir Gowther*: The Process of a Romance." *Chaucer Review* 6 (1971/72), 14–29. [Demonstrates the process of transformation of a conversion story influenced by chivalric ethics.]

Ogle, M. B. "The Orchard Scene in *Tydorel* and *Sir Gowther.*" *Romanic Review* 13 (1922), 37–43. [Comparative study.]

Ravenel, Florence Leftwich. "*Tydorel* and *Sir Gowther.*" *PMLA* 20 (1905), 152–77. [Comparative study with the OF lay.]

Sir Gowther

God, that art of myghtis most,
Fader and Sone and Holy Gost,
That bought man on Rode so dere, — *Cross*
Shilde us from the fowle fende, — *Protect; foul fiend*
That is about mannys sowle to shende — *injure*
All tymes of the yere!
Sumtyme the fende hadde postee — *Once; power*
For to dele with ladies free — *copulate; noblewomen*
In liknesse of here fere, — *their husbands*
So that he bigat Merlyng and mo, — *Merlin; others*
And wrought ladies so mikil wo — *caused; great pain*
That ferly it is to here. — *wondrous; hear*

A selcowgh thyng that is to here, — *marvelous; hear*
That fend nyeght wemen nere — *lay with; so near*
And makyd hom with chyld; — *them*
Tho kynde of men wher thei hit tane,[1]
For of hom selfe had thei nan, — *For they themselves had no form*
Be meydon Maré mylde, — *By maiden Mary*
Therof seyus clerkus, y wotte how; — *clerks say; I know*
That schall not be rehersyd now,
As Cryst fro schame me schyld. — *shield*
Bot y schall tell yow of a warlocke greytt, — *great demon*
What sorow at his modur hart he seyt — *mother's heart; brought*
With his warcus wylde. — *wild deeds*

Jesu Cryst, that barne blythe, — *joyful child*
Gyff hom joy, that lovus to lythe — *Give them; love; listen*
Of ferlys that befell. — *wonders*
A law of Breyten long y soghht, — *lay*
And owt ther of a tale ybroghht,

---

[1] *Then the form (kynde) of men they took there*

That lufly is to tell. *lovely*
Ther wonde a Duke in Estryke, *[once] lived; Austria*
He weddyt a ladé non hur lyke *lady unsurpassed*
For comly undur kell; *beauty; head-dress*
To tho lyly was likened that lady clere, *the lily; bright (innocent)*
Hur rod reyde as blosmes on brere, *Her complexion rosy; briar*
That ylke dere damsell. *same*

When he had weddyd that meydyn schene *beautiful*
And sche Duches withowt wene, *doubt*
A mangere con thei make; *feast did*
Knyghtus of honowr tho furst dey *the first day*
Justyd gently hom to pley *Jousted*
Here shaftes gan thei shake. *Their lances; shatter*
On the morow the lordes gente
Made a riall tournement *royal*
For that lady sake;
Tho Duke hym selfe wan stedys ten.
And bare don full doghty men, *brought down; valiant*
And mony a cron con crake. *cracked many a skull*

When this turment was y-ses, *tournament; over*
Tho ryche Duke and tho Duches *worthy; the*
Lad hor lyfe with wyn; *Led their; joy*
Ten yer and sum dele mare *somewhat more*
He chylde non geyt ne sche non bare, *begot; bore*
Ther joy began to tyne; *wane*
To is ladé sone con he seyn, *To his lady*
"Y tro thu be sum baryn, *I believe you to be somewhat barren*
Hit is gud that we twyn; *separate*
Y do bot wast my tyme on the,
Eireles mon owre londys bee"; *Heirless must*
For gretyng he con not blyn. *weeping; cease*

Tho ladé sykud and made yll chere *The lady sighed*
That all feylyd hur whyte lere, *pale face*
For scho conseyvyd noght; *she*
Scho preyd to God and Maré mylde *She; Mary*
Schuld gyffe hur grace to have a chyld,

On what maner scho ne roghth. *she didn't care*
In hur orchard apon a day
Ho meyt a mon, tho sothe to say, *She met a man; truth*
That hur of luffe besoghth, *love*
As lyke hur lorde as he myght be;
He leyd hur down undur a tre,
With hur is wyll he wroghtth. *her his desire he wrought*

When he had is wylle all don *his pleasure taken*
A felturd fende he start up son, *As a shaggy fiend; lept up quickly*
And stode and hur beheld;
He seyd, "Y have geyton a chylde on the *begotten; you*
That in is yothe full wylde schall bee, *in his youth*
And weppons wyghtly weld." *mightily wield*
Sche blessyd hur and fro hym ran, *crossed herself*
Into hur chambur fast ho wan, *she went*
That was so bygly byld. *firmly built*
Scho seyd to hur lord, that ladé myld, *lady*
"Tonyght we mon geyt a chyld *may beget*
That schall owre londus weld." *rule*

"A nangell com fro hevon bryght *An angel*
And told me so this same nyght,
Y hope was Godus sond; *God's messenger*
Then wyll that stynt all owr stryfe." *resolve*
Be tho lappe he laght his wyfe *By a fold of her robe; seized*
And seyd, "Dame, we schall fonde." *make love*
At evon to beyd thei hom ches, *evening; bed; made their way*
Tho ryche Duke and tho Duches,
And wold no lengur wonde; *wait*
He pleyd hym with that ladé hende, *gracious lady*
And ei yode scho bownden with tho fende, *went; burdened; devil's child*
To God wold losse hur bonde. *Until; release; burden*

This chyld within hur was no nodur, *none other*
Bot eyvon Marlyon halfe brodur, *Than Merlin's*
For won fynd gatte hom bothe; *For one fiend begot them both*
Thei sarvyd never of odyr thyng *never did anything else*
But for to tempe wemen yon. *young*

To deyle with hom was wothe. — *have intercourse; sinful*
Ylke a day scho grette fast — *Each; grew more obviously pregnant*
And was delyverid at tho last
Of won that coth do skathe; — *one; could do harm*
Tho Duke hym gard to kyrke beyre, — *had him taken to the church*
Crystond hym and cald hym Gwother, — *called*
That sythyn wax breme and brathe. — *soon grew fierce; violent*

Tho Duke comford that Duches heynde, — *comforted; diligently*
And aftur melche wemen he sende, — *wet nurses*
Tho best in that cuntré,
That was full gud knyghttys wyffys. — *Who were; wives*
He sowkyd hom so thei lost ther lyvys, — *sucked them*
Sone had he sleyne three!
Tho chyld was yong and fast he wex – — *grew*
The Duke gard prycke aftur sex – — *had sent for six [other wet nurses]*
Hende harkons yee: — *Pay heed, gentle audience*
Be twelfe monethys was gon — *Before*
Nine norsus had he slon — *slain*
Of ladys feyr and fre.

Knyghtus of that cuntré geydyrd hom samun — *banded themselves together*
And seyd to tho Duke hit was no gamun — *joke*
To lose hor wyffus soo; — *their*
Thei badde hym orden for is son — *ordain*
He geytys no more is olde won, — *[That] he practice no more his old habits*
Norsus now no moo. — *[On] no more nurses*
His modur fell afowle unhappe, — *unfortunately*
Upon a day bad hym tho pappe, — *offered him her breast*
He snaffulld to hit soo — *suckled*
He rofe tho hed fro tho brest – — *tore the nipple*
Scho fell backeward and cald a prest,
To chambur fled hym froo.

Lechus helud that ladé yare, — *Physicians; promptly*
Wemen durst gyffe hym souke no mare,
That yong chyld Gowther,
Bot fed hym up with rych fode
And that full mych as hym behovyd, — *as much as he demanded*

Full safly mey y sweyre. *may I swear*
Be that he was fifteen yere of eld *when; age*
He made a wepon that he schuld weld, *wield*
No nodur mon myght hit beyr; *bear*
A fachon bothe of stylle and yron, *curved sword*
Wytte yow wyll he wex full styron *Know; waxed; fierce*
And fell folke con he feyr. *many; terrorize*

In a twelmond more he wex *He grew more in a year*
Then odur chyldur in seyvon or sex, *other children did in six or seven*
Hym semyd full well to ryde;
He was so wekyd in all kyn wyse *wicked in all kinds of ways*
Tho Duke hym myght not chastyse,
Bot made hym knyght that tyde, *time*
With cold brade bronde; *broad sword*
Ther was non in that londe
That dynt of hym durst byde. *blow; could abide*
For sorro tho Duke fell don ded;
His modur was so wo of red *weary of the secret*
Hur care scho myght not hyde.

Mor sorro for hym sche myght have non, *might not endure*
Bot to a castyll of lyme and ston
Frely then scho fled;
Scho made hit strong and held hur thare,
Hor men myght tell of sorro and care,
Evyll thei wer bested, *They were ill-situated*
For wher he meyt hom be tho way,
"Evyll heyle!" myght thei say *Curses!*
That ever modur hom fed;
For with his fachon he wold hom slo *slay them*
And gurde hor horssus backus in too – *strike their; two*
All seche parellys thei dred. *perils*

Now is he Duke of greyt renown,
And men of holy kyrke dynggus down *church he smites down*
Wher he myght hom mete. *Wherever*
Masse ne matens wold he non here *nor matins; hear*
Nor no prechyng of no frere, *friar*

That dar I heyly hette; *solemnly swear*
Erly and late, lowde and styll,
He wold wyrke is fadur wyll *do his father's*
Wher he stod or sete.
Hontyng lufde he aldur best, *He loved hunting best of all*
Parke, wodd and wylde forest,
Bothe be weyus and strete. *byways; highways*

He went to honte apon a day, *hunt*
He see a nonry be tho way *nunnery by*
And thedur con he ryde;
Tho pryorys and hur covent *prioress*
With presescion ageyn hym went *procession; went to meet him*
Full hastely that tyde; *time*
Thei wer full ferd of his body, *very frightened*
For he and is men bothe leyn hom by – *lay with them*
Tho sothe why schuld y hyde? *truth*
And sythyn he spard hom in hor kyrke *then he enclosed them*
And brend hom up, thus con he werke; *burned them; did*
Then went his name full wyde.

All that ever on Cryst con lefe, *did believe*
Yong and old, he con hom greve *caused them grief*
In all that he myght doo:
Meydyns maryage wolde he spyll *destroy by rape*
And take wyffus ageyn hor wyll,
And sley hor husbondus too,
And make frerus to leype at kraggus *jump off cliffs*
And parsons for to heng on knaggus, *hang on hooks*
And odur prestys sloo; *other; slew*
To bren armettys was is dyssyre, *burn hermits*
A powre wedow to seyt on fyre, *poor widow; set*
And werke hom mykyll woo. *do them great*

A nolde erle of that cuntré *An old earl*
Unto tho Duke then rydys hee
And seyd, "Syr, why dose thu soo?
We howpe thu come never of Cryston stryn, *suspect; strain*
Bot art sum fendys son, we weyn, *think*

That werkus hus this woo. — *causes us*
Thu dose never gud, bot ey tho ylle — — *always the bad*
We hope thu be full syb tho deyll." — *think you must be close kin to the devil*
Syr Gowther wex then throo; — *became angry*
Hee seyd, "Syr, and thu ly on mee, — *if you tell lies*
Hongud and drawon schall thu bee — *drawn*
And never qwycke heythyn goo." — *alive go hence*

He gard to putte tho erle in hold — *ordered to be imprisoned*
And to his modur castyll he wold — *set off*
As fast as he myght ryde;
He seyd, "Dame, tell me in hye, — *at once*
Who was my fadur, withowt lye,
Or this schall thoro the glyde"; — *through you*
He sette his fachon to hur hart: — *her heart*
"Have done, yf thu lufe thi qwart!" — *Speak; health*
Ho onswarde hym that tyde — — *She*
"My lord," scho seyd, "that dyed last." — *recently*
"Y hope," he seyd, "thou lyus full fast"; — *I think; lie*
Tho teyrus he lett don glyde.

"Son, sython y schall tho sothe say: — *Son, now I*
In owre orcharde apon a day
A fende gat the thare, — *begot thee*
As lyke my lorde as he myght be,
Undurneyth a cheston tre"; — *chestnut*
Then weppyd thei bothe full sare. — *sorrowfully*
"Go schryfe the, modur, and do tho best, — *confess*
For y wyll to Rome or that y rest — *ere*
To lerne anodur lare." — *teaching*
This thoght come on hym sodenly:
"Lorde, mercy!" con he cry
To God that Maré bare,

To save hym fro is fadur tho fynde; — *fiend*
He preyd to God and Maré hynde, — *gentle*
That most is of posté, — *power*
To bryng is sowle to tho blys
That He boght to all His — *His [people]*

Apon tho Rode tre. *Cross*
Sythyn he went hym hom ageyn *took himself*
And seyd to tho erle, withowt leyn, *lie*
Tho sothe tale tolde thu mee; *truthful*
Y wyll to Rome to tho apostyll, *Pope*
That he mey schryfe me and asoyll; *may confess; absolve*
Kepe thu my castyll free." *safe*

This old erle laft he theyr
For to be is stydfast heyre, *his steadfast heir*
Syr Gwother forthe con glyde; *hastened*
Toward Rome he radly ranne, *readily*
Wold he nowdur hors ne man
With hym to ren ne ryde;
His fauchon con he with hym take,
He laft hit not for weyle ne wrake, *lifted; joy nor pain*
Hyt hong ei be his syde. *ever*
Toward Rome cety con hee seche; *did he journey*
Or he come to tho Powpe speche *Before*
Full long he con abyde.

As sone has he the Pope con see,
He knelys adown apon is kne
And heylst hym full sone; *greets*
He preyd hym with mylde devocyon
Bothe of schryfte and absolyscion; *for confession*
He granttyd hym is bone. *his request*
"Whethon art thu and of what cuntré?"
"Duke of Estryke, lorde," quod hee,
"Be tru God in trone; *By; on throne*
Ther was y geyton with a feynde *begotten*
And borne of a Duches hende;
My fadur has frenchypus fone." *few friendships*

"Y wyll gladly, be my fey!
Art thou Crystond?" He seyd, "Yey,
My name it is Gwother;
Now y lowve God." "Thu art commun hedur,
For ellus y most a traveld thedur

Apon the for to weyre, *admonish*
For thu hast Holy Kyrke destryed." *Holy Church*
"Nay, holy fadur, be thu noght agrevyd,
Y schall the truly swere
At thi byddyng beyn to be,
And hald tho penans that thu leys to me, *assign penance*
And never Cryston deyre." *injure*

"Lye down thi fachon then the fro;
Thou schallt be screvon or y goo, *confessed before I go*
And asoylyd or y blyn." *absolved; cease*
"Nay, holy fadur," seyd Gwother,
"This bous me nedus with mee beyr, *falchion I needs must carry*
My frendys ar full thyn." *very few*
"Wherser thu travellys, be northe or soth, *Wheresoever*
Thu eyt no meyt bot that thu revus of howndus mothe *eat no food; snatch*
Cum thy body within;
Ne no worde speke for evyll ne gud,
Or thu reyde tokyn have fro God, *Until you've received a sign*
That forgyfyn is thi syn."

He knelyd down befor tho Pope stole, *chair of authority*
And solemly he con hym asoyle, *did he absolve him*
Tho sarten sothe to sey. *To tell the very truth*
Meyte in Rome gatte he non *Food*
Bot of a dog mothe a bon, *from a dog's mouth*
And wyghttly went is wey; *quickly; his*
He went owt of that cetè
Into anodur far cuntrè,
Tho testamentys thus thei sey; *witnesses*
He seyt hym down undur a hyll, *set himself*
A greyhownde broght hym meyt untyll *regularly*
Or evon yche a dey. *Before evening every day*

Thre neythtys ther he ley: *nights*
Tho grwhownd ylke a dey *each day*
A whyte lofe he hym broghht; *loaf*
On tho fort day come hym non, *fourth*
Up he start and forthe con gon, *onward he went*

And lovyd God in his thoght. *with*
Besyde ther was a casstell, *Nearby*
Therein an emperowr con dwell,
And thedurwarde he soghht; *thither he proceeded*
He seyt hym down withowt the yate *outside the gate*
And durst not entur in ther atte, *dared*
Thof he wer well wroght. *Though he was powerfully built*

Tho weytus blu apon tho wall, *guards on the wall blew [a signal]*
Knyghttus geydert into tho hall, *gathered*
Tho lord buskyd to his saytte; *hurried; seat*
Syr Gwother up and in con gwon, *went*
At tho dor uschear fond he non, *no usher*
Ne porter at tho yatte, *Nor; gate*
Bot gwosse prystely thoro tho pres, *goes swiftly; crowd*
Unto tho hye bord he chesse, *head table; went*
Ther undur he made is seytt. *under [the table]; his seat*
Tho styward come with yarde in honde, *steward; stick*
To geyt hym thethyn fast con he fonde *deal with him quickly*
And throly hym con threyt *fiercely threatened him*

To beyt hym, bot he wende awey. *beat; unless*
"What is that?" tho Emperour con sey.
"My lord," he seyd, "a mon,
And that tho feyryst that ever y sye; *fairest; saw*
Cum loke on hym, it is no lye,"
And thedur wyghtly he wan. *quickly he went*
Won word of hym he myght not geyt; *One word from*
Thei lette hym sytt and gafe hym meyt. *food*
"Full lytyll gud he can,
And yett mey happon thoro sum chans *Except what; circumstance*
That it wer gyffon hym in penans," *given; penance*
Tho lord thus onsward than. *answered*

When tho Emperowr was seyt and sarvyd *seated; served*
And knyghttus had is breyd karvyd, *cut up*
He sent tho dompmon parte; *mute man*
He lette hit stond and wold ryght non. *would not eat any*
Ther come a spanyell with a bon, *spaniel*

In his mothe he hit bare,
Syr Gwother hit fro hym droghhe, *it from him drew*
And gredely on hit he gnofe, *eagerly; gnawed*
He wold nowdur curlu ne tartte. *would [accept] neither curlew nor quail*
Boddely sustynans wold he non
Bot what so he fro tho howndus wan,
If it wer gnaffyd or mard. *Even if it were chewed or spoiled*

Tho Emperowre and tho Emperrys
And knyghttys and ladys at tho des *high table*
Seyt and hym behelld;
Thei gaffe tho hondus meyt ynoghhe, *enough*
Tho dompe Duke to hom he droghhe, *mute Duke [Gowther]; drew close*
That was is best beld. *comfort*
Among tho howndys thus was he fed,
At evon to a lytyll chambur led *evening*
And hyllyd undur teld; *hidden; a curtain*
At none come into tho hall, *noon he would come*
Hob hor fole thei con hym call; *Hob their fool they called him*
To God he hym con yelde. *yield*

But now this ylke Emperowre
Had a doghtur whyte as flowre,
Was too soo dompe as hee; *also as mute as Gowther*
Scho wold have spokyn and myght noght.
That meydon was worthely wroght, *very beautiful*
Bothe feyr, curteys and free.
A messynger come apon a dey,
Tyll her fadur con he sey,
"My lord wele gretys the;
Tho Sawdyn, that is of mykyll myght *Sultan; great power*
Wyll wer apon the dey and nyghtt *[make] war upon you*
And bren thi bowrus free, *burn; bowers*

And sley thi men bot thu hym sende *unless*
Thi doghttur that is so feyr and heynde, *courteous*
That he mey hur wedde."
Tho Emperowr seyd, "Y have bot won, *one*
And that is dompe as any ston, *she is mute*

Feyrur thar non be feyd; *None fairer could be imagined*
And y wyll not, be Cryst wonde, *by Christ's wounds*
Gyffe hor to no hethon hownde, *her*
Then wer my bale bredde. *would my sorrows be engendered*
Yet mey God thoro Is myght *through His power*
Ageyn to geyt hur spech ryght." *Return to her*
Tho messynger ageyn hym spedde *hastened away*

To tho Sadyn and told hym soo. *Sultan*
Then wakynd ey more wo and wo, *awakened increasing sorrow*
He toke is oste and come nere. *army*
Tho Emperowr, doghtty undur schyld, *courageous*
With anodur kepped hym in tho fyld, *engaged*
Eydur had batell sere. *Each; several battalions*
Syr Gwother went to a chambur smart, *promptly*
And preyd to God in his hart
On Rode that boghtt Hym dere, *Cross*
Schuld sende hym armur, schyld and speyr,
And hors to helpe is lord in weyr *war*
That wyll susstand hym thare. *sustain*

He had no ner is preyr made, *no sooner said his prayer*
Bot hors and armur bothe he hade, *When*
Stode at his chambur dor;
His armur, is sted was blacke color; *his horse*
He leypus on hors, that stythe in stowr, *sturdy in battle [was]*
That stalworthe was and store; *strong*
His scheld apon his schuldur hong,
He toke his speyre was large and long
And spard nodur myre ne more; *shunned neither mere nor moor*
Forthe at tho yatus on hors he went, *pathways*
Non hym knew bot that meydyn gent,
And aftur hur fadur he fore. *rode*

Tho Emperour had a batell kene, *fierce battalion*
Tho Sawden anodur, withowt wene, *doubt*
Assemuld, as was hor kast; *Assembled as was their design*
Bot fro Syr Gwother comun were, *But once*
Mony a crone con he stere *head did he remove*

And hew apon full fast; *cut down*
He gard stedus for to stakur *made horses stagger*
And knyghttus hartys for to flakur *hearts quake in fear*
When blod and brenus con brast; *brains burst*
And mony a heython hed of smott, *heathen head smote off*
And owt of hor sadyls, wylle y wott, *well I know*
Thei tombull at tho last. *tumble*

He putte tho Sawden to tho flyghth
And made tho chasse to it was nyghth, *gave pursuit until*
And sluye tho Sarsyns kene; *slew the fierce Saracens*
Sython rode before tho Emperowr. *Then*
Non hym knew bot that bryghtt in bowr, *lovely [princess]*
Tho dompe meydon schene. *so beautiful*
To chambur he went, dysharnest hym sone, *soon disarmed himself*
His hors, is armur awey wer done,
He ne wyst wher hit myght bene.
In hall he fond his lorde at meyt; *dinner*
He seytt hym down and made is seytt *took his place*
Too small raches betwene. *Two small hunting dogs*

Tho meydon toke too gruhowndus fyn *two fine greyhounds*
And waschyd hor mowthus cleyn with wyn
And putte a lofe in tho ton; *loaf of bread in the one*
And in tho todur flesch full gud; *other fresh meat*
He raft bothe owt with eyggur mode, *wrested; eagerly*
That doghty of body and bon. *worthy one*
He seytt, made hym wyll at es, *well at ease*
Sythyn to chambur con he ches,
In that worthely won. *dwelling*
On tho morne cum a messengere
Fro tho Sawdyn with store chere, *foreboding news*
To tho Emperowr sone he come;

He seyd: "Syr, y bryng yow a lettur:
My lord is commun, wyll take hym bettur,
Yesturdey ye slo his men;
Todey he is commun into tho feyld
With knyghtys that beyrus speyr and schyld,

Thowsandus mo then ten;
On the he will avenied be." *On you; avenged*
"Hors and armour," than said he,
"Hastly had we thenne."
God sende Syr Gwother thro Is myghth *sent; His*
A reyd hors and armur bryght, *red*
He fowlyd thro frythe and fen. *followed; forest; marsh*

When bothe batels wer areyd, *armies; prepared*
Truly, as tho romandys seyd, *romance*
Syr Gwother rode betwene;
Mony a sturdy gard he stombull, *knight he caused to stumble*
Toppe over teyle hor horssus to tombull,
For to wytte withowt wene; *doubt*
He hewde insondur helme and schelde, *hewed in two*
He feld tho baner in tho feld *felled; field*
That schon so bryght and schene; *shining*
He leyd apon tho Sarsyns blake
And gard hor basnettus in too crake; *helmets to crack in two*
He kyd that he was kene. *proved; brave*

"A, Lord God!" seyd tho Emperowre,
"What knyght is yondur so styffe in stowr
And all areyd in red,
Bothe his armur and his sted,
Mony a hethon he gars to bled *causes; bleed*
And dynggus hom to tho deyd, *beat them to death*
And hedur come to helpe me? *hither*
Anodur in blacke yesturdey had we
That styrd hym wyll in this styd, *handled himself well in this place*
Dyscomfytt the Sawden and mony a Sarsyn; *Defeated*
So wyll yondur do, as y wene, *think*
His dyntys ar heyve as leyde; *blows; heavy as lead*

His fochon is full styffe of stele – *falchion*
Loke, he warus his dyntus full wele, *delivers his blows*
And wastus of hom never won." *wastes; never a one*
Tho Emperowr pryckus into tho pres, *gallops, thick of battle*
Tho doghtty knyght with hym he ches,

And byrkons hom flesche and bon. *belabors them*
Tho Sawdyn to a forest fled,
And his ost with hym he led
That laft wer onslon. *Those that were left unslain*
Syr Gwother turnyd is brydyll bryght *bridle*
And rode befor is lorde full ryghtt, *as was fitting*
To chambur then he hym cheys. *returned*

When his armur of wer don, *was taken off*
His hors and hit away wer son, *disappeared*
That he wyst not whare. *didn't know where*
When he come into tho hall,
He fond tho Emperour and is men all
To meyt was gwon full yare; *promptly*
Among tho howndus down he hym seytt,
Tho meydon forthe tho greyhondus feytt, *brought forth*
And leytt as noghtt ware; *behaved as if nothing had happened*
Fedde Hob tho fole, for sothe to sey
Lyke as sche dyd tho forme dey; *previous*
To chambur sython con fare.

Tho Emperour thonkud God of hevun,
That schope tho nyght and tho deyus seyvun, *created; seven days*
That he had soo sped;
Dyscomfyd tho Sawdyn thwys, *twice*
And slen is men most of prys, *most highly valued*
Save thos that with hym fled.
"Anturus knyghtus come us too, *Adventurous*
Aydur dey won of thoo,
Y ne wyst wher thei wer bred; *I do not know; born*
Tho ton in reyd, tho todur in blacke — *The one; the other*
Had eydur of hom byn to lacke *Had either of them been absent*
Full evyll we had ben steyd." *Great evil we would have incurred*

They pypud and trompud in tho hall, *piped; played trumpets*
Knyghtus and ladys dancyd all
Befor that mynstralsy;
Syr Gwother in his chambur ley,
He lyst nowdur dance ne pley, *desired neither*

For he was full wery, — *exhausted*
Bryssud for strokus that he had laghtth — *Bruised; received*
When he in tho batell faghtth,
Amonghe that carefull cry.
He had no thoght bot of is syn,
And how he myght is soule wyn
To tho blys that God con hym by. — *did purchase for him*

Thes lordys to bed con hom bown, — *got ready*
And knyghttys and ladys of renown,
Thus this romans told. — *romance*
On tho morne come a messynger
And seyd to tho Emperour, "Now is wer, — *war*
Thi care mey be full cold;
My lord is comun with his powyr,
Bot yf thu gyff hym thi doghttur dere — *Until*
He wyll hampur the in hold, — *besiege; castle*
And byrkon the bothe blod and bon, — *thrash you*
And leyve on lyfe noght won — *leave no one alive*
Off all thi barons bold."

"Y count hym noght," quod tho Emperour;
"Y schall gare sembull as styff in stour, — *assemble together; strong; warfare*
And meyt hym yf y mey."
Tho doghtty men that to hym dyd long — *belong*
Anon wer armyd, old and yong, — *Soon*
Be undur of tho dey. — *By 9:00 a.m.*
Thei leype on hors, toke schyld and speyr,
Then tho gud knyght Gwotheyr
To God in hart con prey, — *heart*
Schulde sende hym hors and armur tyte; — *quickly*
Sone he had bothe, mylke whyte,
And rod aftur in gud arey. — *well equipped*

Hys to commyngus tho dompe meydon had sene, — *two comings*
And to tho thryd went with wene, — *full knowingly*
No mon hit knew bot God,
For he fard nodur with brag ne bost,
Bot preystely pryckys aftur tho ost, — *without hesitation rides; host*

And foloud on hor trowd. *in their path*
Tho Emperour was in tho voward, *vanguard*
And Gowther rode befor is lord,
Of knyghttys was he odde. *outstanding*
Tho berons wer to tho dethe dongon *struck*
And baners bryght in sladus slongon, *valleys cast down*
With strokus greyt and lowd.

Tho Sawdyn bare in sabull blacke,
Three lyons rampand, withowt lacke, *rampant; peer*
That all of silver schon;
Won was corvon with golys redde, *adorned; red gules*
Anodur with gold in that steyd,
Tho thryde with aser, y wene; *azure*
And his helmyt full rychely frett, *inlaid*
With charbuckolus stonus suryly sett *carbuncle stones securely*
And dyamondus betwene;
And his batell wele areyd,
And his baner brodly dyspleyd;
Sone aftur tyde hom tene. *he came to harm*

Tho gud knyght, Syr Gowtheyr,
He styrd hym styfly in his geyr, *armor*
Ther levyd non doghttear, y wene; *lived none more doughty*
Ylke a dyntte that he smotte *Every*
Throowt steyll helmus it boott, *steel helmets; cut*
He felld bothe hors and mon,
And made hom tombull to tho gronde;
Tho fote men on tho feld con stonde
And then ward radly ranne. *retreated quickly*
Tho Sawdyn for tho Emperourus doghttur
Gard Cryston and hethon to dye in slaghttur: *Caused*
That tyme hym burd wele ban. *he had good reason to curse*

To whyle Syr Gwother freschely faghtte *All the while*
Mony a doghtté hors is deythe ther kaghtte, *caught its death there*
That he myghtte over reche; *overtake*
All that he with his fawchon hytte
Thei fell to tho ground and ross not yette, *arose*

Nor lokyd aftur no leyche. — *physician*
Bot he wold not for yre ne tene — *anger nor injury*
No worde speyke, withowt wene, — *without doubt*
For dowtte of Godus wreke; — *divine vengeance*
If all he hongurt, noght he dyd eytte — *Even though; was hungry*
Bot what he myght fro tho howndus geyt; — *Except*
He dyd as tho Pwope con hym teche.

Syr Gwother, that stythe in stowre, — *fierce one in battle*
Rydys ey with tho Emperour — *ever alongside*
And weyrus hym fro wothe; — *protects; harm*
Ther was no Sarsyn so mykull of strenthe,
That durst come within is speyre lenthe, — *his spear's length*
So doghttey wer thei bothe.
With his fachon large and long
Syche dyntus on them he dong — *struck*
Hor lyfus myghtte thei lothe; — *Their lives; detest*
All that ever abode that becur — *conflict*
Of hor deythus meghtt be secur, — *sure*
He styrd his hondus so rathe. — *swiftly*

That dey he tent noght bot is fyght; — *thought of nothing but his fighting*
Tho Emperour faght with all his myght,
Bot radly was he takon, — *quickly*
And with tho Sawdyn awey was led;
Tho dompe Duke gard hym ley a wed, — *made him a pledge*
Stroke of his hed anon, — *Cut off*
Rescowyd is lord, broght hym ageyn, — *rescued his*
Lovyd be God in hart was ful feyn,
That formod bothe blod and bon.
Ther come a Sarsyn with a speyre,
Thro tho scholdur smott Gotheyr.
Then made the dompe meydon mon; — *moan*

For sorro fell owt of hur toure, — *tower*
Tho doghtur of tho Emperour,
To whyte withowt wene. — *know without a doubt*
A doghtty sqwyer in hur bare; — *squire carried her in*
Of all too deyus hoo styrd no mare — *For two full days she stirred no more*

Then ho deyd had ben. *Than if she were dead*
Tho lord come hom, to meyt was seytt,
And tho doghtty knyght, withowt leytt, *impediment*
That had in tho batell byn,
To chambur he went, dyd of is geyre, *took off his armor*
This gud knyght Syr Gwothere,
Then myssyd he that meydon schene.

Emong tho howndus is meyt he wan;
Tho Emperour was a drury man *grieving*
For his doghttur gent;
He gard erlys and barons go to Rome *commanded*
Aftur tho Pope, and he come sone
To hur enterment, *burial*
And cardynals to tho beryng *funeral*
To assoyle that swett thyng. *absolve*
Syche grace God hur sentt
That scho raxeld hur and rase, *awoke and raised herself up*
And spake wordus that wyse was
To Syr Gwother, varement. *truly*

Ho seyd, "My lord of heyvon gretys the well, *She*
And forgyffeus the thi syn yche a dell, *each part*
And grantys the tho blys;
And byddus the speyke on hardely,
Eyte and drynke and make mery;
Thu schallt be won of His."
Scho seyd to hur fadur, "This is he
That faght for yow deys thre *days*
In strong batell, ywys." *truly*
Tho Pope had schryvon Syr Gother – *absolved*
He lovyd God and Maré ther –
And radly hym con kys, *quickly [the Pope] kissed him*

And seyd, "Now art thu Goddus chyld;
The thar not dowt tho warlocke wyld, *You need not fear; devil*
Ther waryd mot he bee." *vanquished must*
Thro tho Pope and tho Emperour asent *consent*
Ther he weyd that meydyn gent, *wed*

That curtesse was and fre.	*courteous*
And scho a lady gud and feyr,	
Of all hur fadur londus eyr;	*heir*
Beyttur thurte non bee.	*anywhere*
Tho Pope toke his leyfe to weynde,	*took leave to go*
With tham he laft his blessyng,	
Ageyn to Rome went hee.	
When this mangeyre was broght to ende,	*wedding feast*
Syr Gwother con to Estryke wende	*Austria*
And gaff tho old erle all;	
Made hym Duke of that cuntré,	
And lett hym wed his modur fre,	
That ladé gent and small;	*lady*
And ther he made an abbey	
And gaff therto rent for ey,	*support forever*
"And here lye y schall";	*I shall be buried*
And putte therin monkus blake	*[i.e., Benedictines]*
To rede and syng for Godys sake,	
And closyd hit with gud wall.	*enclosed*
All yf tho Pope had hym schryvyn	*Even though*
And God is synnus clene forgevon,	
Yett was his hart full sare	*grieved*
That ever he schuld so yll wyrke	
To bren tho nunnus in hor kyrke,	
And made hor plasse so bare.	*their place; desolate*
For hom gard he make that abbey	*them he ordered construction of*
And a covent therin for ey	*forever*
That mekull cowde of lare,	*much knew of wisdom*
For them unto tho wordus end	*world's*
For hor soulus that he had brend	*their*
And all that Cryston ware.	
And then he went hym hom ageyn,	
And be that he come in Allmeyn	*by the time that; Germany*
His fadur tho Emperour was deyd,	
And he lord and emperowr,	
Of all Cryston knyghttus tho flowre,	*the flower of knighthood*

And with tho Sarsyns dredde.
What mon so bydus hym for Godys loffe doo *asked*
He was ey redy bown thertoo, *always ready*
And stod pore folke in styd, *stood in support of the poor*
And ryche men in hor ryght,
And halpe holy kyrke in all is myght;
Thus toke he bettur reyd. *he followed better counsel*

Furst he reynod mony a yere, *reigned*
An emperour of greyt power,
And whysyle con he wake; *wisely*
And when he dyed, tho sothe to sey,
Was beryd at tho same abbey *buried*
That hymselfe gart make;
And he is a varré corsent parfett, *a truly pious person*
And with Cryston pepull wele belovyd;
God hase done for his sake
Myrrakull, for he has hym hold; *Miracle*
Ther he lyse in schryne of gold
That suffurd for Goddus sake.

Who so sechys Hym with hart fre,
Of hor bale bote mey bee, *Their suffering help may*
For so God hase hym hyght; *promised*
Thes wordus of hym thar no mon wast, *need*
For he is inspyryd with tho Holy Gost,
That was tho cursod knyght;
For he garus tho blynd to see *makes the blind*
And tho dompe to speyke, pardé, *by God*
And makus tho crokyd ryght,
And gyffus to tho mad hor wytte,
And mony odur meracullus yette,
Thoro tho grace of God allmyght.

Thus Syr Gwother coverys is care, *recovers his estate*
That fyrst was ryche and sython bare, *poor*
And effte was ryche ageyn,
And geyton with a felteryd feynd; *Though begotten by; hairy*
Grace he had to make that eynd *end*

That God was of hym feyn. *glad*
This is wreton in parchemeyn, *parchment*
A story bothe gud and fyn
Owt off a law of Breyteyn. *lay*
Jesu Cryst, Goddys son,
Gyff us myght with Hym to won, *dwell*
That Lord that is most of meyn. Amen *omnipotent might*

Explicit Syr Gother

Notes

Abbreviations: R: BL MS Royal 17.B.43; A: Advocates 19.3.1; B: Breul; M: Mills; N: Novelli.

1–14 R provides the first thirteen and a half lines (to the middle of "nyeght" in line 14), missing in A.

3 B omits *on Rode.*

10 The begetting of a child on a mortal woman by a demon or by sorcery is a frequent occurrence in Arthurian romance. Merlin and Arthur are archetypes of those conceived in this way. Merlin, who first appears in Geoffrey of Monmouth's *Historia Regum Britanniae*, is engendered in a nun, a daughter of King Demetia, by a seductive incubus. King Arthur is conceived when Uther Pendragon, with the aid of Merlin's sorcery, appears to Igrayne in the form of her husband. He begets Arthur the same night Igrayne's husband, the Duke of Tintagel, is killed. Uther soon arranges to wed Igrayne, but when Arthur is born the child must be relinquished to Merlin in payment for his services. (See note on lines 61–65 and 97–99 on The Devil's Contract).

17 The belief that demons could engage in shapeshifting at will is expressed during the dialogue between the Summoner and the Friar in Chaucer's Friar's Tale:

> "I wende ye were a yeman trewely.
> Ye han a mannes shap as wel as I;
> Han ye a figure thanne determinat
> In helle, ther ye been in youre estat?"
> "Nay, certainly," quod he, "ther have we noon;
> But whan us liketh we kan take us oon,
> Or elles make yow seme we been shape;
> Somtyme lyk a man, or lyk an ape,
> Or lyk an angel kan I ryde or go.
> It is no wonder thyng thogh it be so;
> A lowsy jogelour kan deceyve thee,
> And pardee, yet kan I moore craft than he."
> (II [D] 1457–1468)

Even the thirteenth-century theologian Thomas Aquinas did not deny that demons could assume human form to have intercourse with mortal women; yet he maintained that the bodies they formed for the purpose could not be considered human and any children begotten in this way could only result from stolen human semen. See *Summa Theologica*, Pars I, Art. III, reply to Obj. 6.

28–29 A reads *ysoughht* in line 28 and *have y broughht* in line 29. M reads the *y* as a pronoun rather than as the first syllable in the participle in both lines, while B reads a pronoun in the first line and omits it in the second line so that the line reads *have broughht*. I have accepted B's first pronoun because the clause needs a subject, but read *ybroughht* as a participle (and omit *have* as being redundant and unmetrical).

31 B interprets *Estryke* and *Ostrych* as *Austria* (p. 118) though N favors the definitions in *OED* and *MED* "which would most probably have pointed to the Baltic region." The *OED* suggests both an eastern kingdom or country and an East Frankish Kingdom.

33 *For comly undur kell*. A similar line is found in *Emaré* (line 303) and in *Pistil of Swete Susan* (line 128). The "kell" or head-dress, a veil intended to hide female beauty, fails to obscure the extraordinary comeliness of any of these exemplary women.

34–35 The upper right section of this leaf of A is torn away and portions of lines 34 and 35 have been supplied by the reading in R.

34 The lily suggests purity and is often associated with the Virgin Mary or female virgin saints in Christian symbolism. In the iconography of the Annunciation, an event at which the Archangel Gabriel appears to the Virgin to announce the impending birth of Christ, the flower is frequently present (see George Ferguson, *Signs & Symbols in Christian Art*).

42–44 A has only nine lines in this stanza. Since this is a tail-rhyme romance in twelve-line stanzas, I agree with B's decision to substitute three lines (42, 43, 44) from R.

46 A: *x* rather than *ten*. I have emended all Roman numerals to their verbal equivalent.

56 Sterility could be grounds for divorce in the Middle Ages though, as James Brundage points out in *Law, Sex, and Christian Society in Medieval Europe*, "several authorities explicitly excluded sterility as a basis of separation" (p. 201). Some critics have seen an allusion to the apocryphal story of Joachim and Anna, who became the parents of the Virgin Mary under similar circumstances. While the aged and barren Anna is in an orchard one day, an angel appears to her and prophesies that she will bear an extraordinary child. Lydgate retells the story in his *Life of Our Lady*, one of the companion texts in the Advocates MS.

61–65 Folklorists have identified several folktale motifs in *Gowther* including the Wish Child and The Devil's Contract. In both of these folktale motifs parents longing for a child pray to God; in some cases the prayer is answered by an angel (e.g., Joachim and Anna), while in others a pact is made with a devil before the child's birth. The child is then subject to diabolic influence from whose dominion it is freed finally either by its own ingenuity or by the intervention of Providence. Stith Thompson in *The Folktale* identifies the Devil's Contract motif in both the legendary tale of *Robert the Devil* and *Sir Gowther* and remarks that "Gowther, or Robert the Devil, was not to blame for his demonic association, since the fault lay entirely with his mother" (p. 269).

71 In medieval romance encounters with supernatural beings frequently take place under a certain kind of tree (e.g., *Sir Orfeo*, *Sir Degaré*, etc.). Often referred to as *ympe* (grafted) trees these trees facilitate interaction between the Otherworld and reality. See note on line 233 for the significance of the chestnut tree.

74 *felturd fende* finds a parallel in *Emaré*: *A fowlle, feltred fende* (line 540). Hairiness is often a characteristic of the devil or those perceived as exhibiting diabolic influence by their wild behavior. Born with a hairy body, Merlin is often characterized as a wild man when he retreats into the woods to watch the wild animals while himself hidden like a beast (see Richard Bernheimer, *Wild Men in the Middle Ages*).

89 *lappe*. The *OED* defines this term as "a piece of cloth, the fold of a robe over the breast, which served as a pocket or pouch." That this pocket or pouch could also serve as a carrier for an infant is suggested in Chaucer's Clerk's Tale:

> . . . that he pryvely
> Sholde this child softe winde and wrappe . . .

> And carie it in a cofre or in a lappe.
> (IV [E] 582-85)

90 *fonde.* Perhaps the poet's choice of *fonde* for "lovemaking" indicates the husband's curiosity or the desire to procreate. The word might also be glossed as "try," or "find out," or "invent."

99 Gowther's kinship to Merlin is explicitly established here. See note to line 10. Merlin and Gowther have different mothers, but the same father. In *Merlin*, a twelfth-century version of the Merlin story by Robert de Boron, the prophet/magician is engendered by a demon on the pious daughter of a wealthy man while she sleeps. However, because she confesses and is signed with a cross at that time, her son's destiny is altered. Though he is born with a hairy body and preternatural knowledge, he is not subject to his father's will to evil.

105 A: *wold* is crossed out before *coth.*

106 *gard* is often used in a modal sense (e.g., caused, ordered, made).

108 A: *barre*; R: *brathe.* N suggests that "*barre* evidently came to the scribe's mind more readily than the original *brathe*" (p. 162). B preferred *brathe*, an emendation with which I agree.

115 R reverses lines 115 and 116. B's emendation follows R here as do I.

129 *snaffulld.* According to the *OED* "snaffle" and its related form "snuffle" means "to make a sniffling noise, to inhale audibly." This is a term, as Novelli suggests, "appropriate for a nursing infant" (p. 162), particularly one with Gowther's voracious appetite.

130 That the infant Gowther is able to tear off his mother's nipple suggests the presence of teeth. Early dentition was often regarded as an indication of a child's extraordinary future and was frequently associated with dog-like attributes. Shakespeare expresses this folkloric belief in *Richard III:*

> That dog, that had his teeth before his eyes.
> To worry lambs, and lap their gentle blood.
> (said of Richard III, Act IV, scene iv, lines 49–50)

In *King Henry VI, Part III*, Gloucester says of himself:

> The midwife wonders and the women cried,
> "Oh, Jesus bless us, he is born with teeth!"
> And so I was; which plainly signified
> That I should snarl, and bite, and play the dog.
> (Act V, scene vi, lines 74–76)

Early dentition could also be a characteristic of vampirism, werewolfism, or the consequence of sorcery. See Paul Barber, *Vampires, Burial, and Death: Folklore & Reality* (New Haven: Yale University Press, 1988), p. 30.

137 A: *behovyd*. B emends to *behode*.

141 A: *No nodur mon myght hit beyr*; B omits *mon* for the sake of the meter. I have retained it for the sake of Gowther's humanity.

142 The falchion Gowther has made for himself has symbolic value. For M it suggests Gowther's "unbridled violence in his unregenerate days, and his militancy in his later career. His refusal to give it up at the Pope's bidding in 289–91 underlines its significance as symbol and talisman; it is an essential part of him, and must go with him on his new quest for forgiveness" (p. 215). E. M. Bradstock, in "The Penitential Pattern in *Sir Gowther*," argues that the falchion, unlike the straight sword of a Christian knight, is of Oriental origin and a weapon the Saracens would carry. Bradstock sees it as "an apt weapon for a ferocious persecutor of Christians. Further, like its Saracen creators who had 'their dark origins in the race of Cain' but were always reclaimable through baptism, and like Gowther himself who was born of a devil, this falchion has the potential for good or evil" (p. 7).

149–50 This is a puzzling passage in that there seems to be no motivation for the Duke's knighting of Gowther. N suggests that this detail is evidence that *Robert the Devil* is a close analogue.

151–52 B emends these two lines with the corresponding lines in R: *He gaf him his best swerd in honde / Ther was no knyght in all that londe*.

157 *Mor sorro*: B follows R and substitutes *dowrey* for *sorro*.

172 Matins is the first of the canonical hours, followed by lauds, prime, terce, sext, none, vespers, and compline.

175 MS: *For late lowde and styll*: B emends to *Erly and* from R.

176 *is fadur wyll.* The question of Gowther's paternity is raised again. The poet reminds us that Gowther's father is a demon whose will he has been destined to carry out. Yet Gowther's baptism brings him into a state of grace that, in effect, cancels diabolic predestination and renders his actions a matter of free will.

179–80 B emends these two lines to correspond with R: *In parke and in wylde forest, / Where he myght it gete.*

181–92 R omits the raping of the nuns in line 188: (*For he and is men bothe leyn hom by)*. R reads:

> As he rode on huntyng uppon a day
> He saw a nonnery bi the highway,
> And theder gan he ride;
> The prioresse and here covent
> With procession agayn him went,
> Trewly in that tyde.
> Thei kneeled down oppon here knee,
> And said "Leige lord, welcome be yee!"
> Yn hert is nowght to hide
> He drofe hem home into here churche,
> And brend hem uppe thus gan he werche,
> His lose spring ful wide. *fame*
> (lines 175–86)

187 That the prioress and her charges should be frightened of Gowther's body underscores his diabolical appearance. The absence of armor suggests Gowther's rejection of chivalric codes of conduct.

193 B emends to: *All that ever on Cryst wold leve.*

196 B emends *maryage* to *maryagys.*

233 *cheston tre.* The choice of tree may be significant. According to George Ferguson's *Signs & Symbols in Christian Art* (New York: Oxford University Press,

1954; rpt., 1961), the chestnut in its husk is surrounded by thorns, but unharmed by them. "For this reason it is a symbol of chastity because this virtue is a triumph over the temptations of the flesh symbolized by the thorns" (p. 29).

254 *stydfast*. B emends to *styward* perhaps to indicate to whom the property is bequeathed. Yet the identity of that person as "this olde erle" in the previous line serves adequately to designate the heir. The poet needs only to signify the quality of that heir's character which he has in his choice of *stydfast.*

256 Gowther's rejection of horse and man underscores both his determination to atone for his transgressions and the solitude that atonement requires.

259 See note to line 142.

296 B omits *that thu revus* to maintain metrical integrity.

301 B emends *Pope stole* to *apostoyle*.

305 The dog, because of its attributes of watchfulness, obedience, and fidelity, could be understood as a symbol of these virtues and for Gowther is a fitting sign of penance. There are many examples of the faithful dog that could have been known to the Gowther poet. One comes from the apocryphal story of Tobias in which the dog accompanies his master on an arduous journey to restore the eyesight of Tobias' father. Another is from the story of St. Roch, a fourteenth-century French hermit who, according to the *Oxford Dictionary of Saints*, ed. David Hugh Farmer (Oxford: Oxford University Press, 1982) "spent much of his life on pilgrimages" (p. 346). While on one of his many journeys, he caught the plague and was fed in the woods by a dog. "In England his memory is recalled in the Sussex place-name (St. Rokeshill) and by screen painting in Devon and Norfolk. These depict him as a pilgrim with a sore on his leg, accompanied by a dog with a loaf of bread in its mouth" (p. 346).

307 In A *cuntré* is crossed out before *ceté*.

309 *testamentys* is glossed by M as *authorities*, but *witnesses* seems a more likely meaning since at this point Gowther needs evidence of his first penitential act rather than validation.

311 Much like a ministering angel to a desert hermit, the greyhound succors Gowther in his neediness. Albertus Magnus in his encyclopedic work, *Man and the Beasts,* defines the special qualities of these dogs: "Greyhounds seldom, if ever, bark; on the contrary, they show disdain for the yelping of small dogs which bark for the sake of showing their prowess as watchdogs. Nor do they rush headlong to greet any newcomer, since they seem to regard such a flurry of activity as beneath their dignity. Moreover, this dog must be fed more milk than whey when it is weaned." See Albert the Great, *Man and the Beasts: De Animalibus* (Books 22–26), trans. James J. Scanlan (Binghamton, NY: Medieval & Renaissance Texts and Studies, 1987), p. 81.

313 The cardinal number three was called by Pythagoras the number of completion indicating beginning, middle, and end. Here it suggests, perhaps, a time of ordeal, like Christ's descent into Hell, though Gowther arises on the fourth day rather than the third.

320 R reads: *The emperor of Almayn thereyn gan dwell.*

324 *Thof.* A: *Of.* B emends to *Thof.* The variation between this line in A and the corresponding line in R is worth noting for the variance in sense as well as diction: A: *Of he wer well wroght*. R: *Though him were woo yn thought.* The line in A suggests that though Gowther is attractive and would have gained admittance based on his appearance he nonetheless assumes a posture of humility and does not force entry but waits until the appropriate signal is given before entering with the rest of the group. When he finally gains admittance he goes to a place under the table and assumes the posture of an obedient dog. The implication of R on the other hand is that despite his heavy heart Gowther chooses to remain outside the gate until a signal is given for general admittance. In this way R places emphasis on Gowther's psychological state rather than on his physical appearance as A does.

331 R: *He presid blythely thorow the prese.*

340 The emphasis on Gowther's fair appearance here justifies the reading of line 324 above. A similar line is found in *Sir Isumbras*: "The faireste mane that ever I seghe" (line 258). It has been suggested by N and others that this tale incorporates a male Cinderella motif. For N "the menial station of the male Cinderella becomes the hero's means of doing penance, and his provision with

armor and his success in the three battles a sign that he is in divine favor" (pp. 32–33).

371 B suggests that the name Hob, a diminutive of Robert, provides a verbal link between *Sir Gowther* and *Robert the Devil.* N rejects the notion as mere coincidence because the name may also be associated with rustics and clowns.

394 B emends to *Yeit mey God gyffe hur thoro Is myght.* In a request reminiscent of the one made by Gowther's mother, the Emperor expresses his keen desire to have his daughter's voice restored. The daughter's muteness differs from Gowther's because it is neither self-imposed nor penitential, but an accident of nature. For this reason the Emperor seeks a corrective from God. In *Robert the Devil* the daughter's muteness is greatly expanded when she attempts several times to reveal Gowther's true identity to her father, but is unable to communicate effectively.

420 In A *fo* is cancelled before *fadur.*

429 R: *Whan blade thorow brenyys brast.*

442 A: *H* is cancelled at the beginning of the line.

445 The juxtaposition of the "two small hunting dogs" (raches) with the "two fine greyhounds" calls attention to the importance of dogs and their attributes in this poem. It may be recalled that a greyhound is the first dog to assist Gowther's penance by bringing him a loaf of bread (like the dog in the *Life of St. Roch*) while the spaniel and the hunting dogs serve as his dinner companions. Gowther's association with hunting dogs seems to complement his own early predilection for hunting prey while his contact with greyhounds suggests an increasing association with the divine. For an interesting discussion of the divine attributes of this breed of dog see Jean-Claude Schmitt, *The Holy Greyhound: Guinefort, Healer of Children Since the Thirteenth Century,* trans. Martin Thom (Cambridge: Cambridge University Press, 1983).

454 The messenger plays a significant supporting role in medieval romance serving as a link between characters, between the human and the supernatural worlds, and between elements of plot.

456 *sone he come.* B emends to *come he sone*, thus maintaining the rhyme.

463–65 B substitutes from R to maintain a consistent twelve-line stanzaic structure. M omits them in his edition, but indicates their presence by ellipsis. He then transfers the three lines to his endnotes and comments on their "corrupt" nature. But though they may be corrupt, something like them must have been part of the original poem.

501 A: *That laft wer on lyve slone*, with *lyve* marked for cancellation.

504 B emends *he hym cheys* to *is gone* to maintain the rhyme scheme. M follows B.

537 A: *Amoghe*. R: *Amonghe.*

554 The epithet *styff in stour* appears several times in the second half of the poem (lines 482, 554, 613). Taken with similar descriptions such as *stalworthe and store*, *doghhty of body and bon*, and *styf and store*, the phrase seems to indicate Gowther's increasing practice of chivalric codes of behavior.

563 Gowther's white suit of armor, the third and most symbolic, completes the color triad. The progression from black to red and finally to white parallels Gowther's moral progression. For a discussion of color symbolism in medieval romance see Jessie Laidlay Weston, *The Three Days' Tournament*, and Shirley Marchalonis, "*Sir Gowther*: The Process of a Romance," *Chaucer Review* 6 (1971/72), 14–29.

566 *with wene*. B emends to *withowt wene.*

575 *baners. A: barons; R: baners.* I prefer R to avoid the repetition of *barons* in line 574.

578 The description here indicates the heraldic symbols on the Sultan's banner.

584 B omits *suryly.*

591 B emends *y wene* to *thanne.*

621 *thei.* A: *the*. M emends to *them*, the sense being that the enemies' lives became painful (*lothe*) to them.

629 N suggests that the sense of this line should be: "The dumb duke made him [the Sultan] remain a hostage," but a more probable reading (concurrent with R) is

leve his wedde, i.e., "leave his hostage." Gowther causes the Sultan to leave his hostage permanently by decapitating him in the next line.

632 B reads: *And lovyd God in hart ful feyn.*

635 Here Gowther is wounded in the shoulder. In *Robert the Devil* the hero is wounded in the thigh, an injury which then becomes an important sign of recognition. The placement of Robert's wound recalls the Scriptural Jacob, wounded in the thigh in his struggle with an angel, the wound of the Fisher King in the Grail stories, and Odysseus' wound in Homer's *Odyssey*. For an interesting discussion of symbolic wounding see Bruno Bettelheim, *Symbolic Wounds: Puberty Rites and the Envious Male* (New York: Collier Books, 1962).

646–47 B reverses these lines.

653 B emends *he come sone* to *sone he come*.

668 The three-day tournament motif, popular in medieval romance, serves as the ultimate test of knightly prowess and carries implications of progressive spiritual refinement. The hero fights incognito in different suits of armor for three consecutive days to prove his worthiness both to serve his lord and to win a noble lady. See Jessie Laidlay Weston, *The Three Days' Tournament: A Study in Romance and Folklore* (London: D. Nutt, 1902).

683 B adds *heynde* at the end of this line to complete the rhyme.

689 *hym*. A: *kym*. B's emendation.

699 Gowther's remorse for his crimes against the nuns is so great that he builds an abbey and a convent in order that all those contained within might pray for the souls of their murdered sisters. It is interesting to note that R, which omits the rape scene, substitutes *monkus grey* for the sisters. In R Gowther builds two abbeys, one for the nuns and another for Cistercian monks. The monks, rather than the sisters, pray for the souls of the dead nuns.

711 The Emperor is actually Gowther's father-in-law, a term not used before the late sixteenth century according to the *OED*.

715 B deletes *so*.

718 B adds *mayntened* before *ryche*. R reads *pouer* rather than *ryche*.

720 *to be* crossed out before *toke*.

730 B changes *has* to *was*.

735 In A this line appears in the upper right margin rather than in its appropriate place in the stanza.

744 A omits any reference to Saint Guthlac while R explicitly identifies Gowther with the English saint:

> There he lyeth in a shryne of gold
> And doth maracles, as it is told,
> And hatt Seynt Gotlake. *is called*
> He make blynd men for to se,
> Wode men to have here wit, parde,
> Crokyd here crucches forsake.
> (lines 679-84)

According to the *Oxford Dictionary of Saints*, Guthlac (c. 673–714), of royal blood from the Mercian tribe of Guthlacingas, became a soldier at age fifteen. After nine years of warfare, however, he decided to become a monk at Repton, a double monastery ruled by Abbess Aelfrith. In about 701 he adopted the hermetic life at Crowland, a site surrounded by fens and marshes and thought to be inhabited by evil spirits. Guthlac fought the demons for fifteen years before he died. At that time Edburga, the new abbess of Repton, sent a shroud and leaden coffin. Guthlac's sister, Pega, attended his burial with several of his disciples. A year later the grave was opened and the body was discovered incorrupt. Guthlac is regarded as one of the most important pre-Conquest saints of England (pp. 184–85).

746 The theme of the vicissitudes of fortune is also found in *Sir Isumbras*, a companion text in A.

Erle of Tolous

Introduction

Although probably composed in the last half of the fourteenth century, the *Erle of Tolous* is found in four fifteenth- and sixteenth-century MSS: Bodleian 6922 (Ashmole 61), Bodleian 6926 (Ashmole 45), Cambridge Ff.2.38, and Lincoln Cathedral 91 (Thornton). The poem is written in the dialect of the Northeast Midlands in tail-rhyme stanzas, a form that places it among a distinctive group of tail-rhyme lays, including *Emaré*, *Sir Launfal*, and *Sir Gowther*. As with many of the Middle English Breton lays, the *Erle of Tolous* boasts a complex intertextuality that enriches its interpretive potential; it appears in numerous analogues in several different languages (Dutch, Latin, French, Catalan, Spanish, Italian, German) in several genres (folktale, legend, chronicle, Scripture, romance, and Breton lay) and incorporates folkloric and literary motifs that extend beyond the boundaries of medieval Europe.[1] Such an extensive intertextual web and widespread dissemination over time suggest a popularity and a cultural adaptability few other poems can claim.

One popular motif around which the narrative revolves has been identified by several scholars variously as that of the Woman Accused of Adultery, the Calumniated Queen, or the Innocent Wife Persecuted Unjustly. In this motif, an innocent

---

[1] The several versions of the narrative have compelled scholars to group them into categories which differ from scholar to scholar. Laura A. Hibbard [Loomis] in *Medieval Romance in England* (New York: Oxford University Press; rpt. Burt Franklin, 1960), for instance, separates them into groups related by similar plot motifs. The first grouping is in Catalan and Spanish and contains the oldest chronicle versions, e.g., the late thirteenth-century *Cronica del Rey En Pere* by Bernat Desclot, the late fifteenth-century *Croniques de Espanya* by Pere Miguel Carbonell, and a sixteenth century version by Pedro Anton Beuter. Loomis groups with these a fifteenth-century romance, *El Conde de Barcelona*, and two seventeenth-century French chronicles, one by Cesar de Nostredame and the other, *La Royalle Couronne des Roys d'Arles*. In the second major grouping she places the four extant Middle English versions listed in the four manuscripts above; into the third group, the French play *Miracle de la Marquise de la Gaudine*. The fourth grouping is somewhat eclectic; it contains a fifteenth-century Danish poem, *Den Kydske Dronning* by Jeppe Jensen, a Latin prose narrative, *Philopertus et Eugenia*, a sixteenth-century French prose romance, *L'Histoire de Palanus, Comte de Lyon*, a German "Volksbuch," and an Italian tale by Bandello, *Amore di Don Giovanni di Mendozza e della Duchessa di Savoia*. Edwin Greenlaw and Paul Christophersen designate the Middle English poem a type which has influenced the development of works such as Shakespeare's *Cymbeline* and the anonymous *Ballad of Sir Aldingar*.

woman — often the wife or daughter of a king or emperor — is falsely accused of an adulterous liaison by one or more malicious people — jealous mothers-in-law, spurned suitors, and evil courtiers. The motive of the villainous accusers is to discredit, embarrass, or tarnish the reputation of the exemplary heroine in order to enhance their own status at court or to save them from their own injudicious actions. When the allegations are made public the heroine is frequently condemned to death or exile by the king or emperor (usually her husband or father), an action that necessitates exoneration and rescue by a champion. Found in popular folktales of various cultures and in several literary works throughout the Middle Ages, the motif is both prolific and popular.[2] A Scriptural version, which at least one scholar claims to be the oft-neglected source for the motif, appears in the apocryphal narrative of *Susanna and the Elders* in which an innocent Susanna, accused of adultery by two lecherous "elders," is tried and eventually rescued by the prophet Daniel.[3] The late fourteenth-century Middle English retelling of the tale, *The Pistel of Swete Susan,* which circulated in the fifteenth century with Chaucer's Man of Law's Tale, suggests the motif's currency in England at the time.[4] But folktale, romance, and Scripture are not the only venues for the motif; frequently it finds expression in chronicle and legend.

Several scholars subscribe to the notion that the basic plot of the *Erle of Tolous* originates in history. They point to an event of the ninth century during the reign of Louis the Pious when Judith, his second wife, was accused of committing adultery with Bernard, Count of Barcelona and son of William of Toulouse. In this incident Judith was banished to a convent, charged with conspiracy to overthrow the French king's edict to divide the kingdom among the sons of his first marriage, in favor of her son Charles the Bald. She was later brought back to court, having lived an exemplary life in the convent, and exonerated when no accuser appeared at her trial in 831. The centrality of the motif of the accused queen, the close association between the names Bernard and Barnard, his place of origin (i.e., Toulous), the identification of two accusers (Hugo, Count of Tours, and Matfrid, Count of Or-

---

[2] For an interesting and comprehensive study of the motif in folktale and literature see Margaret Schlauch, *Chaucer's Constance and Accused Queens* (New York: Gordian Press, 1927).

[3] See Paul Christophersen, *The Ballad of Sir Aldingar: Its Origin and Analogues* (Oxford: Clarendon Press, 1952), pp. 137–42.

[4] Russell A. Peck, *Heroic Women from the Old Testament in Middle English Verse*. Medieval Institute Publications (Kalamazoo: Western Michigan Press, 1991), pp. 73–108. The audience of *Pistel of Swete Susan* "was that newly literate group, composed in part of women, among whom the Wycliffite movement flourished" (p. 73).

leans), and the resolution of the incident by judicial combat (though the actual combat never took place), make the correlation between this historical event and its poetic representation compelling.[5] Some scholars argue that a direct line can be drawn from the earliest chronicle treatment of the event in Bernat Declot's late thirteenth-century *Cronica del Rey en Pere* to the Middle English *Erle*. Yet there are several similar historical incidents which suggest a more complex network of influence and exchange. Laura Hibbard Loomis, for instance, cites plot similarities in the legend of Gundeberg, wife of the Lombard king Arioald in the seventh century, and an eleventh-century legend associated with Gunhild, daughter of Canute and future wife of Emperor Henry III.[6] Paul Christophersen enlarges the list to include two wives of Charlemagne, Sibilla and Hildegard, in addition to other luminous medieval women.[7] The motif of the accused queen is hence not exclusively the provenance of romantic imagination, but rather an apparently recurrent historical event.

The importance of the accused queen motif in the *Erle of Tolous* is evident when the poet points almost immediately to the poem's heroine, introducing her as his subject directly after the conventional exhortation to the audience. This poem is, he says, about "How a lady had grete myschefe / And how sche covyrd [recovered] of hur grefe" (lines 10–11). Her narrative, in fact, formulates the nexus for the stories of the two male protagonists — the Emperor Dyoclysyan and Syr Barnard. A laudatory description of her virtues follows their introduction so that she is immediately intertwined with them. Just as the Emperor is "a bolde man and a stowte" (line 16), and Syr Barnard, the Erle of Tolous, is "an hardy man and a stronge" (line 31), so too the heroine is described, though not by name at first, in equally exemplary terms:

Thys Emperour had a wyfe,
The fayrest oon that evyr bare lyfe, — *fairest one; ever lived*
  Save Mary mekyll of myght — *Except*
And therto gode in all thynge, — *good*
Of almesdede and gode berynge, — *almsdeeds; proper behavior*
  Be day and eke be nyght; — *By; also*

---

[5] Allen Cabaniss, "Judith Augusta and Her Time," *University of Mississippi Studies in English* 10 (1969), 67–109.

[6] Laura A. Hibbard [Loomis], *Medieval Romance in England* (New York: Oxford University Press, 1924), p. 37. For further discussion of the "Judith affair," see Pauline Stafford, *Queens, Concubines, and Dowagers: The King's Wife in the Early Middle Ages* (Athens: University of Georgia Press, 1983), pp. 93–114.

[7] See Paul Christophersen, *The Ballad of Sir Aldingar: Its Origin and Analogues* (Oxford: Clarendon Press, 1952), pp. 137–42.

Of hyr body sche was trewe *true, i.e., faithful*
As evyr was lady that men knewe.
(lines 37–44)

Like many other medieval heroines, Dame Beulybon, whose name is a combination of *belle* [beautiful] and *bon* [good], is exemplary both in physical appearance and in personal conduct. Not only is she the most beautiful woman "that evyr bare lyfe," she is perhaps more significantly, charitable, of "gode berynge," and faithful to her husband, a fact which necessitates her early description as "wyfe" and sets up the circumstance essential for the dramatic calumniation that occurs later in the plot. Short of being the Virgin Mary herself, Beulybon embodies the attributes associated with the Mother of God, sterling qualities both of body and soul. Her exemplary characterization is, in fiction as in fact, crucial to a chivalric ideology that places women at its center.

Chivalry provided a standard of conduct for knights that required rigorous mental and physical training. Knights were expected to perform as well on the battlefield as in courtly society and to serve God as ardently as they serve their earthly lords. Because chivalric requirements demanded physical and moral acuity, a strict and often austere military regimen was accompanied by an equally demanding fitness program for the soul. In Ramón Lull's *Book of the Order of Chivalry*, for example, "justice, wisdom, charity, loyalty, truth, humility, strength, hope, promptness and all other similar virtues" provide a paradigm of values the knight was expected to cultivate and execute by his deeds.[8] Ideally, knights honored their feudal obligations, protected the interests of their lords, and guarded against criminal activities; they were required to protect women, particularly those in distress, widows and orphans, weak or disabled men, and various disempowered others. Throughout the poem Dame Beulybon is placed in situations that expose the strengths and weaknesses of the knights around her. Because she embodies virtues similar to those of the ideal knight, she functions as a standard by which the knights in the poem may be measured.

In the initial situation Dame Beulybon becomes embroiled in a territorial dispute between her husband, the Emperor, and the Earl whose territory the Emperor has unjustly seized. Her position is one of mediation as she attempts to counsel her husband to do the right thing and return the Earl's land to him. The Emperor's action constitutes a violation of chivalric codes of justice as he, in effect, commits a theft of property, an action that marks a fault in the Emperor's virtue, exposing the chink in his moral armor. His unchivalrous theft throws into question his ability to

[8] See *The Book of the Order of Chivalry*, trans. Robert Adams (Huntsville: Sam Houston State University Press, 1991), p. 28.

provide his knights with an example for appropriate chivalric behavior, and seems to activate a trickle-down effect as his knights later demonstrate their interpretations of the code. Beulybon's attempts at mediation allow us to perceive the fault of the Emperor; her implicit sympathy for the wronged Barnard fosters our judgment of the Earl as a paragon of chivalric virtue. Syr Barnard has clearly been wronged and just as clearly needs to rectify the injustice done to him. His overwhelming victory in battle — the slaying of sixty thousand of the Emperor's knights and the taking of many captives, including the Emperor's favorite retainer, Syr Trylabas — establishes his chivalric prowess and anticipates his impending heroism.

In the scene that follows Trylabas's capture, Beulybon's mediatrix position shifts as she becomes the object of the Earl's desire and the proctor for Trylabas's test of virtue. In exchange for his freedom, Sir Trylabas agrees to conduct Barnard to the beautiful Empress and arrange an audience with her. The importance of Trylabas's oath to the Earl should not be underestimated because it functions as the means by which Trylabas's chivalric integrity is tested:

My trowthe y plyght thee;	*oath; promise you*
Y schall holde thy forward gode	*promise*
To brynge the, wyth mylde mode,	*peaceably*
In syght hur for to see;	
And therto wyll y kepe counsayle	
And nevyr more, wythowte fayle,	
Agayne yow to bee;	*Against*
Y schall be trewe, be Goddys ore,	*by God's grace*
To lose myn own lyfe therfore;	
Hardely tryste to mee!"	*Heartily trust me*
(lines 219–28)	

Because the Earl is chivalrous, he immediately, though somewhat naively, subscribes to Trylabas's seemingly sincere pledge to desist opposition, nevermore "agayne yow to bee." Trylabas seems to make a choice of allegiance to Syr Barnard that implicitly negates his previous feudal obligation to the Emperor. Christian ethics make it clear that a knight cannot serve two masters simultaneously, but rather must make a choice if necessity arises. A knight's obligation to perfect his soul as well as his body compels him to speak truthfully and subsequently fulfill his word by his deeds. If a "true" knight gives his word, then it must be understood to be an expression of truth. Trylabas pledges his word, swearing "be Goddys ore" that it is true. Barnard believes Trylabas to be truthful not only because they have taken the same "fraternal" vows, but because Trylabas's pledge is witnessed by the highest of medieval authorities, the Lord to whom all knights pledge themselves above all others.

As in the territorial dispute between the Earl and the Emperor at the beginning of the poem, Dame Beulybon again attempts to mediate opposing sides; she counsels Trylabas to fulfill his promise to the Earl, to maintain his personal integrity, and to recognize the jeopardy to which he has subjected his soul. In this way, she attempts to rectify the wrong done to Barnard by attempting to save his life. She also functions to reveal latent treachery as it exists hidden in the hearts of her husband's retainers; a trusted knight, like Trylabas, willing to violate a chivalric code of conduct, to break an oath even when extended to a perceived enemy, is suspect to Beulybon:

Certys, yf thou hym beglye,	*Certainly if you; beguile*
Thy soule ys in grete paryle,	*Your; peril*
Syn thou haste made hym othe;	*Since; oath*
Certys, hyt were a traytory	*i.e., an act of treason*
For to wayte hym velany;	*lie in wait; treachery*
Me thynkyth hyt were rowthe!	
(lines 292–97)	

Just as the Emperor before him, Trylabas ignores the counsel of the virtuous Empress and makes a choice that perpetuates the trickle-down effect initiated by the Emperor's theft of Barnard's land. Trylabas enlists two thugs, Kaunters and Kaym, to ambush and slay the unsuspecting Earl after his disguised meeting with Beulybon. Trylabas foolishly underestimates his opponent's capabilities, never suspecting that the lovesick Syr Barnard might be the vanquisher rather than the vanquished. Again Barnard proves his mettle in battle as he single-handedly slays all three.

In the crucial scenario leading up to the calumniation of the Empress, two knights assigned to guard the Empress by the Emperor in his absence make an attempt on her virtue. In competition with each other the knights take turns propositioning her. Taken aback by their breach of decorum — "What woman holdyst thou me? . . . Os y were a hore or a scolde?" — she promptly reminds them of the gravity of their actions. Chivalry requires the protection of women and demands that their honor be upheld at all times. These knights have invalidated the high honor of chivalry, an act that in Lull's view constitutes theft:

> A Knight who is a thief steals more from the high honor of chivalry by taking away the reputation of knighthood than does he who steals money or other things. For to steal honor is to impute ill fame and slander and to blame that very thing which is worthy to have recognition and praise (p. 44).

To cover their initial errors, the dishonorable knights attempt to slander and blame the lady who should be worthy of their loyalty and service. Their intent to silence the Empress' voice compounds their crimes; their enlistment of the young carver is symptomatic of how far from the chivalric ideal they have strayed. The position of carver, often assigned to young men attaining to knighthood to teach them the responsibilities of service to another, in a sense, represents the order of chivalry itself. The two knights not only steal the carver's future, but betray the ideological system to which they have vowed their allegiance. Their words are lies as they cleverly disguise their deadly "play" as amusement for the lady's benefit. Just as the chivalrous Earl believed Trylabas's word earlier, so too does the apprentice knight believe the two knights to be speaking truthfully. Eager to please his lady, Sir Antore agrees to enter the sleeping Empress' bedroom, disrobe, and hide behind a curtain awaiting his cue to jump out and make the lady laugh. This is no laughing matter, however, as Antore begins to suspect when the knights of the castle, bidden immediately to the scene, confront him in the Empress' bedroom. Before he can speak out in his own defense Antore is murdered, his life stolen by "That oon thefe wyth a swerde of were." Beulybon's subsequent screams of protest are overridden by the knights' accusations of adultery substantiated by the incriminating evidence of the half-naked corpse lying on her bedroom floor. The slandered Empress is then promptly thrown into prison to await the return of the Emperor.

At this point the narrative abruptly shifts to the Emperor himself as we are offered a brief glimpse into his psyche. But again his character is thrown into question as we wonder why he would leave his wife under the protection of two such untrustworthy knights. As Ramón Lull suggests: "He who commends his sheep to the care of the wolf is a fool — as is he who puts his fair wife in the care of a deceitful Knight" (p. 46). How could such a man protect others if he can't protect his own loved ones Lull asks. The Emperor's subconscious perception of the great danger Beulybon faces manifests itself in a dream he has at the moment of her persecution. In the Emperor's dream her body is being torn apart by two wild boars. The dream proves true: Beulybon's bodily integrity is torn asunder as the two knights conduct their rapacious verbal assault and defile her impeccable reputation. Their allegations point to a serious moral and political crime, treason both private and public. The charges against Beulybon must be addressed directly by the Emperor himself. Just as several of his historical counterparts, the Emperor is bound by his public duty to administer and carry out the laws of the land even if it means punishing his beloved wife. Beulybon, like Judith and so many other notable queens and empresses, seems doomed to be burned at the stake unless a champion can be found to exonerate her from the false charges.

The call for a champion resounds throughout the land and not surprisingly the Earl responds. This time, however, he is cautious and wary, stealthily entering the kingdom in the company of a horsedealer. Syr Barnard is no fool; he wants to be sure of the Empress' innocence before taking up the gauntlet on her behalf. Custom, in fact, required a would-be champion to be a witness to his sponsor's claim.[9] Thus the Earl's subsequent meeting with the abbot of the local monastery, Beulybon's uncle, is not enough to prove her innocence. Rather, he disguises himself as a monk and receives the confession of the Empress directly. To his great satisfaction he discovers that, except for the ring she gave to him as a token of her regard, her conscience is clear. Convinced of her innocence the Earl then openly declares his intent to champion her cause by agreeing to participate in a trial by combat, a chivalric custom that required the accusers to battle the champion of the accused. If the champion won, the case was decided in his favor; the loser suffered the consequences. If the champion lost, he and those he championed were subject to whatever punishment was assigned by the court. Having proven himself formidable in battle before, the Earl wins the day and saves the Empress from a dire fate. The two knights are punished accordingly — burned at the stake — and truth and justice prevail. But that is not the end of the story. Though the Emperor returns the illegally seized land and makes Sir Barnard his steward, the Emperor remains a tainted character; his own actions and the actions of his knights reflect upon his capabilities as a ruler. As if the poet were recognizing the need for complete exculpation he allows the Emperor to live only for three more years, and because there are no heirs, Barnard is unanimously elected Emperor. Having held his love for Beulybon in check for so long Barnard is finally permitted to marry her. Their union is fruitful; they produce fifteen children, "doghty knyghts all bedene" (line 1212), and live in familial bliss for twenty-three years.

Select Bibliography

Manuscripts

Oxford University Library Bodleian 6922 (Ashmole 61). Fols. 28a–38a.

Oxford University Library Bodleian 6926 (Ashmole 45). Fols. 3a–31b.

Lincoln Cathedral 91 (Thornton). Fols. 114b–122a.

Cambridge Ff. 2.38 provides the version presented here. Fols. 63a–70b.

---

[9] George Neilson, *Trial by Combat* (New York: Macmillan & Co., 1891), p. 48.

Critical Editions

Clark, J. H. "A Critical Edition of *The Earl of Toulouse*." *Index to Theses for Higher Degrees* 20 (1969–70), 312. M. Phil., London University.

Hulsmann, F. *Erle of Toulous: Eine neu Edition mit Einleitung und Glossar*. Ph.D. dissertation, Munster. Cited in *Neuphilologische Mitteilungen* 86 (1985), 127.

Lüdtke, Gustav. *The Erle of Tolous and the Emperes of Almayne*. Sammlung englischer Denkmaler 3. Berlin, 1881. [Contains texts from all MSS with extensive introduction, but without textual notes. In German.]

Collections

Fellows, Jennifer, ed. *Of Love and Chivalry: An Anthology of Middle English Romance*. London: Everyman, 1992. Pp. 231–65. [Uses Cambridge Ff.2.38.]

French, Walter Hoyt and Charles B. Hale, eds. *Middle English Metrical Romances*. New York: Russell & Russell, 1964. I, 381–419. [Uses Cambridge Ff.2.38.]

Ritson, Joseph. *Ancient Engleish Metrical Romanceës*. London: Bulmer and Co., 1802. III, 93–144. [Uses Cambridge Ff.2.38.]

Rumble, Thomas, ed. *Breton Lays in Middle English*. Detroit: Wayne State University Press, 1965. Pp. 135–77. [Uses Cambridge Ff.2.38.]

Rickert, Edith, ed. *Early English Romances in Verse: Done into Modern English*. New York: Cooper Square Publishers, 1967. Pp. 80–105. [Illustrated prose translation.]

Related Studies

Cabaniss, Allen. "Judith Augusta and Her Time." *University of Mississippi Studies in English* 10 (1969), 67–109. [Study of chronicle accounts of Judith, concluding that she deserves better representation.]

Christophersen, Paul. *The Ballad of Sir Aldingar: Its Origin and Analogues*. Oxford: Clarendon Press, 1952. [Study of the patterns of influence and cross-influence of this particular ballad, including its relation to *Erle of Tolous*.]

Erle of Tolous

Greenlaw, Edwin A. "The Vows of Baldwin: A Study in Medieval Diction." *PMLA* 21 (1906), 575–636. [Discusses three knightly vows as tests of character. Includes a discussion of the Woman Falsely Accused.]

Hulsmann, Friedrich. "The Watermarks of Four Late Medieval Manuscripts Containing *The Erle of Toulous.*" *Notes and Queries* n.s. 32 (1985), 11–12. [Argues that all watermarks point to date of 1470–1490.]

Reilly, Robert. "*The Earl of Toulouse*: A Structure of Honor." *Mediaeval Studies* 37 (1975), 515–23. [Relates the structure of contrast and comparison to an underlying system of honor.]

Erle of Tolous

Jhesu Cryste, yn Trynyté,
Oonly God and persons thre,
Graunt us wele to spede,
And gyf us grace so to do *give*
That we may come thy blys unto,
On Rode as thou can blede! *Cross; did bleed*
Leve lordys, y schall you telle *Permit [me]*
Of a tale, some tyme befelle *once occurred*
Farre yn unknowthe lede: *land*
How a lady had grete myschefe, *misery*
And how sche covyrd of hur grefe; *recovered from her*
Y pray yow take hede!

Some tyme there was in Almayn *Germany*
An Emperrour of moche mayn; *much might*
Syr Dyoclysyan he hyght; *was called*
He was a bolde man and a stowte; *hardy*
All Chrystendome of hym had dowte, *fear*
So stronge he was in fyght;
He dysheryted many a man, *disinherited*
And falsely ther londys wan, *lands won*
Wyth maystry and wyth myght, *intrigue*
Tyll hyt befelle upon a day, *i.e., it happened*
A warre wakenyd, as y yow say, *war arose; I say to you*
Betwene hym and a knyght.

The Erle of Tollous, Syr Barnard,
The Emperrour wyth hym was harde, *hostile*
And gretly was hys foo. *foe*
He had rafte owt of hys honde *reft, i.e., taken, gouged*
Three hundred poundys worth be yere of londe:
Therfore hys herte was woo.
He was an hardy man and a stronge, *formidable knight*
And sawe the Emperour dyd hym wronge, *saw [that]*

And other men also;
He ordeyned hym for batayle — *prepared himself*
Into the Emperours londe, saun fayle; — *without delay*
And there he began to brenne and sloo. — *burn; slay*

Thys Emperour had a wyfe,
The fayrest oon that evyr bare lyfe, — *i.e., lived*
Save Mary mekyll of myght, — *Except*
And therto gode in all thynge, — *good*
Of almesdede and gode berynge, — *almsdeeds; proper behavior*
Be day and eke be nyght; — *By; also*
Of hyr body sche was trewe — *faithful*
As evyr was lady that men knewe,
And therto moost bryght. — *also; beautiful*
To the Emperour sche can say: — *did*
"My dere lorde, y you pray,
Delyvyr the Erle hys ryght." — *Deliver (return); property*

"Dame," he seyde, "let that bee;
That day schalt thou nevyr see,
Yf y may ryde on ryght, — *properly*
That he schall have hys londe agayne; — *again*
Fyrste schall y breke hys brayne, — *break; brain*
Os y am trewe knyght! — *As*
He warryth faste in my londe; — *makes war vigorously*
I schall be redy at hys honde
Wythyn thys fourteen nyght!" — *fortnight*
He sente abowte everywhare,
That all men schulde make them yare — *prepare themselves*
Agayne the Erle to fyght. — *Against*

He let crye in every syde,
Thorow hys londe ferre and wyde, — *Throughout; far; wide*
Bothe in felde and towne, — *field*
All that myght wepon bere, — *carry weapons*
Sworde, alablast, schylde, or spere, — *crossbow; shield; spear*
They schoulde be redy bowne; — *ready to go*
The Erle on hys syde also
Wyth forty thousand and moo — *more*

Wyth spere and schylde browne. *shield shining*
A day of batayle there was sett;
In felde when they togedur mett,
Was crakydde many a crowne. *cracked; head*

The Emperour had bataylys sevyn; *battalions seven*
He spake to them wyth sterne stevyn *spoke; powerful voice*
And sayde, so mot he thryve, *thrive, i.e., win*
"Be ye now redy for to fyght,
Go ye and bete them downe ryght *beat*
And leveth non on lyve; *leave none alive*
Loke that none raunsonyd bee
Nothyr for golde ne for fee, *Neither; nor; property*
But sle them wyth swerde and knyfe!" *slay*
For all hys boste he faylyd gyt; *threats; nonetheless*
The Erle manly hym mett, *courageously met him*
Wyth strokys goode and ryfe. *abundant*

They reryd batayle on every syde; *joined*
Bodely togedyr can they ryde, *Boldly*
Wyth schylde and many a spere;
They leyde on faste as they were wode, *charged; mad*
Wyth swerdys and axes that were gode;
Full hedeous hyt was to here. *hideous; hear*
There were schyldys and schaftys schakydde, *spears broken*
Hedys thorogh helmys crakydde, *Heads; helmets cracked*
And hawberkys all totore. *hauberks torn to pieces*
The Erle hymselfe an axe drowe; *drew*
An hundred men that day he slowe, *slew*
So wyght he was yn were! *effective; war*

Many a stede there stekyd was; *was slain*
Many a bolde baron in that place
Lay burlande yn hys own blode. *wallowing*
So moche blode there was spylte, *spilled*
That the feld was ovyrhylte *covered*
Os hyt were a flode. *As if it; flood*
Many a wyfe may sytt and wepe,
That was wonte softe to slepe, *used to sleep peacefully*

And now can they no gode. *know no good (i.e., are wretched)*
Many a body and many a hevyd, *head*
Many a doghty knyght there was levyd, *left lying*
That was wylde and wode. *used to be wild; ferocious*

The Erle of Tollous wan the felde; *won; field*
The Emperour stode and behelde:
Wele faste can he flee *Quickly did*
To a castell there besyde.
Fayne he was hys hedde to hyde, *Eager*
And wyth hym Erlys thre; *three Earls*
No moo forsothe scapyd away, *more; escaped*
But they were slayn and takyn that day:
Hyt myght non othyr bee. *not be any other way*
The Erle tyll nyght folowed the chace, *followed; chase*
And sythen he thanked God of hys grace,
That syttyth in Trynyté.

There were slayne in that batayle
Syxty thousand, wythowte fayle, *without doubt*
On the Emperours syde;
Ther was takyn thre hundred and fyfty
Of grete lordys, sekyrly, *certainly*
Wyth woundys grymly wyde; *terribly*
On the Erlys syde ther were slayne
But twenty, sothely to sayne, *Only; to tell the truth*
So boldely they can abyde! *did they face the foe*
Soche grace God hym sende *Such*
That false quarell cometh to evell ende *evil*
For oght that may betyde. *Whatever; happen*

Now the Emperour ys full woo: *sorrowful*
He hath loste men and londe also;
Sore then syghed hee; *Sorely*
He sware be Hym that dyed on Rode, *Cross*
Mete nor drynke schulde do hym no gode,
Or he vengedde bee. *Until; avenged*
The Emperes seyde, "Gode lorde, *Empress*
Hyt ys better ye be acorde *agreed*

Be oght that y can see; *By*
Hyt ys grete parell, sothe to telle, *peril truthfully*
To be agayne the ryght quarell; *opposed to; just cause*
Be God, thus thynketh me!"

"Dame," seyde the Emperoure,
"Y have a grete dyshonoure; *[suffered]; dishonor*
Therfore myn herte ys woo;
My lordys be takyn, and some dede;
Therfore carefull ys my rede: *wretched; deliberation*
Sorowe nye wyll me sloo." *nearly; slay*
Then seyde Dame Beulybon:
"Syr, y rede, be Seynt John, *I advise by*
Of warre that ye hoo; *cease*
Ye have the wronge and he the ryght,
And that ye may see in syght,
Be thys and othyr moo."

The Emperour was evyll payde: *outraged*
Hyt was sothe the lady sayde; *truly just as*
Therfore hym lykyd ylle, *it ill-pleased him*
He wente awey and syghed sore;
Oon worde spake he no more, *Not one word*
But held hym wonder stylle. *amazingly still*
Leve we now the Emperour in thoght:
Game ne gle lyked hym noght, *nor joy pleased*
So gretly can he grylle! *did; grieve*
And to the Erle turne we agayn,
That thanked God wyth all hys mayn, *Who; might*
That grace had sende hym tylle. *sent to him*

The Erle Barnard of Tollous
Had fele men chyvalrous *many*
Takyn to hys preson; *prison*
Moche gode of them he hadde;
Y can not telle, so God me gladde,
So grete was ther raunsome!
Among them alle had he oon,
Was grettest of them everychon,

A lorde of many a towne,
Syr Trylabas of Turky
The Emperour hym lovyd, sekurly, — *confidently*
A man of grete renowne.

So hyt befell upon a day — *came about*
The Erle and he went to play
Be a rever syde. — *By; river*
The Erle seyde to Trylabas,
"Telle me, syr, for Goddys grace,
Of a thyng that spryngyth wyde, — *Of something widely known*
That youre Emperour hath a wyfe,
The fayrest woman that ys on lyfe,
Of hewe and eke of hyde. — *color; skin*
Y swere by boke and by belle,
Yf sche be so feyre as men telle,
Mekyll may be hys pryde."

Then sayde that lord anon ryght,
"Be the ordre y bere of knyght, — *bear as*
The sothe y schall telle the:
To seeke the worlde more and lesse,
Bothe Crystendome and hethynnesse,
Ther ys none so bryght of blee. — *hue*
Whyte as snowe ys hur coloure;
Hur rudde ys radder then the rose-floure, — *complexion; redder than*
Yn syght who may hur see;
All men that evyr God wroght — *created*
Myght not thynke nor caste in thoght — *i.e., imagine*
A fayrer for to bee."

Then seyde the Erle, "Be Goddys grace,
Thys worde in mornyng me mas. — *mourning; makes*
Thou seyest sche ys so bryght;
Thy raunsom here y the forgeve, — *remit*
My helpe, my love, whyll y leve — *live*
Therto my trowthe y plyght, — *pledge*
So that thou wylt brynge me — *Providing that*
Yn safegarde for to bee,

Of hur to have a syght,
An hundred pownde, wyth grete honoure,
To bye the horses and ryche armoure, *purchase*
Os y am trewe knyght!" *Because*

Than answeryd Syr Trylabas,
"Yn that covenaunt in thys place *covenant*
My trowthe y plyght thee;
Y schall holde thy forward gode *promise*
To brynge the, wyth mylde mode, *peaceably*
In syght hur for to see;
And therto wyll y kepe counsayle
And nevyr more, wythowte fayle,
Agayne yow to bee;
Y schall be trewe, be Goddys ore, *by God's grace*
To lose myn own lyfe therfore;
Hardely tryste to mee!" *Firmly trust me*

The Erle answeryd wyth wordys hende: *gracious*
"Y tryste to the as to my frende, *trust you; friend*
Wythowte any stryfe;
Anon that we were buskyd yare, *Soon; prepared nimbly*
On owre jurney for to fare, *journey*
For to see that wyfe;
Y swere be God and Seynt Andrewe,
Yf hyt be so y fynde the trewe,
Ryches schall be to the ryfe." *plentiful*
They lettyd nothyr for wynde not wedur,[1]
But forthe they wente bothe togedur,
Wythowte any stryfe.

These knyghtys nevyr stynte nor blanne, *stopped; tarried*
Tyll to the cyté that they wan,
There the Emperes was ynne.
The Erle hymselfe for more drede
Cladde hym in armytes wede, *hermit's clothing*

[1] *They delayed neither for wind nor [foul] weather*

Thogh he were of ryche kynne, — *kin*
For he wolde not knowen bee. — *be known*
He dwellyd there dayes three
And rested hym in hys ynne. — *inn*
The knyght bethoght hym, on a day, — *(Trylabas) thought to himself*
The gode Erle to betray; — *good*
Falsely he can begynne.

Anone he wente in a rese — *nervous rush*
To chaumbur to the Emperes,
And sett hym on hys knee;
He seyde, "Be Hym that harowed helle, — *harrowed hell*
He kepe yow fro all parelle, — *peril*
Yf that Hys wylle bee!"
"Madam," he seyde, "be Jhesus,
Y have the Erle of Tollous;
Oure moost enemye ys hee." — *foremost*
"Yn what maner," the lady can say,
"Ys he comyn, y the pray?
Anone telle thou me." — *Tell me why he has come*

"Madam, y was in hys preson; — *prison*
He hath forgevyn me my raunsom, — *granted*
Be God full of myght —
And all ys for the love of the!
The sothe ys, he longyth yow to see, — *truth*
Madam, onys in syght! — *once*
And hundred pownde y have to mede, — *as reward*
And armour for a nobull stede;
Forsothe y have hym hyght — *promised*
That he schall see yow at hys fylle,
Ryght at hys owne wylle;
Therto my trowthe y plyght.

Lady, he ys to us a foo; — *foe*
Therfore y rede that we hym sloo; — *suggest; slay*
He hath done us gret grylle." — *caused; grief*
The lady seyde, "So mut y goo, — *must*
Thy soule ys loste yf thou do so;

Thy trowthe thou schalt fulfylle,
Sythe he forgaf the thy raunsom *Since*
And lowsydd the owt of preson, *loosed (released) you*
Do away thy wyckyd wylle!

To-morne when they rynge the masbelle, *mass bell*
Brynge hym into my chapelle,
And thynke thou on no false sleythe; *trick*
There schall he see me at hys wylle,
Thy covenaunt to fulfylle;
Y rede the holde thy trowthe!
Certys, yf thou hym begyle, *beguile*
Thy soule ys in grete paryle, *peril*
Syn thou haste made hym othe; *oath*
Certys, hyt were a traytory, *an act of treason*
For to wayte hym wyth velany; *lie in wait for; treachery*
Me thynkyth hyt were rowthe!"

The knyght to the Erle wente;
Yn herte he helde hym foule schente *foully disgraced*
For hys wyckyd thoght.
He seyde, "Syr, so mote y the, *might I thrive*
Tomorne thou schalt my lady see; *Tomorrow morning*
Therfore, dysmay the noght: *do not dismay*
When ye here the masbelle, *hear; call to Mass*
Y schall hur brynge to the chapelle;
Thedur sche schall be broght.
Be the oryall syde stonde thou stylle; *By; oriel (passageway)*
Then schalt thou see hur at thy wylle,
That ys so worthyly wroght." *worthily wrought*

The Erle sayde, "Y holde the trewe,
And that schall the nevyr rewe,
As farre forthe as y may."
Yn hys herte he waxe gladde: *grew*
"Fylle the wyne," wyghtly he badde, *eagerly*
"Thys goyth to my pay!" *goes to my liking*
There he restyd that nyght;
On the morne he can hym dyght *prepare himself*

Yn armytes array; *hermit's*
When they ronge to the masse,
To the chapell conne they passe,
To see that lady gay.

They had stonden but a whyle,
The mowntaunse of halfe a myle, *In the time required to ride half a mile*
Then came that lady free;
Two erlys hur ladde;
Wondur rychely sche was cladde,
In golde and ryche perré. *jewels*
Whan the Erle sawe hur in syght,
Hym thoght sche was as bryght
Os blossome on the tree;
Of all the syghtys that ever he sye,
Raysyd nevyr none hys herte so hye,
Sche was so bryght of blee! *fair of countenance*

Sche stode stylle in that place
And schewed opynly hur face *showed*
For love of that knyght.
He beheld ynly hur face; *closely*
He sware there be Goddys grace,
He sawe nevyr none so bryght.
Hur eyen were gray as any glas;
Mowthe and nose schapen was
At all maner ryght;
Fro the forhedde to the too, *forehead; toe*
Bettur schapen myght non goo,
Nor none semelyer yn syght. *seemlier*

Twyes sche turnyd hur abowte *Twice; around*
Betwene the Erlys that were stowte, *strong*
For the Erle schulde hur see.
When sche spake wyth mylde stevyn, *voice*
Sche semyd an aungell of hevyn, *angel; heaven*
So feyre sche was of blee! *countenance*
Hur syde longe, hur myddyll small; *middle, i.e., waist*
Schouldurs, armes therwythall,

Fayrer myght non bee;
Hur hondys whyte as whallys bonne, *whale's bone*
Wyth fyngurs longe and ryngys upon;
Hur nayles bryght of blee. *hue*

When he had beholden hur welle,
The lady wente to hur chapell,
Masse for to here;
The Erle stode on that odur syde; *other*
Hys eyen fro hur myght he not hyde, *He couldn't take his eyes off her*
So lovely sche was of chere! *countenance*
He seyde, "Lorde God, full of myght,
Leve y were so worthy a knyght, *Would that*
That y myght be hur fere, *companion*
And that sche no husbonde hadde,
All the golde that evyr God made
To me were not so dere!"

Whcn thc massc comc to cndc,
The lady, that was feyre and hende, *gracious*
To the chaumbur can sche fare; *did she return*
The Erle syghed and was full woo
Owt of hys syght when sche schulde goo;
Hys mornyng was the mare. *mourning; more*
The Erle seyde, "So God me save,
Of hur almes y wolde crave,
Yf hur wylle ware; *If she were willing*
Myght y oght gete of that free,
Eche a day hur to see
Hyt wolde covyr me of my care." [1]

The Erle knelyd down anon ryght
And askyd gode, for God allmyght,
That dyed on the tree. *Who died*
The Emperes callyd a knyght:

[1] *Whatever I might receive from that generous person / Every time I were to see her / It would assuage (redeem) me from my sorrow (poverty)*

"Forty floranse that ben bryght, *florins*
Anone brynge thou mee."
To that armyte sche hyt payde; *hermit*
Of hur fyngyr a rynge she layde *From*
Amonge that golde so free;
He thankyd hur ofte, as y yow say.
To the chaumbyr wente that lady gay,
There hur was leveste to bee.

The Erle wente home to hys ynnys, *lodgings*
And grete joye he begynnys
When he founde the rynge;
Yn hys herte he waxe blythe *grew happy*
And kyssyd hyt fele sythe, *many times*
And seyde, "My dere derlynge, *precious darling*
On thy fyngyr thys was!
Wele ys me, y have thy grace
Of the to have thys rynge!
Yf evyr y gete grace of the Quene
That any love betwene us bene,
Thys may be our tokenyng."

The Erle, also soone os hyt was day, *as it*
Toke hys leve and wente hys way *Took his leave*
Home to hys cuntré;
Syr Trylabas he thanked faste:
"Of thys dede thou done me haste,
Well qwyt schall hyt bee."
They kyssyd togedur as gode frende; *good friends*
Syr Trylabas home can wende,
There evell mote he thee! *evil befall him*
A traytory he thoght to doo *treachery*
Yf he myght come thertoo;
So schrewde in herte was hee!

Anon he callyd two knyghtys,
Hardy men at all syghtys; *by all accounts*
Bothe were of hys kynne.
"Syrs," he seyde, "wythowt fayle,

Yf ye wyl do be my counsayle, *by my counsel*
Grete worschyp schulde ye wynne;
Knowe ye the Erle of Tollous?
Moche harme he hath done us;
Hys boste y rede we blynne; *boast; advise; squelch*
Yf ye wyll do aftur my redde, *i.e., listen to my counsel*
Thys day he schall be dedde,
So God save me fro synne!"

That oon knyght Kaunters, that odur Kaym;
Falser men myght no man rayme, *coerce*
Certys, then were thoo; *than; those*
Syr Trylabas was the thrydde;
Hyt was no mystur them to bydde *need; wait*
Aftur the Erle to goo.
At a brygge they hym mett; *bridge*
Wyth harde strokes they hym besett,
As men that were hys foo; *foe*
The Erle was a man of mayn: *strength*
Faste he faght them agayne,
And soone he slew two.

The thrydde fledde and blewe owt faste; *i.e., got winded*
The Erle ovyrtoke hym at the laste: *overtook*
Hys hedd he clofe in three. *clove*
The cuntrey gedryrd abowte hym faste, *gathered; quickly*
And aftur hym yorne they chaste: *eagerly; pursued*
An hundred there men myght see.
The Erle of them was agaste: *surprised*
At the laste fro them he paste; *passed*
Fayne he was to flee; *Glad*
Fro them he wente into a waste; *wilderness area*
To reste hym there he toke hys caste: *took his cares*
A wery man was hee. *weary*

All the nyght in that foreste
The gentyll Erle toke hys reste:
He had no nodur woon. *no other dwelling*
When hyt dawed, he rose up soone *dawned*

And thankyd God that syttyth in trone, *on throne*
That he had scapyd hys foon; *escaped; enemies*
That day he travaylyd many a myle, *traveled*
And ofte he was in grete parylle,
Be the way os he can gone,
Tyll he come to a fayre castell,
There hym was levyst to dwelle, *most pleased*
Was made of lyme and stone.

Of hys comyng hys men were gladde.
"Be ye mery, my men," he badde,
"For nothyng ye spare;
The Emperour, wythowte lees, *lies (i.e., to tell the truth)*
Y trowe, wyll let us be in pees. *peace*
And warre on us no mare." *make war; more*
Thus dwellyd the Erle in that place
Wyth game, myrthe, and grete solase, *mirth; solace*
Ryght os hym levyst ware. *Just as it suited him*
Let we now the Erle alloon,
And speke we of Dame Beulyboon,
How sche was caste in care. *thrown into despair*

The Emperoure lovyd hys wyfe
Also so moche os hys own lyfe,
And more, yf he myght;
He chose two knyghtys that were hym dere, *dear to him*
Whedur that he were ferre or nere, *Whether; far; near*
To kepe hur day and nyght. *i.e., guard*
That oon hys love on hur caste: *one*
So dud the todur at the laste, *did; other*
Sche was feyre and bryght!
Nothyr of othyr wyste ryght noght,
So derne love on them wroght, *secretly; affected them*
To dethe they were nere dyght. *nearly brought*

So hyt befell upon a day,
That oon can to that othyr say,
"Syr, also muste y thee, *might I thrive*
Methynkyth thou fadyste all away, *i.e., you're wasting away*

Os man that ys clongyn in clay, *shriveled*
So pale waxeth thy blee!" *countenance*
Then seyde that other, "Y make avowe, *a vow*
Ryght so, methynketh, fareste thou,
Whysoevyr hyt bee;
Tell me thy cawse, why hyt ys,
And y schall telle the myn, ywys: *truly*
My trouthe y plyght to thee." *confess*

"Y graunte," he seyde, "wythowt fayle,
But loke hyt be trewe counsayle!" *make sure it be*
Therto hys trowthe he plyght.
He seyde, "My lady the Emperes,
For love of hur y am in grete dystresse;
To dethe hyt wyll me dyght." *condemn*
Then seyde that othyr, "Certenly,
Wythowte drede, so fare y *Without a doubt*
For that lady bryght;
Syn owre love ys on hur sett,
How myght owre bale beste be bett? *suffering; eased*
Canste thou rede on ryght?"

Then seyde that othyr, "Be Seynt John,
Bettur counsayle can y noon,
Methynkyth, then ys thys:
Y rede that oon of us twoo
Prevely to hyr goo *Privately*
And pray hur of hur blys; *beg; favor*
Y myselfe wyll go hyr tylle; *to her*
Yn case y may gete hur wylle,
Of myrthe schalt thou not mys;
Thou schalt take us wyth the dede: *catch us*
Leste thou us wrye sche wyll drede, *betray us; be afraid*
And graunte the thy wylle, ywys."

Thus they were at oon assent; *agreed*
Thys false thefe forthe wente *This; thief*
To wytt the ladyes wylle. *test*
Yn chaumbyr he founde hyr so free; *noble*

He sett hym downe on hys knee,
Hys purpose to fulfylle.
Than spake that lady free, *Then spoke*
"Syr, y see now well be the, *by you*
Thou haste not all thy wylle;
On thy sekeness now y see;
Telle me now thy prevyté, *secret*
Why thou mornyst so stylle." *mourn*

"Lady," he seyde, "that durste y noght *dare I not*
For all the gode that evyr was wroght, *good*
Be grete God invysybylle, *invisible*
But on a booke yf ye wyll swere *swear*
That ye schull not me dyskere, *disclose, i.e., tell on me*
Then were hyt possybyll." *it would be possible*
Then seyde the lady, "How may that bee?
That thou darste not tryste to mee, *dare not trust*
Hyt ys full orybylle. *horrible*
Here my trowthe to the y plyght:
Y schall heyle the day and nyght, *conceal you*
Also trewe as boke or belle."

"Lady, in yow ys all my tryste; *trust*
Inwardely y wolde ye wyste
What payne y suffur you fore; *suffer for you*
Y drowpe, y dare nyght and day; *pine; sulk*
My wele, my wytt ys all away, *well-being; mind*
But ye leve on my lore; *Unless; believe; words*
Y have yow lovyd many a day,
But to yow durste y nevyr say — *I never dare speak*
My mornyng ys the more! *grief*
But ye do aftur my rede, *counsel*
Certenly, y am but dede:
Of my lyfe ys no store." *value*

Than answeryd that lovely lyfe: *Then; person*
"Syr, wele thou wottyst y am a wyfe: *certainly you know*
My lorde ys Emperoure;
He chase the for a trewe knyght, *chose*

To kepe me bothe day and nyght *guard*
Undur thy socowre. *protection*
To do that dede yf y assente, *deed*
Y were worthy to be brente *burned*
And broght in grete doloure; *misery*
Thou art a traytour in thy sawe, *words*
Worthy to be hanged and to-drawe
Be Mary, that swete floure!" *By*

"A, madam!" seyde the knyght,
"For the love of God almyght,
Hereon take no hede! *don't be offended*
Yn me ye may full wele tryste ay; *trust*
Y dud nothyng but yow to affray, *did; frighten*
Also God me spede!
Thynke, madam, youre trowthe ys plyght
To holde counsayle bothe day and nyght
Fully, wythowte drede;
Y aske mercy for Goddys ore! *sake*
Hereof yf y carpe more, *complain*
Let drawe me wyth a stede!" *Let me be pulled apart by horses*

The lady seyde, "Y the forgeve; *forgive you*
Also longe os y leve, *live*
Counsayle schall hyt bee;
Loke thou be a trewe man
In all thyng that thou can,
To my lorde so free."
"Yys, lady, ellys dyd y wronge,
For y have servyd hym longe,
And wele he hath qwytt mee." *compensated*
Hereof spake he no mare,
But to hys felowe can he fare,
There evyll must they the! *evil; suffer*

Thus to hys felowe ys he gon,
And he hym frayned anon, *questioned soon*
"Syr, how haste thou spedde?" *fared*
"Ryght noght," seyde that othyr:

"Syth y was borne, lefe brothyr,
Was y nevyr so adredde; *frightened*
Certys, hyt ys a boteles bale *hopeless cause*
To hur to touche soche a tale
At borde or at bedde." *table*
Then sayde that odur, "Thy wytt ys thynne: *other; thin*
Y myselfe schall hur wynne:
Y lay my hedde to wedde!" *head; wager*

Thus hyt passyd ovyr, os y yow say,
Tyl aftur on the thrydde day
Thys knyght hym bethoght:
"Certys, spede os y may,
My ladyes wylle, that ys so gay,
Hyt schall be thorowly soght." *thoroughly probed*
When he sawe hur in beste mode,
Sore syghyng to hur he yode, *went*
Of lyfe os he ne roght. *as if he cared not*
"Lady," he seyde, "wythowte fayle,
But ye helpe me wyth yowre counsayle,
Yn bale am y broght." *Into woe*

Sche answeryd full curtesly,
"My counsayle schall be redy.
Telle me how hyt ys;
When y wott worde and ende,
Yf my counsayle may hyt mende,
Hyt schall, so have y blysse!"
"Lady," he seyde, "y undurstonde
Ye muste holde up yowre honde
To holde counsayle, ywys." *I think*
"Yys," seyde the lady free, *Yes; noble*
"Thereto my trouthe here to the,
And ellys y dudde amys." *Or else I did amiss*

"Madam," he seyde, "now y am in tryste; *trust*
All my lyfe thogh ye wyste, *know*
Ye wolde me not dyskevere; *reveal*
For yow y am in so grete thoght, *i.e., mental anguish*

Yn moche bale y am broght, *grief*
Wythowte othe y swere; *oath*
And ye may full wele see,
How pale y am of blee: *color*
Y dye nere for dere; *nearly die of suffering*
Dere lady, graunt me youre love,
For the love of God, that sytteth above,
That stongen was wyth a spere." *pierced*

"Syr," sche seyde, "ys that youre wylle?
Yf hyt were myne, then dyd y ylle;
What woman holdyst thou me? *What kind of woman do you think I am*
Yn thy kepeyng y have ben:
What haste thou herde be me or sene *heard about me*
That touchyth to any velanye,
That thou in herte art so bolde
Os y were a hore or a scolde? *As if; whore; a gossip*
Nay, that schall nevyr bee!
Had y not hyght to holde counsayle, *promised*
Thou schouldest be honged, wythowt fayle,
Upon a galowe tree."

The knyght was nevyr so sore aferde *afraid*
Sythe he was borne into myddyllerde, *middle Earth*
Certys, os he was thoo.
"Mercy," he seyde, "gode madam!
Wele y wott y am to blame;
Therfore myn herte ys woo!
Lady, let me not be spylte; *condemned*
Y aske mercy of my gylte! *for; guilt*
On lyve ye let me goo."
The lady seyde, "Y graunte wele;
Hyt schall be counseyle, every dele,
But do no more soo."

Now the knyght forthe yede *went*
And seyde, "Felowe, y may not spede. *I've had no luck*
What ys thy beste redde? *advice*
Yf sche telle my lorde of thys,

We be but dedde, so have y blys:
Wyth hym be we not fedde. — *nourished*
Womans tonge ys evell to tryste; — *i.e., unsafe*
Certys, and my lorde hyt wyste, — *if; knew*
Etyn were all owre bredde. — *Eaten*
Felow, so mote y ryde or goo,
Or sche wayte us wyth that woo, — *Before; inflicts*
Hurselfe schall be dedde!"

"How myght that be?" that othur sayde;
"Yn herte y wolde be wele payde, — *well satisfied*
Myght we do that dede." — *deed*
"Yys, syr," he seyde, "so have y roo, — *repose*
Y schall brynge hur wele thertoo;
Therof have thou no drede. — *fear*
Or hyt passe dayes three, — *Before three days pass*
In mekyll sorowe schall sche bee: — *much*
Thus y schall qwyte hur hur mede." — *pay her her reward*
Now are they bothe at oon assente
In sorow to brynge that lady gente:
The devell mote them spede! — *reward them*

Sone hyt drowe toward nyght; — *Soon; drew*
To soper they can them dyght, — *supper; prepare themselves*
The Emperes and they all;
The two knyghtys grete yapys made, — *jests*
For to make the lady glade,
That was bothe gentyll and small;
When the sopertyme was done,
To the chaumbyr they went soone,
Knyghtys cladde in palle — *i.e., rich fabrics*
They daunsed and revelyd, os they noght dredde,
To brynge the lady to hur bedde:
There foule muste them falle!

That oon thefe callyd a knyght
That was carver to that lady bryght;
An erleys sone was hee; — *earl's son*
He was a feyre chylde and a bolde; — *handsome; confident*

Twenty wyntur he was oolde:
In londe was none so free. — *well-endowed*
"Syr, wylt thou do os we the say? — *as I tell you*
And we schall ordeygne us a play, — *invent; game*
That my lady may see.
Thou schalt make hur to lagh soo, — *laugh*
Thogh sche were gretly thy foo,
Thy frende schulde sche bee."

The chylde answeryd anon ryght:
"Be the ordur y bere of knyght,
Therof wolde y be fayne, — *amenable*
And hyt wolde my lady plese, — *If*
Thogh hyt wolde me dysese, — *distress*
To renne yn wynde and rayne."
"Syr, make the nakyd save thy breke; — *except your breeches*
And behynde the yondur curtayn thou crepe,
And do os y schall sayne;
Then schalt thou see a joly play!" — *jolly*
"Y graunte," thys yonge knyght can say, — *Okay*
"Be God and Seynte Jermayne." — *Germaine*

Thys chylde thoght on no ylle:
Of he caste hys clothys stylle; — *Off*
And behynde the curtayn he went.
They seyde to hym, "What so befalle, — *Whatever happens*
Come not owt tyll we the calle."
And he seyde, "Syrs, y assente."
They revelyd forthe a grete whyle;
No man wyste of ther gyle — *knew; guile*
Save they two, veramente. — *Except those; truly*
They voyded the chaumber sone anon; — *vacated*
The chylde they lafte syttyng alone, — *left sitting*
And that lady gente.

Thys lady lay in bedde on slepe; — *asleep*
Of treson toke sche no kepe, — *notice*
For therof wyste sche noght. — *knew*
Thys chylde had wonder evyr among

Why these knyghtys were so longe:
  He was in many a thoght.
"Lorde, mercy! How may thys bee?
Y trowe they have forgeten me, *suspect*
  That me hedur broght;
Yf y them calle, sche wyll be adredd,
My lady lyeth here in hur bede,
  Be Hym that all hath wroght!"

Thus he sate stylle as any stone:
He durste not store nor make no mone *move; moan*
  To make the lady afryght.
Thes false men ay worthe them woo!,
To ther chaumbur can they goo
  And armyd them full ryght;
Lordys owte of bedde can they calle
And badde arme them, grete and smalle:
  "Anone that ye were dyght,
And helpe to take a false traytoure
That wyth my lady in hur bowre *bedroom*
  Hath playde hym all thys nyght."

Sone they were armyd everychone; *everyone*
And wyth these traytours can they gone,
  The lordys that there wore. *were there*
To the Emperes chaumber they cam ryght
Wyth torchys and wyth swerdys bryght
  Brennyng them before. *Burning*
Behynde the curtayne they wente;
The yonge knyght, verrament,
  Nakyd founde they thore. *there*
That oon thefe wyth a swerde of were *war*
Thorow the body he can hym bere, *Through; thrust*
  That worde spake he no more.

The lady woke and was afryght,
Whan sche sawe the grete lyght
  Before hur beddys syde.
Sche seyde, "Benedycyté!" *Bless us*

Syrs, what men be yee?"
And wonder lowde sche cryedd.
Hur enemyes mysansweryd thore *i.e., spoke abusively*
"We are here, thou false hore: *whore*
Thy dedys we have aspyedd! *deeds; witnessed*
Thou haste betrayed my lorde;
Thou schalt have wonduryng in thys worde: *exile (wandering)*
Thy loos schall sprynge wyde!" *infamy*

The lady seyde, "Be Seynte John,
Hore was y nevyr none, *Whore*
Nor nevyr thoght to bee."
"Thou lyest," they seyde, "thy love ys lorne" — *lost*
The corse they leyde hur beforne — *corpse*
"Lo, here ys thy lemman free! *promiscuous lover*
Thus we have for they hym hytt;
Thy horedam schall be wele quytte: *whoredom; proven*
Fro us schalt thou not flee!"
They bonde the lady wondyr faste *bound*
And in a depe preson hur caste: *deep prison*
Grete dele hyt was to see! *sadness*

Leve we now thys lady in care, *distress*
And to hur lorde wyll we fare, *husband*
That ferre was hur froo. *far; from*
On a nyght, wythowt lette, *doubt*
In hys slepe a swevyn he mett, *dream; dreamed*
The story telleth us soo.
Hym thoght ther come two wylde borys *wild boars*
And hys wyfe all toterys *That; tore all to pieces*
And rofe hur body in twoo; *ripped*
Hymselfe was a wytty man, *intelligent*
And be that dreme he hopyd than *knew with certainty*
Hys lady was in woo.

Yerly, when the day was clere, *Early*
He bad hys men all in fere *bade; all together*
To buske and make them yare. *arm; prepare themselves*
Somer horsys he let go before *Pack horses; sent ahead*

And charyettes stuffud wyth stoore *wagons; provisions*
Wele twelve myle and mare.
He hopud wele in hys herte *was certain*
That hys wyfe was not in querte; *safety*
Hys herte therfore was in care; *deeply concerned*
He styntyd not tyll he was dyght, *stopped; prepared*
Wyth erlys, barons, and many a knyght;
Homeward can they fare. *did; proceed*

Nyght ne day nevyr they blanne, *ceased*
Tyll to that cyté they came
There the lady was ynne.
Wythowt the cyté lordys them kepyd; *Outside; awaited*
For wo in herte many oon wepyd: *wept*
There teerys myght they not blynne. *Their tears; stop*
They supposyd wele yf he hyt wyste
That hys wyfe had soche a bryste, *misfortune*
Hys yoye wolde be full thynne; *joy*
They ladden stedys to the stabyll, *lead the steeds*
And the lorde into the halle,
To worschyp hym wyth wynne. *joy*

Anon to the chaumbur wendyth he:
He longyd hys feyre lady to see,
That was so swete a wyght. *person*
He callyd them that schoulde hur kepe: *have guarded*
"Where ys my wyfe? Ys sche on slepe? *asleep*
How fareth that byrde bryght?"
The two traytours answeryd anone, *immediately*
"Yf ye wyste how sche had done, *knew; behaved*
To dethe sche schulde be dyght." *death; condemned*

"A, devyll!" he seyde, "how soo,
To dethe that sche ys worthy to go?
Tell me, in what manere."
"Syr," they seyd, "be Goddys ore, *by God's grace*
The yonge knyght Syr Antore,
That was hur kervere, *carver*
Be that lady he hath layne, *With; has lain*

And therfore we have hym slayne;
We founde them in fere; — *together (copulating)*
Sche ys in preson, verrament; — *truly*
The lawe wyll that sche be brente, — *demands; burned*
Be God, that boght us dere." — *redeemed*

"Allas!" seyde the Emperoure,
"Hath sche done me thys dyshonoure?
And y lovyd hur so wele!
Y wende for all thys worldys gode — *I believed; world's good*
That sche wolde not have turned hur mode: — *i.e., been unfaithful*
My joye begynnyth to kele." — *joy; cool*
He hente a knyfe wyth all hys mayn; — *seized; strength*
Had not a knyght ben, he had hym slayn, — *himself*
And that traytour have broght owt of heele. — *(see note)*
For bale hys armes abrode he bredde — *despair; opened*
And fell in swowne upon hys bedde; — *swoon*
There myght men see grete dele. — *torment*

On the morne be oon assente,
On hur they sett a perlyament — *parliament*
Be all the comyn rede.
They myght not fynde in ther counsayle — *counsel*
Be no lawe, wythowt fayle,
To save hur fro the dede.
Then bespake an olde knyght,
"Y have wondur, be Goddys myght,
That Syr Antore thus was bestedde, — *situated*
In chaumbyr thogh he naked were;
They let hym gyf none answere,
But slowe hym, be my hedde! — *slew*

Ther was nevyr man, sekurly, — *certainly*
That be hur founde any velany, — *villainy*
Save they two, y dar wele say; — *Except those*
Be some hatered hyt may be; — *By; hatred*
Therfore doyth aftur me — *i.e., as I say*
For my love, y yow pray.
No mo wyll preve hyt but they twoo; — *No one else; prove*

Therfore we may not save hur fro woo,
For sothe, os y yow say,
In hyr quarell but we myght fynde — *cause; unless*
A man that were gode of kynde — *nature*
That durste fyght agayn them tway." — *two*

All they assentyd to the sawe: — *suggestion*
They thoght he spake reson and lawe.
Then answeryd the Kyng wyth crowne,
"Fayre falle the for thyn avyse." — *Blessings on you*
He callyd knyghtys of nobyll pryce — *esteem*
And badde them be redy bowne — *quickly prepared*
For to crye thorow all the londe,
Bothe be see and be sonde, — *by sea; shore*
Yf they fynde mowne — *could*
A man that ys so moche of myght,
That for that lady dar take the fyght,
"He schall have hys warison." — *reward*

Messangerys, y undurstonde,
Cryed thorow all the londe
In many a ryche cyté,
Yf any man durste prove hys myght — *Whether*
In trewe quarell for to fyght,
Wele avaunsed schulde he bee. — *advanced in rank*
The Erle of Tullous harde thys telle, — *heard; proclamation*
What anger the lady befell; — *grief*
Thereof he thoght grete pyté.
Yf he wyste that sche had ryght,
He wolde aventure hys lyfe to fyght — *risk*
For that lady free.

For hur he morned nyght and day,
And to hymselfe can he say
He wolde aventure hys lyfe: — *risk*
"Yf y may wytt that sche be trewe, — *know*
They that have hur accused schull rewe, — *be sorry*
But they stynte of ther stryfe." — *Unless; stop*
The Erle seyde, "Be Seynte John,

Ynto Almayn wyll y goon, *Germany; go*
Where y have fomen ryfe; *abundant enemies*
I prey to God full of myght
That y have trewe quarell to fyght,
Owt of wo to wynne that wyfe." *rescue*

He rode on huntyng on a day,
A marchand mett he be the way, *merchant*
And asked hym of whens he was. *where he was from*
"Lorde," he seyde, "of Almayn."
Anon the Erle can hym frayne *ask*
Of that ylke case: *same*
"Wherefore ys yowre Emperes *Why*
Put in so grete dystresse?
Telle me, for Goddys grace.
Ys sche gylté, so mote thou the?" *guilty; may you prosper*
"Nay, be Hym that dyed on tree,
That schope man aftur Hys face." *created; image*

Then seyde the Erle, wythowte lett, *hesitation*
"When ys the day sett
Brente that sche schulde bee?"
The marchande seyde sekyrlyke, *assuredly*
"Evyn thys day thre wyke, *three weeks*
And therfore wo ys mee."
The Erle seyde, "Y schall the telle:
Gode horsys y have to selle, *Good*
And stedys two or thre:
Certys, myght y selle them yare, *quickly*
Thedur wyth the wolde y fare, *Thither*
That syght for to see."

The marchand seyd wordys hende: *favorable*
"Into the londe yf ye wyll wende,
Hyt wolde be for yowre prowe, *advantage*
There may ye selle them at your wylle."
Anon the Erle seyde hym tylle,
"Syr, herkyn me nowe:
Thys jurney wylt thou wyth me dwelle *journey*

Twenty pownde y schall the telle *promise you*
To mede, y make avowe!" *As reward*
The marchand grauntyd anon; *agreed instantly*
The Erle seyde, "Be Seynt John,
Thy wylle y alowe." *approve*

The Erle tolde hym in that tyde *time*
Where he schulde hym abyde, *wait for him*
And homeward wente hee.
He busked hym, that no man wyste, *armed himself*
For mekyll on hym was hys tryste. *great; him [the merchant]; trust*
He seyde, "Syr, go wyth mee!"
Wyth them they toke stedys sevyn — *seven horses*
Ther were no fayre undyr hevyn *none fairer*
That any man myght see.
Into Almayn they can ryde:
As a coresur of mekyll pryde *horsedealer*
He semyd for to bee.

The marchand was a trewe gyde; *guide*
The Erle and he togedur can ryde,
Tyll they came to that place.
A myle besyde the castell
There the Emperoure can dwelle,
A ryche abbey ther was;
Of the abbot leve they gatt *permission; got*
To sojorne and make ther horsys fatt; *sojourn*
That was a nobyll case!
The abbot was the ladyes eme; *uncle*
For hur he was in grete wandreme, *sorrow*
And moche mornyng he mase. *[with] mourning he was overwhelmed*

So hyt befell upon a day,
To churche the Erle toke the way,
A masse for to here.
He was a feyre man and an hye; *tall*
When the abbot hym sye, *saw him*
He seyde, "Syr, come nere:
Syr, when the masse ys done,

Y pray yow, ete wyth me at noone,
  Yf yowre wylle were."
The Erle grauntyd all wyth game;
Afore mete they wysche all same, *before eating; wash together*
  And to mete they wente in fere. *dine; together*

Aftur mete, as y yow say,
Into an orchard they toke the way,
  The abbot and the knyght.
The abbot seyde and syghed sare; *sorely*
"Certys, Syr, y leve in care *live*
  For a lady bryght;
Sche ys accusyd — my herte ys woo! —
Therfore sche schall to dethe goo,
  All agayne the ryght; *against*
But sche have helpe, verrament, *Unless*
In fyre sche schall be brente *fire; burned*
  Thys day sevenyght." *i.e., in a week*

The Erle seyde, "So have y blysse,
Of hyr, methynkyth, grete rewthe hyt ys, *pity*
  Trewe yf that sche bee!"
The abbot seyde, "Be Seynte Poule, *Paul*
For hur y dar ley my soule *wager*
  That nevyr gylté was sche;
Soche werkys nevyr sche wroght *Such deeds*
Neythyr in dede nor in thoght, *practice; thought*
  Save a rynge so free *Except; graciously*
To the Erle of Tullous sche gafe hyt wyth wynne, *gladness*
Yn ese of hym and for no synne: *For his comfort*
  In schryfte thus tolde sche me." *confession*

The Erle seyde, "Syth hyt ys soo, *Since*
Cryste wreke hur of hur woo, *avenge*
  That boght hur wyth Hys bloode! *Who redeemed*
Wolde ye sekyr me, wythowt fayle, *assure*
For to holde trewe counsayle,
  Hyt myght be for yowre gode."
The abbot seyde be bokes fele *by many books*

And be hys professyon, that he wolde hele, *embrace*
   And ellys he were wode. *Or else; mad*
"Y am he that sche gaf the rynge
For to be oure tokenynge. *token*
   Now heyle hyt, for the Rode! *conceal; Cross*

Y am comyn, lefe syr, *dear sir*
To take the batyle for hyr, *fight in her cause*
   There to stonde wyth ryght;
But fyrste myselfe y wole hur schryve, *confess*
And yf y fynde hur clene of lyve, *i.e., guiltless*
   Then wyll my herte be lyght.
Let dyght me in monkys wede *me be dressed; monk's garb*
To that place that men schulde hyr lede,
   To dethe to be dyght; *For; prepared*
When y have schrevyn hyr, wythowt fayle, *confessed*
For hur y wyll take batayle,
   As y am trewe knyght!"

The abbot was nevyr so gladde;
Nere for joye he waxe madde; *Nearly; went crazy*
   The Erle can he kysse;
They made meré and slewe care. *merry; set aside*
All that sevenyght he dwellyd thare
   Yn myrthe wythowt mysse. *interruption*
That day that the lady schulde be brent,
The Erle wyth the abbot wente
   In monkys wede, ywys;
To the Emperour he knelys blyve, *knelt humbly*
That he myght that lady schryve: *confess*
   Anon resceyved he ys. *received*

He examyned hur, wyttyrly, *questioned; intelligently*
As hyt seythe in the story; *says*
   Sche was wythowte gylte.
Sche seyde, "Be Hym that dyed on tree,
Trespas was nevyr none in me
   Wherefore y schulde be spylte; *executed*
Save oonys, wythowte lesynge,

To the Erle of Tollous y gafe a rynge:
Assoyle me yf thou wylte; *Absolve*
But thus my destanye ys comyn to ende,
That in thys fyre y muste be brende;
There Goddys wylle be fulfyllyt."

The Erle assoyled hur wyth hys honde, *absolved*
And sythen pertely he can up stonde *then boldly*
And seyde, "Lordyngys, pese! *peace*
Ye that have accused thys lady gente,
Ye be worthy to be brente."
That oon knyght made a rees: *rush*
"Thou carle monke, wyth all thy gynne, *churlish; trickery*
Thowe youre abbot be of hur kynne, *Though; kin*
Hur sorowe schalt thou not cees; *cease*
Ryght so thou woldyst sayne
Thowe all youre covent had be hyr layne; *monastery; by her lain*
So are ye lythyr and lees!" *liar; false*

The Erle answeryd, wyth wordys free,
"Syr, that oon y trowe thou bee
Thys lady accused has.
Thowe we be men of relygyon,
Thou schalt do us but reson *be held accountable*
For all the fare thou mas. *accusations you make*
Y prove on hur thou sayst not ryght.
Lo, here my glove wyth the to fyght!
Y undyrtake thys case;
Os false men y schall yow kenne; *expose (make known)*
Yn redde fyre for to brenne; *for to be burnt*
Therto God gyf me grace!"

All that stoden in that place
Thankyd God of hys grace,
Wythowte any fayle.
The two knyghtys were full wrothe: *very angry*
He schulde be dedde, they swere grete othe; *swore; oath*
But hyt myght not avayle. *i.e., to no avail*
The Erle wente there besyde

And armyd hym wyth mekyll pryde,
Hys enemyes to assayle.
Manly when they togedur mett, *Fiercely*
They hewe thorow helme and basenet
And martyrd many a mayle. *i.e., ruined; chainmail*

They redyn togedur, wythowt lakk, *fail*
That hys oon spere on hym brakk; *own; broke*
That othyr faylyd thoo;
The Erle smote hym wyth hys spere; *hit*
Thorow the body he can hym bere: *Through*
To grounde can he goo.
That sawe that odyr, and faste can flee; *other*
The Erle ovyrtoke hym undur a tre *overtook*
And wroght hym mekyll woo;
There thys traytour can hym yylde *yield*
Os recreaunt yn the fylde;
He myght not fle hym froo. *from him*

Before the Emperoure they wente
And there he made hym, verrament,
To telle for the noonys. *at once*
He seyde, "We thoght hur to spylle, *destroy*
For sche wolde not do oure wylle,
That worthy ys in wonnys." *behavior*
The Erle answeryd hym then,
"Therfore, traytours, ye schall brenne
Yn thys fyre, bothe at onys!" *once*
The Erle anon them hente, *seized*
And in the fyre he them brente,
Flesche, felle, and boonys. *skin; bones*

When they were brent bothe twoo,
The Erle prevely can goo
To that ryche abbaye.
Wyth joye and processyon
They fett the lady into the towne, *brought*
Wyth myrthe, os y telle may.
The Emperoure was full gladde:

"Fette me the monke!" anon he badde, *Fetch*
"Why wente he so awaye?
A byschoperyke y wyll hym geve, *bishopric*
My helpe, my love, whyll y leve, *live*
Be God that owyth thys day!" *governs*

The abbot knelyd on hys knee
And seyde, "Lorde, gone ys hee
To hys owne londe;
He dwellyth wyth the pope of Rome;
He wyll be glad of hys come, *arrival*
Y do yow to undurstonde." *hope you*
"Syr abbot," quod the Emperoure,
"To me hyt were a dyshonoure;
Soche wordes y rede thou wonde; *advise you cease*
Anone yn haste that y hym see,
Or thou schalt nevyr have gode of me,
And therto here myn honde!" *i.e., I swear it*

"Lorde," he seyde, "sythe hyt ys soo *since*
Aftur hym that y muste goo,
Ye muste make me sewrté, *an assurance*
Yn case he have byn youre foo,
Ye schall not do hym no woo;
And then, also mote y thee, *may I prosper*
Aftur hym y wyll wynde, *go*
So that ye wyll be hys frende,
Yf youre wylle bee."
"Yys," seyd the Emperoure full fayne, *Yes; happily*
"All my kynne thogh he had slayne, *even though*
He ys welcome to mee."

Then spake the abbot wordys free:
"Lorde, y tryste now on thee:
Ye wyll do os ye sey; *as you say*
Hyt ys Syr Barnard of Tollous,
A nobyll knyght and a chyvalrous,
That hath done thys jurney."
"Now certys," seyde the Emperoure,

"To me hyt ys grete dyshonoure;
Anon, Syr, y the pray — *i.e., promise you*
Aftur hym that thou wende:
We schall kysse and be gode frende,
Be God, that owyth thys day!"

The abbot seyde, "Y assente."
Aftur the Erle anon he wente,
And seyde, "Syr, go wyth mee:
My lorde and ye, be Seynt John,
Schull be made bothe at oon, — *as one*
Goode frendys for to bee."
Therof the Erle was full fayne;
The Emperoure came hym agayne
And sayde, "My frende so free,
My wrath here y the forgeve,
My helpe, my love, whyll y leve, — *live*
Be Hym that dyed on tree!"

Togedur lovely can they kysse;
Therof all men had grete blysse: — *happiness*
The romaunse tellyth soo.
He made hym steward of hys londe
And sesyd agayne into hys honde — *returned*
That he had rafte hym froo. — *taken*
The Emperoure levyd but yerys thre; — *three years*
Be alexion of the lordys free, — *election*
The Erle toke they thoo.
They made hym ther Emperoure,
For he was styffe yn stoure — *fierce; battle*
To fyght agayne hys foo.

He weddyd that lady to hys wyfe;
Wyth joye and myrthe they ladde ther lyfe
Twenty yere and three.
Betwene them had they chyldyr fifteen, — *children*
Doghty knyghtys all bedene, — *indeed*
And semely on to see. — *handsome*
Yn Rome thys geste cronyculyd ywys; — *story is chronicled truly*

A lay of Bretayne callyd hyt ys,
And evyr more schall bee.
Jhesu Cryste to hevyn us brynge,
There to have owre wonnyng! *dwelling*
Amen, amen, for charytee!

Here endyth the Erle of Toullous
and begynneth Syr Egyllamoure of Artas.

Notes

Abbreviations: B: Bodleian 6922 (Ashmole 61); Bo: Bodleian 6926 (Ashmole 45); C: Cambridge, T: Thornton, H: Halliwell; L: Lüdtke, F&H: French & Hale.

15 Syr Dyoclysyan probably refers to the third century Roman leader, Gaius Aurelius Valerius Diocletianus. According to the *Oxford Classical Dictionary*, Diocletian rose through the ranks to become Emperor Numerian's bodyguard. He distinguished himself initially by avenging Numerian's death, striking down the praetorian prefect, Aper, a name which also means "wild boar." The naming of a boar may have particular intertextual significance since a companion text in the Cambridge MS, the *Seven Sages of Rome*, not only points to Dioclesian,

Some tyme ther was a noble man
Who name was clepyd Dyaclysyan,

but contains a short didactic narrative about a wild boar ("Aper" appears in the margin). But Diocletian's most famous contribution to the Roman Empire was his establishment of a tetrarchy, a four-part joint rulership. He established himself Augustus in the East, took Galerius to be his Caesar, and elevated an old comrade who had proven valorous in combat, to Augustus in the West and assigned Constantius Chlorus to be his Caesar. The two Caesars were bound to their Augusti by marriage with their daughters . . . Diocletian's genius was as an organizer, and many of his administrative measures lasted for centuries. The tetrarchy was an attempt to provide each part of the Empire with a ruler and to establish an ordered, non-hereditary succession (p. 346).

In T the *Erl of Toulous* appears under the title heading, *Romance of Dyoclicyane* with the subtitle *Erl of Toulous and the Empress Beaulibone* while in C the title appears as an incipit: *Here foloweth the Erle of Tolous*.

25 Mortimer J. Donovan, in *The Breton Lay: A Guide to Varieties*, notes that *Syr Barnard* points to a legendary ninth-century love affair between Count Bernard of Barcelona and Empress Judith, second wife of Louis the Pious:

Bernard I, count of Barcelona and Toulouse, was made prime minister with the connivance of Empress Judith, second wife of Louis le Debonnaire, who used him to

> forward plans for her son Karl. The two conspirators of the poem are identified with Hugo, Count of Tours, and Matfrid, Count of Orleans. The Empress was accused of adultery with Bernard and at an assembly in 831 cleared herself when, according to law, no accuser appeared. Although Bernard was ipso facto exonerated, he asked the privilege of a duel with any accuser, but, none coming, never fought. (p. 207)

According to Allen Cabaniss in "Judith Augusta and Her Time," *University of Mississippi Studies in English* 10 (1969), 67–109, the Empress Judith was "banished to Poitiers and required to take the veil at St. Radegunda's convent of the Holy Cross . . . . For six or seven months Empress Judith suffered, like an earlier Heloise, restriction to cloister life at St. Radegunda, deprivation of her husband and son, separation from her lover Bernard, if lover he was, and above all loss of the recent gay life at court" (p. 88). She was released from her vows by Pope Gregory IV and stood trial before the emperor, his sons, and barons of the empire. "The assembly was asked if anyone wished to make indictment of her. Not a single voice was lifted, although less than a year before there had been riotous clamor against her. Judith thereupon solemnly purged herself by oath of any charge that might have been alleged against her. Once again she was wife as well as empress" (p. 92).

29 Three hundred pounds worth of land would have been an extraordinary acquisition.

37–38 The Emperor's wife, Beulybon, is being compared with yet subordinated to the Virgin Mary, who, in the late Middle Ages, was understood to be both an icon of female perfection and a mediatrix. According to Adelaide Harris in *The Heroine of the Middle English Romances* (Norwood: Norwood Editions, 1978), the analogy is a medieval romance convention (see note for line 188).

33–48 Thomas Aquinas lists three conditions necessary to sanction a just war: the authority of a sovereign, a just cause, and a rightful intention, (*Summa Theologica*, Pars II, Q. 40, Art. I). Romances often challenged those conditions; as Beulybon's response to her husband's actions suggests. See also Margaret Gist's *Love and War in the Middle English Romance* (Philadelphia: University of Pennsylvania Press, 1947), p. 114.

65 All other MSS read *swordys and schylde*.

79 C: *raumsomyd.* F&H emend to *raunsonyd.*

83 According to F&H *manly* suggests virtue, character, dignity, and courageous behavior.

86 C: *Bodely.* L emends to *Boldely.*

93 A hauberk is a tunic of chain mail worn as protective garb over the torso. As with all pieces of armor, it conveyed symbolic significance. In Ramón Lull's *Book of the Order of Chivalry,* for example, it represents a "castle and fortress against vices and weaknesses. For just as a castle or fort is walled in, so a hauberk is firm and closed on all sides to remind a noble Knight that he should not enter with his courage into treason nor any other vice" (p. 67).

95 C uses the Roman numeral for hundred (C) here as in line 124.

113 This line constitutes an addition from T. F&H supply the line in parentheses and I have followed them in order to maintain both poetic and stanzaic integrity.

137 *no gode*. L omits *no*.

151 In T the Empress is named in the title (see note for line 15). Beulybon's name, a combination of *belle* meaning "beautiful" and *bon* meaning "good," suggests that she complies with conventional notions of the medieval romance heroine (see note for line 188). Laura A. Hibbard [Loomis] sees evidence in the heroine's name for a lost French original (*Medieval Romance in England,* p. 36).

152 *Seynt John*. Though there are many saints by the name of John, including John the Baptist, this is probably a reference to John the Evangelist, a.k.a. John the Apostle, the author of the Gospel and Epistles bearing his name as well as the *Book of Revelation*. According to the *Oxford Dictionary of Saints* he was immensely popular:

> One hundred and eighty-one ancient churches and not a few modern ones are dedicated to him. He must have been a very familiar figure to medieval people through being represented on rood-screens, while the iconography of medieval apocalypses often include a series of pictures of his life. He is often represented in the West with John the Baptist as on the stole of Cuthbert, embroidered at Winchester during the 9th century. (p. 228)

174 During the Hundred Years War fought between England and France (1337-1453) ransoming became a popular mode of raising revenue not only for the aristocracy but also for ordinary folks. Desmond Seward in *The Hundred Years War* (New York: Atheneum, 1978) writes:

> A prince or nobleman commanded an enormous price, but the market was not restricted to magnates; a fat burgess or an important cleric could be an almost equally enviable prize . . . . For ransoming was often more like the kidnap racket of modern times, and small tradesmen and farmers had their price; even ploughmen fetched a few pence. (p. 80)

Geoffrey Chaucer, when taken prisoner during an expedition to Brittany, was held ransom. Edward III contributed £16 for his release (p. 98). Later the poet wrote in the Tale of Melibee:

> "There is ful many a man that crieth 'Werre! Werre!'
> that wot ful litel what werre amounteth." (*CT* VII 1039)

175 F&H add *alle* from T.

179 F&H supply this line from T.

182 F&H's conjecture that "play" suggests hawking is probably correct not only because hawking constitutes a common leisure activity for aristocrats in the Middle Ages, but because there is a direct correlation between avian and human hierarchies. According to *De Arte Venandi Cum Avibus*, a thirteenth-century hunting manual (reiterated in Juliana Berners' tract on hawking in *The Boke of Albans* in the fifteenth century), social status is indicated by particular species of hunting bird:

Emperor	eagle
King	gerfalcon and its tercel
Prince	falcon gentle and its tercel
Duke	rock falcon
Earl	peregrine falcon
Baron	bastard
Knight	saker
Squire	lanner
Lady	merlin
Young man	hobby
Yeoman	goshawk
Poor man	male goshawk
Priest	sparrowhawk
Holy water clerk	musket
Servant	kestrel

For further discussion of falconry see Robin Oggins, "Falconry and Medieval Social Status," *Mediaevalia* 12 (1989), 43–55. It is interesting to note that an activity often thought of as strictly aristocratic should have a designation for people belonging to non-aristocratic social circles, e.g., the "poor man." Hawks were so highly treasured that it was a felony to steal one.

188 In compliance with conventions of medieval romance, the heroine is described as the "fayrest woman" alive. Standards for beauty found in romance narratives include grey eyes, a small waist, a complexion "bryght of blee" and as white as "whale's bone" (see lines 340–43, 353–57). According to Adelaide Harris, in addition to these attributes, "no heroine of romance has dark hair. Even in *Tristan,* where contrast would be effective, both Iseult of Ireland and Iseult of Brittany are blondes" (p. 14).

190 *by boke and by belle.* F&H note that "a similar ceremony is in *Richard Coeur de Lion*, line 605. The Saracens in the 'Chanson' swear on the Koran, line 610. Most of the articles mentioned here are used in *Ywain*, lines 3907ff. The penalty for swearing falsely was violent death sent from heaven. See *Joseph of Arimathea*, line 362; Chaucer's Man of Law's Tale, *CT* 11[B], lines 666–76. In *Amis and Amiloun*, lines 1250–60, the punishment is leprosy" (p. 81). According to Addis & Arnold's *Catholic Dictionary*:

> Many solemn oaths ordered by the Church are made more solemn by touching the Gospels; and in the Middle Ages persons swearing often touched the Blessed Sacrament, relics, the sacred vessel, etc.

The Dictionary of Medieval Knighthood & Chivalry sheds more light on the significance of this practice:

> The intense veneration of relics caused them to be adopted as the most effective means of adding security to oaths; because the simple oath was given such little respect these adjuncts came to be regarded as an essential feature of the oath and the oath was divested of its binding force without them (p. 347).

210 F&H supply this line from T.

219 Chivalry relies upon, among other things, the validity of oral contracts among knights and their superiors.

232 *we*. The pronoun is inserted above the line in a later hand. Medieval scribes often omit pronomial subjects, especially with incipient verbs, but here the *we* suits the meter.

235 *Seynt Andrewe*. Andrew was popular throughout the Middle Ages. Legend indicates that his relics were transferred from Patras in Achaia, the place of his crucifixion, by Regulas, an eighth-century Pope to Fife, Scotland now known as St. Andrews. Fife became an important center of evangelism and pilgrimage.

244 The word *for* appears as an insertion above the line.

280 *mut*. L emends to mot. The honorable Beulybon recognizes that it would be a grave sin to forswear an oath, since the promise was made with God as witness.

286 It was customary to attend mass upon rising.

288 All other MSS read *slouth*.

296 F&H add *wyth*.

307 *oryall*. The *MED* defines *oriel* as a bay window, recess (in a building or ship); a balcony, gallery, loft; a small private room. Joseph Ritson suggests that the windows were occasionally ornamented with painted glass.

320 F&H suggest that the "chapel probably was attached to the buildings of Diocletian's castle. The oriel seems to have opened off the vestibule" (p. 393).

340 F&H note that this eye color is blue, while Larry D. Benson in *The Riverside Chaucer* suggests that the true color is "uncertain," but acknowledges the frequency with which grey is used to describe the eyes. That the color — whatever it might be — constitutes a special feminine attribute, perhaps deriving from the grey-eyed Athena of classical Greek tradition, is of no dispute. Chaucer uses the term in the *Romaunt of the Rose* to describe the watchful eyes of the beautiful maiden at the garden door. Note the color of her hair as well:

> A mayden curteys openyde me.
> Hir heer was as yelowe of hewe *yellow; hue*
> As ony basyn scoured newe,

Hir flesh tendre as is a chike,
With bente browis smothe and slyke *smooth; sleek*
And by mesure large were
The opening of hir yen clere
Hir nose of good proporcioun *proportion*
Her yen greye as a faucoun. *eyes grey; falcon*
(lines 538–46)

And again in the Prioress' description in the *Canterbury Tales*: "hir nose tretys, hir eyen greye as glas" (GP, line 152).

355 Joseph Ritson's nineteenth-century note on whale's bone is interesting:

> This allusion is not to what we now call whale-bone, which is well-known to be black, but to the ivory of the horn or tooth of the Narwhal, or sea-unicorn.

Modern science knows whale's bone to be white (perhaps Ritson is referring to baleen, the dark-colored transverse palatal plates used to make women's corsets in the nineteenth century), but the rest of his comment is probably accurate. Albertus Magnus in *Man and the Beasts* lists the *Narwhal* under *Monoceros* and describes it as "a sea creature endowed with a single horn in the front of its head, with which it can pierce fish and even some boats" (p. 363). Anne Clark in *Beasts and Bawdy* (New York: Taplinger, 1975) elaborates:

> The narwhal, which is sometimes called the sea-unicorn, has a long tusk which is twisted in this way. These, and the horns of the rhinoceros or other animals, were often either genuinely mistaken for the horns of unicorns, or were fraudulently offered for sale under that name. (p. 48) Ground into a powder the "unicorn" horn was famous both as a remedy for poison and as an aphrodisiac.

377 *y wolde*. C: *he wolde*. F&H follow L's emendation as do I since the Earl seems to be indicating his own desire.

379 C: *y not*. F&H comply with L's emendation as do I.

389 C: *Of on*. F&H and L omit *on* thereby eliminating an inherent contradiction.

398 C: *kyssyd hyt*. F&H emend to *hyt kyssyd* to improve the meter. L reads *kyssys hyt*.

430 L notes variations on the name *Kaunters* found in the other MSS: *Kamiters, Camtres, Kanteres, Kankerus*. There seems to be no precedent for the name which is not the case with *Kaym*. The *Index of Arthurian Names* lists several variations on *Kaym*, e.g., *Kaymes, Caym, Cayn,* etc. which appear in Arthurian works. All are variations on Cain, the murderous son of Adam.

572 *hanged and to-drawe*. The official punishment for treason. *MED* cites John Trevisa's translation of Higden's *Polychronicon* as example of what the procedure entailed: "He was first i-compned and then to drawe with horses, and than an honged by the throte, and than i-quartered and to deled to dyvers places of Engelond" (8.267); and *Brut*-1333 (Rawlinson B. 171), 209–23: "Sir Gilbert of Midelton was atteint, and take, and honede & drawe [eviscerated] and his body quartarede, and his hevede smyten of an sette oppon a spere . . . and the iiij quarters sent to iiij citees of England." This method of execution appears in the *Song of Roland*, where Ganelon is drawn and quartered for his treachery and betrayal of Roland and Charlemagne.

602 *lefe brothyr*. A "leve [dear/faithful] brother" is a sworn friend.

625 *worde*. F&H note that this may be a "possible blunder for the usual *orde and ende*" (I, p. 402).

703 This line is added by F&H.

707 According to the *MED* the carver is one who attends a superior at the table by cutting up his/her meat and serving food; one who waits table. The duties of a carver appear in John Russell's *Book of Nurture*, a medieval instruction manual for boys:

> My son, thy knife must be clean and bright; and it beseems thee to have thy hands fair washed. Hold always thy knife surely, so as not to hurt thyself, and have not more than two fingers and the thumb on thy keen knife . . . (as quoted in *The Babees Book: Medieval Manners for the Young*, ed. Edith Rickert, pp. 58–59).

730 *Seynte Jermayne*. F&H note that this St. Germaine refers to Germanus of Auxerre, who "led a British army against the Picts and the Scots in 429 A.D. His name is preserved in several Welsh place-names" (p. 405). Other significant details may include his rise to the governorship of Auxerre, an Armorican border province. According to the *Oxford Dictionary of Saints*:

> On the death of Amator, bishop of Auxerre, in 418, Germanus was chosen as his successor . . . he directed British forces in battle, when they won the famous 'Alleluia victory' against a combination of Picts and Saxons, apparently without bloodshed. A year later he was in Ravenna pleading the cause of the rebellious Bretons to the Emperor (p. 180).

Another possibility may be Germanus of Man, who Celtic scholars believe was "born in Brittany c. 410, went to Ireland to stay with Patrick in 440, came to Wales and lived in the monastery of Brioc and Illtud c. 450, left Gaul to meet Patrick in Britain c. 462, where he engaged in a magic contest with Gwrtheyrn, returned to Ireland and became bishop of Man c. 466" (p. 169). He is often confused with Germanus of Auxerre.

731 There are several theories of age operating in the Middle Ages. See J. A. Burrow's *The Ages of Man: A Study in Medieval Writing and Thought* (Oxford: Clarendon Press, 1986). That a twenty-year-old carver is referred to as a child suggests his novice status rather than his degree of maturity. See also *Sir Degaré, Floris and Blanchfleur.* In *Love and War in the Middle English Romances*, Margaret Gist comments that romance heroes are often older when they initiate their adventures than might occur in real life wherein people married at an early age, e.g., twelve for girls and fourteen for boys (p. 27).

758 *ay worthe them woo.* This portion of the line derives from T. F&H's emendation.

759 *To ther.* All MSS read: *To hur.* L's emendation, followed by F&H.

768 C: *traytour.*

771 Other MSS read: *swerdys and torchys.*

785 *mysanswery d.* F&H gloss "spoke abusively," though the sense might also be "spoke deceitfully," as they viciously bring her own words home to her (see lines 653 and 786).

789 *wonduryng.* F&H gloss as *wandering.* But *wondering* is possible too, as if to say that she will be made a spectacle — "a marvel" — in her infidelity.

809 F&H read *berys* rather than *borys.* Though the word appears to be *berys* in C, I have emended it to conform with T. External evidence including commentary and the related tale of Diocletian in the *Gesta Romanorum* support my emendation. Also boars with their tusks are more commonly associated with the ravishing of women. See Chaucer's *Troilus and Criseyde*, V. 1436–84.

813 F&H gloss *hopyd than* as "knew with certainty" rather than "hoped that." To maintain consistency, they gloss *hopud* in line 822 similarly, though there is a marked difference between absolute knowledge of any situation and the uncertainty hoping implies.

818 It was customary for long-distance travellers to carry an extraordinary supply of provisions to compensate for a lack of adequate accommodations along the way.

851 *they seyde.* C: *he seyde*. L's emendation, followed by F&H.

852 *Syr Antore*. The name may allude to the giantslayer in *Libeaus Desconus* or may be another name for Arthur.

856 *in fere.* "Together," though possible, is too neutral a gloss. "Keeping company" or "copulation" is the implication of the conniving knights.

865–88 *kele*. C: *kelee*. F&H's emendation.

867 *Had not . . . hym slayn.* The two lines are corrupt. F&H gloss: "had not a knight interferred, he would have slain his informant, and thus discomfited the traitor" (I, p. 409). Or, perhaps the sense is: had a knight not been present the Emperor would have slain himself [*hym slayn*] and destroyed the traitor as well. Or, conceivably, line 868 might imply that, had the Emperor slain himself, the traitor would have gone scot-free [*broght owt of heele*: "released from constraint"].

873 The motif of the Woman Falsely Accused is found in a number of other romances, most notably *Octavian, Oliva, Gaudine, Sir Aldingar,* and *Avowing of Arthur*. See Edwin A. Greenlaw, "The Vows of Baldwin: A Study of Medieval Fiction," *PMLA* 21 (1906), 575–636.

881 *he naked.* C: *they naked.* L's emendation, followed by F&H.

1035 *hele*. F&H gloss as "conceal," though that sense of *helen* does not suit the context well. "Embrace" or "preserve" seem the more likely meanings. See *MED helen* v(1). 3b or v(2). 1d.

1039 *heyle*. "conceal." Given the fact that the priest has just revealed the contents of his niece's confession, the Earl has good reason to request secrecy.

1041 Trial by combat was customary in a chivalric dispute of this kind. It necessitated a contest between two knights fought with weapons of war until one of the two was unable to fight any longer. According to Broughton's *Dictionary of Medieval Knighthood & Chivalry* this method of settling disputes flourished under Edward III (1327–1377), whose interest in chivalry inspired him to create the Order of the Garter.

1047 That the priest reveals the secrets of the confessional to a stranger here is perhaps a mark of his trust in his niece and her virtue rather than a breech of his office. But if it is a breech of office it is minor compared to his letting the Earl hear confession subsequently.

1065 F&H and others acknowledge a direct source to be non-extant.

1095 Tantamount to throwing down the gauntlet, this act constitutes a public challenge. By picking it up, the opponent accepts the challenge.

1110 *basenet*. A protective head-covering worn under the helmet.

1133 *them*. C: *hym*. L's emendation, followed by F&H.

1145 *byschoperyke*. A province under the authority of a bishop or archbishop, a bishopric constitutes a generous gift.

1154 *Syr*. L emends to *Syr [abbot]*, to fill out the line metrically; followed by F&H.

1164 In C *thee* is obliterated by a smudge.

1198 Many scholars have noted the romance as non-extant.

1199 The steward in medieval romance is often portrayed negatively. In *Sir Orfeo* that convention is reversed when Orfeo confers temporary kingship upon his steward, later tests him, discovers and acknowledges his loyalty. And, here, the steward is certainly good.

1200 *sesyd.* According to the *MED seisin* means to "endow in legal or formal possession of a kingdom, land, feudal estate, goods, etc."

1203 The election takes place because the Emperor and Beulybon have no heirs. Just as the steward in *Sir Orfeo*, Sir Barnard proves himself to be a worthy candidate for rulership.

1208 This line recalls a similar line in *Emaré*: *wedde her to his wife*. See also Henry Weber's edition of *Seven Sages of Rome*, line 3343.

1215 L notes that *Rome* may suggest *romance*. H concurs by noting the difference between the manuscripts and the printed edition which reads "In romance this chronicle is" suggesting that the "boke of Rome" is a volume written in a Romance language, probably French. This conclusion, however, discourages consideration of other possibilities, i.e., the *Gesta Romanorum* or the *Seven Sages of Rome*, a companion text in C. Both contain stories of Diocletian and may be, if not direct sources, then indirect resources. In the *Gesta Romanorum* the tale begins:

> When Diocletian reigned, he decreed that whatsoever woman committed adultery should be put to death.

In addition, *rome* is not capitalized in the MS; its capitalization is a modern editorial decision. In line 1151 it clearly refers to the city.

1215 The poem is being specifically associated with Breton lay.

1219 L notes the variations in endings in two MSS: *Amen qd Rate* in B and *Sic transit gloria mundi* in Bo. The ending to T is missing.

Sir Cleges

Introduction

Sir Cleges is preserved in two fifteenth-century manuscripts, one early (c. 1400), the other twenty-five to thirty years later. Though both have been identified as originating in the East Midlands, the earlier version (Advocates) exhibits linguistic features pointing to a more specific origin in the South while the later Bodleian 6922 (Ashmole 61) is from the North. The differences between the two versions are significant; both poems tell the story of Sir Cleges, but vary in dialect, diction, and dramatic representation. These variations have led at least one scholar, G. H. McKnight, to conclude that neither derives from the other, but rather each harkens back to a common lost original.[1] The narratives then, according to McKnight, developed independently of one another through separate tracts of oral transmission. The nuances in dialect between the two seem to bear this out. Yet any consideration of the non-dialectic variations such as diction and dramatic representation — facilitated by a close examination of A. C. Treichel's dual edition[2] — indicates not only separate lines of development, but suggests the possibility for differing perspectives on the issues the narrative raises, differences which encourage questions about changing attitudes of both audience and poet. How, for instance, does the idea of charity or almsgiving change over time? What are the attitudes toward women, minstrels, and the poor? What is the significance of a belief in miracles? For this volume I have chosen the Bodleian MS because it is more complete (it includes the ending Advocates lacks), and it provides a more comprehensive substrate for asking these kinds of questions.

Despite the existence of two manuscripts and an unknown source, *Sir Cleges* is a poem often described as "unique" or "original." Laura Hibbard Loomis, for example, sees the poem's uniqueness in the mixing of "humor, piety, and romance";[3] Mary

---

[1] See George H. McKnight, *Middle English Humorous Tales in Verse* (Boston: Heath, 1913; rpt. New York: Gordian Press, 1971), pp. 38–59.

[2] A. Treichel, *"Sir Cleges*: Eine mittelenglische Romanze," *Erlanger Studien* 22 (1896), 345–89.

[3] Laura A. Hibbard [Loomis], *Medieval Romance in England* (New York: Oxford University Press, 1924; rpt. New York: Burt Franklin, 1960), pp. 79–80.

Housum claims its originality lies in its combination of three folk motifs,[4] while others determine its uncommon status to reside in generic hybridization — fabliaux, *conte devot*, family drama, Christmas story. All scholars concur that the poet's hybridization of discursive elements is the secret to the poem's success. Yet the intertextuality that *Sir Cleges* demonstrates by establishing likeness to other narratives, both literary and folkloric, seems to argue against originality or uniqueness, and rather for commonality and synthesis. *Sir Cleges* is not original or unique because it stands alone as an independent creation, uncommon only in its method of composition, but because it resonates the sonorities of other narratives, genres, and modes of discourse; it is literally uncommon in its degree of commonality. Folk motifs play an important role in *Sir Cleges*, adding substance and direction to the narrative while pointing to the formidable oral tradition informing the poem. These motifs remind us of the viable presence of that oral/aural mode of discourse and the interactive aspect of medieval poetry read aloud and often performed to groups of attentive and responsive listeners, an audience not exclusively made up of courtly aristocrats, but of diverse ordinary folks. *Cleges*' claim to an uncommon commonality, therefore, is possible not only by its intertextuality but because it speaks to "common people," a burgeoning fifteenth-century lay audience, of what must have been common concerns: their place in the social hierarchy, their customs and practices, aspects of daily life, and their dreams for the future. It offers an uncommon glimpse into a medieval nuclear family — their familial relations one to another, their charity, their hope, and their faith in miracles. It is a Christmas story that expresses the meaning of family solidarity, the dignity of poverty, the necessity of undiscriminating kindness, the intrinsic value of human integrity, and the satisfaction in the meting out of justice.

Three major folk motifs have been identified in *Sir Cleges*: The Spendthrift Knight, The Miraculous Cherries/Unseasonable Fruit, and the Strokes Shared. The Spendthrift Knight, a motif that concerns a knight whose generosity exceeds the bounds of common sense is found in *Sir Amadace*, *Sir Launfal*, *The Knight and His Wife*, and *A True Tale of Robin Hood*. In these Middle English poems the motif establishes the necessary conditions for the hero's rehabilitation — a fall into poverty and despair — then a return to a better condition for himself and those around him. In *Sir Amadace* the knight's destitution results from his charitable and chivalrous action toward a despairing widow who is prevented from burying her husband's corpse until she pays his debts to a wicked merchant. Amadace comes to her rescue, pays the debts and funeral expenses, and is left profoundly poverty-stricken, a condition from which he

[4] Mary Elizabeth Housum, *A Critical Edition of Middle English Sir Cleges* (Ph.D. dissertation, Catholic University, 1988). The three motifs are the Spendthrift Knight, the Unseasonal Fruit, and the Strokes Shared.

recovers only with the aid of the "grateful dead." Likewise, in Thomas Chestre's *Sir Launfal*, and later in *Sir Lambewell*, the hero gives away his newly acquired wealth to all who ask and creates a state of poverty he would not be able to overcome were it not for his rescue by a fairy mistress. In *The Knight and His Wife*, the knight's poverty, resulting from feasts he gives on behalf of the Virgin, compels him to seek the forest for shame to be rescued only by the intervention of the Virgin herself. In the ballad *A True Tale of Robin Hood* the hero, Lord Robert Hood, Earl of Huntington, consumes his wealth "For wine and costly cheere," an act which results in his being outlawed and forced to live by stealth.

The cause for the knight's fall into poverty in *Cleges* is, as in the previous narratives, his uncontrolled liberality. Cleges holds elaborate feasts particularly at Christmas time to which everyone is invited: "Hys mete was redy to every man / That wold com and vyset hym than" (lines 22–23). An open house and a reputation for generosity attract a clientele for Cleges which, over the course of "ten or twelve years," literally eats him out of house and home. His real estate holdings dwindle to a single manor; he would rather sell than desist in his almsgiving and hospitality until finally he's unable to pay his debts. Like those heroes in the narratives above, Cleges confronts an economic crisis with consequences that extend beyond himself. He is left with nothing, no means by which to support his family, and little hope for engineering his own restitution. It is clear by this point in the poem that Cleges' spendthrift days must end for his life or the narrative to continue. The motif of the Spendthrift Knight creates an economy of exchange among these narratives that momentarily facilitates interaction. Once the moment is over, the motif spent, however, the poems differ widely in their concerns and emphases.

One of the primary concerns of *Cleges* is in the strength and integrity of the family unit. Cleges is a family man, happily married to Dame Clarys, a woman of admirable attributes; together they are the parents of two children. As a married couple they demonstrate a deep concern for one another and their children, and a genuine interest in the needs of others. Clarys shares Cleges' compassionate attitudes toward the poor; they both participate in almsgiving forming a kind of medieval social welfare system, a locus of distribution, that takes care of those who meet with hard times — "squyres, that traveyled in lond of werre / And wer falleyn in poverte bare" (lines 16–17), "pore" men, friars, and minstrels, groups of people in a state of powerlessness and dependency on the kindness of others. Cleges and Clarys together "cheryd many a wyght" (line 33), for to them everyone had something of value to offer. Both are able to read beyond surfaces to discern the intrinsic worth of those who come to them for succor and supper. So too do they recognize the intrinsic value of their children. One of the most poignant scenes in the poem depicts the parents playing with their children — an altogether rare scene in medieval poetry — in an attempt to maintain emotional equilibrium in the face of profound loss:

With myrth thei drofe the dey awey	*they drove; day*
The best wey that they myght.	
With ther chylder pley thei dyd	*their children play they did*
And after evensong went to bede	
At serteyn of the nyght.	*At an appropriate time*
(lines 158–62)	

But medieval romance demands that the hero incur great difficulty so that his rehabilitation and return to a better condition, the substance of the plot, may the better be facilitated. The poet of *Sir Cleges* sets up the knight's fall into poverty and subsequent despair quickly so that the rest of the story might focus on his ability to overcome the obstacles put before him. Many romances require the hero to fight dragons, oppose vicious giants, or submit to extraordinary tests in order to prove himself worthy enough to win the lady and live happily ever after.[5] Not so in *Cleges*. Here the hero fights the psychological assault of poverty resolvable finally not by anything he can act against — no dragon to slay, or giant to defeat — but rather by an act of faith. Cleges' trial is one that requires not only personal fortitude and emotional support from his family, but mediation from a higher authority; this hero cannot orchestrate his own restitution, but must rely upon a miracle from God. For this the poet incorporates the Miraculous Cherries or Unseasonable Growth motif.

This motif concerns the discovery and acknowledgment of unseasonable fruit, a motif common to several Celtic saints' legends.[6] Sometimes the motif takes the form of miraculous flowering as in the legend of Joseph of Arimathea when Joseph's staff planted in the earth was thought to blossom profusely every Christmas Eve. As a cherry motif it appears in an amusing scene in the *Ludus Coventriae* or *Play of Corpus Christi* (N-town cycle) in the fifteenth play known as *The Birth of Christ*. The miracle occurs on the road to Bethlehem when Mary spies "unseasonable" fruit.[7] When

---

[5] *Sir Degaré, King Horn,* and *Beves of Hampton*, for example.

[6] Unseasonable growth motifs linked to Celtic folklore and hagiography include Sts. Ciaranus of Saigir, Kentigern, Barrus, Berrachus, Aidus, and Brynach. See C. Loomis Grant, "Unseasonable Growth in Hagiology," *Modern Language Notes* 53 (1938), 591–94.

[7] Sherwyn T. Carr, "The Middle English Nativity Tree: The Dissemination of a Popular Motif," *Modern Language Quarterly* 36 (1975), 133–47. Carr traces the motif to the apocryphal *Pseudo-Matthew*, which "was for the whole of Europe a major source of legends concerning the lineage, birth, and education of the Virgin, and of stories purporting to describe Christ's early life" (p. 135).

Joseph tries to gather the fruit, he discovers that the tree is too high and complains indignantly: "Let hym pluk yow cheryes [who] begatt yow with childe." The tree then bows down to deliver its fruit into Mary's hands, whereupon Joseph is dutifully repentant for his presumption.

A similar incident takes place in a popular ballad called "The Cherry Tree Carol," when the unborn Christ child commands the tree to bend down and offer its fruit to the expectant mother. In the *Secunda Pastorum* of the Wakefield master a comic prefiguration of the generous gift of the Magi takes place when Coll, the eldest shepherd exhorts the Christ child to "Have a bob of cherys!" Given in the winter, clearly out of season, the cherries, along with the holly and a ball, replace the frankincense, gold, and myrrh traditionally associated with the kings at Christ's nativity. The fruity gift resonates as symbolically as do gifts of rare and precious objects, at least to those who believe in miracles and are able to read the signs correctly. Though Cleges is aware that fruit spontaneously grown out of season indicates something of import, he has difficulty interpreting the miracle that occurs in his garden just after he has said a prayer on behalf of those suffering in poverty. He takes the bough to Clarys and expresses his anxiety over just having complained to God:

"Lo, dame, here is a nowylté; — *novelty*
In ouer garthyn upon a tre — *our garden*
  Y found it sykerly — *truly*
Y ame aferd, it is tokenyng — *I am afraid; omen*
Be cause of ouer gret plenyng — *our; complaining*
  That mour grevans is ny." — *more grievance; coming*
His wyfe seyd: "It is tokenyng — *a token (sign)*
Off mour godness, that is comyng. — *Of more goodness*
  (lines 217–24)

To Cleges the cherries signify an omen "that mour grevans is ny," while Clarys interprets the sign as a miracle, a "tokenyng off mour godness." She then offers a course of action that will get Cleges back on track, suggesting that he take the gift to King Uther for recompense as was customary. She directs their son to follow his father carrying the basket containing the precious fruit and as two poor shepherds, horseless and armed only with walking staffs, they make their way to Uther's castle.

The third motif, the Strokes Shared, is widely disseminated and is known to numerous cultures and nationalities beyond the geographic boundaries of Europe.[8] Basically, the motif involves the discovery of a precious object and its presentation

[8] See John R. Reinhard, "Strokes Shared," *Journal of American Folklore* 36 (1928), 380–400.

to an overlord with the expectation of reward; the extortion by hindering servants, also a component of the motif, would consume all the profits, so the clever discoverer asks for strokes rather than money. The distribution of strokes and the receiving of a proper reward conclude the plot. Variations of the motif are found in *Gesta Romanorum* (*How the King's Son Won his Reward*), in John Bromyard's *Summa Praedicantium* (a collection of exempla used in sermons), and in a French tale called *Le Vilain au Buffet*. In *Cleges* the motif is played out in an amusing scenario with the porter, the usher, and the steward, servants who exemplify in their attempts to extort a portion of Cleges' reward the selfishness that opposes charity and social welfare. Their avaricious behavior stands in sharp contrast to Cleges' generosity at the outset of the story. In their abuse of the power and responsibility of their positions the hindering servants obstruct the feudal family, the kinship of king and knight, king and servant, and king and subject; they impede the distribution of wealth among the king's subjects by undermining a system dependent upon individual adherence to chivalric ethics and codes of behavior. The avaricious servants discriminate against Cleges for all the wrong reasons: his "pore clothyng," his unassuming manner, his vulnerability. The porter scornfully directs him to "beggars' row," the usher threatens to beat him, and the steward commands his immediate departure, calling him "Herlot" (line 355) and "Cherle"(line 331). All three officers are unable to recognize any intrinsic value in the person before them; they read external signs in a literal manner concluding that the poor man requesting an audience with the king is unworthy of such an honor. Like Chaucer's virtuous Knight, who is likewise plainly dressed and "meeke as is a mayde" (I [A] 69), Cleges' virtues lie in his inner fortitude and magnanimous spirit.

Though the officious servants are unable to recognize the intrinsic worth of a good man, they are able to recognize the extrinsic value of the cherries in Cleges' basket; fruit out of season is indeed a valuable gift for the king and worth the extortion attempts which set up the humorous payback. Cleges, in a display of business savvy worthy of a medieval merchant, strikes a bargain with the servants and their demands for an appropriate return for their services. The payback scene offers them as satisfying a dispensation of social justice as any dishonest middle man might deserve.

Although *Cleges* is not usually placed in the company of Breton lays, its attention to minstrels and minstrelsy, an emphasis that has caused several scholars to call the poem a minstrel tale, is one of its integral features. Cleges' largesse is extended to all minstrels, itinerant members of medieval society, whose very mobility functioned in real life as a nexus between courtly society and the lower classes. Minstrels drew their stories from the sources available to them; they brought to court the stories of ordinary folk as well as stories of aristocrats, stories derived from life experience as well as pure fictions, stories from the past as well as the present. They often performed their tales as actors in a play and were rewarded by audience response and tokens in the form of garments, cups, or other articles of value. It is their performances that Marie de France wished to preserve from being lost by the wayside. Not only are minstrels mentioned during Cleges' days of good fortune, "mystrellus wold not be behynd" (line 46), but they signal the advent of the miracle about to happen:

And as he walkyd uppe and done — *up; down*
Sore sygheng, he herd a sowne — *Pitifully sighing; sound*
  Off dyverse mynstralsy, — *Of diverse*
Off trumpers, pypers and nakerners, — *trumpeters, pipers; drummers*
Off herpers notys and gytherners, — *harpers' music; cythernists*
  Off sytall and of sautrey. — *citole; psaltery*
Many carrals and grete dansyng — *carols; dancing*
In every syde herd he syng. — *Everywhere he heard singing*
  (lines 97–104)

Resonating the uninhibited joy of David and, later, the Son of David, as they entered Jerusalem triumphantly, the "joy and mirth" expressed by the performances of these unseen minstrels lends an air of buoyant Christmas optimism to an otherwise despairing scene. The mood-elevating aspect of music has a positive psychological effect on Cleges and casts him into a frame of mind more accepting of events that are beyond his control; he becomes optimistic, if only momentarily.

But if the power of music elevates the human spirit it also reminds us to cast our thoughts beyond the present moment to imagine the future or remember the past. In *Sir Cleges* minstrels are reminders of the living presence of poetry and music of another time. The *mise en scene* of the poem places it firmly in the Christian past at a time when the Celtic bardic tradition was strong. In this way the minstrel functions as a mediator between past and present, various oral traditions and written poetry. Thus it is not surprising that the poem's "harper" facilitates the identification of Cleges as a knight King Uther thought long dead:

  "My lege, withouten les, — *lie*
Somtyme men callyd him Cleges;
  He was a knyght of youre. — *yours*
I may thinke, when that he was
Full of fortone and of grace,
  A man of hye stature." — *high status*
  (lines 493–98)

Then, as if Cleges were a minstrel himself, he tells the story of retribution so compellingly that the "lordes lewghe [laugh], both old and yenge" (line 517), and, like many a talented minstrel, he is amply rewarded for his services. But, as if in a last gesture to remind us that Cleges does not act exclusively alone, the poet returns to the obedient son and Dame Clarys. Uther bestows upon Cleges' son a "colere forte were" (line 554) and a "hundryth pownd of rente" (line 555), the means for a young man to establish an identity and a place of his own in medieval society. Upon Clarys the King bestows a "cowpe of gold" (line 550), an item of great intrinsic value and a token of "joy and myrthe" (line 552). Dame Clarys is not to be forgotten either for her role as mediatrix or for her role as wife and mother, for she forms the nucleus of the family around which her husband and their children revolve. Hers is an unliberated position by modern standards to be sure, but one which is — at least in this medieval poem — honored and respected.

Select Bibliography

Manuscripts

National Library of Scotland Edinburgh MS 19.1.11 (Advocates). Fols. 71a–79b.

Oxford MS Bodleian 6922 (Ashmole 61). Fols. 67b–73a. [The entire MS is written by a single scribe identified as Rate and features drawings of a pike and a flower after several of the pieces.]

Critical Editions

Ginn, R.K.G. "A Critical Edition of the Two Texts of *Sir Cleges*." *Index to Theses for Higher Degrees* 18. Queen's University of Belfast, 1967–68, 317.

Treichel, A. "*Sir Cleges*: Eine mittelenglishce Romanze." *Erlanger Studien* 22 (1896), 345–89.

Housum, Mary Elizabeth. *A Critical Edition of Middle English Sir Cleges*. Ph.D. dissertation, Catholic University, 1988.

Introduction

Collections

French, Walter Hoyt, and Charles Brockway Hale, eds. *Middle English Metrical Romances*. New York: Prentice-Hall, 1930. II, 877–95.

McKnight, George H. *Middle English Humorous Tales in Verse*. Boston: Heath, 1913; rpt. New York: Gordian Press, 1971. Pp. 38–59; 171–80.

Morley, Henry. *Shorter English Poems*. London: Cassell, Petter & Galpin, 1876. Pp. 23–40.

Weber, Henry William. *Metrical Romances of the Thirteenth, Fourteenth & Fifteenth Centuries Published from Ancient Manuscripts*. Edinburgh: Constable, 1810. I, 329–53.

Related Studies

Carr, Sherwyn T. "The Middle English Nativity Cherry Tree: The Dissemination of a Popular Motif." *Modern Language Quarterly* 36 (1975), 133–47. [Demonstrates that the nativity tree associated with *Ludus Conventriae* is the common source for both *Cleges* and the "Cherry Tree Carol."]

Loomis, C. Grant. "*Sir Cleges* and Unseasonable Growth in Hagiology." *Modern Language Notes* 53 (1938), 591–94. [Explores the development and dissemination of this folk motif.]

Reinhard, John R. "Strokes Shared." *Journal of American Folklore* 36 (1928), 380–400. [Traces the dissemination of a widespread, popular folk motif.]

Modernizations and Translations

Curry, Jane Louise. *The Christmas Knight*. Illustrated by DyAnne DiSalvo-Ryan. New York: Maxwell Macmillan Books, 1993. [An illustrated children's adaptation.]

Darton, F. J. Harvey, ed. *A Wonder Book of Romance*. New York: F. A. Stokes, 1907.

Hadow, Grace Eleanor and W. H. eds. *The Oxford Treasury of English Literature*. Oxford: Clarendon Press, 1906–08. Pp. 37–50. [From Weber's edition.]

Sir Cleges

Krapp, George Philip, ed. *Tales of True Knights*. New York: Century, 1921.

Weston, Jessie. *Libeaus Desconus and Sir Cleges*. London: D. Nutt, 1902.

Sir Cleges

Lystyns, lordynges, and ye schall here *hear*
Off ansytores, that before us were, *Of ancestors*
Bothe herdy and wyght. *hardy; strong*
In tyme of Uter and Pendragoun, *Uther Pendragon*
Kyng Artour fader of grete renoune, *Arthur's father*
A sembly man of syght. *handsome; to look upon*
He had a knyghht, hyght Sir Clegys; *called*
A doughtyere man was non at nedys *stronger; in time of need*
Of the Ronde Tabull ryght. *virtuous (lawful)*
He was man of hy statoure *high stature*
And therto feyre of all fetour, *fair; feature*
A man of mekyll myght. *great power*

Mour curtas knyght than he was one *More courteous*
In all this werld was ther non;
He was so gentyll and fre. *noble; freeborn*
To squyres, that traveyled in lond of werre *struggled in wartime*
And wer fallyn in poverté bare, *were; poverty*
He gaff them gold and fe. *gave; fee*
Hys tenantes feyre he wold rehete; *nourish (cheer up)*
No man he wold buske ne bete; *quarrel with nor punish*
Meke as meyd was he. *Meek (humble); maid*
Hys mete was redy to every man, *larder*
That wold com and vyset hym than; *present himself*
He was full of plenté.

The knyght had a gentyll wyff, *noble wife*
A better myghht non be of lyfe
Ne non semblyere in syght. *more beautiful*
Dame Clarys hyght that lady; *was called*
Off all godnes sche had treuly *Of*
Glad chere bothe dey and nyght.

Grete almusfolke bothe thei were *almsgivers*
Both to pore man and to frere; *friars*
They cheryd many a wyght: *cheered; person*
Fore them had no man ought lore, *On account of them; lost*
Whether thei wer ryche ore pore,
Of hym thei schuld have ryght. *restitution*

Every yere Sir Clegys wold
In Crystynmes a fest hold *Christmas*
In the worschype of that dey. *honor; day*
As ryall in all thynge, *royal*
As he hade ben a kynge. *As if*
For soth, as I you saye,
Ryche and pore in that contré *country*
At that fest thei schuld be; *feast*
There wold no man sey nay.
Mynstrellus wold not be behynd,
Myrthys wer thei may fynd. *where*
That is most to ther pay. *their delight*

Mynstrellus, when the fest was don,
Schuld not withoutyn gyftes gon, *go without gifts*
That wer both rych and gode,
Hors and robys and rych rynges,
Gold and sylver and other thynges,
To mend with ther mode. *benefit; spirit*
Ten yere our twelve sych festes thei held *[For] ten or; they*
In worschype of Hym, that all weld *who rules all*
And fore us dyghed upon the Rode. *died; Rood (Cross)*
Be than his gode began to slake, *But then; fortune; fall away*
Sych festes he gan make,
The knyght of jentyll blode. *noble blood*

To hold hys feste he wold not lete; *desist*
Hys rych maners to wede he sete; *manors as security; put up*
He thought hymselve oute to quyte.[1]

---

[1] *He thought to rid himself of debt by that means*

Thus he festyd many a yere
Both gentyll men and comenere *commoner*
In the name of God allmyght.
So at the last, soth to sey, *to tell the truth*
All hys gode was spendyd away;
Than he had bot a lyte. *but little left*
Thoff hys god were ne hond leste, *Though; goods; nearly lost*
In the wyrschyp he made a feste;
He hopyd, God wold hym quyte. *defray the expense (redeem him)*

Hys ryalty he forderyd ay, *royal estate; frittered away*
To hys maners wer sold awey, *Until; manors were*
That hym was left bot one,
And that was of lytell valew, *worth*
That he and hys wyfe so trew
Oneth myght lyfe therone. *Scarcely; live*
Hys men, that wer so mych of pride,
Weste awey onne every syde; *Fell away*
With hym ther left not one.
To duell with hym ther left no mo *dwell*
Bot hys wyfe and his chylder two. *children*
Than made he mekyll mone. *a great moan*

It fell on a Crystenmes Eve,
Syre Clegys and his wyfe,
They duellyd by Cardyff syde. *i.e., in the region of*
When it drew towerd the none, *noon*
Syre Clegys fell in swownyng sone; *into a swoon suddenly*
Wo bethought hym that tyde, *time*
What myrth he was wonte to hold, *joy; could have*
And he, he had hys maners solde,
Tenandrys and landes wyde. *Tenancies; extensive property*
Mekyll sorow made he ther; *Great*
He wrong hys hondes and wepyd sore, *wrung; wept sorrowfully*
Fore fallyd was hys pride. *Utterly gone*

And as he walkyd uppe and done *up; down*
Sore sygheng, he herd a sowne *Pitifully sighing; sound*
Off dyverse mynstralsy, *diverse*

Off trumpers, pypers, and nakerners, *trumpeters, pipers; drummers*
Off herpers notys and gytherners, *harpers' music; cythernists'*
  Off sytall and of sautrey. *citole; psaltery*
Many carrals and grete dansyng *carols; dancing*
In every syde herd he syng, *Everywhere he heard singing*
  In every place, treuly.
He wrong hys hondes and wepyd sore; *wrung*
Mekyll mon he made ther, *Great moan; there*
  Sygheng full pytewysly. *piteously*

"A, Jhesu, Heven Kyng,
Off nought Thou madyst all thyng; *Out of nothing*
  I thanke The of Thy sonde. *for; sending (message)*
The myrth, that I was won to make *expected*
In this tyme fore Thi sake,
  I fede both fre and bond, *freeborn; bonded*
And all, that ever com in Thi name,
They wantyd nother wylde ne tame, *neither wild nor domestic game*
  That was in any lond,
Off rych metys and drynkes gode.
That longes for any manus fode, *Whoever desires; man's food*
  Off cost I wold not wonde." *Because of; withhold*

Als he stode in mournyng so, *As*
And hys wyfe com hym to,
  In armys sche hym bente. *enfolded*
Sche kyssed hym with glad chere
And seyd: "My trew wedyd fere, *companion*
  I here wele what ye ment. *hear; complain about*
Ye se wele, sir, it helpys nought,
To take sorow in your thought;
  Therefore I rede ye stynte. *advise; cease*
Let your sorowe awaye gon
And thanke God of Hys lone *loan*
  Of all that He hath sent.

"Be Crystes sake, I rede ye lynne *counsel to desist*
Of all the sorow that ye be ine,
  Agene this holy dey.

Now every man schuld be mery and glad
With sych godes, as thei had; *they have*
Be ye so, I you pray.
Go we to ouer mete belyve *our dinner eagerly*
And make us both mery and blythe, *merry; joyful*
Als wele as ever we may. *As well*
I hold it fore the best, trewly;
I have made owre mete treuly,
I hope, unto your pay." *to your liking*

"Now I assent," quothe Cleges tho, *then*
In with hyre he gan go *her; did*
Somwhat with better chere.
When he fell in thought and care, *Whenever; anxiety*
Sche comforth hym ever mour,
Hys sorow fore to stere. *efface*
After he gan to wex blyth *grow happy*
And wyped hys terys blyve, *quickly*
That hang on hys lyre. *cheek*
Than thei wesch and went to mete *washed; dinner*
With sych god as thei myght gete
And made mery chere. *cheer*

When thei had ete, the soth to sey, *eaten*
With myrth thei drofe the dey awey, *they drove; day*
The best wey that they myght.
With ther chylder pley thei dyde *their children play they did*
And after evensong went to bede
At serteyn of the nyght. *At an appropriate time*
The sclepyd to it rong at the chyrche, *They slept until [the bell]*
Godes servys forto wyrche, *service; work*
As it was skyll and ryght. *reasonable*
Up thei ros and went thether,
They and ther chylder together, *their children*
When thei were redy dyght. *prepared*

Syre Cleges knelyd on hys kne;
To Jhesu Cryst prayd he
Be chesyn of hys wyfe: *For the discretion (choice, resolve)*

"Grasyos Lord," he seyd tho, *Gracious*
"My wife and my chylder two,
  Kepe us out of stryffe!"
The lady prayd hym ageyn; *on his behalf*
Sche seyd: "God, kepe my lord fro peyn *husband; pain*
  Into everlastyng lyffe!"
Servys was don and hom their wente; *done; home they went*
The thankyd God omnipotent; *They*
  They went home so ryfe. *quickly*

When he to hys palys com, *palace*
He thought his sorow was overgon; *gone forever*
  Hys sorow he gan stynt. *stop*
He made hys wyfe before hym gon
And hys chylder everychon;
  Hymselve alone he wente
Into a garthyn ther besyde; *garden; beside*
He knelyd adoun in that tyde *moment*
  And prayd to God verament. *earnestly (truly)*
He thankyd God with all hys hert
Of all desesyd in poverté, *[who] suffer*
  That ever to hym He sente.

As he knelyd oune hys kne *on his knee*
Underneth a chery tre,
  Makyng hys praere, *prayer*
He rawght a bowghe in hys hond, *reached for a bough with his hand*
To ryse therby and upstond; *help him rise; stand up*
  No lenger knelyd he ther.
When the bowghe was in hys hond,
Gren levys theron he fond *Green leaves; found*
  And ronde beryes in fere. *berries in abundance*
He seyd: "Dere God in Trinyté,
What maner beryes may this be, *kind of berries might these*
  That grow this tyme of yere? *time; year*

"I have not se this tyme of yere, *seen*
That treys any fruyt schuld bere, *trees should bear any fruit*
  Als ferre as I have sought." *As far*

He thought to tayst it, yff he couthe *taste; if; could*
One of them he put in hys mouthe;
  Spare wold he nought.
After a chery it relesyd clene, *As; released clean*
The best that ever he had sene,
  Seth he was man wrought. *Since; born*
A lytell bow he gan of slyfe *bough; to cut off*
And thought he wold schewe it hys wyfe; *show*
  In hys hond he it brought.

"Lo, dame, here is a nowylté; *novelty*
In ouer garthyn upon a tre *our garden*
  Y found it sykerly. *truly*
Y ame aferd, it is tokenyng *I am afraid; omen*
Be cause of ouer grete plenyng, *our; complaining*
  That mour grevans is ny." *more grievance; coming*
His wyfe seyd: "It is tokenyng *a token*
Off mour godness, that is comyng; *Of more goodness*
  We schall have mour plenté.
Have we les our have we mour, *less or; more*
Allwey thanke we God therfore; *Always*
  It is the best, treulye."

The lady seyd with gode chere: *good cheer*
"Late us fyll a panyere *Let us fill a basket*
  Off the frute, that God hath sente.
Tomorrow, when the dey do spryng, *day begins*
Ye schall to Cardyff to the Kyng,
  Full feyre hym to presente.
Sych a gyft the may hafe ther, *Such; have there*
That we schall the beter fare; *we shall fare better*
  I tell you, verament." *truly*
Syr Clegys grantyd sone therto:
"Tomorowe to Cardyff I wyll go *agreed*
  After your entent." *As you advise*

The morne, when it was dey lyght, *morrow, i.e., next day*
The lady had the pannyere dyght; *basket prepared*
  To hyre eldyst son seyd sche: *her eldest*

"Take up this pannyere gladly
And bere it at thy bake esyly — *on your back easily*
After thi fader so fre."
Syr Clegys than a staff he toke;
He had no hors, so seyth the boke,
To ryde hys jorneye,
Nether sted ne palferey, — *steed; palfrey*
Bot a staff was his hakney, — *Nothing but; hackney*
As maner in poverté. — *In the manner of poverty*

Syre Cleges and hys son gent — *noble*
The ryght wey to Cardyfe went — *straight way*
On Crystenmes Dey.
To the castell gate thei com full ryght,
As thei wer to mete dyght, — *were preparing for dinner*
At none, the soth to sey. — *noon; truth*
As Sir Cleges wold in go, — *Just as he was*
In pore clothyng was he tho, — *then*
In a symple aray. — *simple array*
The porter seyd full spytously: — *scornfully*
"Thow schall withdraw the smertly, — *remove yourself promptly*
I rede, withoute deley, — *advise; delay*

Els, be God and Seynt Mary, — *Or else*
I schall breke thi hede smertly, — *break your head*
Go stond in begers route. — *stand in the beggars' class*
Iff thou draw any mour inwerd, — *any further inward*
Thow schall rew it afterwerd; — *regret*
I schall the so cloute." — *so [thoroughly] beat you*
"Gode sir," seyd Sir Cleges tho,
"I pray you, late me in go: — *let*
Thys is withouten doute: — *doubt*
The Kyng I have a present browght
Fro Hym, that made all thinge of nought; — *From; out of nothing*
Behold and loke aboute!" — *look*

The pourter to the pannyere wente; — *porter*
Sone the lyde up he hente; — *Quickly; lid; lifted*
The cherys he gan behold.

Wele he wyst, fore his commyng,	*Well; knew*
Fore hys present to the Kyng,	
Grete gyftes have he schuld.	*Great gifts*
He seyd: "Be Hym that me dere bought,	
In at this gate commys thou nought,	
Be Hym that made this mold,	
The thyrd parte bot though graunte me	*unless you grant*
Off that the Kyng wyll gyff the,	*Of whatever; will give you*
Whether it be sylver our gold."	*or*
Syre Cleges seyd: "Therto I sente."	*consent*
He gave hym leve, and in he wente	*[The porter]; permission*
Withouten mour lettyng.	*delay (hindrance)*
In he went a grete pas;	*He entered a great hallway*
The offycers at the dore was	*officer; door*
With a staff standyng.	
In com Sir Cleges so wyght;	*boldly*
He seyd: "Go, chorle, out of my syght,	*churl*
Without any mour lettyng	*delay*
I schall the bete every lythe,	*beat you; limb*
Hede and body, withoutyn grythe,	*regret*
And thou make mour presyng."	*If you advance any further*
"Gode sir," seyd Sir Cleges than,	
"For Hys love, that made man,	
Sese your angry mode,	*Cease; mood*
For I have a presante brought	
Fro Hym, that made all thyng of nowght	
And dyed upon the Rode.	*Cross*
Thys nyght this fruyt grew;	
Behold, whether I be fals our trew;	*false or true*
They be gentyll and gode."	*noble; good*
The usschere lyfte up the lyde smertly;	*usher; lifted; promptly*
The feyrest cherys, that ever he sey,	*fairest cherries; saw*
He mervyllyd in his mode.	*admired; mind*
The usschere seyd: "Be Mary suete,	*By; sweet*
Thou comyst not in this halle on fete,	*You; during the feast*
I tell the, sykerly,	

Bot thou graunte me, without wernyng, *Unless; refusal*
The thyrd parte of thi wyneng *winning*
  When thou comyst ageyn to me." *i.e., return*
Syre Cleges sey non other wone, *said no other word*
Bot ther he grantyd hym anon; *But; agreed immediately*
  It wold non other weys be. *It would be no other way*
Than Sir Cleges with hevy chere *sober countenance*
Toke his son and his pannyere;
  Into the hall went he.

The stewerd stert fast in the hall, *steward started forth quickly*
Among the lordes in the halle
  That weryd ryche wede. *Who wore rich clothing*
He went to Sir Cleges boldly
And seyd: "Who made the so herdy, *you; [fool]hardy*
  To come hether, our thou were bede?" *before you were invited*
"Cherle," he seyd, "thou arte to bolde. *too*
Withdraw the with the clothes olde
  Smertly, I the rede." *Instantly, I advise you*
He seyd: "Sir, I have a presant brought
Fro that Lord that us dere bought
  And on the Rode gan bled." *did bleed*

The stewerd stert forth wele sone *came; immediately*
And plukyd up the lyde anon, *plucked up; swiftly*
  Als smertly as he mought. *As quickly; might*
The stewerd seyd: "Be Mary dere, *By*
Thys saw I never this tyme of yere,
  Seth I was man i-wrought. *Since; born*
Thow schall cum no nere the Kyng, *come no nearer*
Bot if thou grante me myn askyng, *Until*
  Be Hym that me dere bought. *By Him who*
The thyrd parte of the Kynges gyfte
I wyll have, be my thryfte,
  Or els go truse the oute!" *throw yourself*

Syre Cleges stode and bethoughht hym than: *thought to himself*
And I schuld parte betwyx thre men, *If*
  Myselve schuld haue no thyng. *nothing*

Fore my traveyll schall I not gete, *trouble; get nothing*
Bot if it be a melys mete." *tasty dinner*
  Thus thought hym sore sygheng. *sorely sighing*
He seyd: "Herlot, has thou no tong? *He [the steward]; Harlot; tongue*
Speke to me and tary not long
  And grante me myn askyng,
Or with a staff I schall the twake *beat you*
And bete thi ragges to thi bake *ribs into your back*
  And schofe the out hedlyng!" *shove you out headfirst*

Syre Cleges saw non other bote, *recourse*
Hys askyng grante hym he mote, *demand; must*
  And seyd with syghyng sore:
"What that ever the Kyng rewerd,
Ye schall have the thyrd parte,
  Whether it be lesse our more." *or*
When Sir Cleges had seyd that word,
The stewerd and he wer acorde *were in agreement*
  And seyd to hym no more.
Up to the Kyng sone he went;
Full feyre he proferd hys presente,
  Knelyng onne hys kne hym before.

Syre Cleges uncoveryd the pannyere
And schewyd the Kyng the cherys clere, *bright*
  Upon the ground knelyng.
He seyd: "Jhesu, ouer Savyoure, *our Saviour*
Sente you this fruyt with grete honour
  Thys dey onne erth growyng."
The Kyng saw the cherys fressch and new,
And seyd: "I thanke the, swete Jhesu,
  Here is a feyre newyng." *novelty (i.e., something new)*
He comandyd Sir Cleges to mete, *dinner*
A word after with hym to speke, *speak*
  Without any feylyng. *without fail*

The Kyng therfore made a presente
And send unto a lady gente,
  Was born in Corneweyle. *Cornwall*

Sche was a lady bryght and schen; *radiant (lovely)*
After sche was hys awne Quen, *Afterward; own*
  Withouten any feyle. *Without fail*
The cherys wer served throughe the hall; *throughout*
Than seyd the Kyng, a lord ryall: *royal*
  "Be mery, be my conseyle! *counsel*
And he that brought me this present,
I schall make hym so content
  It schall hym wele avayle." *avail him well*

When all men wer merye and glad,
Anon the Kyng a squyre bade: *Soon thereafter; commanded*
  "Bryng hym me beforne,
The pore man that the cherys brought."
Anon he went and taryd nought, *tarried not*
  Withouten any scorne; *contempt*
He brought Cleges before the Kyng.
Anon he fell in knelyng, *As soon as*
  He wend hys gyft had be lorn. *knew; payment; lost*
He spake to the Kyng with wordes felle; *humble*
He seyd: "Lege lord, what is your wylle?
  I ame your man fre borne."

"I thanke the hertely," seyd the Kyng,
"Off the grete presentyng, *For*
  That thou hast to me do. *you have given*
Thow hast honouryd all my feste
With thi deyntes, moste and leste, *dainties*
  And worschyped me allso. *honored; also*
What that ever thou wyll have, *Whatever you want*
I wyll the grante, so God me save,
  That thin hert stondes to, *desires*
Whether it be lond our lede *land or people*
Or other gode, so God me spede. *goods*
  How that ever it go."

He seyd: "Gare mersy, lege Kyng! *Grant mercy liege*
Thys is to me a hye thing, *a great honor*
  Fore sych one as I be.

Forto grante me lond our lede   *Were you to grant me land or holdings*
Or any gode, so Gode me spede,
  Thys is to myche fore me.   *too much*
Bot seth that I schall ches myselve,   *But if I might choose [for] myself*
I aske nothyng bot strokes twelve,
  Frely now grante ye me,
With my staff to pay them all
Myn adversarys in this hall,
  Fore Seynt Charyté."

Than ansuerd Uter the Kyng;
He seyd: "I repent my grantyng,   *retract*
  The covenand, that I made."   *covenant*
He seyd: "Be Hym that made me and the,
Thou had be better take gold our fe;   *or goods*
  Mour nede therto thou hade."
Syr Cleges seyd withouten warryng;   *hesitation*
"Lord, it is your awne graunteyng;   *own granting*
  I may not bc dclcyd."   *overridden*
The Kyng was angary and grevyd sore;   *vexed; sorely grieved*
Never the les he grante hym thore,   *there*
  The dyntes schuld be payd.   *blows; paid*

Syre Cleges went into the hall
Among the grete lordes all,
  Withouten any mour.
He sought after the stewerd;
He thought to pay hym his rewerd,
  Fore he had grevyd hym sore.
He gafe the stewerd sych a stroke,   *gave; such*
That he fell doune lyke a bloke   *down like a block*
  Among all that there were,
And after he gaff hym strokes thre;
He seyd: "Sir, for thi curtassé,   *courtesy*
  Stryke thou me no mour!"

Out of the hall Sir Cleges wente:
To pay mo strokes he had mente,   *more; intended*
Withowtyn any lette.   *hesitation*

To the usschere he gan go;
Sore strokes gaffe he tho, — *Painful; gave*
When thei togeder mette, — *met*
That afterwerd many a dey
He wold wern no man the wey — *hinder*
So grymly he hym grete. — *fiercely (see note)*
Syr Cleges seyd: "Be my thryfte, — *By my good luck*
Thou hast the thyrd parte of my gyfte,
Ryght evyn as I the hyght." — *as I promised you*

To the porter com he yare; — *eagerly*
Foure strokes payd he thare;
His parte had he tho. — *share; then*
Aftyrwerd many a day
He wold wern no man the wey. — *hinder*
Nether to ryde ne go.
The fyrst stroke he leyd hym onne, — *laid on him*
He brake atwo hys schulder bone — *broke in two*
And hys ryght arme also.
Syre Cleges seyd: "Be my thryfte,
Thow hast the thyrd parte of my gyfte;
Covenant made we so."

The Kyng was sett in hys parlere, — *seated; chamber*
Myrth and revell forto here; — *Joy; revelry; hear*
Syre Cleges theder wente. — *thither*
An harper had a geyst i-seyd, — *told a story*
That made the Kyng full wele apayd, — *pleased*
As to hys entente. — *According to his desire*
Than seyd the Kyng to this herpere:
"Mykyll thou may ofte tyme here,
Fore thou hast ferre wente. — *travelled afar*
Tell me trew, if thou can:
Knowyst thou thys pore man,
That this dey me presente?"

He seyd: "My lege, withouten les, — *lie*
Somtyme men callyd hym Cleges;
He was a knyght of youre. — *yours*

I may thinke, when that he was
Full of fortone and of grace,
A man of hye stature." *high status*
The Kyng seyd: "This is not he in dede; *in fact*
It is long gon that he was dede, *It's long been thought; dead*
That I lovyd paramour. *Whom; very much*
Wold God that he wer wyth me; *I wish to God*
I had hym lever than knyghtes thre: *would rather have him*
That knyght was styff in stoure." *staunch in battle*

Syre Cleges knelyd before the Kyng;
For he had grantyd hym hys askyng, *Because*
He thankyd hym curtasly. *courteously*
Spesyally the Kyng hym prayd, *Specially; inquired of him about*
The thre men that he strokes payd, *to whom*
Wherefore it was and why.
He seyd: "I myght not com inwerd,
To I grantyd iche of them the thryd parte *Until; each*
Off that ye wold gyff me. *whatever; give*
Be that I schuld have noght myselve;
To dele among theym strokys twelve
Me thought it best, trewly."

The lordes lewghe, both old and yenge, *laughed; young*
And all that there wer wyth the Kyng,
They made solas inowghe *pleasure; enough*
They lewghe, so thei myght not sytte; *laughed [so hardily]; sit*
They seyd: "It was a nobull wytte, *noble joke*
Be Cryst we make a vow."
The Kyng send after hys stewerd
And seyd: "And he grante the any reward,
Askyth it be the law."
The stewerd seyd and lukyd grym: *looked grim*
"I thynke never to have ado with hym; *want nothing to do*
I wold I had never hym knaw." *wish; known him*

The Kyng seyd: "Withouten blame,
Tell me, gode man, what is thi name,
Before me anon ryght?"

"My lege," he seyd, "This man you tellys,
Som tyme men called me Sir Cleges;
I was your awne knyght." *own*
"Arte thou my knyghht, that servyd me,
That was so gentyll and so fre, *noble; gracious*
Both strong, herdy and wyght?" *manly*
"Ye, lord," he seyd, "so mote I the, *so might I thrive*
Tyll God Allmyght hath vyset me; *Until; blessed*
Thus poverté hath my dyght." *Thereafter; has been my lot*

The Kyng gaffe hym anon ryght
All that longes to a knyght, *belongs*
To aray hys body with. *clothe*
The castell of Cardyff also
With all the pourtenans therto, *appurtenances*
To hold with pes and grythe. *peace; mercy*
Than he made hym hys stuerd *steward*
Of all hys londys afterwerd,
Off water, lond and frythe. *land; royal forest*
A cowpe of gold he gafe hym blythe, *cup; joyfully*
To bere to Dam Clarys hys wyfe, *carry home*
Tokenyng of joy and myrthe. *As a token*

The Kyng made hys son squyere *squire*
And gafe hym a colere forte were *collar to wear*
With a hundryth pownd of rente.
When thei com home in this manere, *manner*
Dame Clarys, that lady clere,
Sche thankyd God verament. *truly*
Sche thankyd God of all maner, *in every way*
Fore sche had both knyght and squyre
Somwhat to ther entente.
Upon the dettys that they hyght, *debts; incurred*
They payd als fast as thei myght, *as*
To every man wer content. *Until; was*

A gentyll stewerd he was hold; *known as*
All men hym knew, yong and old,
In lond wer that he wente. *wherever*

There fell to hym so grete ryches,
He vansyd hys kynne, mour and les, *advanced*
The knyght curtas and hend. *refined*
Hys lady and he lyved many yere *years*
With joy and mery chere,
Tyll God dyde fore them send. *Until; sent for them*
Fore ther godnes, that thei dyd here, *good works; on earth*
There saulys went to Heven clere, *Their souls; shining*
There is joy withouten ende.
Amen. *Where there*

Notes

Sir Cleges is extant in two fifteenth-century MSS (see introduction). The version presented in this volume is Bodleian 6922, which is more complete than the Edinburgh version. The entire MS is written by a single scribe identified as Rate and features drawings of a pike and a flower after several of the pieces.

Abbreviations: B: Bodleian MS 6922 (Ashmole); A: Advocates MS; Mc: McKnight; T: Treichel; H: Housum.

1 *Lystyns lordynges*. B: *ystyns lordynges*; T's emendation. A: *Will ye lystyn, and ye schyll here*. The line constitutes a conventional exhortation to the audience suggesting the orality/aurality of the poem as the reader gains the attention of the audience.

1–79 A number of scholars have noted the similarity between the initial situation of *Sir Cleges* and that of *Sir Amadace*; the two poems share the motif of the Spendthrift Knight. Both Amadace and Cleges give generously even after they incur great debt. See also *Sir Launfal* contained in this volume.

2 *Off ansytores, that before us were*. A: *Of eldyrs, that before us were*. One of the features of B is the scribal proclivity for writing double *f*. Thus "of" appears as *off*. H notes that *ansytores* and *eldyrs* refer to "ancestors and in general to those who lived in former times." She points out a distinction in the two terms that implies a gap in composition time between the two MSS. "The use of *eldyrs* to mean 'ancestors' seems to have become less common around the end of the fourteenth century. The *MED* does not list any fifteenth-century citation of *eldyrs* meaning 'ancestors'."

3 *herdy and wyght*. A stereotype of what ancestors were thought to be and a conventional expression in romance and Breton lay.

4–5 *Uter and Pendragoun*. A: *In the tyme of kynge Uter*. Mc suggests that the evocation of the name Pendragon in B refers to Uther's brother, which is his explanation for the separation of the names. However, the surname is often attached to Uther himself who, with the aid of Merlin, became the legendary father of

King Arthur, as line five suggests. Arthur's mother is Igraine of Cornwall to whom a reference is made later in the poem (lines 386–89). H suggests that the double naming in B is a scribal error and is originally intended to suggest one man, Uther Pendragon, Arthur's father.

6 *A sembly man of syght.* A: *A semely man in sight.* H notes the frequency with which *semely* along with a variation of "see" is found in tail-rhyme poetry. The term is used again in line 27 to describe Dame Clarys.

7 *knyghht, hyght.* The scribe commonly uses yogh to indicate a palatal or velar fricative, which I have transcribed as *gh*.

Clegys. A: *Cleges.* Mc points out that Cleges is an uncommon name found a few times in Malory's *Morte d'Arthur* and the *Awntyrs of Arthur.* Jessie Weston and Mary Housum note the similarity to Chrétien de Troyes' title character in *Cliges*, but point out the lack of similarity in plot. The *MED* defines *clege* as a noun meaning "horsefly," which may be a joking comment on Cleges' horselessness later in the poem.

9 The evocation of the Round Table as well as the earlier evocation of Uther Pendragon places the narrative within the Arthurian tradition, though it is not often recognized as part of the Arthurian cycle, but rather as an apocryphal, independent narrative such as Thomas Chestre's *Sir Launfal.* The Round Table is more often understood to be the invention of King Arthur.

10 *hy statoure.* A: *hight stature.* Mc suggests that "high stature" is a literary convention describing the physical attributes of the protagonist. The phrase, used again at line 498, suggests a possible pun meaning both physical height and lofty status in the community.

13 *he was one.* The sense is that in his country Cleges is in a class apart from others — all alone in his kind, beyond the capability of anyone else.

13–15 The attributes of a knight, i.e., courtesy and gentilnesse or nobility, constitute necessary character traits both for a romantic hero and for an actual knight. In addition to "generosity," *fre* indicates Cleges' socio-economic status, namely that he is freeborn.

14 *In all this werld.* A: *In all the lond.* The phrase in B expands the boundaries of Cleges' reputation.

16–17 Cleges makes a practice of honoring those who did not fare well during the war.

18 *gold and fe.* In feudal English law a *fee* is a parcel of land or an estate held on condition of homage and service to a superior lord, by whom it is granted and in whom the ownership remains. The term is synonymous with *fief* and *feudal benefice.* Fee often appears in conjunction with something else of intrinsic value, usually gold.

19 *Hys tenantes feyre he wold rehete.* A: *The pore pepull he wold releve.* B's reading points to Cleges as a property owner, a status that plays an important role in this economy of manors/manners. The reading in A provides evidence of Cleges' charity to the poor.

20 *No man he wold buske ne bete.* A: *And no man wold he greve.*

H notes the variations in meaning of the word *buske* and its association with other words, e.g., *busken*, "to hasten," *busshen* "to push, press," and *busten*, "to bruise, beat." The *MED*, which cites only *Sir Cleges*, defines it as "to oppress, flog." The difference in meaning of the two lines is notable; the reading of B foreshadows Cleges' mode of justice later in the poem.

21 *Meke as meyd was he.* A: *Meke of maners was hee.*

In the *Canterbury Tales* Chaucer's exemplary knight is described similarly to the reading in B:

> And though that he were worthy, he was wys,
> And of his port as meeke as is a mayde.
> (General Prologue, 68–69)

27 *Ne non semblyere in syght.* A: *And mery sche was on sighte.* The description of Clarys in B parallels that of Cleges in line six.

28 Dame Clarys, as her name suggests, illuminates the narrative with her good sense, patience, and cheerful optimism. Mc expresses admiration by comparing her to such stalwart female characters as Le Freine, Emaré, Constance, and

Griselda, though he finds Clarys "the most human of them all" (p. 74). Another worthy comparison may be Dame Beulybon in *Erle of Tolous*, who demonstrates a remarkable fortitude in response to a false accusation of adultery. H notes no other romance heroine of this exact name, but one Old French verse romance in which Cleges appears as a character is called *Clarice* after the hero; other sources of inspiration may be the Old French verse romance *Claris et Laris*, Clarice, the protective friend of Blanchefleur, in *Floris and Blanchefleur*, or the briefly mentioned character in *Piers Plowman*, Clarys of Cokkeslane. Given the themes of the poem, Clarys could allude to St. Clare, the thirteenth-century Franciscan nun who founded the Order of Poor Clares in Assisi shortly after the death and canonization of St. Francis.

31–32 *Grete almusfolke bothe thei were.* A: *Almus gret sche wold geve.* B defines both Cleges and Clarys as almsgivers. Almsgiving to the poor was both an indication of charity and an official activity.

32 *Both to pore man and to frere.* A: *The pore pepull to releve.* A distinction is being made in B between the ordinary poor and mendicants, orders of friars who embrace poverty voluntarily. Fraternal orders include the Franciscans, the Dominicans, the Augustinians, and the Carmelites. According to the *MED*, *frere* could also refer to knights of a brotherhood such as the Templars or Hospitallers, an order founded by St. Julian the patron saint of hospitality.

34–36 The sense seems to be: For Claris and Cleges no person would suffer loss, whether rich or poor; for such people they would provide restitution.

38–39 It was customary on feast days for double portions to be served to guests as a sign of the king's liberality and good will. Largesse was particularly encouraged at Christmas. Compare Christmas feasts in *Sir Gawain and the Green Knight* and *Sir Perceval of Galles*.

40–42 A lacuna appears in B. I have emended by supplying the missing passage from A.

46–54 Minstrels often performed in return for room and board and whatever remuneration a lord might offer for the entertainment. Most often reward consisted of robes and garments, but occasionally a valuable gold cup was given.

47 A: *For there they myghht most myrthis fynd.*

48 *ther pay*. A double sense is possible here: Minstrels will be there since they find their greatest pleasure amidst such mirth; or, since that is where they find greatest recompense.

52 *rynges*. B: *thynges*. T emends to *rynges*. I follow the emendation to maintain the alliteration and to avoid redundancy.

55 In B Roman numerals indicate cardinal numbers. I have emended all Roman numerals to their verbal equivalents.

56 *In worschype of Hym, that all weld.* A: *In the worschepe of Mari myld*. The disparity between MSS in the object of worship, i.e., Christ or the Virgin Mary, is interesting, perhaps indicating the interchangeability between the two in medieval piety, particularly at Christmas. Mary is evoked three more times in both MSS in exclamatory expressions.

58 *slake*. B: *schake*. T emends to *slake* to concur with the reading in A as well as for sense.

65 *Both gentyll men and comenere*. A: *Many a knyght and squire*. B expands the range of Cleges' largesse beyond strict delineations of class and estate.

68 The folk motif of the Spendthrift Knight has been noted as present in this and other poems, e.g., Thomas Chestre's *Sir Launfal*, the later *Sir Lambewell*, *Sir Amadace*, *The Good Knight and His Jealous Wyfe*, and the fifteenth-century ballad *The True Tale of Robin Hood*. H notes the occurrence of the motif "in the folktales and literature of many European cultures as well as far away as Japan" (p. 67).

78 A: *Might not leve there on*.

79 Mc marks this as the point of differentiation from the plot of *Sir Amadace*. Amadace's wealth is lost as a result of his charity toward a widow who is prevented from burying the corpse of her husband until she pays his debts and funeral costs. Amadace's fortune is restored by the ghost of the dead man disguised as a White Knight rather than by an equally grateful but living king as in *Sir Cleges*. In *Sir Launfal*, the hero's wealth is restored by a fairy mistress.

80 *Weste awey onne every syde*. A: *Gan slake awaye on every syde*. Either reading points to the unreliability of fair-weather friends.

82–83 B: *To duell with hym ther left no mo / Bot hys wyfe and his chylder two*. A: *But he and his childyrn too; / Than was his hart in mech woo*. B is more explicit in describing Cleges' family including two children and his wife, who play a significant supporting role in the narrative.

86 *Syre Clegys and his wyfe*. A: *A kynge bethowght hym full evyn*.

87 *Cardyff syde*. Cardiff is a city in Wales associated with the Arthurian cycle as are Carleon and Carlisle.

88 *none*. Noon often precipitates unusual occurrences in medieval narratives, e.g., *Sir Orfeo*. See John Block Friedman's "Orpheus, Eurydice and the Noon-day Demon," *Speculum* 41 (1966), 22–24.

89 Swooning is not uncommon in medieval romance. H notes other poems which incorporate the trope: *Sir Launfal, Sir Eglamour, Amis and Amiloun, Sir Landevale, Sir Degaré*. Also Constance and Griselda in Chaucer's Man of Law's Tale and the Clerk's Tale or both Troilus and Crisyde in their romance.

93 B: *Tenandrys and landes wyde*. A: *And his renttes wyde*.

96 *Fore fallyd was his pride*. Hanspeter Schelp, who categorizes *Sir Cleges* as an exemplary romance, argues that Cleges' pride is his downfall. [See *Exemplarische Romanzen im Mittelenglishchen* (Göttengen: Vandenhaeck & Ruprecht, 1967), pp. 93–97.]

99 *dyverse mynstralsy*. There are a number of similar listings of musical instruments in other romances. See *Sir Launfal, Emaré, Pearl, Squire of Low Degree, Richard Coeur de Lyon, Libeaus Desconus, Thomas of Erceldoune, Kyng Alisaunder, Buke of Houlate, Sir Degrevant*. Chaucer's Manciple's Tale lists the musical instruments similarly: "Bothe harpe, and lute, and gyterne, and sautrie" (line 268). Though the instruments differ among the poems, the frequency with which they occur in these narratives indicates the importance of music to everyday as well as festive medieval life.

101 *notys*. The *MED* (sb. 2d) suggests that *notys* in this line might refer to a musical instrument on grounds that A reads *luttis;* but that interpretation accords neither with the syntax of the line nor the sense of the series which presents performers and music rather than instruments. Line 102 does, however, mention instruments, as it does in A. But in B the progression in the series moves from musicians (line 100) to their music (line 101) to their instruments (line 102).

102 *sytall.* B: *sycall*; T's emendation.

103 In the Middle Ages carols included dancing. Men and/or women formed a circle and danced as they sang. A famous scene of carolling is staged in *Handlyng Synne* to serve as an example of wicked behavior.

119 *That longes for any manus fode.* A: *That myght be gott, be the rode*. In his prayer Cleges demonstrates his philosophy of charity. He will give to anyone in "any lond" (line 117) who has experienced misfortune and hunger. He is not only generous but undiscriminating in his generosity.

125 *My trew wedyd fere*. A: *my trew fere*.

130–32 There is a three-line lacuna in B which I have replaced with the corresponding passage in A.

145 *tho*. B: *the*; T's emendation.

148 *fell*. B: *sell*; T's emendation.

149 *comforth*. H observes that "comfort" implies more than "to cheer, or console," its primary meaning. Rather, it carries connotations of spiritual strength since "Clarys is leading her husband away from despair."

166–68 These three lines are missing in A.

171 *Be chesyn*. The phrase is rich with possible meanings. The sense could be that Cleges prays because of his wife's admonition, or choice, or resolve, or chastisement; or it could mean that he prayed on behalf of his wife, or in appreciation of her discretion, or in gratitude for the choice of wife that Christ, his gracious Lord, has bestowed upon him.

172 *seyd.* B: *feyd;* T's emendation.

179 *The thankyd God omnipotent.* A: *And thanked God with good entent.*

180 *They went home so ryfe.* A: *And put away penci.*

185 *hys.* B: *hy*; T's emendation.

191–92 *Of all desesyd in poverté / That ever to hym He sente.* A: *Of his dysese and hys povertt / That to hym was sent.* In B Cleges prays explicitly for those other than himself which is the implication of A.

193–201 The motif of the Miraculous Cherries has been traced by Sherwin Carr to *Pseudo-Matthew*, an apocryphal gospel, and demonstrated in *The Birth of Christ* or *Joseph and the Midwives*, the fifteenth play of the N-Town mystery cycle, sometimes called the *Ludus Coventriae* or *The Play Called Corpus Christi.* A similar motif appears in "The Cherry Tree Carol," Ballad 54, printed in F. J. Child's edition of *The English and Scottish Popular Ballads*. In the play, the miracle occurs enroute to Bethlehem when Mary spies a cherry tree (see introduction).

In "The Cherry Tree Carol" the unborn child commands the tree to bend down and offer its fruit:

> O then bespoke the babe,
> within his mother's womb:
> "Bow down then the tallest tree,
> for my mother to have some."

The motif has also been noted in the Wakefield Master's *Secunda Pastorum* in The Towneley Cycle (see introduction).

194 *chery-tre*. Cherry trees were commonly found in medieval English gardens; cherry festivals were often held in orchards during cherry season. Reference to the fruit appears twice in John Gower's *Confessio Amantis*, in a discussion of teachers of religion and morality and again while speaking of love's delicacies.

> Thei prechen ous in audience
> That noman schalle his soule empeyre,
> For al is bot a chirie feire.

(Prologue, 452–54)

Somtime I drawe into memoire
Hou sorwe mai noght evere laste;
And so comth hope in ate laste,
Whan I non other fode knowe
And that endureth bot a throwe,
Riht as it were a cherie feste;
(VI, 886-91)

The fruit also appears in an elaborate description of the *hortus conclusus* in *The Pistel of Swete Susan*: "The chirie and the chestein that chosen is of hewe" (line 93).

In *Piers Plowman* cherries are the food of the poor:

Al the pore peple · pese-coddes fetten,
Bake benes in bred · thei brouhten in heor lappes
Chibolles, cheef mete · and ripe chiries monye,
And proferde Pers this present · to plese with hungur.
(ed., Skeat, A text, VII, 279–82; see also B VI 294-97.
The line is omitted in the C text.)

A "ripe cherry" is likened to the material world in *A Father's Instructions to His Son*, a companion piece in B: "Son, set nought by this world's weal, for it fares as a ripe cherry."

The cherry is recognized in Christian iconography as symbolic. According to George Ferguson's *Signs & Symbols in Christian Art* (New York: Oxford University Press, 1954) the cherry "symbolizes the sweetness of character which is derived from good works. It is often called the Fruit of Paradise. A cherry, held in the hand of the Christ Child, suggests the delights of the blessed" (p. 29).

200–01 The motif of Unseasonable Growth has hagiological and folkloric resonances. C. Grant Loomis notes the Celtic legends of St. Ciaranus of Saigir, St. Kentigern, St. Barrus, St. Aidus, and St. Brynach, while Clement Miles, in *Christmas in Ritual and Tradition, Christian and Pagan* (London: T. F. Unwin, 1912), acknowledges an ancient belief in England of trees blossoming at Christmas. The belief is connected with a well-known legend of Joseph of Arimathea. Miles writes: "When the saint settled at Glastonbury he planted his staff in the earth and it put forth leaves; moreover it blossomed every Christmas Eve" (p. 268).

211 The cherry pit is left in Cleges' mouth, evidence of the kind of fruit this is.

220–25 Cleges interprets the sign as a portent, while Clarys interprets it as a miracle.

235 It was customary for rewards to be given for gifts offered to the King.

242 *pannyere*. The *OED* defines the term as:

> a basket of considerable size for carrying provisions, fish, or other commodities; in later use mostly restricted to those carried by a beast of burden (usually in pairs, one on each side, slung across the back), or on the shoulders of a man or woman.

255 There seems to be an error in chronology. If the miracle occurs on Christmas Day then Cleges' journey to deliver the gift to King Uther takes place on Boxing Day, the day after Christmas.

262 The porter's duties include screening those desiring an audience with the king. Mc notes that "the minstrel was well accustomed to the ill treatment of porters, and the surly porter appears frequently in minstrel story [sic]" (p. 77). H notes that the Hindering Servant motif often appears with the Shared Strokes motif but also separately. These servants, including here the usher and the steward, prohibit heroes of several Middle English narratives from entering the castle, e.g., *Sir Gowther*, *Octavian*, *Sir Tristrem*, *Robert of Cisyle*, *Beves of Hampton.*

267 *begers route.* A frequent motif in medieval narrative, many heroes often become beggars or are disguised as beggars. In *Sir Orfeo*, Orfeo assumes the beggar's disguise to test his steward; in *King Horn* the hero goes to beggar's row:

> He sette him wel loghe
> In beggeres row.
> (lines 1080–81)

In *Piers Plowman*, Will experiences poverty first hand:

> Ich haue mete more than ynough · ac nought so moche worship
> As tho that seten atte syde-table · or with the souereignes of the halle
> But sitte as a begger bordeless · bi myself on the grounde.

(ed., Skeat, B text, XII, 199–201)

267 B: *Go*. T emends to *To*.

275 Cleges claims here and subsequently that his gift is from God Himself.

293 *offycers*. A: *usscher*. The office of usher called for an ability to distinguish class difference in order to seat people appropriately at table; or as F&H note "[to keep] the rabble from annoying guests at a feast." According to John Russell's *Book of Nurture*, a fifteenth-century treatise on the duties of domestic employees of the king including carvers, chamberlains, ushers, etc.:

> An usher or marshal, without fail, must know all the estates of the Church, and the excellent estate of a king with his honourable blood. This is a notable nurture, cunning, curious and commendable . . . and now I will show you how they should be grouped at table in respect of their dignity, and how they should be served. (As quoted in *The Babees Book: Medieval Manners for the Young*, ed., Edith Rickert, pp. 69–71.)

316 *wernyng*. A: *lesyng*. The variant readings are worth noting. A implies that the usher expects Cleges to lie; B expects compliance.

337 *stewerd*. The steward acted as his lord's representative in decision making regarding household or manorial matters. Often held by a freeman it was a position requiring absolute trust and unwavering loyalty.

352 *traveyll*. A: *labor*.

355 *Herlot*. Contrary to modern associations of this word with female prostitution, in Middle English it means "a man of no fixed occupation, an idle rogue, a vagabond or beggar." Used as a term of abuse it connoted, "scoundrel, knave, rogue, reprobate, base fellow, coward." In the General Prologue of the *Canterbury Tales*, Geoffrey Chaucer describes the Summoner as: "a gentil harlot and a kynde; / A bettre felawe sholde men noght fynde" (I [A] 647-48). Larry D. Benson in *The Riverside Chaucer* glosses harlot "buffoon, jester," which casts the term in a more positive light.

358–59 B: *Or with a staff I schall the twake / And bete thi ragges to thi bake*. A: *Ar wyth a staffe I schall the wake / Thàt thy rebys schall all to quake*. The physicality of the retribution provided by B renders the scene more graphically than the reading of A.

384 *Without*. B: *With*. T's emendation.

386 *a lady gente*. The allusion seems to be to Igraine, who becomes Uther's queen and Arthur's mother.

403 *He brought Cleges before the Kyng*. A: *Whan he cam before the kynge*. In B the King sends the squire to retrieve Cleges; in A the squire seems to get lost along the way.

428 *strokes twelve*. The motif of Shared Strokes is found in a number of cultures in various degrees of sophistication according to John R. Reinhard in "Strokes Shared," *Journal of American Folklore* 36 (1928), 380–400. But the four most often cited as related stories are from John Bromyard's *Summa Praedicantium*, a collection of exempla for preaching, where the story is found under the heading, "Invidia"; *How the King's Son Shared His Reward*, found in the *Gesta Romanorum;* a French tale, *Le Vilain au Buffet*; and *Lucky They Are Not Peaches*, printed in W. A. Clouston's *Popular Tales and Fictions: Their Migrations and Transformations* (Edinbugh and London: W. Blackwell and Sons, 1887), vol. II.

432 *Fore Seynt Charyté*. A: *For send charyte*. As one of three theological virtues (Faith and Hope are the other two), Charity is fittingly personified as a saint. H notes how common the expression is in Middle English romance, e.g., "For love of seynt charyté" (*Sir Isumbras*, line 156), "For seynt charite" (*Amis and Amiloun*, line 1608). J.O. Halliman in *Thornton Romances* (London: J. B. Nichols and Son, 1844), p. 272, cites its use by Shakespeare: "By Gis and by Saint Charity" (*Hamlet*, Act IV, Scene 5); and Spenser: "Ah! dear Lord, and sweet Saint Charitee! / That some good body once would pity me" (*Shephard's Calendar*, May, line 247).

440 *graunteyng*. B: *graunte*; T's emendation.

442 B: *The Kyng was angary and grevyd sore*. A: *The kynge was sory therfore*. B's reading demonstrates a more complex emotional response.

444 *The dyntes schuld be payd.* A: *Therefore he was full sade.* That Cleges' debt should be paid in "dyntes" is an important detail that the B poet/scribe does not overlook.

448 A describes the steward as *proud*; B does not.

454 *strokes thre.* There are four blows in all (a third of the twelve).

465 *him grete.* The resonances of word choice here are rich, ranging from "greeted him," "honored him," "welcomed or rewarded him," to "insulted, challenged, or struck him" or "made him weep" or "groan."

466 B: *Syr seyd*; T adds *Cleges.*

481 *hys parlere.* A private chamber separated from the main dining hall, a segregation of the King from his court that William Langland, author of *Piers Plowman*, finds lamentable:

> Elyng is the halle · vche daye in the wyke,
> There the lord ne the lady · liketh noughte to sytte
> Now hath vche riche a reule · to eten bi hym-selue
> In a pryue parloure · for pore mennes sake,
> Or in a chambre with a chymneye · and leue the chief halle,
> That was made for meles · men to eten inne.
> (ed., Skeat, B, X, 93–99)

484 *a geyst i-seyd.* H observes a significant variance between MSS in this passage. While in A the harper sings a song of Cleges, in B the subject of the song is not mentioned.

496 *thinke.* B: *thnke.*

517–20 H observes that a similar situation occurs in Northern *Octavian* "where Clement, the bourgeois stepfather of the hero, angered at the expenses of his stepson's knighting, beats part of the emperor's retinue, in this case the minstrels, and causes the court to laugh at him": "Thereatt all the kynges loghe / There was joye and gamen ynoghe" (lines 1165–66).

545 Compare *Sir Orfeo* and its positive portrayal of the steward. In the *Erle of Tolous* Sir Barnard proves himself worthy to be bequeathed the Emperor's holdings.

554 *colere.* The investiture of a collar, often including a pair of spurs, signifies the making of a squire. The attainment of the position was not restricted to those of noble birth but open to peasants, tradesmen, and common soldiers. See *Squire of Low Degree.* A squire's training often included the singing and writing of poems, as in the case of Chaucer's Squire in the General Prologue of the *Canterbury Tales.*

566 *old.* B: *hold;* T's emendation.

569 *kynne.* B: *lynne*; T's emendation.

576 *Amen.* A is incomplete. Many of the companion pieces in B including a fragment of *Erle of Tolous* read: *Amen quod Rate.* There is some disagreement among scholars about the identity of the scribe or author. F. J. Furnivall, who reads the initial letter of the name as K rather than R, suggests that the scribe may be female: *Quoth Kate.* "The same name occurs at the end of the three next poems as they appear in Bodleian MS 6922 (Ashmole 61). It is probably a corruption, unless we have here one of the rare instances of a woman copyist." (As quoted in *The Babees Book: Medieval Manners for the Young,* ed. Edith Rickert, p. 183.) But H disspells the possibility with a specific name — John Rathe.

Appendix A

The Lay of the Ash Tree

From: *Lays of Marie de France and Other French Legends*, trans. Eugene Mason (1911).

Now will I tell you the Lay of the Ash Tree, according to the story that I know.

In ancient days there dwelt two knights in Brittany, who were neighbours and close friends. These two lords were brave and worthy gentlemen, rich in goods and lands, and near both in heart and home. Moreover each was wedded to a dame. One of these ladies was with child, and when her time was come, she was delivered of two boys. Her husband was right happy and content. For the joy that was his, he sent messages to his neighbour, telling that his wife had brought forth two sons, and praying that one of them might be christened with his name. The rich man was at meat when the messenger came before him. The servitor kneeled before the daïs, and told his message in his ear. The lord thanked God for the happiness that had befallen his friend, and bestowed a fair horse on the bringer of good tidings. His wife, sitting at board with her husband, heard the story of the messenger, and smiled at his news. Proud she was, and sly, with an envious heart, and a rancorous tongue. She made no effort to bridle her lips, but spoke lightly before the servants of the house, and said,

"I marvel greatly that so reputable a man as our neighbour, should publish his dishonour to my lord. It is a shameful thing for any wife to have two children at a birth. We all know that no woman brings forth two at one bearing, except two husbands have aided her therein."

Her husband looked upon her in silence for awhile, and when he spoke it was to blame her very sternly.

"Wife," he said, "be silent. It is better to be dumb, than to utter such words as these. As you know well, there is not a breath to tarnish this lady's good name."

The folk of the house, who listened to these words, stored them in their hearts, and told abroad the tale, spoken by their lady. Very soon it was known throughout Brittany. Greatly was the lady blamed for her evil tongue, and not a woman who heard thereof — whether she were rich or poor — but who scorned her for her malice. The servant who carried the message, on his return repeated to his lord of what he had seen and heard. Passing heavy was the knight, and knew not what to do. He doubted his own true wife, and suspected her the more sorely, because she had done naught that was in any way amiss.

The lady, who so foully slandered her fellow, fell with child in the same year. Her neighbour was avenged upon her, for when her term was come, she became the mother of two daughters. Sick at heart was she. She was right sorrowful, and lamented her evil case.

"Alas," she said, "what shall I do, for I am dishonoured for all my days. Shamed I am, it is the simple truth. When my lord and his kinsfolk shall hear of what has chanced, they will never believe me a stainless wife. They will remember how I judged all women in my plight. They will recall how I said before my house, that my neighbour could not have been doubly a mother, unless she had first been doubly a wife. I have the best reason now to know that I was wrong, and I am caught in my own snare. She who digs a pit for another, cannot tell that she may not fall into the hole herself. If you wish to speak loudly concerning your neighbour, it is best to say nothing of him but in praise. The only way to keep me from shame, is that one of my children should die. It is a great sin; but I would rather trust to the mercy of God, than suffer scorn and reproach for the rest of my life."

The women about her comforted her as best they might in this trouble. They told her frankly that they would not suffer such wrong to be done, since the slaying of a child was not reckoned a jest. The lady had a maiden near her person, whom she had long held and nourished. The damsel was a freeman's daughter, and was greatly loved and cherished of her mistress. When she saw the lady's tears, and heard the bitterness of her complaint, anguish went to her heart, like a knife. She stooped over her lady, striving to bring her comfort.

"Lady," she said, "take it not so to heart. Give over this grief, for all will yet be well. You shall deliver me one of these children, and I will put her so far from you, that you shall never see her again, nor know shame because of her. I will carry her safe and sound to the door of a church. There I will lay her down. Some honest man shall find her, and — please God — will be at the cost of her nourishing."

Great joy had the lady to hear these words. She promised the maiden that in recompense of her service, she would grant her such guerdon as she should wish. The maiden took the babe — yet smiling in her sleep — and wrapped her in a linen cloth. Above this she set a piece of sanguine silk, brought by the husband of this dame from a bazaar in Constantinople — fairer was never seen. With a silken lace they bound a great ring to the child's arm. This ring was of fine gold, weighing fully an ounce, and was set with garnets most precious. Letters were graven thereon, so that those who found the maid might understand that she came of a good house. The damsel took the child, and went out from the chamber. When night was come, and all was still, she left the town, and sought the high road leading through the forest. She held on her way, clasping the baby to her breast, till from afar, to her right hand, she heard the howling of dogs and the crowing of cocks. She deemed that she was near a town, and went the lighter for the hope, directing her steps, there, whence the noises came. Presently the damsel entered in a fair city, where was an Abbey, both great and rich. This Abbey was worshipfully ordered, with many nuns in their office and degree, and an Abbess in charge of all. The maiden gazed upon the mighty house, and considered its towers and walls, and the church with its belfry. She went swiftly to the door, and setting the child upon the ground, kneeled humbly to make her prayer.

"Lord," said she, "for the sake of Thy Holy Name, if such be Thy will, preserve this child from death."

Her petition ended, the maiden looked about her, and saw an ash tree, planted to give shadow in a sunny place. It was a fair tree, thick and leafy, and was divided into four strong branches. The maiden took the child again in her arms, and running to the ash, set her within the tree. There she left her, commending her to the care of God. So she returned to her mistress, and told her all that she had done.

Now in this Abbey was a porter, whose duty it was to open the doors of the church, before folk came to hear the service of God. This night he rose at his accustomed hour, lighted candles and lamps, rang the bells, and set wide the doors. His eyes fell upon the silken stuff within the ash. He thought at first that some bold thief had hidden his spoil within the tree. He felt with his hand to discover what it might be, and found that it was a little child. The porter praised God for His goodness; he took the babe, and going again to his house, called to his daughter, who was a widow, with an infant yet in the cradle.

"Daughter," he cried, "get from bed at once; light your candle, and kindle the fire. I bring you a little child, whom I have found within our ash. Take her to your breast; cherish her against the cold, and bathe her in warm water."

The widow did according to her father's will. She kindled a fire, and taking the babe, washed and cherished her in her need. Very certain she was, when she saw that rich stuff of crimson samite, and the golden ring about the arm, that the girl was come of an honourable race. The next day, when the office was ended, the porter prayed the Abbess that he might have speech with her as she left the church. He related his story, and told of the finding of the child. The Abbess bade him to fetch the child, dressed in such fashion as she was discovered in the ash. The porter returned to his house, and showed the babe right gladly to his dame. The Abbess observed the infant closely, and said that she would be at the cost of her nourishing and would cherish her as a sister's child. She commanded the porter strictly to forget that he took her from the ash. In this manner it chanced that the maiden was tended of the Abbess. The lady considered the maid as her niece, and since she was taken from the ash, gave her the name of Frêne. By this name she was known of all, within the Abbey precincts, where she was nourished.

When Frêne came to that age in which a girl turns to a woman, there was no fairer maiden in Brittany, nor so sweet a damsel. Frank, she was, and open, but discreet in semblance and in speech. To see her was to love her, and to prize her smile above the beauty of the world. Now at Dol there lived a lord of whom much good was spoken. I will tell you his name. The folk of his country called him Buron. This lord heard speak of the maiden, and began to love her, for the sweetness men told of her. As he rode home from some tournament, he passed near the convent, and prayed the Abbess that he might look upon her niece. The Abbess gave him his desire. Greatly was the maiden to his mind. Very fair he found her, sweetly schooled and fashioned, modest and courteous to all. If he might not win her to his love, he counted himself the more forlorn. This lord was at his wits end, for he knew not what to do. If he repaired often to the convent, the Abbess would consider of the cause of his comings, and he would never again see the maiden with his eyes. One thing only gave him a little hope. Should he endow the Abbey of his wealth, he would make it his debtor for ever. In return he might ask a little room, where he might abide to have their fellowship, and, at times, withdraw him from the world. This he did. He gave richly of his goods to the Abbey. Often, in return, he went to the convent, but for other reasons than for penitence and peace. He besought the maiden, and with prayers and promises, persuaded her to set upon him her love. When this lord was assured that she loved him, on a certain day he reasoned with her in this manner.

"Fair friend," said he, "since you have given me your love, come with me, where I can cherish you before all the world. You know, as well as I, that if your aunt should perceive our friendship, she would be passing wrath, and grieve beyond measure. If my counsel seems good, let us flee together, you with me, and I with you. Certes, you shall never have cause to regret your trust, and of my riches you shall have the half."

When she who loved so fondly heard these words, she granted of her tenderness what it pleased him to have, and followed after where he would. Frêne fled to her lover's castle, carrying with her that silken cloth and ring, which might do her service on a day. These the Abbess had given her again, telling her how one morning at prime she was found upon an ash, this ring and samite her only wealth, since she was not her niece. Right carefully had Frêne guarded her treasure from that hour. She shut them closely in a little chest, and this coffret she bore with her in her flight, for she would neither lose them nor forget.

The lord, with whom the maiden fled, loved and cherished her very dearly. Of all the men and servants of his house, there was not one — either great or small — but who loved and honoured her for her simplicity. They lived long together in love and content, till the fair days passed, and trouble came upon this lord. The knights of his realm drew together, and many a time urged that he should put away his friend, and wed with some rich gentlewoman. They would be joyous if a son were born, to come after to his fief and heritage. The peril was too great to suffer that he remained a bachelor, and without an heir. Never more would they hold him as lord, or serve him with a good heart, if he would not do according to their will.

There being naught else to do, the lord deferred to this counsel of his knights, and begged them to name the lady whom he needs must wed.

"Sir," answered they, "there is a lord of these parts, privy to our counsel, who has but one child, a maid, his only heir. Broad lands will he give as her dowry. This damsel's name is Coudre, and in all this country there is none so fair. Be advised: throw away the ash rod you carry, and take the hazel as your staff. The ash is a barren stock; but the hazel is thick with nuts and delight. We shall be content if you take this maiden as your wife, so it be the will of God, and she be given you of her kinsfolk."

Buron demanded the hand of the lady in marriage, and her father and kin betrothed her to the lord. Alas! it was hid from all, that these two were twin sisters. It was Frêne's lot to be doubly abandoned, and to see her lover become her sister's husband. When she learned that her friend purposed taking to himself a wife, she made no outcry against his falseness. She continued to serve her lord faithfully, and was diligent in the business of his house. The sergeant and the varlet were marvellously wrathful, when they knew that she must go from amongst them. On the day appointed for the marriage, Buron bade his friends and acquintance to the feast. Together with these came the Archbishop, and those of Dol who held of him their lands. His betrothed was brought to his home by her mother. Great dread had the mother because of Frêne, for she knew of the love that the lord bore that maiden, and feared leste her daughter should be a stranger in her own hall. She spoke to her son-in-law, counselling him to send Frêne from his house, and to find her an honest man for her husband. Thus there would be quittance between them. Very splendid was the feast. Whilst all was mirth and jollity, the damsel visited the chambers, to see that each was ordered to her lord's pleasure. She hid the torment in her heart, and seemed neither troubled nor downcast. She compassed the bride with every fair observance, and waited upon her right daintily. Her courage was marvellous to that company of lords and ladies, who observed her curiously. The mother of the bride regarded her also, and praised her privily. She said aloud that had she known the sweetness of this lady, she would not have taken her lover from her, nor spoiled her life for the sake of the bride. The night being come the damsel entered in the bridal chamber to deck the bed against her lord. She put off her mantle, and calling the chamberlains, showed them how their master loved to lie. His bed being softly arrayed, a coverlet was spread upon the linen sheets. Frêne looked upon the coverlet: in her eyes it showed too mean a garnishing for so fair a lord. She turned it over in her mind, and going to her coffret she took therefrom that rich stuff of sanguine silk, and set it on the couch. This she did not only in honour of her friend, but that the Archbishop might not despise the house, when he blessed the marriage bed, according to the rite. When all was ready the mother carried the bride to that chamber where she should lie, to disarray her for the night. Looking upon the bed she marked the silken coverlet, for she had never seen so rich a cloth, save only that in which she wrapped her child. When she remembered of this thing, her heart turned to water. She summoned a chamberlain.

"Tell me," she said, "tell me in good faith where this garniture was found."

"Lady," he made replay, "that you shall know. Our damsel spread it on the bed, because this dossal is richer than the coverlet that was there before."

The lady called for the damsel. Frêne came before her in haste, being yet without her mantle. All the mother moved within her, as she plied her with questions.

"Fair friend, hide it not a whit from me. Tell me truly where this fair samite was found; whence came it; who gave it to you? Answer swiftly, and tell me who bestowed on you this cloth?"

"Lady, my aunt, the Abbess, gave me this silken stuff, and charged me to keep it carefully. At the same time she gave me a ring, which those who put me forth, had bound upon me."

"Fair friend, may I see this ring?"

"Certes, lady, I shall be pleased to show it."

The lady looked closely on the ring, when it was brought. She knew again her own, and the crimson samite flung upon the bed. No doubt was in her mind. She knew and was persuaded that Frêne was her very child. All words were spoken, and there was nothing more to hide.

"Thou art my daughter, fair friend."

Then for reason of the pity that was hers, she fell to the ground, and lay in a swoon. When the lady came again to herself, she sent for her husband, who, all adread, hastened to the chamber. He marvelled the more sorely when his wife fell at his feet, and embracing him closely, entreated pardon for the evil that she had done.

Knowing nothing of her trespass, he made reply,

"Wife, what is this? Between you and me there is nothing to call for forgiveness. Pardon you may have for whatever fault you please. Tell me plainly what is your wish."

"Husband, my offence is so black, that you had better give me absolution before I tell you the sin. A long time ago, by reason of lightness and malice, I spoke evil of my neighbour, whenas she bore two sons at a birth. I fell afterwards into the very pit that I had digged. Though I told you that I was delivered of a daughter, the truth is that I had borne two maids. One of these I wrapped in our stuff of samite, together with the ring you gave me the first time we met, and caused her to be laid beside a church. Such a sin will out. The cloth and the ring I have found, and I have recognised our maid, whom I had lost by my own folly. She is this very damsel — so fair and amiable to all — whom the knight so greatly loved. Now we have married the lord to her sister."

The husband made answer.

"Wife, if your sin be double, our joy is manifold. Very tenderly hath God dealt with us, in giving us back our child. I am altogether joyous and content to have two daughters for one. Daughter, come to your father's side."

The damsel rejoiced greatly to hear this story. Her father tarried no longer, but seeking his son-in-law, brought him to the Archbishop, and related the adventure. The knight knew such joy as was never yet. The Archbishop gave counsel that on the morrow he would part him and her whom he had joined together. This was done, for in the morning he severed them, bed and board. Afterwards he married Frêne to her friend, and her father accorded the damsel with a right good heart. Her mother and sister were with her at the wedding, and for dowry her father gave her the half of his heritage. When they returned to their own realm they took Coudre, their daughter, with them. There she was granted to a lord of those parts, and rich was the feast.

When this adventure was bruited abroad, and all the story, the Lay of the Ash Tree was written, so called of the lady, named Frêne.

Appendix B

The Lay of Sir Launfal

From: *Lays of Marie de France and Other French Legends*, trans. Eugene Mason (1911).

I will tell you the story of another Lay. It relates the adventures of a rich and mighty baron, and the Breton calls it, The Lay of Sir Launfal.

King Arthur — that fearless knight and courteous lord — removed to Wales, and lodged at Caerleon-on-Usk, since the Picts and Scots did much mischief in the land. For it was the wont of the wild people of the north to enter the realm of Logres, and burn and damage at their will. At the time of Pentecost, the King cried a great feast. Thereat he gave many rich gifts to his counts and barons, and to the Knights of the Round Table. Never were such worship and bounty shown before at any feast, for Arthur bestowed honours and lands on all his servants — save only on one. This lord, who was forgotten and misliked of the King, was named Launfal. He was beloved by many of the Court, because of his beauty and prowess, for he was a worthy knight, open of heart and heavy of hand. These lords, to whom their comrade was dead, felt little joy to see so stout a knight misprized. Sir Launfal was son to a King of high descent, though his heritage was in a distant land. He was of the King's household, but since Arthur gave him naught, and he was of too proud a mind to pray for his due, he had spent all that he had. Right heavy was Sir Launfal, when he considered these things, for he knew himself taken in the toils. Gentles, marvel not overmuch hereat. Ever must the pilgrim go heavily in a strange land, where there is none to counsel and direct him in the path.

Now, on a day, Sir Launfal got him on his horse, that he might take his pleasure for a little. He came forth from the city, alone, attended by neither servant nor squire. He went his way through a green mead, till he stood by a river of clear running water. Sir Launfal would have crossed this stream, without thought of pass or ford, but he might not do so, for reason that his horse was all fearful and trembling. Seeing that he was hindered in this fashion, Launfal unbitted his steed, and let him pasture in that fair meadow, where they had come. Then he folded his cloak to serve him as a pillow, and lay upon the ground. Launfal lay in great misease, because of his heavy thoughts, and the discomfort of his bed. He turned from side to side, and might not sleep. Now as the knight looked towards the river he saw two damsels coming towards him; fairer maidens Launfal had never seen. These two maidens were richly dressed in kirtles closely laced and shapen to their persons and wore mantles of goodly purple hue. Sweet and dainty were the damsels, alike in raiment and in face. The elder of these ladies carried in her hands a basin of pure gold, cunningly wrought by some crafty smith — very fair and precious was the cup; and the younger bore a towel of soft white linen. These maidens turned neither to the right hand nor to the left, but went directly to the place where Launfal lay. When Launfal saw that their business was with him, he stood upon his feet, like a discreet and courteous gentleman. After they had greeted the knight, one of the maidens delivered the message with which she was charged.

"Sir Launfal, my demoiselle, as gracious as she is fair, prays that you will follow us, her messengers as she has a certain word to speak with you. We will lead you swiftly to her pavilion, for our lady is very near at hand. If you but lift your eyes you may see where her tent is spread."

Right glad was the knight to do the bidding of the maidens. He gave no heed to his horse, but left him at his provand in the meadow. All his desire was to go with the damsels, to that pavilion of silk and divers colours, pitched in so fair a place. Certainly neither Semiramis in the days of her most wanton power, nor Octavian, the Emperor of all the West, had so gracious a covering from sun and rain. Above the tent was set an eagle of gold, so rich and precious, that none might count the cost. The cords and fringes thereof were of silken thread, and the lances which bore aloft the pavilion were of refined gold. No King on earth might have so sweet a shelter, not though he gave in fee the value of his realm. Within this pavilion Launfal came upon the Maiden. Whiter she was than any altar lily, and more sweetly flushed than the new born rose in time of summer heat. She lay upon a bed with napery and coverlet of richer worth than could be furnished by a castle's spoil. Very fresh and slender showed the lady in her vesture of spotless linen. About her person she had drawn a mantle of ermine, edged with purple dye from the vats of Alexandria. By reason of the heat her raiment was unfastened for a little, and her throat and the rondure of her bosom showed whiter and more untouched than hawthorn in May. The knight came before the bed, and stood gazing on so sweet a sight. The Maiden beckoned him to draw near, and when he had seated himself at the foot of her couch, spoke her mind.

"Launfal," she said, "fair friend, it is for you that I have come from my own far land. I bring you my love. If you are prudent and discreet, as you are goodly to the view, there is no emperor nor count, nor king, whose day shall be so filled with riches and with mirth as yours."

When Launfal heard these words he rejoiced greatly, for his heart was litten by another's torch.

"Fair lady," he answered, "since it pleases you to be so gracious, and to dower so graceless a knight with your love, there is naught that you may bid me do – right or wrong, evil or good – that I will not do to the utmost of my power. I will observe your commandment, and serve in your quarrels. For you I renounce my father and my father's house. This only I pray, that I may dwell with you in your lodging, and that you will never send me from your side."

When the Maiden heard the words of him whom so fondly she desired to love, she was altogether moved, and granted him forthwith her heart and her tenderness. To her bounty she added another gift besides. Never might Launfal be desirous of aught, but he would have according to his wish. He might waste and spend at will and pleasure, but in his purse ever there was to spare. No more was Launfal sad. Right merry was the pilgrim, since one had set him on the way, with such a gift, that the more pennies he bestowed, the more silver and gold were in his pouch.

But the Maiden had yet a word to say.

"Friend," she said, "hearken to my counsel. I lay this charge upon you, and pray you urgently, that you tell not to any man the secret of our love. If you show this matter, you will lose your friend, for ever and a day. Never again may you see my face. Never again will you have seisin of that body, which is now so tender in your eyes."

Launfal plighted faith, that right strictly he would observe this commandment. So the Maiden granted him her kiss and her embrace, and very sweetly in that fair lodging passed the day till evensong was come.

Right loath was Launfal to depart from the pavilion at the vesper hour, and gladly would he have stayed, had he been able, and his lady wished.

"Fair friend," said she, "rise up, for no longer may you tarry. The hour is come that we must part. But one thing I have to say before you go. When you would speak with me I shall hasten to come before your wish. Well I deem that you will only call your friend where she may be found without reproach or shame of men. You may see me at your pleasure; my voice shall speak softly in your ear at will; but I must never be known of your comrades, nor must they ever learn my speech."

Right joyous was Launfal to hear this thing. He sealed the covenant with a kiss, and stood upon his feet. Then there entered the two maidens who had led him to the pavilion, bringing with them rich raiment, fitting for a knight's apparel. When Launfal had clothed himself therewith, there seemed no goodlier varlet under heaven, for certainly he was fair and true. After these maidens had refreshed him with clear water, and dried his hands upon the napkin, Launfal went to meat. His friend sat at table with him, and small will had he to refuse her courtesy. Very serviceably the damsels bore the meats, and Launfal and the Maiden ate and drank with mirth and content. But one dish was more to the knight's relish than any other. Sweeter than the dainties within his mouth was the lady's kiss upon his lips.

When supper was ended, Launfal rose from table, for his horse stood waiting without the pavilion. The destrier was newly saddled and bridled, and showed proudly in his rich gay trappings. So Launfal kissed, and bade farewell, and went his way. He rode back towards the city at a slow pace. Often he checked his steed, and looked behind him, for he was filled with amazement, and all bemused concerning this adventure. In his heart he doubted that it was but a dream. He was altogether astonished, and knew not what to do. He feared that pavilion and Maiden alike were from the realm of faery.

Launfal returned to his lodging, and was greeted by servitors, clad no longer in ragged raiment. He fared richly, lay softly, and spent largely, but never knew how his purse was filled. There was no lord who had need of a lodging in the town, but Launfal brought him to his hall, for refreshment and delight. Launfal bestowed rich gifts. Launfal redeemed the poor captive, Launfal clothed in scarlet the minstrel. Launfal gave honour where honour was due. Stranger and friend alike he comforted at need. So, whether by night or by day, Launfal lived greatly at his ease. His lady, she came at will and pleasure, and, for the rest, all was added unto him.

Now it chanced the same year, about the feast of St. John, a company of knights came, for their solace, to an orchard, beneath that tower where dwelt the Queen. Together with these lords went Gawain and his cousin, Yvain the fair. Then said Gawain, that goodly knight, beloved and dear to all.

"Lords, we do wrong to disport ourselves in this pleasaunce without our comrade Launfal. It is not well to slight a prince as brave as he is courteous, and of a lineage prouder than our own."

Then certain of the lords returned to the city, and finding Launfal within his hostel, entreated him to take his pastime with them in that fair meadow. The Queen looked out from a window in her tower, she and three ladies of her fellowship. They saw the lords at their pleasure, and Launfal also, whom well they knew. So the Queen chose of her Court thirty damsels — the sweetest of face and most dainty of fashion — and commanded that they should descend with her to take their delight in the garden. When the knights beheld this gay company of ladies come down the steps of the perron, they rejoiced beyond measure. They hastened before to lead them by the hand, and said such words in their ear as were seemly and pleasant to be spoken. Amongst these merry and courteous lords hasted not Sir Launfal. He drew apart from the throng, for with him time went heavily, till he might have clasp and greeting of his friend. The ladies of the Queen's fellowship seemed but kitchen wenches to his sight, in comparison with the loveliness of the Maiden. When the Queen marked Launfal go aside, she went his way, and seating herself upon the herb, called the knight before her. Then she opened out her heat.

"Launfal, I have honoured you for long as a worthy knight, and have praised and cherished you very dearly. You may receive a queen's whole love, if such be your care. Be content: he to whom my heart is given, has small reason to complain him of the alms."

"Lady," answered the knight, "grant me leave to go, for this grace is not for me. I am the King's man, and dare not break my troth. Not for the highest lady in the world, not even for her love, will I set this reproach upon my lord."

When the Queen heard this, she was full of wrath, and spoke many hot and bitter words.

"Launfal," she cried, "well I know that you think little of woman and her love. There are sins more black that a man may have upon his soul. Traitor you are, and false. Right evil counsel gave they to my lord, who prayed him to suffer you about his person. You remain only for his harm and loss."

Launfal was very dolent to hear this thing. He was not slow to take up the Queen's glove, and in his haste spake words that he repented long, and with tears.

"Lady," said he, "I am not of that guild of which you speak. Neither am I a despiser of woman, since I love, and am loved, of one who would bear the prize from all the ladies in the land. Dame, know now and be persuaded, that she, whom I serve, is so rich in state, that the very meanest of her maidens, excels you, Lady Queen, as much in clerkly skill and goodness, as in sweetness of body and face, and in every virtue."

The Queen rose straightway to her feet, and fled to her chamber, weeping. Right wrathful and heavy was she, because of the words that had besmirched her. She lay sick upon her bed, from which, she said, she would never rise, till the King had done her justice, and righted this bitter wrong. Now the King that day had taken his pleasure within the woods. He returned from the chase towards evening, and sought the chamber of the Queen. When the lady saw him she sprang from her bed, and kneeling at his feet, pleaded for grace and pity. Launfal — she said — had shamed her, since he required her love. When she had put him by, very foully had he reviled her, boasting that his love was already set on a lady, so proud and noble, that her meanest wench went more richly, and smiled more sweetly, than the Queen. Thereat the King waxed marvellously wrathful, and swore a great oath that he would set Launfal within a fire, or hang him from a tree, if he could not deny this thing, before his peers.

Arthur came forth from the Queen's chamber, and called to him three of his lords. These he sent to seek the knight who so evilly had entreated the Queen. Launfal, for his part, had returned to his lodging, in a sad and sorrowful case. He saw very clearly that he had lost his friend, since he had declared their love to men. Launfal sat within his chamber, sick and heavy of thought. Often he called upon his friend, but the lady would not hear his voice. He bewailed his evil lot, with tears; for grief he came nigh to swoon; a hundred times he implored the Maiden that she would deign to speak with her knight. Then, since the lady yet refrained from speech, Launfal cursed his hot and unruly tongue. Very near he came to ending all this trouble with his knife. Naught he found to do but to wring his hands, and call upon the Maiden, begging her to forgive his trespass, and to talk with him again, as friend to friend.

But little peace is there for him who is harassed by a King. There came presently to Launfal's hostel those three barons from the Court. These bade the knight forthwith to go with them to Arthur's presence, to acquit him of this wrong against the Queen. Launfal went forth, to his own deep sorrow. Had any man slain him on the road, he would have counted him his friend. He stood before the King, downcast and speechless, being dumb by reason of that great grief, of which he showed the picture and image.

Arthur looked upon his captive very evilly.

"Vassal," said he, harshly, "you have done me a bitter wrong. It was a foul deed to seek to shame me in this ugly fashion, and to smirch the honour of the Queen. Is it folly or lightness which leads you to boast of that lady, the least of whose maidens is fairer, and goes more richly, than the Queen?"

Launfal protested that never had he set such shame upon his lord. Word by word he told the tale of how he denied the Queen, within the orchard. But concerning that which he had spoken of the lady, he owned the truth, and his folly. The love of which he bragged was now lost to him, by his own exceeding fault. He cared little for his life, and was content to obey the judgment of the Court.

Right wrathful was the King at Launfal's words. He conjured his barons to give him such wise counsel herein, that wrong might be done to none. The lords did the King's bidding, whether good came of the matter, or evil. They gathered themselves together, and appointed a certain day that Launfal should abide the judgment of his peers. For his part Launfal must give pledge and surety to his lord, that he would come before this judgment in his own body. If he might not give such surety then she should be held captive till the appointed day. When the lords of the King's household returned to tell him of their counsel, Arthur demanded that Launfal should put such pledge in his hand, as they had said. Launfal was altogether mazed and bewildered at this judgment, for he had neither friend nor kindred in the land. He would have been set in prison, but Gawain came first to offer himself as his surety, and with him, all the knights of his fellowship. These gave into the King's hand as pledge, the fiefs and lands that they held of his Crown. The King having taken pledges from the sureties, Launfal returned to his lodging, and with him certain knights of his company. They blamed him greatly because of his foolish love, and chastened him grievously by reason of the sorrow he made before men. Every day they came to his chamber, to know of his meat and drink, for much they feared that presently he would become mad.

The lords of the household came together on the day appointed for his judgment. The King was on his chair, with the Queen sitting at his side. The sureties brought Launfal within the hall, and rendered him into the hands of his peers. Right sorrowful were they because of his plight. A great company of his fellowship did all that they were able to acquit him of this charge. When all was set out, the King demanded the judgment of the Court, according to the accusation and the answer. The barons went forth in much trouble and thought to consider this matter. Many amongst them grieved for the peril of a good knight in a strange land; others held that it were well for Launfal to suffer, because of the wish and malice of their lord. Whilst they were thus perplexed, the Duke of Cornwall rose in the council, and said,

"Lords, the King pursues Launfal as a traitor, and would slay him with the sword, by reason that he bragged of the beauty of his maiden, and roused the jealousy of the Queen. By the faith that I owe this company, none complains of Launfal, save only the King. For our part we would know the truth of this business, and do justice between the King and his man. We would also show proper reverence to our own liege lord. Now, if it be according to Arthur's will, let us take oath of Launfal, that he seek this lady, who has put such strife between him and the Queen. If her beauty be such as he has told us, the Queen will have no cause for wrath. She must pardon Launfal for his rudeness, since it will be plain that he did not speak out of a malicious heart. Should Launfal fail his word, and not return with the lady, or should her fairness fall beneath his boast, then let him be cast off from our fellowship, and be sent forth from the service of the King.'

This counsel seemed good to the lords of the household. They sent certain of his friends to Launfal, to acquaint him with their judgment, bidding him to pray his damsel to the Court, that he might be acquitted of this blame. The knight made answer that in no wise could he do this thing. So the sureties returned before the judges, saying that Launfal hoped neither for refuge nor for succour from the lady, and Arthur urged them to a speedy ending, because of the prompting of the Queen.

The judges were about to give sentence upon Launfal, when they saw two maidens come riding towards the palace, upon two white ambling palfreys. Very sweet and dainty were these maidens, and richly clothed in garments of crimson sendal, closely girt and fashioned to their bodies. All men, old and young, looked willingly upon them, for fair they were to see. Gawain, and three knights of his company, went straight to Launfal, and showed him these maidens, praying him to say which of them was his friend. But he answered never a word. The maidens dismounted from their palfreys, and coming before the daïs where the King was seated, spake him fairly, as they were fair.

"Sire, prepare now a chamber, hung with silken cloths, where it is seemly for my lady to dwell; for she would lodge with you awhile."

This gift the King granted gladly. He called to him two knights of his household, and bade them bestow the maidens in such chambers as were fitting to their degree. The maidens being gone, the King required of his barons to proceed with their judgment, saying that he had sore displeasure at the slowness of the cause.

"Sire," replied the barons, "we rose from Council, because of the damsels who entered in the hall. We will at once resume the sitting, and give our judgment without more delay."

The barons again were gathered together, in much thought and trouble, to consider this matter. There was great strife and dissension amongst them, for they knew not what to do. In the midst of all this noise and tumult, there came two other damsels riding to the hall on two Spanish mules. Very richly arrayed were these damsels in raiment of fine needlework, and their kirtles were covered by fresh fair mantles, embroidered with gold. Great joy had Launfal's comrades when they marked these ladies. They said between themselves that doubtless they came for the succour of the good knight. Gawain, and certain of his company, made haste to Launfal, and said,

"Sir, be not cast down. Two ladies are near at hand, right dainty of dress, and gracious of person. Tell us truly, for the love of God, is one of these your friend?"

But Launfal answered very simply that never before had he seen these damsels with his eyes, nor known and loved them in his heart.

The maidens dismounted from their mules, and stood before Arthur, in the sight of all. Greatly were they praised of many, because of their beauty, and of the colour of their face and hair. Some there were who deemed already that the Queen was overborne.

The elder of the damsels carried herself modestly and well, and sweetly told over the message wherewith she was charged.

"Sire, make ready for us chambers, where we may abide with our lady, for even now she comes to speak with thee."

The King commanded that the ladies should be led to their companion, and bestowed in the same honourable fashion as they. Then he bade the lords of his household to consider their judgment, since he would endure no further respite. The Court already had given too much time to the business, and the Queen was growing wrathful, because of the blame that was hers. Now the judges were about to proclaim their sentence, when, amidst the tumult of the town, there came riding to the palace the flower of all the ladies of the world. She came mounted upon a palfrey, as white as snow, which carried her softly, as though she loved her burthen. Beneath the sky was no goodlier steed, nor one more gentle to the hand. The harness of the palfrey was so rich, that no king on earth might hope to buy trappings so precious, unless he sold or set his realm in pledge. The Maiden herself showed such as I will tell you. Passing slim was the lady, sweet of bodice and slender of girdle. Her throat was whiter than snow on branch, and her eyes were like flowers in the pallor of her face. She had a witching mouth, a dainty nose, and an open brow. Her eyebrows were brown, and her golden hair parted in two soft waves upon her head. She was clad in a shift of spotless linen, and above her snowy kirtle was set a mantle of royal purple, clasped upon her breast. She carried a hooded falcon upon her glove, and a greyhound followed closely after. As the Maiden rode at a slow pace through the streets of the city, there was none, neither great nor small, youth nor sergeant, but ran forth from his house, that he might content his heart with so great beauty. Every man that saw her with his eyes, marvelled at a fairness beyond that of any earthly woman. Little he cared for any mortal maiden, after he had seen this sight. The friends of Sir Launfal hastened to the knight, to tell him of his lady's succour, if so it were according to God's will.

"Sir comrade, truly is not this your friend? This lady is neither black nor golden, mean nor tall. She is only the most lovely thing in all the world."

When Launfal heard this, he sighed, for by their words he knew again his friend. He raised his head, and as the blood rushed to his face, speech flowed from his lips.

"By my faith," cried he, "yes, she is indeed my friend. It is a small matter now whether men slay me, or set me free; for I am made whole of my hurt just by looking on her face."

The Maiden entered in the palace – where none so fair had come before – and stood before the King, in the presence of his household. She loosed the clasp of her mantle, so that men might the more easily perceive the grace of her person. The courteous King advanced to meet her, and all the Court got them on their feet, and pained themselves in her service. When the lords had gazed upon her for a space, and praised the sum of her beauty, the lady spake to Arthur in this fashion, for she was anxious to begone.

"Sire, I have loved one of thy vassals – the knight who stands in bonds, Sir Launfal. He was always misprized in thy Court, and his every action turned to blame. What he said, that thou knowest; for over hasty was his tongue before the Queen. But he never craved her in love, however loud his boasting. I cannot choose that he should come to hurt or harm by me. In the hope of freeing Launfal from his bonds, I have obeyed thy summons. Let now thy barons look boldly upon my face, and deal justly in this quarrel between the Queen and me."

The King commanded that this should be done, and looking upon her eyes, not one of the judges but was persuaded that her favour exceeded that of the Queen.

Since then Launfal had not spoken in malice against his lady, the lords of the household gave him again his sword. When the trial had come thus to an end the Maiden took her leave of the King, and made her ready to depart. Gladly would Arthur have had her lodge with him for a little, and many a lord would have rejoiced in her service, but she might not tarry. Now without the hall stood a great stone of dull marble, where it was the wont of lords, departing from the Court, to climb into the saddle, and Launfal by the stone. The maiden came forth from the doors of the palace, and mounting on the stone, seated herself on the palfrey, behind her friend. Then they rode across the plain together, and were no more seen.

The Bretons tell that the knight was ravished by his lady to an island, very dim and very fair, known as Avalon. But none had had speech with Launfal and his faery love since then, and for my part I can tell you no more of the matter.

Appendix C

Sir Landevale

Based on Bodleian MS Rawlinson C 86, with Bliss's additional lines from *Sir Launfal* or by his own invention to complete rhymes, marked by brackets. The scribe occasionally transposes letters; we have retransposed them silently.

Sothly, by Arthurys day — *Truly*
Was Bretayne yn grete nobylé, — *nobility*
For yn hys tyme a grete whyle
He sojourned at Carlile; — *Carlisle*
He had with hym a meyné there, — *company*
As he had ellyswhere,
Of the Rounde Table the knyghtys alle,
With myrth and joyc yn hys hallc.
Of eache lande yn the worlde wyde — *From*
There came men on every syde,
Yonge knyghtys and squyers
And othir bolde bachelers,
Forto se that nobley
That was with Arthur allwey,
For ryche geftys and tresoure — *gifts*
He gayf to eache man of honoure. — *gave*

With hym there was a bachiller,
[And hadde ybe well many a yer],
A yonge knyght of muche myght:
Sir Landevale, forsoith, he hight, — *truly he was called*
Sir Landavale spent blythely,
And gaf geftys largely; — *generously*
So wildely his goode he sette — *charity*
That he felle yn grete dette.
[Then gan he to make his mone:] — *lament*
"Who hath no good, goode can he none! —
And I am here in uncuth londe, — *strange circumstance*
And no gode have under honde;

Men will me hold for a wreche.
Where I become, I ne reche!" *don't care*
He lepe upon a coursier, *lept; horse*
Withoute grome or squier, *groom*
And rode forthe yn a mornynge
To dryve awey longynge.
Then he takyth toward the west, *goes*
Betwene a water and a forest.
The sonne was hote that underntyde; *noonday*
He lyght adowne, and wolde abyde, *lay down; would rest*
For he was hote yn the weddir. *weather*
Hys mantelle he toke and folde togeder; *mantle (cloak)*
Than lay downe that knyght so free
Undre the shadow of a tree.
"Alas!" he said, "No good I have!
How shalle I doo? I can not crave! *beg*
All the knyghtys that ben so feers, *fierce*
Of the Rounde Table they were my pyers. *peers*
Every man of me was glade,
And now they be for me full saide." *sad*
"Alas! Alas!" was his songe:
Sore wepyng his hondis he wronge. *hands; wrung*
Thus he lay yn sorow full sore;
Than he sawe, comynge oute of holtys hore, *woods gray*
Owte of the forest cam mydyns two, *maidens*
The fayrest on grounde that myght goo. *earth*
Kyrtyls they had of purpyl sendelle, *Belts*
Smalle i-lasid, syttyng welle; *Intricately laid, well appointed*
Mantels of grene velvet
Frengide with golde were wele i-sette; *Fringed*
They had on atyre therwithalle,
And eache of them a joly cornalle; *crown*
With facys white as lelyfloure, *lily flower*
With ruddy, rede as rose, coloure, *complexion*
Fayrer women never he see —
They semyd angels of hevin hie. *heaven high*
That one bare a golde basyne, *one bore; basin*
That othir a towail, riche and fyne. *towel*
To hymwarde come the maydyns gent;

The knyght anon agaynse hem went.
"Welcome!" he said, "damsels fre."
"Sir knyght," they seide, "Wel thu be!
My lady, that is as bright as floure,
The gretith, Landavale, paramour; — *[Your] lover greets you*
Ye must come and speke with her,
Yef it be your wille, Sir." — *If*
"I graunt," he said "blythely," — *eagerly*
And went with them hendly. — *readily*
Anone he in that forest sy — *saw*
A pavylione, i-pight an hy, — *pitched*
With treysour i-wrought on every syde,
Al of werke of the faryse; — *fairies*
Eche pomelle of that pavilione
Was worth a citie, or a towne.
Upon the cupe an heron was,
A richer nowher ne was; — *None richer was there*
In his mouthe a carboucle, bright — *carbuncle (gem)*
As the mone that shone light. — *moon*
Kyng Alexander the conquerour,
Ne Salamon yn hys honour,
Ne Charlemayn, the riche kyng, — *Charlemagne*
They had never suche a thing.
He founde yn that pavilione
The kyngys doughter of Amylione;
That ys an ile of the fayré — *isle; fair*
In occian, full faire to see. — *ocean*
There was a bede of mekylle price, — *bed; great*
Coveride with purpille byse; — *cloth*
Thereon lay that maydyn bright,
Almost nakyde, and upright.
Al her clothes byside her lay:
Syngly was she wrappyde, parfay,
With a mauntell of hermyne, — *ermine*
Coveride was with alexanderyne. — *alexandrine*
The mauntelle for hete downe she dede
Right to hir gyrdillestede. — *i.e., waist*
She was white as lely in May,
Or snowe that fallith yn wynterday;

Blossom on brere, ne no floure, *branch*
Was not like to her coloure;
The rede rose whan it is newe
To her rud is not of hewe; *complexion*
Her heire shon as gold wire — *hair*
Noman can tell her atyre. *describe*
"Landavale," she seid, "myn hert swete,
For thy love now I swete.
There is kyng ne emperour — *[neither]; nor*
And I lovyd hym par amor
As moche as I do the — *you*
But he wolde be full glad of me."
Landevale behelde the maydyn bright;
Her love persyde hys hert right. *pierced; heart instantly*
He sette hym down by her syde;
"Lady," quod he, "whatso betyde,
Evermore, lowde and stylle,
I am redy at your wylle."
"Sir knyght," she said "curteyse and hende, *gracious*
I know thy state, every ende. *i.e., dilemma*
Wilt thow truliche the to me take, *truly*
And alle other for me forsake?
And I wille geve the grette honoure, *give you*
Gold inought, and grete tresoure. *enough*
Hardely spende largely, *Heartily spend freely*
Gife geftys blythely! *Give gifts*
Spende and spare not, for my love!
Thow shalt inought to thy behove."
Tho she saide to his desyre;
He clyppide her abowte the swire, *embraced; neck*
And kyssyde her many a sith; *time*
For her profer he thankyd hir swyth. *quickly*
This lady was son up sette, *i.e., stood up*
And bad hir maydyns mete fette, *dinner fetch*
And to this handys water clere; *i.e., washed their hands*
And sothyn went to soupere. *then; supper*
Bothe they togedirs sette.
The maydyns servyd theym of mete;
Of mete and dryng they had plentie, *food; drink*

Of alle thing that was deynté.
After soper the day was gone;
To bedde they went both anone;
Alle that nyght they ley yn fere *entwined*
And did what thir wille were —
For pley they slepyde litille that nyght. *Because of play*
Tho it began to dawe light, *dawn*
"Landavale," she said, "goo hens now." *go forth*
Gold and sylver take with you,
Spend largely on every man.
I wille fynd you inough than,
And when ye wille, gentil knyght,
Speke with me any night,
To sum derne stede ye goo, *magical (i.e., supernatural) place*
And thynke on me soo and soo
Anon to you shalle I tee. *come*
Ne make ye never bost of me! *boast*
And yff thou doyest, be ware beforn *be forewarned*
For thow has my love forlorn." *lost*
  The maydeyns bringe hys horse anone;
He toke hys leve, and went sone.
Of tresoure he hath grete plentie,
And ridith forth ynto the cieté.
He comythe home to hys in, *lodging*
And mery he makyth hym therin.
Hymsylf he clothyde fulle richely,
Hys squyer, hys yoman, honestly.
Landavale makyth nobile festys; *noble feasts*
Landevale clothys the pore gestys; *guests*
Landevale byith grette stedys; *steeds*
Landevale gevythe riche wedys; *gives; clothes*
Landevale rewaredithe religiouse, *ecclesiastics*
And acquitethe the presons; *prisoners*
Landevale clothes gaylours; *jailers*
Landevale doith each man honours.
Of his largesse eche man wote, *wondered*
But how it comyth noman wote. *knows*
And he wille, derne or stelle, *If; secretly; quietly*
Hys love ys redy at his wylle.

Upon a tyme, Sir Gawyne *Gawain*
The curteys knyght, and Sir Ewayne *Ywain*
And Sir Landavale with them also,
And othir knyghtys twenté or moo,
Went to play theym on a grene
Under the towre where was the quene.
Thyse knyghtys with borde playd tho;
Atte the last to daunsyng they goo. *dance*
Sir Landevale was tofore i-sette;
For his largesse he was lovyd the bette. *best*
The quene hersylf beheld [this alle;]
"Yender," she said "ys Landavalle; *Yonder*
Of alle the knyghtys that bene here
There is none so faire a bachylere; *bachelor*
And he have noder leman ne wyfe, *neither lover nor wife*
I wold he lovyde me as his life. *wish*
Tide me good or tyde me ille, *Befall*
I wille assay the knyghtys wille." *test*
She toke with her a company
Of faire laydys thyrty;
She goith adowne anonerighte
Forto daunce with the knyghte.
The quene yede to the first ende, *went*
Betwene Landavale and Gawyne so hende, *gracious*
And all her maydens forth aright,
One be one betwyxt eche knyght. *by; between*
Whan the daunsynge was i-slakyde,
The quene Landavale to concelle hath takyde: *counsel*
"Shortely," she saide, "Thu gentil knyght,
I the love with alle my myght,
And as moche desire I the yere *you eagerly*
As the kyng, and moche more.
Gode [hap is to the tanne] *Good fortune; befallen you*
To love more me than any woman."
"Madame," he said, "be God, nay!
I wil be traitoure never, parfay!
I have do the kyng othe and feaulté *oath; fealty*
He shall not be traid for me!" *betrayed by*
"Fy!" said she, "Thow fowle coward!

An harlot ribawde I wote thou harte; *observe; you are*
That thow livest it is pité:
Thow lovyst no woman, ne no women the!"
The knyght was agreved thoo;
He her ansurid and said, "Noo!
Madame," quod he, "Thu saist thi wille, *say what you*
Yet can I love dern and stelle, *secretly; with quiet discretion*
And am i-loved, and have a leman *loved; lover*
As gentille and as faire as any man.
The semplest maide with her, I wene,
Over the may be a quene."
Tho was she ashamyd and wrothe. *angry*
She clepid her maydens bothe;
To bede she goith alle drery. *sad*
For doole she wold dye, and was sory. *dolor (sorrow)*
  The kyng came from huntyng,
Glade and blithe yn alle thing,
And to the quene can he tee. *go*
Anone she fell upon her knee;
Wonder lowde can she crie,
"A! helpe me, lorde, or I die!
I spake to Landavale on a game, *playfully*
And he besought me of shame;
As a foule viced tratoure *traitor*
He wold have done me dishonoure;
And of a leman bost he maide:
That werst maide that she hade
Myght be a quene over me —
And alle, lorde, in dispite of the!" *despite; you*
  The kyng wax wondir wrothe, *amazingly angry*
And forthewithe swore hys othe *oath*
That Landavale shulde bide be the lawe, *abide by*
Be bothe hangyd and drawe;
And commanded four knightys
To fetche the traitoure anonrightys, *immediately*
They four fechyng hym anone —
But Landavale was to chamber gone.
Alas! he hath hys love forlorne,
As she warnyd hym beforne.

Ofte he clepid her, and sought, *Often; called*
And yet it gaynethe hym nought.
He wept and sobbet with rufulle cry, *sobbed*
And on hys kneys he askythe mercy;
[He bet hys body and hys hedde ek,] *beat; head also*
And cursed hys mouth that of hir spake.
"O!" he said, "Gentille creature!
How shalle my wrechyd body endure,
That worldys blysse hath forlore,
And he[r] that I am under arest for
With suche sorowe? — alas that stounde!
With that he fel dede on the grounde, *i.e., fainted*
So long that the knyghtys comyn,
And ther so they hym namyn, *accused*
And as theff hym ladde soo: *thief*
Than was his sorow doble woo. *double sorrow*
He was brought before the kyng.
Thus he hym grete at the begynnyng:
"Thow atteynt, takyn traytoure,
Besoughtest thou my wiff of dishonoure?
That she was lothely thou dedist upbrayde,
That of thy leman the lest mayde *least*
Was fayrer than ys my wyffe!
Therefore shalt thu lose thy lyffe." *lose your life*
  Landavale ansuryd at hys borde *answered*
And told hym the sothe, every worde, *them; truth*
That it was nothing so,
And he was redy forto die tho
That all the countrey wold looke.
Twelve knyghtys were drevyn to a boke *driven; book*
The sothe to say and no leese,
Alle togedir as it was.
This twelve wist withouten wene
All the maner of the quene:
The kyng was good, alle aboute,
And she was wyckyd, oute and oute, *through and through*
For she was of suche comforte
She lovyd men ondir her lorde; *i.e., in her lord's command*
Therby wist thei it was alle

Longe on her, and not on Landevalle.
Herof they quytten hym as treue men,
And sithe spake they farder then,
That yf he myght hys leman bryng,
Of whom he maide knolishyng, *[resoundingly] made known*
And yef her maydeynse bryght and shyne
Werne fairer than the quene
In maykyng, semblaunt and hewe, *form, appearance; hue*
They wold quyte hym gode and true: *acquit*
Yff he ne myght stonnd thertille,
Thann to be at the kyngys wille
This verdite thei gef tofore the kynge. *verdict*
The day was sett her forto brynge:
Borowys he founde to com agene, *Supporters*
Sir Gawyne and Sir Ewyne.
"Alas!" quod he, "Now shalle I die:
My love shalle I never see with ee." *eye*
Ete ne drynke wold he never, *Eat*
But wepyng and sorowyng evir.
Syres, sare sorow hathe he nom! *taken*
He wold hys endyng day wer com, *wished his ending (death)*
That he myght ought of life goo. *out*
Every man was for hym woo, *sorry*
For larger knyght than he *a more generous*
Was ther never yn that countrey.
The day i-sett com on hyynge; *quickly*
His borowys hym brought before the kyng.
The kyng lett recorte tho *had recorded*
The sewt and the answer also, *suit (charge)*
And bad hym bryng his borowis in syghte; *supporters*
Landevalle sayde that he ne myghte.
Tho were comaundyd the barons alle *Then*
To gyve judgement on Sir Landevalle.
Then sayd the Erle of Cornwaylle,
That was att the councelle:
"Lordyngys, ye wott the kyng oure lorde;
His oune mowth berythe recorde
That, yf we go by the lawe.
Landevale is worthy to be drawe;

Butt greatt vilany were therupon
To fordo such a man, *slay*
That is more large and fre *Who; generous; noble*
Then eny of us that here be. *Than any*
Therfore, by oure reade, *counsel*
We wolle the kyng in suche a way lede
That he shalle comaunde hym to goo
Oute of this land for evermo."
While they stode thus spekyng,
They sawe in fere cum rydyng *in company*
Two maydyns, whyte as flower,
On whyte palfrays, with honour;
So fayre creaturys with ien *eyes*
Ne better attyryde were never seen.
Alle ther judgyde theym so sheen *All there; gorgeous*
That over Dame Gaynour they myght be a queen. *Guinevere*
Then sayde Gawen, that curteys knyght,
"Landevale, care the nowyght! *not*
Here comyth thy leman, kynde i-core, *chosen of nature*
For whom thow art anoiede sore." *suffering greatly*
Landevale lokyd and said, "Nay, i-wysse!
My leman of hem ther non is." *lover is not among them*
Thise maidens come so riding
Into the castelle, before the king;
They light adown, and grete hym so, *dismounted*
And besought hym of a chamber tho,
A place for their lady that was cummyng.
Than said Arthour, the nobill king, *noble*
"Who is your lady, and what to done?" *do you want*
"Lord," quod they, "ye may wetyne sone." *find out soon*
The king lete for her sake
The fairest chamber to be take;
Thise maidens gon to bowre on hye.
Than said the king to his baronye,
"Have i-do, and gyve judgement!" *give*
The barones saide, "Verament,
We have beholde these maidens bright;
We will do anoneright."
A new speche began they tho: *speech (i.e., debate)*

Summe said wele, and summe said not so; *yes; no*
Summe wolde hym to dethe deem, *death condemn*
The king their lorde for to queme; *please*
Summe hym wolde make clere — *clear*
And while they spake thus in fere, *together*
Other maidens ther commyn tho
Welle more fairer than the other two,
Riding upon moiles of Spayne, *mules; Spain*
Bothe sadellys and bridels of Almayne; *Germany*
They were iclothed in atire,
And eache a man had grete desire
To beholde her gentrise, *excellence*
They came in so faire assise. *fashion*
Than sade Gawyn the hende,
"Landevale, broder, heder thou wende! *come here*
Here comyth thy love; thou maist wel se
That one herof, I wote, ys she!"
Landevale, with dropyng thought: *i.e., disappointment*
"Nay, alas! I know them nought;
I ne wote who they beith,
Ne whens they come, ne whethir they lith."
These maidens reden ynto the paleys, *palace*
Right afore the kyngys deys, *dais*
And gretith hym and his quene ek. *also*
That one of them thise wordys spake: *one; spoke*
"Sir riche Kyng Arthure,
Lete dight thyn hall with honoure, *decorate*
Bothe rofe and grounde and wallys *roof; walls*
With clothys of gold and riche pallys;
Yet it is lothely, yef thou so doo,
My lady forto light therto."
The kyng said, "So shalle it be:
My lady ys welcom, and soo be ye."
He bade Sir Gawyne bryng hem yn fere
With honour there the othir were. *where*
The quene therfore trowid of gyle, *believed guilefully*
That Landevale shud be holpyn in a while *rescued*
Of his leman that ys comyng:
She cried, and saide: "Lorde and kyng!

And thow lovyst thyn honour *If you love your*
I were avenged on that tratour;
To sle Landevale thu woldest not spare.
Thy barons do thy besmare." *besmear you*
While she spake thus to the kynge
They saw where came ridynge
A lady, herself alle alone
On erthe fayrer was never none
On a white palfrey comlye;
There nesse kyng that hath gold ne fee *is no; property*
That myght by that palfrey *might purchase*
Withoute sellyng of lond awey.
This lady was bright as blossome on brere,
Her ieene lofsum, bright and clere; *eyes lovely*
Jentylle and jolyffe as birde on bowgh, *Gentle; jolly*
In alle thing faire ynowgh.
As rose in May her rude was rede, *countenance*
Here here shynyng on her hede *Her hair; her head*
As gold wyre yn sonn bright; *thread in the sun*
In this worlde nas so faire a wight.
A crowne was upon her hede,
Al of precious stones and gold rede; *red gold*
Clothid she was yn purpylle palle,
Her body gentille and medille smale;
The pane of hir mantelle inwarde *trim*
On hir harmes she foldid owtewarde, *arms*
Whiche wel becam that lady.
Thre white grehoundys went hyr by; *greyhounds*
A sparowhauke she bare upon hir hande;
A softe paas her palfrey comaunde. *easy gait*
Throw the citie rode she,
For every man shuld hir see;
Wiff and childe, yong and olde, *Wife*
Al come hir to byholde.
There was man ne woman that myght
Be wery of so faire a sight! *weary*
Also sone as Landevale hir see,
To all the lordys he cryed on he:
"Now comyth my love, now comyth my swete!

Now comyth she my bale shalle beete! *bail*
Now I have her seyne with myne ee, *seen with my eye*
I ne reke when that I dye." *I don't care*
  The damselle com rydyng stoute, *boldly*
Alone yn the citie throwoute,
Throw the palys ynto the halle,
Ther was the kyng and the quene alle.
Her four maidens with gret honoure
Agayne her came oute of the bowre, *Toward*
And helde her steroppys so; *stirrops*
The lady dyd alight tho, *dismount then*
And they gently can hyr grete,
And she hym with wordys swete. *them; words sweet*
The quene and othir ladyes stoute
Behelde her all aboute;
They to her were allso donne *Compared to her they were dull*
As the monelyght to the sonne. *moonlight; sun*
Than every man had gret deynté
Her to beholde, and preseith hir beauté
Than saide the lady to the kynge:
"Sir, I com for suche a thinge:
My trew leman, Sir Landevalle,
Is accusyd amonges you all
That he shuld with tratoury
Beseche the quene of velony.
That ys fals, by Seynt Jame! *false*
He bad her not, but she bad hyme! *propositioned*
And of that othir, that he saide *i.e., As for that other charge*
That my lothliest maide
Was fairer than the quene,
Loke anone yf yt so bene!"
The kyng beheld and sawe the southe, *truth*
Also erlys and barons bothe;
Every lorde said than
Landevale was a trew man.
When the jugement gyvyne was, *given*
At the kyng her leve she takys, *From*
And lepe upon hir palfrey *lept*
And betoke them to Gode and goode day: *commended*

The kyng fulle fare, and alle his,
Besechit hir, withoutyne mys, — *Beseeched*
Longer to make sojournyng. — *i.e., stay longer*
She said, "Nay!" and thankyd the kyng.
Landevale saw hys love wold gone:
Upon hir horse he lepe anone,
And said, "Lady, my leman bright!
I wille with the, my swete wight, — *creature*
Whedir ye ride or goo — — *Wherever*
Ne wille I never parte you fro!"
"Landevale," she said, withoutyn lette, — *hesitation*
"Whan we first togedire mete,
With dern love, withouten stryfe, — *secret*
I chargyd you yn all your lyffe
That ye of me never speke shulde; — *you should never speak of me*
How dare ye now be so bolde
With me to ride withoute leve? — *permission*
Ye ought to thyng ye shuld me greve." — *think*
"Lady," he said, "faire and goode!
For His love that shed His blode,
Forgef me that trespace, — *trespass*
And put me hole yn your grace!" — *wholly*
Than that lady to hym can speke,
And said to hym wyth wordys meke,
"Landevale, lemman, I you forgyve
That trespace while ye leve. — *live*
Welcom to me, gentille knyghte!
We wolle never twyn, day ne nyghte." — *part*
So they rodyn evenryghte,
The lady, the maydyns, and the knyghte:
Loo, howe love is lefe to wyn — *destined; win*
Of wemen that arn of gentylle kyn! — *women who are; nature*
The same way have they nomyn — *taken*
Ryghte as before she was comyn;
And thus was Landevale broughte from Cardoylle,
With his fere into a joly yle — *companion; happy isle*
That is clepyde Amylyone — *called Avalon*
That knowith every Brytane. — *known [by]; Briton*
Of hym syns herde never man — — *i.e., No man has heard of them since*

No further of Landevalle telle I can;
Butt God, for His greatt mercy,
Bryng us to His blysse on highe.
  Amen
  Explicit

Glossary

This is a select glossary, designed to help readers with words which are not always glossed in the margins of the text and with words which might, in particular contexts, be misconstrued with synonyms, homonyms, and words with similar spellings.

ac *but*
aferd(e) *afraid*
agen (ayen ayeyn) *again; in return; toward; (prep.) against*
aither *either; each*
als *as, also*
amorewe *the next day*
anon(e) *soon, immediately*
apayd *pleased*
ar (er) *before*
areyd *arrayed*
askyng *request*
as(s)oyle *absolve*
assemuld *assembled*
aventour(e) *adventure*

bacinet *a lightweight steel helmet worn under an outer battle helmet*
batail (batayle) *battle*
batell *battalions*
be *by*
be(n) is, be, been
befalle (bifalle) *happened*
behynd *neglected; wanting*
beyre *born, carried*
belyve *joyously*
bestadde *beset*
betere *better*
beth *is*
betwyx *between, amongst*
byddus *bids*
bitawt (bitaught) *bestowed*
bith *is; was*
ble *color, hue; countenance*
blys *bliss*
blithe (blythe) *happy, happily*
boke *book*
borowes *sureties, guarantees*
bour *bower, chamber*
bowen *prepared*
bren *burn*
brente *burned*
burgeys *burgess*
but (bot) *except; unless*

certys *surely, certainly*
chere *countenance, face, expression, mood, news*
cherys *cherries*
ches (cheys) *goes; returns; chose, chooses*
clepede *called; embraced*
cler(e) bright, glorious, innocent
colere *hue; gold chain, badge of honor*
comoun *common, low*
con *did*
cours *course*

couth *know, knew*
couthen *to know, knew*
covenaunt *covenant, promise*
Cryston *Christian*
crystond *christened*
crounes *crowns, skulls*
curta(y)s *courteous*
curtesly *courteously*

dedus *deeds*
del(e) *part; portion; sorrow*
dele *deal, dispense, give; have intercourse*
dey *day*
dinte (dyntte) *blow*
dyscomfyd *defeated*
doghty (doughty, doghtté) *strong, valiant*
doht *went*
doyth *do, act*
dolour *misery*
dompe *dumb, mute*
dout(e) (dowte) *doubt; fear*

eft (effte) *once more; after*
ei (ey) *ever, always*
eyt *eat*
ek *also*
eld *old*
elles *otherwise, else*
er *before*
erliche *early*
erlys *earls*
erthly *earthly; mortal*
Estryke *Austria*

fachon (fawchon) *curved sword, falchion*
fallyd (feylyd) *failed, fell*
fay (fey) *fairy; faith*
fayry *the fairy world, the Other world*
fein (feyn) *glad; eager*
feld (fyld) *field, battlefield*
fele(fell) *many*
fende *fiend, devil*
fer (ferre) *far; (adj.) fierce*
fere *companion; (adj.) fair.* **in fere** *together, in company*
ferly (ferli) *wondrous*
ferthe *fourth*
feyre *fair*
fin *fine, precious*
fir (fer, fure) *fire*
florines *florins (coins)*
fond(e) *found, discovered; established; invented*
foo *foe*
foon *foes*
for *because*
forgevon *forgiven*
forgyffeus *forgives*
forthi *therefore; (conj.) because*
fot *foot*
fre (free) *noble, generous*
frythe *forest*
fro *from*

gan *began; did*
gard (gart) *made; ordered*
gars *makes, causes*
gatis (yatus) *gates*
geyst *geste, story*
geyr *gear, armor*
gent (gentil) *noble*
gest *guest*
gyff *give*
gyffus *gives*
gossibbe *godparent*

greved *grieved*
gud *good*

her *their*
heddys *heads*
hedur *hither*
hele *health; heal*
helm(e) *helmet*
helud *healed*
hem (hom) *them*
hend(e) *courteous; polite; (adv) diligently*
her(e) *her; their; (v.) hear*
herpere *harper*
hette *(to be) called, named*
hert(e) *heart*
hethon *heathen*
heved *head*
hewe *hue, complexion*
hie *hie; hasten*
hye *she*
hyght *is/was called; promised*
hi(i) *they; he; she*
him *him; it; himself*
hir(e) *her*
his (is) *his; its*
hit *it*
ho (hoo) *she*
holde *have*
hom *home; them*
honde *hand*
hongurt *hungered*
hor *their; whore*
hou *how; (pron.) they*
howndes *hound[']s*
hur *her; herself*

ibrout *brought*
ich *I*
icham *I am*
ich(e) (yche) *each*

ifere *together*
ilke (ylke) *same*
iment *intended*
inough (anowgh) *enough*
is *is; his*
ismiten *hit*
isowt *sought*
ispoused *married*
iwis (ywys) *indeed, surely, truly*
iwite *know*
iwrout *made*

justeth *jousted*
justi (iusti, justus) *joust*

kynde *nature; people*
kynne *kin*
kyrke *church*

ladde *led*
laft *left; lifted*
lemman *lover*
lees (les, leighe) *lies, false*
les *lost*
lesen *to lose; to loosen*
lesynge *lying; falsehood*
leve *leave; permission; (n.) dear, beloved*
levedi *lady*
lever *rather*
leveste (levyst) *most pleased*
lightlich *lightly, easily*
lyke *like, resemble*
loffe *love*
lore *learning*
lorn *lost*
loverd *lord*

mannys *man's*
marchaunt(e) *merchant*

mare *more*
maugré *despite*
meydyn *maiden*
meyné *company, household*
mekyll (muchel, mochel, mychyll, myche) *very; great*
mende *heal, help*
mervel *marvel, wonder; (adj.) marvelous, strange*
mester *skill, action*
mete *meat, dinner, food; (v.) meet*
metes (metys) *meats, food, dinner*
mide *with*
myrthys *happiness*
mo *more; others*
mold *earth, world*
mon(e) *moan*
mot *may, might, must*
mothe *mouth*

nam(m) *took*
nom *went; name*
nowdur *neither*
nowt *not; nothing*

o *of; on; upon; one*
on *one*
oonys *once*
or *or; before; ere*
ordre *order*
os *as*

pannyere *basket*
paramour *lover; (adv.) fervently*
paraventure *by chance*
parylle *peril*
part(e) *part; some*
pavyloun *pavilion, tent*
pel (pal) *cloth, robe*
penans *penance*
per *peer*
powre *poor*
press (pres) *throng, crowd*
preson *prison*
prest *priest; (adj.) ready*
prevely *privately*
price (pryse) *excellence*
pryde *pride; magnificence; ornamentation*
prystely *swiftly*

quit (quite, qwite) *pay, repay, compensate*
quytte *proven*

radly *quickly*
rede *advice, counsel*
redy *available, given*
ren (renne) *run; course*
renowne *reputation, fame*
rentes *rents (from land)*
resseyved *received, welcomed*
revus *takes; snatches*
ridend *riding*
ryght *just; correct; (adv.) steadfastly; righteously; entirely*
ronge *rang (bells)*

sain *say*
samun *together*
scapyd *escaped*
schene (shene) *beautiful; shining*
scho *she*
schryne *shrine*
schryvon *absolved; confessed*

sechen *sought*
sechys *seeks*
segh(e) *saw*
seyn *seen; said*
sekurly *with certainty*
sekyrlyke *certainly*
semly (sembly, semblaunt) *handsome; beautiful*
sen(e) *seen; since*
servise *service*
seth *saw; said*
sese *cease*
sewrté *surety, assurance*
shype *ship*
sigge *say*
syghed *sighed*
sike(a)nd *sighing*
sikerly *surely*
sylke *silk*
syn *since*
sithe (sythe) *times*
sithen (sethen, sythen) *since, then*
sle *slay*
slowgh (slough) *slew*
smite *hit*
sometime *once*
son(e) *son; sun; (adv.) immediately; quickly*
sond *sand*
sond(e) *message, sending; blessing; mercy*
soper *supper*
sore *sorrowfully*
sothe *truth*
sothly *truly*
souke *suck*
sowle (saulys) *soul, souls*
spoused *married*
staleworth *stalwart*
stede *place, step; horse*
stedes (stedys) *steeds*
stere *guide; restrain*
styfly *strenuously; bravely*
stynt(e) *stop*
styrd *handled; moved, stirred*
stirt *jumped, rushed*
stond(e) *occasion, time*
stout *strong, bold*
strengere *stronger*
sustynans *sustenance*
swich (syche) *such*
swithe *quickly*
swonygne (sowenyng) *swooning, fainting*

taperes *tapers, candles*
teche *teach*
tellys *tells; explains*
tempe *tempt*
testymonyeth *testifies, witnesses*
teyrus (teres) *tears*
thar *need*
the *thee, you*
thede *people*
thedur (thider) *thence; there*
thenche *think; reflect*
tho *those; then; the*
thore *there*
thous *this; those*
thowght(h)ur *daughter*
thridde *third*
thryfte *luck*
thynne *thin*
tide (tyde) *time*
to *to; two*
tofore *before*
tokyn *token; sign*

tosprong *broke apart*
tryste *trust*
trone *throne*
trow(e) *true; (v.) trust, believe*
trumpud *trumpeted*
tvay *two*

unbounde *delivered*
undernom (undernam) *perceived*
unthur *under, beneath*
unthurstond *understand*
uschear (usschere) *usher*
uyset *beset*

vansyd *advanced; promoted*
venesoun *venison*
verraiment *truly*

wan *won; came*
ware *was*
wawes *waves*
wax (wex) *grew; became*
wede(s) *garment(s); armor*
wedow *widow*
weld *wield; govern; conquer*
wend(e) *knew; thought; go*
wepende (wepinde) *weeping*
wer *war; (v.) were*
wered *wore*
werke *work; do; deed*
wher *where; wherever; whether*
wyght *person; man; manly*
wiste (wyste) *knew*
wold (wolde) *would; power world*
wond(e) *wound; wrapped; went; wait*
wonder (wondur) *marvel, marvelously*
wone *dwell*
wonne *won*
wonnyng *dwelling*
worschyp *honor; fame*
worthy *worthy; (n.) noble one*
wot *know*
wreton *written*
wronge *wrong, evil; (v.) wrung*
wrought *made, created*

yaf *gave*
yare *ready, prepared*
yede *went*
yhe *she, they*
yhe *yes, yeah*
yif (yyf) *if*
yive *give*
ynne *in; inn*
yoye *joy*
ywis *truly, certainly, indeed*
yynge *young*